D0935857

MANAGING EMERGENT PHENOMENA

Nonlinear Dynamics in Work Organizations

MANAGING EMERGENT PHENOMENA

Nonlinear Dynamics in Work Organizations

Stephen J. Guastello
Marquette University

LEA
LAWRENCE ERLBAUM ASSOCIATES, PUBLISHERS
2002 Mahwah, New Jersey London

302.35
G91m

Senior Acquisitions Editor: Anne Duffy
Editorial Assistant: Karen Wittig
Cover Design: Kathryn Houghtaling Lacey
Textbook Production Manager: Paul Smolenski
Full-Service & Composition: TechBooks
Text and Cover Printer: Edwards Brothers Incorporated

This book was typeset in 10/12 pt. Times, Italic, Bold, Bold Italic. The heads were typeset in Americana and Americana Bold.

Copyright © 2002 by Lawrence Erlbaum Associates, Inc.
All rights reserved. No part of this book may be reproduced in any form, by photostat, microfilm, retrieval system, or any other means, without prior written permission of the publisher.

Lawrence Erlbaum Associates, Inc., Publishers
10 Industrial Avenue
Mahwah, New Jersey 07430

Library of Congress Cataloging-in-Publication Data

Guastello, Stephen J.
Managing emergent phenomena : nonlinear dynamics in work organizations / Stephen J. Guastello.
p. cm.
Includes bibliographical references and index.
ISBN 0-8058-3163-0 (alk. paper)
1. Industrial management—Mathematical models. 2. Psychology, Industrial—Mathematical models. 3. Industrial safety—Mathematical models. 4. Organizational behavior—Mathematical models. 5. Chaotic behavior in systems—Mathematical models. 6. Nonlinear theories. I. Title.

HD30.25 .G8 2001
302.3′5—dc21 2001040313

Books published by Lawrence Erlbaum Associates are printed on acid-free paper, and their bindings are chosen for strength and durability.

Printed in the United States of America
10 9 8 7 6 5 4 3 2 1

Dedicated to Denise and Andrea

University Libraries
Carnegie Mellon University
Pittsburgh, PA 15213-3890

Contents

Preface

The year 2001 marks the 20th anniversary of the first journal article on nonlinear dynamics in organizational behavior. The topic was a butterfly catastrophe model of equity in organizations, which was intended as a theoretical integration of some basic psychology, work behaviors, and nonlinear dynamical elements. The first plausible statistical methods for testing any such theory came soon afterward.

Two important developments took place 10 years later. First, I was able to show that a growing range of catastrophe models for discontinuous change, each theoretically grounded in their own way, could account for a substantial amount of behavior variance that could not be accounted for by common linear and static approaches to the same problem. Second, there was a suddenly growing interest within the organizational behavior community in a wider range of nonlinear dynamics that could be applied to a still wider range of organizational phenomena. The hunt for chaos was on; social scientists searched for it in the economy, in the city, in the workplace, in the mind, and in the living room sofa.

Unfortunately, the mathematicians and physicists who gave us chaos only gave us simulations and algorithms that required many thousands of noise-free observations. We needed statistical methods that were suitable to psychological and organizational data. Although the schism in the knowledge base could give some graduate students a nightmare or two, it gave me one of those deja vu moments. By the time the moment had passed, I had harnessed nonlinear regression to evaluate the possibility of chaos and other dynamics in real data.

Thus, in 1995 I published *Chaos, Catastrophe, and Human Affairs: Applications of Nonlinear Dynamics to Work, Organizations, and Social Evolution.* The book compiled the best substantiated pieces of nonlinear theory and research in the psychology of work behavior (or industrial/organizational psychology and some of us prefer)—plus some new speculations and temptations. The statistical methods for catastrophes, chaos, and so forth were explained and illustrated in the course of the exposition. In the cases in which nonlinear dynamics models were accepted as better explanations of phenomena, the nonlinear models were more accurate by an average of 2:1 in terms of statistical variance accounted for compared to the best linear counterpart.

Meanwhile, the interest in chaos mutated to an interest in complexity. When "complexity" is not being used as a management buzzword, it refers to processes of self-organization. Systems take on structures and consolidate behavior patterns without any influence from the outside. Instead, we need to set the preconditions for structure and patterning to occur. Thus, the phrase "order for free" is fairly accurate. Like other uses of the word "free" in our society, it hides a lot of effort and skill that is required to do the job. The elementary dynamics of attractors, bifurcation, chaos, and catastrophe remain at least as important as they once were; they have become a part of the understanding of how self-organization occurs.

In any case, the self-organizing behavior patterns are examples of emergence: Something that suddenly materializes where nothing resembling it existed before. It is matter of contemporary philosophical debate, however, as to how many kinds of emergence there are, and whether they are all synonymous with self-organization. Fortunately, we do not have to rely on a conclusion of that debate to build what has been built here.

This book is not a new edition of the previous one. It is a new story woven from the lessons of the past and many nonlinear ideas that have gelled in the last six years. I am furthermore pleased to report that many more people with provocative ideas have contributed to this fast-developing and extensive theory of organizational behavior. The predictive advantage for the new material remains 2:1. The contribution to our understanding of human collective behavior is also large.

Before turning to the first page, I would like to thank all my research assistants and colleagues who whispered smart stuff in my e-mail from time to time. They are all accomplished in their own right, and their best shots are cited here.

MANAGING EMERGENT PHENOMENA

Nonlinear Dynamics in Work Organizations

1

Scenes from the Nonlinear House of Panic

Our understanding of social groups and organizations has progressed by gradual increments over the last century and then, suddenly, there was a very different theory—one that emphasizes the footprints of change and the many shapes and sizes that there could be. *Nonlinear dynamical systems theory* (NDS), which is also known colloquially as *chaos theory* or *complexity theory*, is the study of the events that change over time and space. By *nonlinear* we are calling attention to the uneven change of events over time, and the disproportionate responses that systems make when we try to affect or control them in some manner. Sometimes a small intervention has a dramatic impact. Sometimes a large plan accomplishes very little.

THE RISE AND FALL OF BUREAUCRACY

NDS's contributions to organizational theory are best appreciated against a backdrop of the previous major landmarks in organizational science. Less than a century ago, *bureaucracy* was considered an improvement over the way organizations had been managed previously (Weber, 1946). Bureaucracy meant that there was a *division of labor*. Each member of the organization performed tasks that began somewhere and ended somewhere else. The ambiguity regarding who was responsible for what was, in principle, extricated.

Bureaucracies assigned *clear responsibility* for decisions to job *roles*. By making clear assignments, it was possible to make decisions efficiently within the boundaries of policies that were set by people in other job roles. The definition of policies for the use by other organizational members removed the necessity of restating a policy every time an example of a decision had to be made. It also produced a *hierarchical structure*.

The nature of a role meant that there was a disconnection between the set of actions denoted by the role and the human being who was incumbent in that role. This disconnection was thought to ensure that decisions were results of policy rather than individual whim, nepotism, or other kinds of organizational politics. The system of roles would also provide equal treatment of personnel and clients. Bureaucracy delivered on its expectations to a great extent, although the extrication of politics from organizations was a fantasy. There were human costs to this efficiency as well.

Bureaucracy and its system of roles were based on a value for rationality. Rationality was the basis of efficiency, and was in turn based on an assumption of a mechanistic system. We are thus confronted with some glaring psychological questions: What is rationality? What is irrationality? Is one always better than the other? Why do we think so? Why do bureaucracies occasionally produce irrational or counterproductive results?

The beginnings of two long answers to the foregoing questions first appeared in the 1950s. One response was that of *bounded rationality*, whichstates that humans can only process so much information well, and beyond that point we should not expect much more in the way of rationality. The artificial intelligence movement tried to plug the holes in human rationality.

The other response to the gap in bureaucratic rationality was the *humanization* movement. People have feelings, emotional reactions, and personalities, none of which are going to disappear through any act of management. Rather, it is the not-traditionally-rational aspects of human nature that are critical to great accomplishments. Emotional reactions can be rational responses to irrational situations. As a result, more of an organization's objectives can be accomplished with less managerial command and control, rather than more. The nature of bounded rationality, contributions of artificial intelligence, and humanization approaches to organizational management are unpacked in later chapters.

The structure of bureaucracy and the liquidity of humanization eventually melted together into what might be called *organic* forms of organizations. Now there was an awareness that a work organization was a life form, rather than a machine. The organization was still driven by its rationality, but it was kept alive by its subrational verve.

In the wave of thinking that culminated in the late 1990s, the organization is a *complex adaptive system*, which recognized nonlinear patterns of behavior

(Anderson, 1999; Dooley, 1997; Guastello, 1995a). Now that organizations are recognized as being alive, we can proceed to questions regarding how they stay that way. How does an organization interpret signals and events in its environment? More importantly, how does it utilize the events in its environment to its own benefit? How does it harness its capabilities as a living system to make effective responses? How and when does it change itself from one form to another in order to enhance its viability as a big collective living organism? How is it affected by other organizational life forms?

Conventional psychology and organizational science have tackled these questions to some extent. Much more is left to NDS, which has produced new knowledge about organizations. Ultimately, the objective of the following chapters is to produce a viable theory of organizations that integrates NDS principles with the best findings from other sources.

ENTER THE HOUSE OF PANIC

A city is a complex system. Every morning people roll out of bed, run some water, jump into some clothes, and head off to work. Trucks and horse-drawn carts make deliveries and fight for parking spaces. Switches turn on. The block smells like bread and pastry—or maybe it's the smell of the brewery getting started for the day. The sky is still dark.

A newspaper editor and a reporter slurp coffee. They were up most of the night finishing a story that seemed important. It was too late to go to bed and wake up again, so they just stayed up. They wisecracked about something you had to be there to appreciate. A vibration rattled coffee cups that no one was touching. Waitresses disappeared. The editor and the reporter stifled their jokes in midsyllable.

Over the previous 50 years, the 400,000 residents of San Francisco had become used to ground tremors that would have terrorized the tourists. Citizens had once debated whether wood frame houses were safer than brick and steel structures. Their preferences eventually leaned toward brick and steel. The post office had recently built an elaborate new facility on land that was reclaimed from the nearby water. Hills around the city were lowered to bring a vast low-lying area above sea level. Some street level building entrances became subcellars while other became third story windows as a result of the regrading. The city's gas and water lines were set in pathways of reclaimed ground, which some people characterized as "jelly."

The city had grown to 10 times its original size during the gold rush of 1849 and shortly afterward. The luck of the prospectors, and the instability that went with it, generated an economy that centered on living in the present and living well whenever possible. The lives and futures of San Franciscans were less predictable than lives in other cities of that era, but for many the slim chance of something great happening was a step up from the certainty of going nowhere. San Francisco was a vibrant center for worldwide immigration. By 1906 it had amassed the largest population of Chinese outside of China itself. The occasional devastation from earthquakes and the steady growth of a luckless and unemployed population contributed to the mentality of living in the present.

Farmers and merchants eventually followed, mostly from the Eastern direction. The land supported large and successful crops of fruits and vegetables. Some people amassed great wealth and channeled it into fine real estate, social development, and institutions of art, science, and higher education. Perhaps the transition toward stable architecture was as much a reflection of the growing stability of the society as it was the result of lessons learned from the quakes.

The tremors permeated the region and lasted nearly 3 minutes. During those 3 minutes the earth opened its mouth and swallowed large sections of San Francisco, and continued to do so over the next week as the tremors returned in 30-second bursts at irregular intervals. By all accounts, the greatest damage was caused by fires, which raged instantly all over the city. The ruptured gas lines fueled they fires, which fed on themselves as they spread. In the early hours of the disaster, the fire response was able to pump water from the harbor to quell the fires closest to the water. The water could not be pumped nearly as far as it was needed, or to nearly as many locations; the water lines around the city were instantly ruptured along with the gas lines.

Figure 1.1 is a scene from Market Street that was depicted in a photograph (from Morris, 1906). People evacuated themselves as best as they could with no motorized transportation. Frame buildings crashed around them. "Mr. J. P. Anthony, as he fled from the Ramona Hotel, saw a score or more people crushed to death, and as he walked the streets at a later hour saw bodies of the dead being carried in garbage wagons and all kinds of vehicles to the improvised morgues, while hospitals and storerooms were already filled with the injured" (Morris, 1906, p. 115). Other eyewitnesses gave reports that were every bit as gruesome.

The tall white building furthest from the camera in Fig. 1.1 was comparatively unscathed, as were the post office, the mint, and customs house. The telegraph facility in the post office turned out to be a crucial link to the outside world along with newspapers and reporters who moved their base of operations to Oakland during the crisis. City Hall, on the other hand, was a total loss.

Municipal fire fighters quickly determined that they were unable to control the spread of the fires by conventional means, and the path of the fire indicated that the devastation was only going get worse in a hurry. Fortunately, Mayor Eugene Schmitz made contact with General Funston at the nearby Presidio. Funston responded with a team of demolition experts who were able to control the spread of the fire by blowing up blocks of buildings that lay in the path of the spreading fire. Figure 1.2 is a portrait of Mayor Schmitz. The original caption read: "Mayor Schmitz, by his untiring efforts and great executive ability, brought order out of chaos" (Morris, 1906, p. 104).

The tourists, who were staying at the hotels, were the first to pack their belongings and leave if they could do so. Their first response was to head for

FIG. 1.1. San Francisco under siege from earthquake and fire. Reprinted from Morris (1906). In the public domain.

FIG. 1.2. Mayor Eugene Schmitz of San Francisco. Reprinted from Morris (1906). In the public domain.

the harbor to catch a ferry to Oakland. The ferry could only accommodate a small number of people at a time.

Citizens who survived responded first by securing their own lives, those of their families and neighbors, and their homes. The shock of the disaster drove some people insane, and they too had to be counted as casualties. Disaster relief teams suddenly appeared. There is no clear record of exactly how they appeared. Some were outgrowths of civic organizations that were already organized. Others emerged for the occasion. The police and military conscripted any freely roaming men to the nearest rubble pile to dig out survivors.

The maintenance of law and order was given a high priority and a clear enforcement policy. The military and the police were under orders to shoot looters on sight. In the early days of the ordinance, common citizens were also given the power to terminate looters. It soon became apparent, however, that the citizens had little skill in law enforcement and that they had coagulated into lynch mobs. The revised directive assigned all execution powers to the police or military.

The criminal challenge was at least as formidable as the other challenges of the situation. One team of bandits was apprehended while trying to break into the mint. An eyewitness discovered the body of a woman in a hotel's wreckage. A looter who wanted the gem stone it must have held had amputated her ring finger. It was unclear whether she was already dead or just unconscious when her finger was cut off. In spite of the best intentions of the police and military, mistakes were still made. People who were rummaging through what was left of their own homes were unfortunately shot as looters too.

Food was scarce. A loaf of bread, if a store was lucky enough to still have one, sold for 20 times the usual price. Again, police intervened to liberate food supplies for the starving. As soon as news of the earthquake escaped the city, food and medical supplies poured in from sources all over the United States and Canada. Businesses with headquarters in foreign countries made contributions as well. City parks were turned into lodging for the homeless and food distributions centers (Fig. 1.3).

The reconstruction of the city was an equally formidable task, and one that required a very different set of management requirements. Figure 1.4 is a view of what was left of Van Ness Avenue. The shell of city hall appears in the distance. Fortunately, Mayor Schmitz was successful in framing attractive offers to architects, engineers, and other professionals of exceptional talent who poured into the city region to rebuild its physical presence and social fabric.

PRINCIPLES OF NONLINEAR DYNAMICS, CHAOS, AND COMPLEXITY

The foregoing tale of the San Francisco earthquake of 1906 captures a number of issues that face managers and social architects in less dramatic, but more widespread, circumstances. NDS is a *general systems theory*, which means that it contains general principles that describe and predict events that are very different in their obvious appearances. Parallels inevitably exist between the functioning of business organizations nonhuman ecology, biological structures, and other collectives of humans or animals that form around different objectives. General systems thinking (e.g., Miller, 1978; L. von Bertalanffy, 1968) thus identifies common themes regarding the behavior of living systems and for generating explanations for phenomena that had not been forthcoming through the conventional analysis of localized problems.

FIG. 1.3. Care for the homeless of San Francisco in the aftermath of the earthquake. Reprinted from Morris (1906). In the public domain.

FIG. 1.4. Ruins of San Francisco. Reprinted from Morris (1906). In the public domain.

General systems theories often begin, or culminate, in relationships that can be mathematically defined. Some theorists emphasize the mathematical content more than others do, depending on what they are trying to accomplish. NDS is clearly of mathematical origin. Fortunately, however, we will use the *products* of its mathematics in our study of organizations. The products take the form of relationships that we can describe in pictures. The specialized math promotes the analysis of data that we observe in the laboratory or in real-world situations. In other words, we can test our claims in a scientific manner that can tell us whether our specific principles of dynamics apply to the situations we are trying to study.

Principles of Elementary Dynamics

NDS's central principles can be grouped into those that pertain to elementary dynamics, and those the address complex systems and emergent phenomena. The elementary dynamics include the particular phenomenon of chaos, which gave rise to the name "chaos theory." The second group, which is usually invoked under the rubric of "complexity theory," cannot be fully appreciated without elementary dynamics.

The consensus today is that the subject matter of NDS can be traced to the pivotal work of Henri Poincaré, a mathematician from the 1890s. His study of astrophysical dynamical processes produced the first observation of mathematical chaos on the one hand, and a highly visual approach to mathematics on the other. Many of the topologies that he studied were so complex that it was not possible to write equations for them. It was not until the development of differential topology that it was possible to fill in this major gap.

Poincaré's phenomena did not have a cute name, like "chaos." Mathematicians did not revisit this group of phenomena until the early 1960s, when Lorenz, a meteorologist, drew our attention to the *strange attractor*. Li and Yorke (1975) introduced "chaos" into the general systems vocabulary; the formal definitions of chaos and other key terms will be saved for the next chapter. In any case, we arrive at the first two principles:

1. *Many seemingly random events are actually the result of deterministic processes that we can describe using simple equations*. It is no small trick to find the equations.
2. *Small differences in the initial conditions of a situation can evolve into radically different system states later on in time*.

The next NDS principle pertains to *catastrophes*. Catastrophes are sudden and discontinuous changes in events. The underlying math and the original exposition about how they can be used is attributed to René Thom (1975). Many of the first applications in the social sciences are credited to E. C. Zeeman (1977).

3. *All discontinuous events can be modeled by one of seven elementary topological forms, which vary in complexity.*

The next four NDS principles involve fractals. Fractals are geometric structures that have fractional dimensions. Their underlying math and their many possible uses are credited to Benoit Mandelbrot whose landmark work was done in the 1960s and 1970s.

4. *Seemingly random shapes*, such as those found in living tissue structures, lightning bolts, plant structures, and the shape of islands and other landscapes, *can actually be generated by relatively simple equations that characterize fractal structures.*

5. *Fractal structures are self-repeating over space, levels of magnitude, or, more generally, scale.*

6. *The boundaries of a chaotic phenomenon are fractal in shape.* This is one of several connections between fractal geometry and other nonlinear dynamics.

7. *The complexity of a fractal form is given by its dimension.* There are several garden varieties of dimension, although the ones that characterize information and turbulence are perhaps the most relevant to human organizations.

Principles of Complex Systems

Galileo, Darwin, and Newton attained their historic stature for several reasons: Their scientific contributions produced specific answers to questions of widely shared concern. They developed methods and tools for studying their topics (e.g. a telescope here, a branch of mathematics there). Their findings contained surprises that shook society's fundamental understanding of its world and its place within the world. The combination of new scientific questions, methods, and worldview produced what Kuhn (1972) regarded as a scientific paradigm.

In a previous scientific epoch, Newton produced a concept of the mechanical system that was the result of many parts. If we understood how each part functioned, we could, therefore, understand the whole system. The general systems thinking of the late 20th century, and NDS in particular, has pretty much discovered the limits to the mechanical systems reasoning. To progress any further, we need to adopt a worldview that was advocated by psychologists studying perception: "The whole is greater than the sum of its parts." This general rule, which is attributed to Kohler, Koffka, and Wertheimer from the early part of the 20th century, plays out in the next group of NDS principles.

8. *Systems that are in a nonequilibrium state create their own structures through one of several processes of self-organization.*

9. *The parts of a system are continually interacting with each other and shaping each other's behavior.*

In Darwin's view of the development of biological species, the process of evolution and natural selection was slow and gradual. Gaps that existed in the historical chain of species evolution were attributed to missing links that would one day be found. Today we think otherwise:

10. *The evolution of systems is in some respects slow and gradual, but slow and gradual effects culminate into sudden and discontinuous changes of events and conditions.* This principle of punctuated equilibrium characterizes patterns of sociotechnical development as well. Two more principles should be added for good measure.

11. *Some dynamical events are reversible, but many are not.*

12. *Principles of NDS are testable in the same sense that any other scientific principle can be tested.* It has been possible to show that, in the cases where an NDS explanation was adopted on empirical groups, rather than intuitive grounds only, the NDS explanation was, on the average, twice as accurate as the conventional explanation (Guastello, 1992a, 1995a). This line of reasoning is expanded in later chapters along with the other NDS principles listed here.

PREVIEW OF COMING ATTRACTIONS

The next chapter of this book elaborates NDS principles. They center on concepts such as attractors, bifurcations, chaos, fractals, self-organization, dimensions, and turbulence. Some illustrative examples are sprinkled in. More frequently, however, it is more useful to work through the general principles on their own terms and preview the places later on where the principles are exploited in their full forms.

Chapter 3 describes the challenges for testing NDS ideas. The methodology that has served the purpose best is the method of structural equations. Fortunately, we have limited sets of structural models that cover a wide range of territory. The broad approach is to identify statistical equations that capture the dynamics of interest, and determine how well they fit the data generated in the laboratory or the field. Those results are compared against those produced with a conventional linear model, or alternative nonlinear models in cases where there is more than one possible NDS explanation.

Chapter 4 introduces the substance of organizational theory, with a particular emphasis on organizational change. There we encounter the nature of organizational development as it has been handed to us from thinkers of the past, NDS interpretations of old and new phenomena, and illustrative empirical or experiential examples. In particular, we call attention to the counterpoint between the organization's conscious efforts and its unconscious contents, and how the latter shapes the development of the former.

Chapter 5 concerns human motivation. To a great extent, the background psychological theories were integrated into an NDS theory in previous work. Chapter 5 recounts the main points and expands the NDS theory of motivation to incorporate the notion of utility in decision making. In order to do that the butterfly catastrophe model of motivation in organizations is integrated for the first time with game theory for strategic decisions. What results is a theory that now includes dynamics of cooperation and competition and evolutionary, or long-run, processes. The motivation chapter also contains an illustrative test of the theory in the context of personnel selection. As part of that story, we can observe how the important variables that affect personnel retention change over time. In essence, we have variables that *emerge* within a given situation. The last phase of the motivation theory is that of motivational *flow*. The flow concept emphasizes the emotional side of motivated behavior and how the intrinsic values of work and life activities change over time and why.

Chapter 6 concerns creative thought, which is one of the critical assets of a complex adaptive system. The creative experience occurs in a complex environment of ideas, people, chance events that shape the flow of ideas, and the demands of a problem situation. A good deal of attention is paid to the cognitive process of developing ideas as they play out within the individual mind and in a creative problem-solving group.

Chapter 7 examines the social network. Ideas, whether creative or otherwise, flow between people, and this communication flow makes the difference between a real group, which has a continuing existence, and a bunch of people who happen to be in the same room. The dynamics that hold a group of individuals together play out in networks of organizations that have continuing business with each other.

Chapter 8 explores the phenomenon of coordination, in which two or more events that are supposed to happen at the same time, or in a particular sequence, actually happen that way. Interestingly, the fundamental aspects of coordination among humans is not too different from coordinated activities among nonhumans. Much of the phenomenon transpires without leaders and without verbal communication. When the critters can talk, a more complex state of affairs sometimes occurs, but sometimes talking does not help much.

Leaders emerge in Chapter 9, which draws connections between elementary leadership theory and the NDS counterpart to leadership. Leaders emerge while other aspects of the group are solidifying their structure. Although the nonlinear dynamics seem to be very similar for different types of group tasks (e.g., creative problem solving versus production), the important variables in the process are grouped differently.

A hierarchical structure is formed when a leader emerges. There is a system of roles, even if it is not a formal system. Chapter 10 explores the production dynamics of organizations that have two or three layers of hierarchy. Sometimes management groups can navigate the turbulent flows, and sometimes they are not so skilled at it.

Chapter 11 considers some NDS topics in economics, which represent the contributions of the environment to the experience of the complex adaptive system.

Theories of organizational behavior in the past have only waved their hands with a mumble about "economics." They often gave us the impression that "economics" had "something to do with markets," as if market behaviors comprised the beginning and end of economics. Thus, markets and the dubious assumptions of rationality are considered first. From there we move on to macroeconomic themes of unemployment and inflation, which are entwined. (There are more dynamics occurring beyond "markets for labor" or "markets for money.")

In previous chapters, information is treated as the stuff that flows between members of a social unit. Here it is considered as a market entity of its own that shapes, or is shaped by, the structures of organizations that use it. The last section of the chapter concerns the dynamics of natural resources and organizational decisions that might pertain to those resources.

Chapter 12 pulls together many ideas from earlier chapters into the theme of prediction and control of dynamical processes. Here we examine viewpoints on the best methods for controlling or creating chaos, or for inducing self-organization processes. The chapter includes a compilation of NDS phenomena and the control variables that affect them insofar as good answers have been produced through research. The final section of Chapter 12 addresses emergency management as it is known today through the lens of NDS.

2

Nonlinear Dynamical Systems Theory

This chapter presents the concepts of attractors, bifurcation, equilibria and stability, fractals, self-organization, and catastrophes. The global picture describes the continuity between highly volatile chaotic processes and simpler ideas of equilibria and stability. Of necessity, this chapter will bear some resemblance to Chapter 2 of *Chaos, Catastrophe, and Human Affairs* (Guastello, 1995a). One main difference, however, is that some of the more exotic dynamics presented previously have been thrown overboard in favor of the smaller number of simpler dynamics that have found fairly wide applicability in applied psychology. The dynamics of self-organization play a greater role this time around. Hopefully, the range of dynamics in use is a temporary state of affairs arising from this still-early stage of theoretical development and experimental analysis. At the same time, however, the contributions of NDS to substantive theories are not so primitive that they can be dusted off as provocative speculations. Rather, they are growing together in a way that permits a comprehensive social science theory.

The presentations that follow emphasize qualitative analysis of phenomena. I tread lightly on the equations and original mathematical thinking. Fortunately, applied science uses the products of the mathematics; this is not necessary to revisit proofs and such. Several books serve as general references for the sections of attractors, bifurcations, and chaos: R. H. Abraham and C. Shaw (1992) and F. D.

Abraham, R. H. Abraham, and Shaw (1990), Kaplan and Glass (1995), Nicolis and Prigogine (1989), Puu (2000a), and Thompson and H. B. Stewart (1986).

ATTRACTORS AND STABILITY

An *attractor* is a piece of space. It has a special property such that if an object gets too close to this space, the object is pulled into it and does not leave it, except under special conditions. The perimeter of the space of an attractor is the attractor's *basin*. If the object does not fly close enough to the perimeter of the basin, the object keeps going on its merry way. The pathways of objects flying outside the perimeter, or within the basin of the attractor are collectively known as the *vectorfields*.

The notion of an attractor overlaps in meaning with the more archaic term *equilibrium*, although the latter is less specific in terms of formal topological dynamics. According to Goldstein (1995), "equilibrium" originated in ancient Greek writing with the meaning of a *balance of forces*. That essential meaning carries through into 20th century economics. Economists, along with the rest of us, will recognize that not all equilibria are unchanging and stable. Some forms of balance, (such as some of the Nash equilibria in game theory in Chapter 5) are fragile. Hence, in common language we speak of "upsetting a delicate balance" or we instruct each other, "not to breathe on it or it will fall apart." Thus, as Goldstein continues, *stability* and *equilibrium* are not synonymous, and any simple attempt to use the two terms with equivalent meaning could present confusion. Although it is sometimes useful to continue to think of equilibrium states, which imply a balance of some sort, alongside the concept of attractor, it is also a good idea to keep the two concepts separated when making the distinction between a mathematical abstraction and a physical realization of the abstraction.

Systems that are *stable* are unlikely to change in any appreciable way, if at all. An *instability* implies that a change will take place, that the results are not predictable, and that a particular result is not likely to occur again in repeated experiments. The classical topological definition, of Andronov and Pontryagin from the 1930s, is that "...[A] dynamical system (vector field or map) is structurally stable if nearby systems have qualitatively the same dynamics" (Wiggins, 1988, p. 58). In other words, if all objects' trajectories in a vectorfield are behaving the same way, then the system is structurally stable. My introduction of probability words such as "likely," "unlikely," and "same" is done with the goal of connecting statistical concepts with topological concepts. Two types of attractors are considered next: the fixed point attractor and the limit cycle. Both are structurally stable. Repellors and saddles, which are considered later, are not structurally stable.

Fixed-Point Attractors

Fixed-point attractors behave in much the same way as a magnet in the presence of iron filings. With *fixed-point* attractors, a behavior will gravitate toward a steady state or a constant value. Figure 2.1 shows a common type of fixed-point

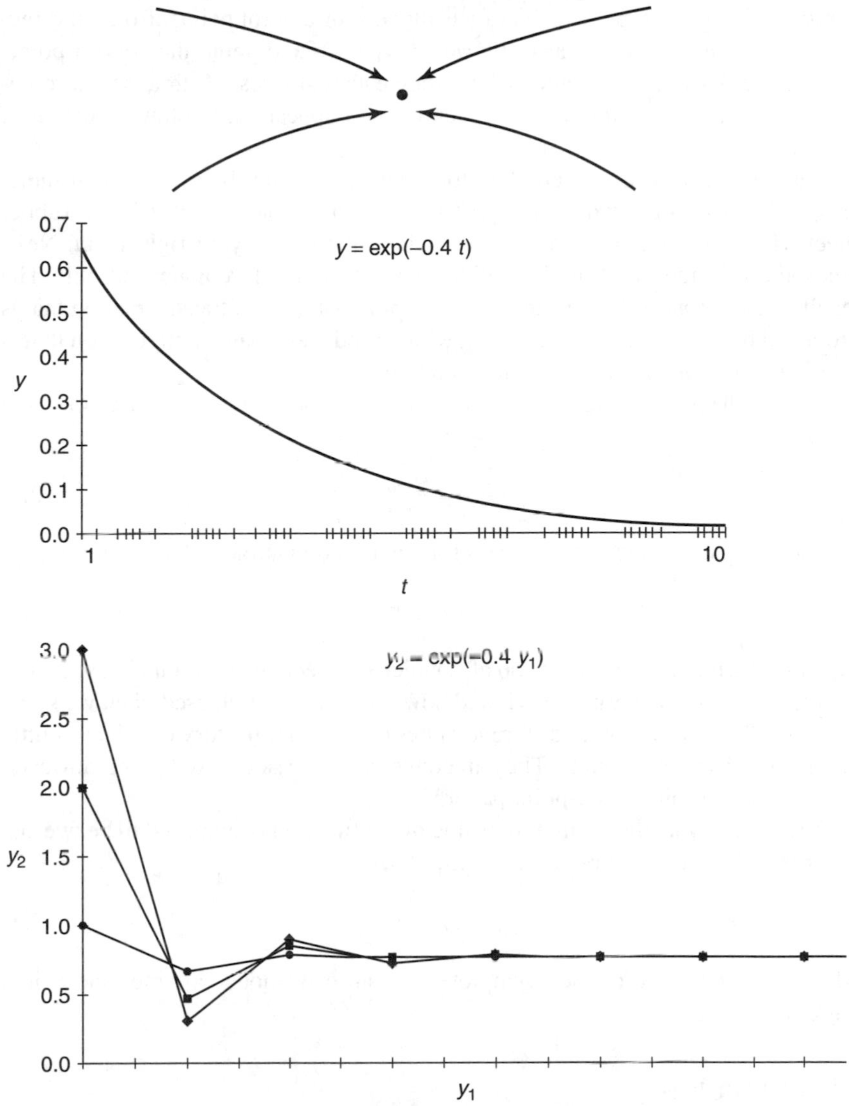

FIG. 2.1. A fixed-point attractor. *Top*: Its phase portrait. *Center*: Asymptotic stability is reached for an exponential function of time. *Bottom*: Asymptotic stability is reached for an exponential affine transformation and several initial conditions.

attractor, the *radial* type, which attracts objects, or control points, from all directions to its center. There is also the *spiral* type of fixed point, the control points spiral inward toward the center where they eventually rest. A time series representation of a fixed-point attractor phenomenon appears in the lower portion of Fig. 2.1.

The paths that lead into an attractor's center need not be symmetrical radial or spiral paths. For instance, imagine that the upper panel Fig. 2.1 is a rubber sheet. Hold the upper right and lower right corners with your right hand. Next, pinch the left side in the middle with your thumb and forefinger and pull. The result is a *homeomorphism* of the original spiral path, i.e., a transformation that is produced by stretching a rubber sheet, which produces a path configuration that is *topologically equivalent* to the initial version.

The middle panel of Fig. 2.1 shows a time series for a fixed-point attractor based on Eq. 2.1:

$$y = e^{-at} \tag{2.1}$$

The bottom panel shows a time series for a fixed-point attractor based on Eq. 2.2:

$$y_2 = e^{y_1 t}. \tag{2.2}$$

Equation 2.2 is a recursive function of y, which is especially important in dynamics. It says that if we know y at Time 1, and how much time has elapsed, then we know y at Time 2. If we start with different values of y, each trajectory oscillates a little bit, and by different amounts. They all converge on the same fixed point, however, and represent a spiral fixed-point pattern.

If we know what the asymptotic value of the function is supposed to be, we can describe a fixed-point attractor using Eq. 2.3:

$$y_2 = K/(1 + e^{\theta x}), \tag{2.3}$$

where K is the value of the asymptote, x is an exogenous variable, and θ is a regression weight.

Limit Cycles

A limit cycle is an attractor that holds objects in a limit cycle around the attractor center. A limit cycle can be created by taking several magnets and arranging them in a closely packed circle such that their basins are contiguous. When a control point is fired into their joint basin, its path stabilizes to a limit cycle around the entire configuration. A limit cycle would characterize the path of moons around a planet, or a planet around a sun. Biological events that we observe as steady oscillations over time are, in essence, limit cycles. In real life, however, two or more limit cycles are commonly coupled together (Koyama, Yoneyama, Sawada,

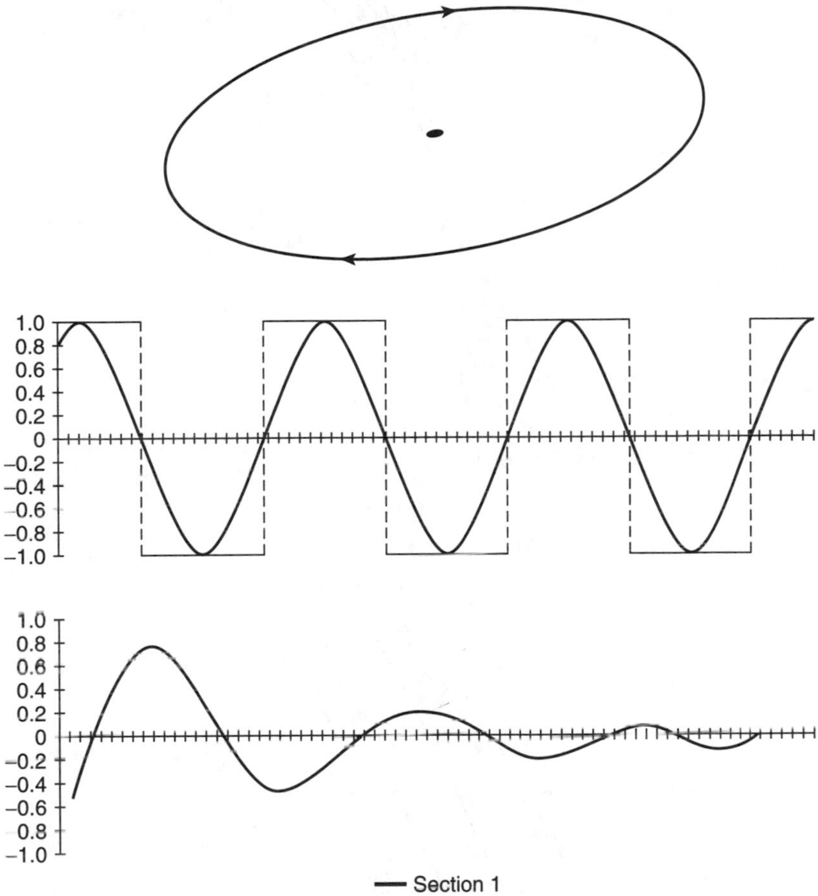

FIG. 2.2. A limit cycle, or periodic attractor. *Top*: Its phase portrait. *Center*: Its time series is a regular sine wave; peaks and valleys become flattened when the function is really a bistable oscillator. *Bottom*: The time series for a dampened oscillator becomes a fixed point.

& Ohtomo, 1994). A limit cycle is depicted in the upper panel of Fig. 2.2. The middle panel of Fig. 2.2 is a sine function, which is the standard limit cycle. (Fourier analysis is the standard method of decomposing a complex waveform into sinusoidal components.) Its function is

$$y = \sin(x), \tag{2.4}$$

where x could be time, or t, in this case. The flattened regions of the function were added to depict what would happen if the continuous function were to be

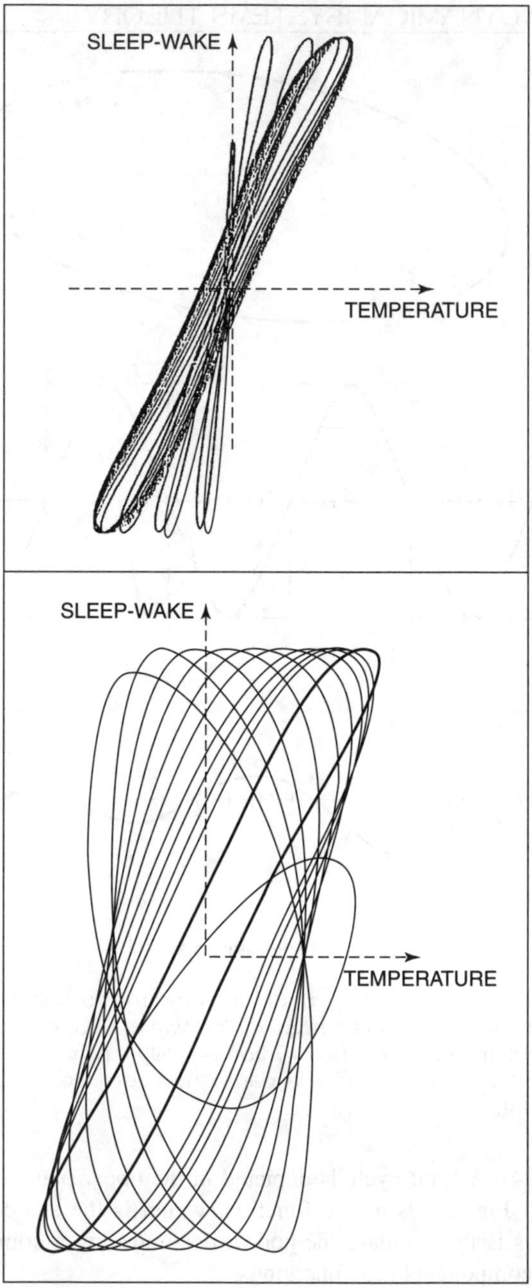

FIG. 2.3. Phase portrait of an oscillator involving two variables. *Upper*: Circadian rhythm for a normally regulated person. *Lower*: The two variables become uncoupled under conditions of jet lag. Reprinted with permission (Abraham et al. 1990, p. III-72 and III-74).

discretized into a two-state situation. See later sections of this chapter regarding repellors and catastrophe theory.

The lower portion of Fig. 2.2 is a *dampened oscillator*, which is similar to what occurs to the pendulum of a mechanical clock that has not been wound for a while. The dampened oscillator bears some resemblance to the spiral attractor, and in practice it might be challenging to tell the two phenomena apart. To do so would require some prior knowledge of the system. Was it oscillating regularly before something happened to it to dampen it? Or did the control point just quickly roll down the sink?

Phase Portraits

The graphic of the control points' paths in the neighborhood of one or more attractors is called its *phase portrait*. Phase portraits can be drawn by plotting a behavior value at time t on the Y-axis against the value of the same behavior at time $t-1$ on the X-axis. For more complex dynamics, the *change* in behavior from time $t-1$ to t can be plotted on the Y-axis against the value of behavior differences at a previous pair of time frames ($t-2, t-1$) on the X-axis. A phase portrait of a fixed-point attractor would show trajectories moving into the center. A limit cycle would be round or elliptic.

Phase portraits need not be restricted to the one-variable case. The example given in Fig. 2.3 (from Abraham et al., 1990) depicts a limit cycle for circadian rhythm, where change in body temperature is plotted against change in wakefulness–sleepiness (arousal). In the upper panel, the phase portrait depicts regular repeated limit cycles. The lower portion depicts what happens in the condition of jet lag. One physiological process is heading in one direction while the other physiological process is heading in another. Eventually, the two processes resynchronize, and the person "recovers."

Often, however, researchers have a time series that should be projected into more than two dimensions, but exactly how many of these *embedding dimensions* are appropriate is unknown. There is some work in progress on efficient methods for finding the most appropriate embedding dimension (Abarbanel, 1996; Abraham, 1997; Guastello & Bock, 2001). Until then, however, there is a convenient theorem to rely on that states that all information about the dimensional complexity of a time series is contained in the time series itself. "Information" would include the embedding dimension, lag structures. For a general proof of the relationship between secondary behaviors in dynamical systems and lag functions of primary behaviors, see Packard, Crutchfield, Farmer, and R.S. Shaw (1980).

INSTABILITIES AND BIFURCATION

Repellors and saddles, which are considered next, are unstable, according to the topological definition, because the trajectories of points are all behaving differently. In the case of the repellor, points are flying in all directions except toward the central

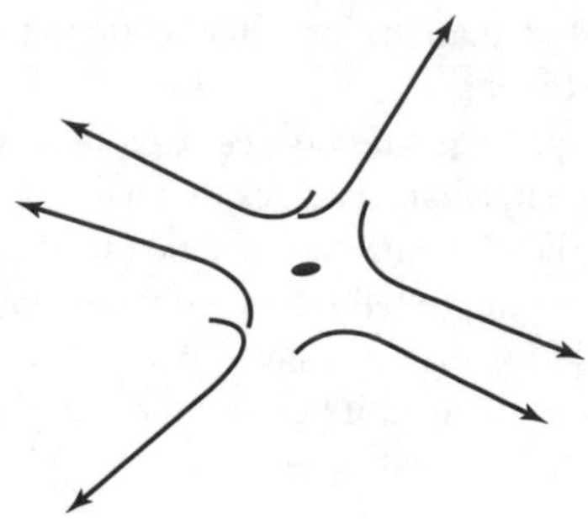

FIG. 2.4. Phase portrait of a repellor.

point. In the case of the saddle, trajectories are showing both attraction and repellor dynamics. Bifurcations are patterns of instability that divide a dynamic field.

Repellors

Repellor forces have the opposite effect on control points. Objects that get too close to a *repellor* force are ejected from the center to somewhere outside the repellor's *separatrix*, which is special name for a repellor's basin. Repellors can generate spiral or radial-hyperbolic paths. A radial repellor is shown in Figure 2.4.

Repellors and limit cycles can be readily confused at first glance, but there are distinguishing subtleties. Historically, science used to believe that there was a dynamic called centrifugal force: If we swing a bucket of water around our head the water stays in the bucket (more or less) until we stop swinging. Centrifugal force was thought to explain the water remaining in the bucket by positing a force that propels objects away from a center. Newton later showed, however, that the real dynamic was centripetal force, or a lack of an attractor in the center. Centripetal behavior is essentially a limit cycle. Objects placed in the vacant center spiral out toward the orbit. Objects outside the orbit are drawn into the same orbit. Limit cycles are potentially confused with *hysteresis*, which is the oscillation between two attractors that are separated by a repellor. Hysteresis dynamics are considered later in this chapter in the context of catastrophe theory.

Saddle Points

Saddle points have characteristics of both repellors and attractors. In Fig. 2.5, an object is drawn into the saddle, but once it arrives, it is repelled into places unknown. A saddle dynamic can be generated by perturbing the motion of a pendulum. When unperturbed, a pendulum will swing an arc, forming a limit cycle pattern. If we perturb the path by interjecting a force transversal to the main arc, the pendulum swings in a figure-8, as shown in the lower panel of Figure 2.5. The pinch point between the lobes of the "8" is the saddle point. In the perturbed pendulum dynamic, the lobes of the "8" represent attractors; virtual separatrices appear in the far field.

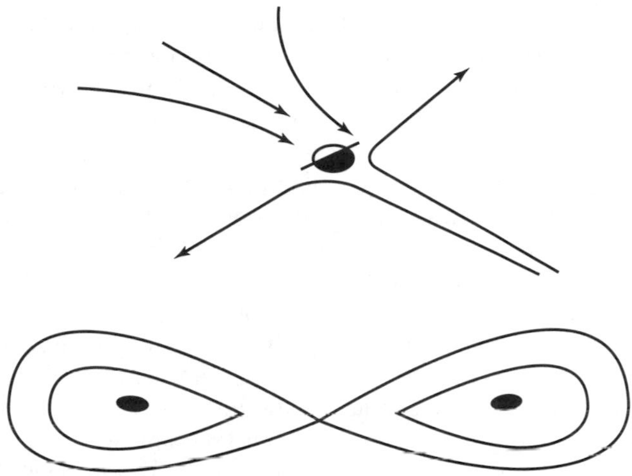

FIG. 2.5. Phase portraits for two types of saddles. *Upper*: Points are attracted, then repelled. *Lower*: The saddle created by a perturbed pendulum; the saddle is central point between two attractor areas.

Saddle points are commonly observed in human negotiations or other game theory applications (Chapter 5). Two players are faced with a range of situations. Some of the outcomes are favorable to one player, while other outcomes are favorable to the other player; favorable outcomes are represented by attractor basins. Undesirable outcomes for both players are represented by the separatrices. The saddle point occurs where the two attractor basins meet, the saddle represents a possible deal between the two parties. In real human terms, the trick is to define the terms of agreement that comprise the saddle. In less difficult negotiations, the saddle point is a "thick" point, which negotiation specialists call a "gray area"; for instance, see Oliva, Peters, & Murthy (1981).

Sadtchenko (2000) identified a saddle point in the course of a (generic) product life cycle. Once a product is introduced (and we assume it is successful enough to remain in the market), the demand for the produce increases until demand reaches a critical saddle point where saturation begins to set in. The producing organization should choose that moment to introduce the next wave of innovations. The market for the newer technology now begins to grow, while the market for the older technology starts to dwindle.

Bifurcation

Bifurcation theory is itself a subtopic of topology that goes a great distance toward explaining why chaos and discontinuous changes of behavior occur. Abraham and Shaw (1992) classify bifurcations into three categories: *subtle*, *catastrophic*, and *explosive*. In a dynamical scheme, a bifurcation is typically observed when control points begin to follow a common pathway, but diverge into two or more directions. Alternatively, one might observe a distinct change in the whole dynamical scheme and the attractors represented within it. Abraham and Shaw noted that, initially, they thought that there were only two types of bifurcations, subtle and catastrophic, but further thought led them to separate catastrophic from explosive types. Because of the limited number of well-studied examples of each, they are included together in Section 2.5. I could easily make a case for identifying subtypes of the subtle bifurcations as well, and the following narrative will eventually explain.

Subtle bifurcations appear to fall into two broad categories. One involves the transformation of an attractor from one type to another. For instance, if we take a weak limit cycle and perturb it, or stretch the "rubber," so that we pull the extreme corners away from the center, the attractor is transformed into a spiral repellor. If the direction of the perturbation is reversed, such that dynamic vectors are introduced that point toward the center rather than away from it, the limit cycle becomes a point attractor.

Another example of a subtle bifurcation is the *Hopf bifurcation*, in which a point attractor evolves into a repellor. One of the defining characteristics of a limit cycle is the absence of points in its geometric center. The local dynamical field may show the vacated center in the vacinity of the bifurcation, but the orbiting dynamics of the limit cycle are not yet visible; thus a Hopf bifurcation may also reflect a transition to a limit cycle. Additionally, in the *Neimark bifurcation*, the speed of a periodic attractor suddenly doubles; if the periodic function were a sound, the sound would be heard to jump an octave in pitch.

All bifurcations share a common trademark, which is the existence of a critical point, or *bifurcation point*, beyond which the effect of the bifurcation structure begins to take place. The bifurcation point itself is highly unstable; a control point located exactly at the bifurcation point could go almost anywhere in the phase space. The value of an accurate dynamical scheme for a real system would be its ability to specify conditions to predict where the control point will actually go at those uncertain moments.

The location of a bifurcation point in phase space is measured by a *control parameter*, which, when taken literally, implies a handle by which one might control a dynamical system. The bifurcation point is thus a critical value of a control parameter. Control parameters, furthermore, are distinguishable from *order parameters*. Order parameters represent multiple behavioral outcomes from the same dynamical process. Although multiple order parameters were intimated in the jet lag example, we might remain happy campers by continuing to think in terms of single order parameters—at least until we work our way up to the more complex models.

A second form of subtle bifurcation is the type where a dynamical field becomes parsed between regions occupied by attractor basins and separatrices. The bifurcation in that context does not refer to the transformation of attractor complexity or stability, but to the direction of possible paths that control point might take. Catastrophe theory addresses a group of those phenomena.

Catastrophic bifurcations are dynamics where a control parameter governs whether an attractor appears in a dynamical field or not. An example is the *blue sky catastrophe*, where an attractor appears "out of the blue" (Abraham & Shaw, 1992). Examples in the social sciences have not been recorded yet.

Explosive bifurcations are dynamics where one dynamic collides with another to produce a third and very different dynamic. An example is the *annihilation bifurcation* in which a repellor is located within its boundary. The repellor grows in size; growth is controlled by a parameter. The repellor eventually collides with the limit cycle, resulting in a fixed point attractor in the center where the repellor used to be (Abraham & Shaw, 1992). There is one known application of the annihilation bifurcation in the social sciences that pertains to urban development and renewal (Guastello, 1995a, pp. 46–47).

Logistic Map

Figure 2.6 shows the logistic map, which can be viewed as the master plan underlying dynamic processes as they make the transition from global stability to

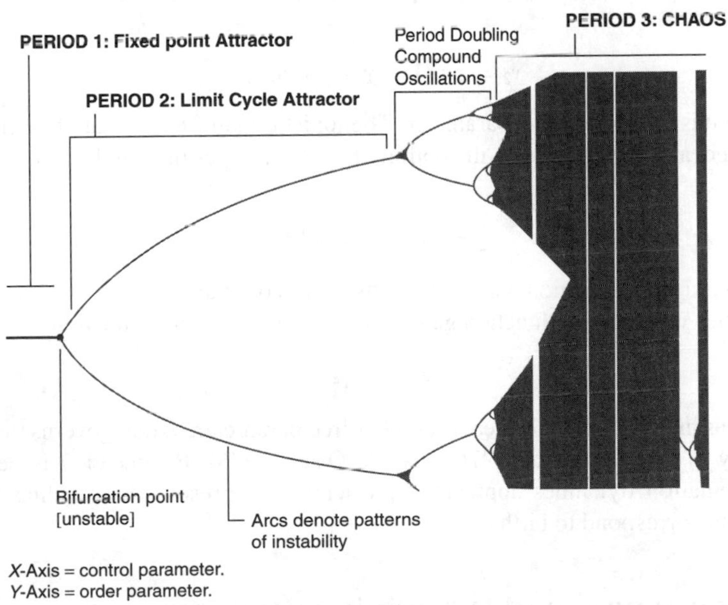

FIG. 2.6. Diagram of the logistic map function showing increasingly complex dynamics as a control parameter increases in value.

full-blown chaos (May, 1976). In the region of the diagram labeled as Period 1, the system is globally stable with dynamics characteristic of a single point attractor.

The bifurcation point marks the transition between Periods 1 and 2. In Period 2, the terrain of the system is marked by a bifurcation and separatrix whereby the system is divided into two attractor basins. The two attractors are located above and below the "pitchfork." A virtual separatrix is located between the prongs. A control parameter is governing the transition of the system from one period to another. The behavior of a system in Period 2 could take the form of a saw-toothed oscillation between the upper and lower boundaries of the pitchfork. Alternatively, trajectories of a behavior could diverge toward attractors on either side of the separatrix.

Toward the end of Period 2, where the control parameter has increased further in value, the bifurcation pattern bifurcates again, dividing the system into four smaller attractor regions. There is a third bifurcation as well, which divides the topography into eight attractor regions. This is the *period doubling* regime. The dynamics of period doubling show oscillations within oscillations.

Period 3 is the region of full-scale chaos (Li & Yorke, 1975). The topology bears little resemblance to the relative order of Periods 1 or 2, or the period doubling configuration. Of particular interest, however, are the windows of relative order that striate the chaotic region. The windows contain ordered trajectories that create a path, with additional bifurcations, from one chaotic period to another.

The equation for the logistic map is relatively simple, and usually represented as:

$$y_2 = cy_1(1 - y_1) = cy_1 - cy_1^2, \tag{2.5}$$

where c is the bifurcation parameter. The logistic map function can be expanded to reflect a dynamic that has the option of going into period doubling or not, such as

$$y_2 = cy_1(1 - y_1)(1 - y_1), \tag{2.6}$$

which is a cubic function that allows substitution of coupled dynamics into one or the other y_1 term. The function generalizes as an exponential function,

$$y_2 = cy_1e^{ayt}, \tag{2.7}$$

whereas in Equation (2.7) there is another free parameter, a, that governs the complexity of function (May 1976; May & Oster, 1976). Parameter a is negative in population dynamics applications, wherein a represents a crowding factor; c would correspond to birth rate.

Conservative and Dissipative Systems

At this juncture it is valuable to introduce the entropy concepts that characterize physical realizations of chaos and bifurcation (Nicolis & Progogine, 1989). In the case of Period 1 dynamics, the system is at rest. As an energy force is applied, such as heat to water, we observe nothing at first, until bubbles that mark the beginning of the boiling process begin to occur. The bubbles rise from the bottom of the beaker, to which heat is applied; a convection process is now taking place where the hot water and air bubbles rise to the top and the cool water from the top is pushed to the bottom. The process continues until the water is boiling throughout the container, the water turns to gaseous water vapor, and heat is *dissipated* into the environment.

Virtually all terrestrial physical systems are dissipative systems like the common one just described. A conservative system is just the opposite; no energy transfers from the system to its environment. If the motion of a pendulum were a true conservative system, the pendulum would swing forever, once it was started. In reality, there is a small amount of friction in the system, which dissipates energy. Thus, the pendulum eventually slows to rest at a fixed point. Conservative systems are convenient abstractions for topological studies, but dissipative processes need to be introduced to define real world systems that might be based on properties of particular conservative systems.

Systems containing increasing amounts of energy increase in entropy of internal randomness. Bifurcations serve the purpose of reducing entropy by allowing the system to split into two or more local topologies, each with lower entropy (Agu, 1983; Thompson, 1982). In the case of boiling water, the phase transition from liquid to gas is the result of a bifurcation that underlies a catastrophe manifold; catastrophe dynamics are explained later in this chapter.

CHAOS AND CHAOTIC ATTRACTORS

The logistic map dropped us off in a state of chaos by the time we reached Period 3. Next, let's see what that means. It is important to remember that not all chaos is a chaotic attractor. Therefore, we consider first the properties of chaos generally, then add the special properties of a chaotic attractor.

Properties of Chaos

Many seemingly random events are actually explicable by simple deterministic equations. The logistic map with $c > 3.56$ is an example, but there are others. A chaotic time series is characterized by three properties: sensitivity to initial conditions, boundedness, and nonrepeatability (Kaplan & Glass, 1995).

The idea of *sensitivity to initial conditions*, also known as *sensitive dependence*, works as follows: Take two points that are arbitrarily close together. As they are iterated through a function, they become further apart. Figure 2.7 depicts an example. The function is an iterative exponential growth function:

$$y_2 = e^{(0.4y_1)}. \tag{2.8}$$

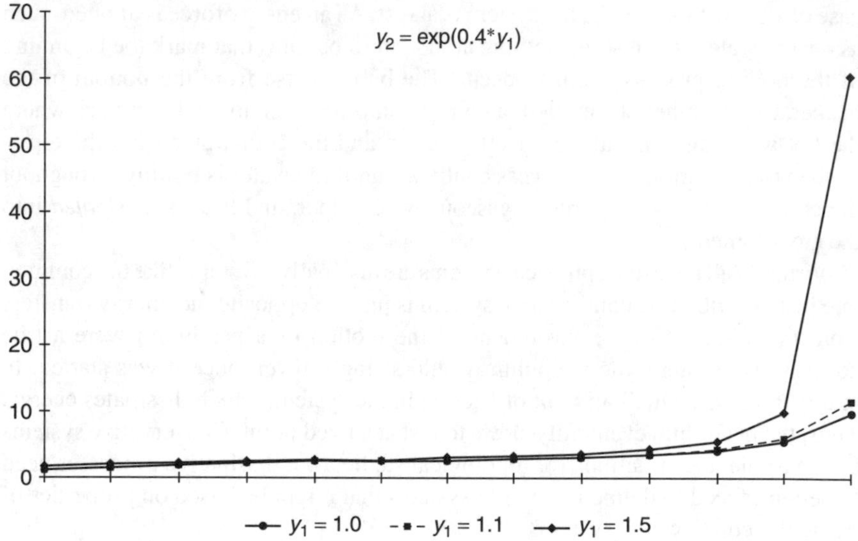

FIG. 2.7. Sensitivity to initial conditions and exponential expansion.

The three trajectories are initial values of 1.0, 1.1, and 1.5. For 11 out of 12 iterations the three functions track each other closely while expanding gradually. On the twelfth, however, they diverge markedly.

Lorenz (1963) discovered sensitive dependence while experimenting with a system of three interrelated equations for describing weather patterns. The equation set required iterative calculations, meaning that initial values of a variable were fed through the equations, then the outcome was fed through the equation again, and so on repeatedly. Lorenz stopped his computer to take a work break. When he returned, he restarted the sequence with the last output value. When the calculations resumed, he noticed the their time series pattern was completely different from the sequence that he had interrupted. It turned out that the computer was calculating to six decimal places, but only printing to three decimal places. All the critical activity was taking place in the unseen decimal places. The discovery led Lorenz to identify an important and distinctive characteristic of chaotic attractors and of chaos in general. Small changes in initial values of a variable lead to large differences in later outcomes. Thus, if any small measurement errors occur when measuring the initial conditions, or even later on, the successive iterations of the function would amplify the deviations. Thus, there is an inherent link between chaos and uncertainty or some definitions of randomness.

Boundedness is another important property of chaos. Figure 2.8 is a time series generated from Equation 2.5 with $c = 4.0$. Notice that the values of x vary markedly over time, and in erratic patterns, but the values never exceed the upper and lower bounds that are implied.

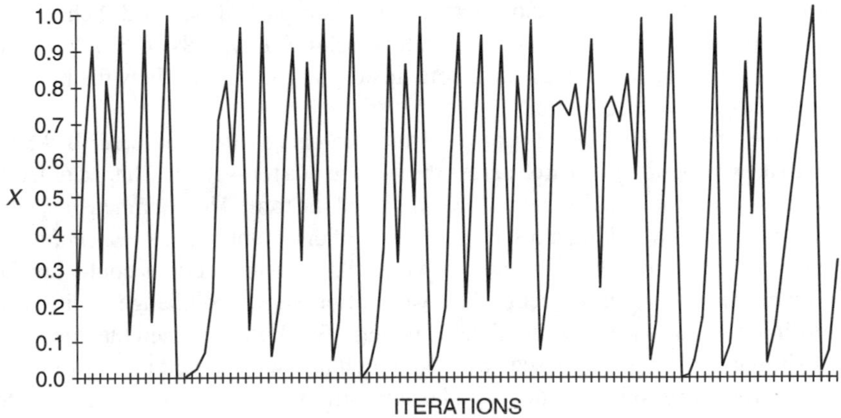

FIG. 2.8. Time series for a chaotic function.

Nonrepeatability is another earmark of chaos. Stated simply, the pattern of numbers shows no repetition. There are a couple caveats to this principle, however. The number series does not repeat so long as the numbers are calculated to a sufficient number of decimal places. If we truncate the values too briefly, we obtain the appearance of repetition (Metzger, 1994).

Another caveat comes from one of the pathways to producing chaos. If we couple three or more oscillators together, we have the minimum conditions to produce chaos (Newhouse, Ruelle, & Takens, 1978; Ueda, 1983). This is not a sufficient condition, however; much depends on the particular combination of oscillators chosen for the occasion (Puu, 1993, 2000a). Nonetheless, we can analyze a hypothetically chaotic time series by searching for qualitative patterns that do repeat at least once. This form of analysis has become known as the method of orbital decomposition (Guastello, 2000a; Guastello, Hyde, & Odak, 1998; Lathrop & Kostelich, 1989; Pincus, 2001). Repetition is a matter of degree in this framework also; the odds of a sequence of observations repeating declines with the length of the sequence.

Chaotic Attractors

Chaotic attractors display the properties of sensitive dependence, boundedness, and nonrepeatability. The sensitive dependence concept has become overstated, according to Abraham et al. (1990). Once a control point enters the basin of an attractor it follows the regime of the attractor, and it no longer matters what the control point was doing before entering the basin.

Chaotic attractors are structurally stable. They attract points and hold them inside just as any other attractor might do. Once inside, the trajectories follow the characteristic motions: Points that veer too close to the outer edge are pulled inward. Those that veer too close to the center are pushed outward. Schools of fish and herds of land animals behave in this fashion (Reynolds, 1987). It would be good to back up a few paces in chaotic history in order to see how the internal chaotic flows were discovered.

In one of the first examples of deterministic chaos after Poincaré, Birkhoff (1932) drove a periodic function across the surface of a torus (bagel shaped object), causing a spiral-like rotation around the outside of the torus. He examined the paths of the trajectories by taking transversal sections of one point in thickness (*Poincare sections*). The places where trajectories passed through the sections could then be compared from section to section and were often shown to change position in two-dimensional space in no predictable pattern. Birkhoff imagined that the torus was similar to a bagel composed of rolled dough that was twisted into its toroidal form. A forced periodic function then became still more complex from section to section, and other topological forms were similarly explored.

Smale (1964) generalized the toroidal forcing concept as the limit of periodic functions driving periodic functions; that concept became a prototype of the chaotic attractor. His now-famous illustration of the horseshoe dynamic utilizes a repeated stretching and folding dynamic. Begin with a straight strip of "dough," stretch it and fold it into three parts, tucking the end third between the first and second. Next, stretch it again transverse to the long axis of the first folding and repeat the wrapping move; then continue the pattern *ad infinitum*. If one were to mark a point on the initial strip of dough and follow it along in a three-dimensional space, its path would be chaotic by the nonrepeating path definition.

Some of the classic chaotic attractors are depicted in Fig. 2.9. They all involve at least three interlaced equations such as $dx/dt = \mathrm{f}(y, z)$, $dy/dt = \mathrm{f}(x, z)$, $dz/dt = \mathrm{f}(x, y)$. I'll refrain from an incantation of their equations because nothing so glamorous has been found in real organizational data yet. If you think you have one, just dust off the books cited earlier in this chapter and move quickly into Chapter 3 of this book to get started testing your theory. Meanwhile the critters in Fig. 2.9 are the Lorenz attractor, the Henon, the Rossler, the Henon-Heiles, and the Henon horseshoe.

The attractors in Fig. 2.9 were all discovered before 1980. Two recent lines of chaos-related investigation are worth mentioning before moving on. Sprott (1997) found that there are 19 vector fields for flow phenomena that are all structurally simpler than the Lorenz attractor. The phase portrait of simplest one of all (Linz & Sprott, 1999) bears a striking resemblance to the Rossler attractor, but with some loss of detail.

Kauffman and Sabelli (1998; also Sabelli, 2001; Sabelli & Kauffman, 1999) discovered a function that can produce dynamics that are more volatile than Period 3 of the logistic map. Their initial objective was to examine the transition between Period 3 chaos to the "stripe" (see Fig. 2.6) that contains four backward bifurcations (or *unifurcations*), and the subsequent transition to Period 4 dynamics.

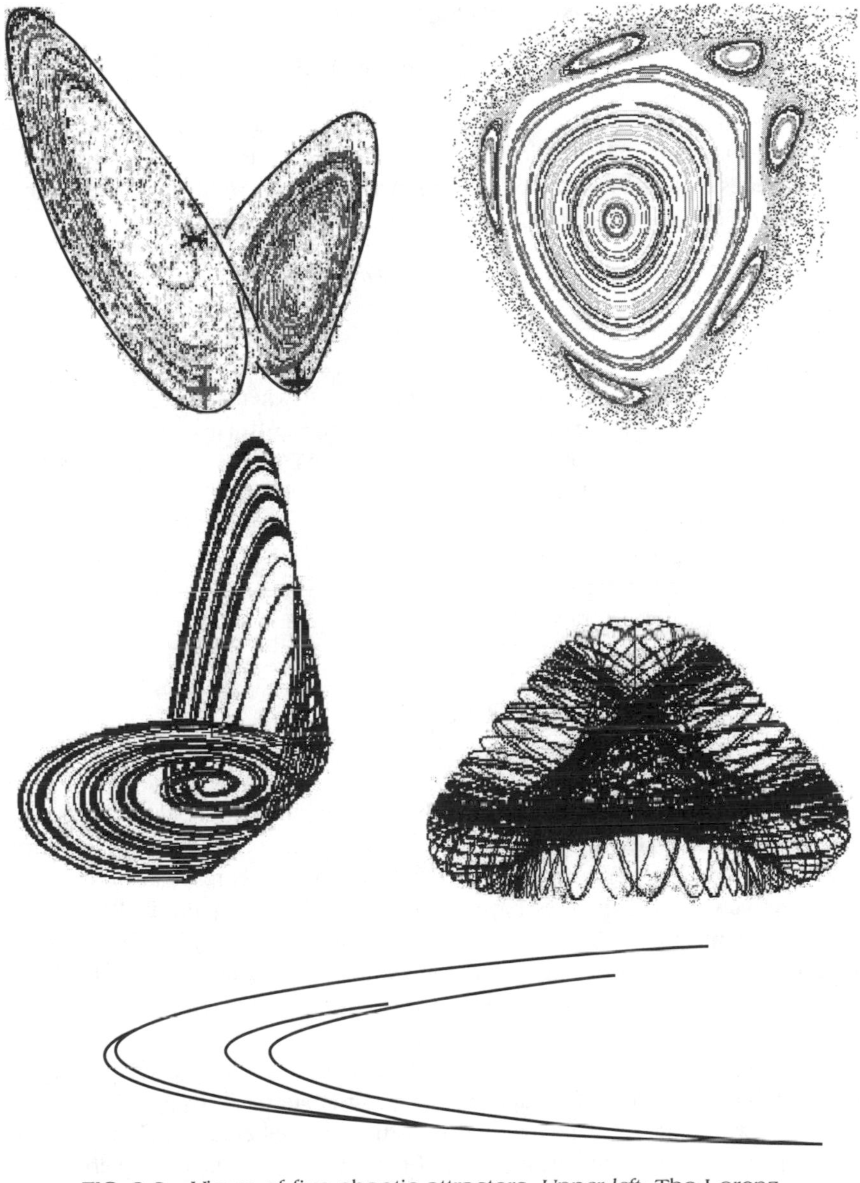

FIG. 2.9. Views of five chaotic attractors. *Upper left*: The Lorenz attractor. *Upper right*: Henon attractor. *Center Left*: Rossler attractor. *Center right*: Henon–Heiles attractor. *Lower*: Henon horseshoe.

Those transitions, they found, occur in the system:

$$A_{t+1} = A_t + g_t \sin(A_t). \tag{2.9}$$

They call Equation 2.9 the "biotic" equation to foreshadow some plausible biological applications: The biotic equation is a *forced oscillator* that produces chaotic series of A when $g > 4.603$. The function becomes asymmetrical when a constant q is introduced:

$$A_{t+1} = A_t + g_t \sin(q + A_t). \tag{2.10}$$

They report that the oscillations in the stock market appear to be examples of such asymmetrical biotic patterning. Similarly, electrocardiogram patterns are asymmetrical, and thought to result in cardiac arrest when q becomes too large. Because new dynamics appear as g and q are varied, Kauffman and Sabelli (1998) have speculated on several other potential applications. The asymmetry constant is also interpretable as a feedback function. As such it bears some resemblance to the dampened oscillator, except that is works in the opposite direction of amplifying, rather than dampening oscillatory behavior.

Finally chaotic attractors have one more property that cannot be missed. The shape of their basins is a fractal. Fractals are considered next.

FRACTALS

Fractals are geometric structures with fractional dimensionality. They were studied most intensely by Mandelbrot (1983) beginning in the early 1950s, although there was a sleepy line of relevant work by Cantor, Koch, and Hausdorff in the 1880–1920 period. Although the study of fractals is responsible for a lot of pretty pictures, the pictures have not done much yet for the understanding of work organizations. There are concepts of fractal origin, however, that play important roles in NDS studies of organizations. A few artful examples from Sprott's *Fractal of the Day* web site appear in Fig. 2.10; for reference see Sprott (2001).

Mandelbrot (1983) observed that simple geometric questions, such as "How long is the coast of Britain?" do not have necessarily simple answers. The coast of Britain, as with other real land forms, is ragged. If we make a crude ellipse around the periphery of the island, one measure of perimeter is obtained. If we choose to measure around the zigs and zags of the land form in 1-kilometer units, a larger measure is obtained. If we measure the same coast in 1-meter units, capturing all the subtle nonlinearities, the measurement is longer still.

The underlying theme is the measure of *scale*. Working with a particular level of scale produces a particular measure. Mandelbrot (1983) further observed that

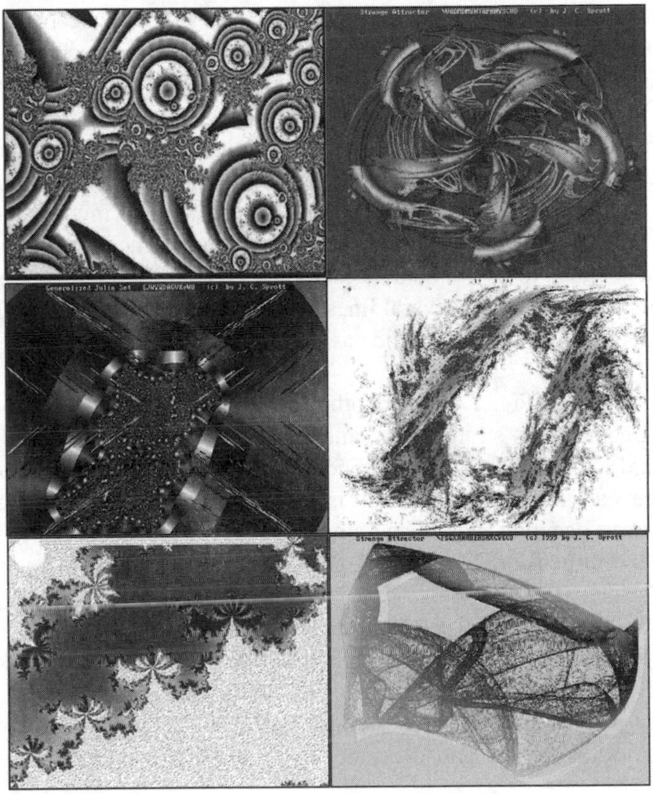

FIG. 2.10. Examples of fractals from the Fractal of the Day Web Site by J. C. Sprott, *http//sprott.physics.wisc.edu*. Reprinted with permission.

boundaries between pairs of countries in Europe have been reported to be different lengths even though the actual boundaries did not change between the reports. Different scales were used at different times of measurement, with the smaller country tending to use smaller scales of measurement.

Fractal Structure

The essential fractal structure is a self-referential or recursive function. Not only does it repeat itself across space, but the resulting geometric forms build upon the same spatial structure at different levels of scale. It is an essential premise of Mandelbrot's (1983) work that naturally occurring geometry is not the results of chance or randomness. According to Mandelbrot, the concept of randomness entered the English language through a medieval French idiom meaning "the motions of a horse that the rider cannot control." The essence of randomness is, therefore, that the observer is not controlling motions or activities of some sort, and has little to do with whether the actual process is actually occurring by chance.

The first historical example of such a recursive fractal function is Cantor's dust, which emulates the distribution of cosmic dust particles. The dust can be created by taking a straight line, dividing it into thirds, throwing the middle third away, and repeating the process for the remaining line segments *ad infinitum*. The "thirds" do not need to be of equal size. Additional complexity can be introduced by middle-third-decimating several lines in several directions at once. The result will be a space full of dust that could easily resemble the "snow" on a badly tuned television.

The Koch curve (Fig. 2.11) is another construction based on a middle-third principle. Begin with a straight line, and divide it into three parts. Push the end thirds inward so that the middle third buckles and folds. Repeat the process for all line segments ad infinitum. The result is a crinkly line that is no longer straight. The Koch curve occupies more than a single linear dimension, but does not occupy the entire two-dimensional space of a plane. Its dimensionality is actually equal to 1.26.

The process of making a Koch curve can be generalized to operations performed on a triangle, or other regular closed geometric form, to produce Koch islands. The islands serve as prototypes for real land formations and the topological analysis thereof. But why stop with planar islands? Entire landscapes can be produced in two to three dimensions. Landscapes occupy at least two dimensions, but do not

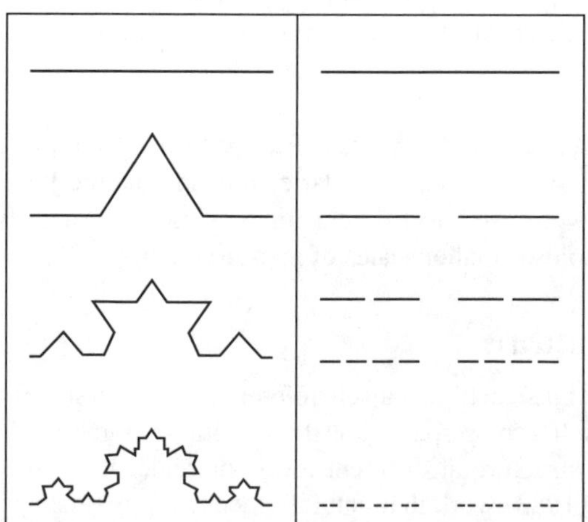

FIG. 2.11. Fractals created by middle-third decimation. *Left*: Koch curve. *Right*: Cantor dust.

uniformly utilize the third, which is why we have mountains and plains. Canyons can be regarded as "negative mountains."

Trees, leaves, seashells, lightning, cell structures, and so on can be defined as fractals, and computer-generated through "forgeries." With fractal forgeries, a computer does not need to store the entire bitmap image of an image, only the algorithm for generating the image. The more exciting line of research, however, is in the development of algorithms that track gradual shifts in biological form along a small number of parameters. The shifts in form, and the parameter values by implication, could be the result of an evolutionary mutation process (Kocic, 2001), which has been historically difficult to track.

Fractals and Chaos

Fractal geometry and nonlinear dynamics were eventually connected when Feigenbaum (1978) discovered an important principle of the logistic map. The pattern of bifurcations comprises a self-similar geometry that qualifies the whole pattern as a fractal. The bifurcations within the period doubling regime differ from each other and from the main bifurcation on the basis of their scale only. That property allowed Feigenbaum to isolate universal constants that marked critical values of the bifurcation parameter at which a bifurcation could be assured to take place. For instance chaos would always set in when $c > 3.6$ in Equation 2.14.

The fractal nature of the logistic map soon inspired additional work directed at describing the fractal nature of basins containing chaotic attractors (Farmer, Ott, & Yorke, 1983; Girault, 1991; Mandelbrot, 1977, 1983). The Lorenz attractor, for instance, is thought to have a dimensionality of 2.06. In any event, the dimensionality of an attractor is now regarded as a measure of the attractor's complexity, and the complexity of the process that generated it. The exact relationship between dimensionality and the complexity of a process is, unfortunately, not exact.

Fractal Dimensions

The calculation of fractal dimension is important not only for understanding and utilizing fractal geometry, but also for assessing the complexity of an attractor, or other phenomena that are expressed in a spatial series or a time series. The concept of fractal dimension dates back to Hausdorff (1919), and was later modified by Mandelbrot (1983). The fractal dimension is defined as

$$D_f = \lim_{l \to 0} \frac{\log[1/M(l)]}{\log l}. \quad (2.11)$$

Imagine that a fractal image is covered with cubes with sides of length l. $M(l)$ is a function of the *embedding dimension*, ε. A true line will require $\varepsilon = 1$, a surface $\varepsilon = 2$, volume $\varepsilon = 3$, and so forth. The number of squares required to cover a point is proportional to $M(l)$, where

$$M(l) = 1/l^{-\varepsilon}. \tag{2.12}$$

The *correlation dimension* has led to an often-used algorithm for calculating attractor dimension (Grassberger & Procaccia, 1983). They define dimension as

$$D_c = \lim_{l \to 0} \frac{\log \|u_i\|_y}{\log l}, \tag{2.13}$$

where l represents the diameter of a circle rather than the side of a square, and $\|u_i\|_y$ denotes the average value of $1/M(l)$ over all points in a time or spatial series of points. Although D_c was meant to approximate D_f, it is now known that $D_c < D_f$ (Girault, 1991; Kugiumtzis, Lillekjendlie, & Christophersen, 1994).

When applied to a time series, however, Equation 2.13 produces unreliable results depending on the amount of noise present in the data, and whether the data are over-sampled or undersampled (Theiler & Eubank, 1993). It is also difficult to determine the correct rate of sampling when tests are being made on standard attractor formulae, such as those that produced the chaotic attractors in Fig. 2.10. Because smooth mapping exist in the near neighborhood of an attractor (Wiggins, 1988); overly short time intervals would lead to a bias toward the linearity conclusion. Choice of time interval can seriously affect the definitions of attractors that one might extract from an analysis (Yee, Sweby, & Griffiths, 1991). When studying real systems (which is what we are doing here), Theiler & Eubank (1993) recommended that the rate of sampling be set relative to the physical properties of the system that is generating the data. For instance, if the system produces values every 2 seconds, a 2-second interval is appropriate. Similarly, if a particular type of economic data is generated every quarter of the year, then four observations per year would be appropriate.

Inverse Power Law

Another way to reach the correlation dimension is to rely on the principle of scale. If we take a frequency distribution of events and order the events by size, we would notice that the large examples of the event are relatively infrequent. The small examples would be more frequent. Next let the size of the event be X in Equation 2.14, which is the *inverse power law*:

$$\text{Freq}(X) = aX^{-b}. \tag{2.14}$$

The parameters a and b can be estimated by nonlinear regression. The value of b that we obtain from that procedure is the fractal dimension. The examples of the inverse power law are widespread and varied according to Bak (1996) and West and Deering (1995).

Some folks obtain the inverse power law function by transforming Equation 2.14 into Equation 2.15:

$$\log(\text{Freq}[X]) = -b\log[X] + a. \tag{2.15}$$

Although the two forms are mathematically equivalent, they are only statistically equivalent in the unlikely case where there is no noise. The product-moment correlation coefficient, r, is used in place of b in Equation 2.15. As we know, the value of r is large when there is no noise in the data and small otherwise. In other words, this calculation of the fractal dimension is confounded with the level or noise (or psychometric error). The two entities are not confounded in nonlinear regression, however.

Lyapunov Exponents and Dimensions

Although chaotic attractors exhibit fractional dimensionality, at least to a small degree, the presence of a fractional D_f is not a sufficient test of chaos. The property of sensitivity to initial conditions is still missing. The *Lyapunov exponent* is based on a concept of entropy, which is the rate at which information that allows a forecast of a variable y is lost. It is calculated (Kaplan & Glass, 1995, pp. 334–335; Puu, 2000a, p. 157) by taking pairs of initial conditions y_1 and y_2 and their iterates one step ahead in time, which would be y_2 and y_3. If the ratio of absolute values of differences

$$L \approx |y_3 - y_2|/|y_2 - y_1| \tag{2.16}$$

is less than 1.0, then the series is contracting. If the value of the function is greater than 1.0, then the function is expanding and sensitive dependence is present. The Lyapunov exponent, λ, is thus

$$\lambda \approx \ln[L]. \tag{2.17}$$

For an ensemble of trajectories in a dynamical field, Lyapunov exponents, λ_i, are computed for all values of y. If the largest value of λ is positive, and the sum of λ_i is negative, then the series is chaotic.

Calculation 2.17 is made on the entire time series and averaged by taking the geometric mean of N values where N is the last entry in the time series. Or, rearranging the terms:

$$\lambda = (1/N)\sum_{N=1}^{N} \ln(L)|. \tag{2.18}$$

The foregoing calculations generalize as:

$$y = e^{\lambda t}, \tag{2.19}$$

which is actually insensitive to initial conditions. A positive value of λ indicates an expanding function, which is to say, chaos. A negative λ indicates a contracting process, which could be fixed point or limit cycle. Dimension, D_L becomes a function of the largest value of λ in the series (Frederickson, Kaplan, E.Yorke, & J. Yorke, 1983; Kugiumtzis et al., 1994; Wiggins, 1988):

$$D_L = e^{\lambda}. \tag{2.20}$$

The Lyapunov exponent an indicator of turbulence (Ruelle, 1991) such as the turbulence that occurs in air and fluid flows. It is tempting to digress here into the relationships between entropy, neg-entropy, information as defined by Shannon (1948), topological entropy, and the Lyapunov exponent. Because we are not going to rely on those relationships in any deliberate way in this book, I should simply suggest a few references where the connections can be found (Guastello, 2000; Guastello, Hyde et al., 1998; Lathrop & Kostelich, 1989; Ott, Sauer & Yorke, 1994; Puu, 2000a).

SELF-ORGANIZATION AND COUPLED DYNAMICS

A system in a state of chaos will reduce its internal entropy by making feedback loops among its subsystems. A self-organized system is one that contains several subsystems that are interconnected by feedback loops. Figure 2.12 shows a dynamical scheme representing four interconnected subsystems. A *dynamical scheme* is a representation of complex dynamics in a self-organized or coupled-dynamic system. The three subsystems could be hooked together in other ways as well, but the important point is that the output parameter for one of the subsystems becomes the

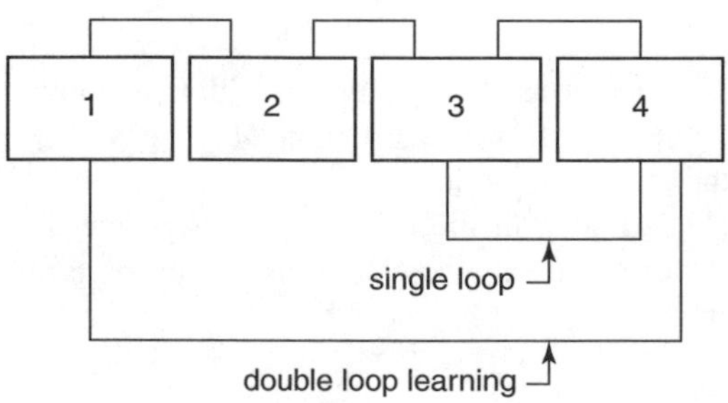

FIG. 2.12. A self-organized system containing four subsystems and one of many possible configurations of feedback loops. This diagram contrasts single- and double-loop learning in human systems.

input parameter for another. Also critical is the circularity in the feedback loop; this form of reciprocal causation changes a dynamical scheme from fundamentally linear to nonlinear.

Feedback Loops and Coupled Dynamics

Let's take a closer look at the feedback loops. A negative feedback loop keeps a system stable within certain boundaries. A positive feedback loop accelerates a behavior, and could lead to bifurcation and chaos. Senge (1980) is credited for identifying the role of feedback loops in social systems and managerial behavior. The idea, however, is at least as old as the thermostat.

Figure 2.12 is configured for a system that could describe single- and double-loop learning in organizations (Argyris & Schon, 1978). Subsystem 1 is the goal-defining and goal-setting phase of a decision process. The results of Subsystem 1 feed into Subsystem 2, which makes a particular plan to achieve the goals. The results of Subsystem 2 feed into Subsystem 3, which executes the necessary actions. The actions of Subsystem 3 are, in essence, waves of information released into the environment, which is signified by Subsystem 4. In single-loop learning (which is considered as an organizational phenomenon in Chapter 4), feedback from the environment affects the action mechanism, which sharpens its efforts to produce a better result if necessary. Single loop learning does not affect the general plan or the goals and assumptions of the system. Double-loop learning, however, *does* affect the goals and assumptions of the system. In doing so, it affects every other link in the decision–action chain.

There is no reason to assume that the output of any subsystem is steady, oscillating, chaotic, or otherwise indicative of any other specific and friendly dynamical pattern. The dynamics of one output do become the input for another subsystem, however. The output of the secondary subsystem will reflect, in part, the dynamics of its input. The general set of relationships can be called *coupled dynamics*. We have already encountered examples in the form of dampened oscillators and forced oscillators. Coupled dynamics gave rise to the general notion of complex systems, which in turn includes mechanisms of self-organization. A few mechanisms of self-organization are considered next: synergetics, catalysts, the rugged landscape, and the sand pile.

Synergetics

Coupled dynamics are central to Haken's (1984) *synergetics*, which is the study of nonlinear dynamics in interacting subsystems. The springboard concept is the *driver–slave* relationship. A driver is usually observed as a relatively slow dynamic that modulates the behavior of a faster-moving slave. For instance, we could have a periodic oscillator driving a chaotic slave. The result would be a broadly periodic function that, when it reaches a certain point, turns on the fast-moving chaotic behavior. An example of that dynamic occurred in a study of the output of creative problem-solving groups (Guastello, 1998a); see Chapter 6.

According to Haken (1988), the flow of information across subsystems is the common feature among all forms of self-organization. When a system reaches a sufficient level of entropy, hierarchical structures emerge that act as drivers. Drivers in the "upper" level of the hierarchy control the dynamics of the "lower" level.

The emergence of a hierarchical structure follows the same mathematical and physical dynamics as a phase transition, such as the transition of a solid to a liquid. The Ginzberg–Landau model for chemical phase transitions (Thompson, 1982) describes conditions of high and low potential energy within a system as a function of two control parameters:

$$f(y) = y^4/4 - by^2/2 - ay, \tag{2.21}$$

which happens to be the integral and potential function of the cusp catastrophe model; see later on this chapter. The main outcomes of Equation 2.21 are shown in Fig. 2.13.

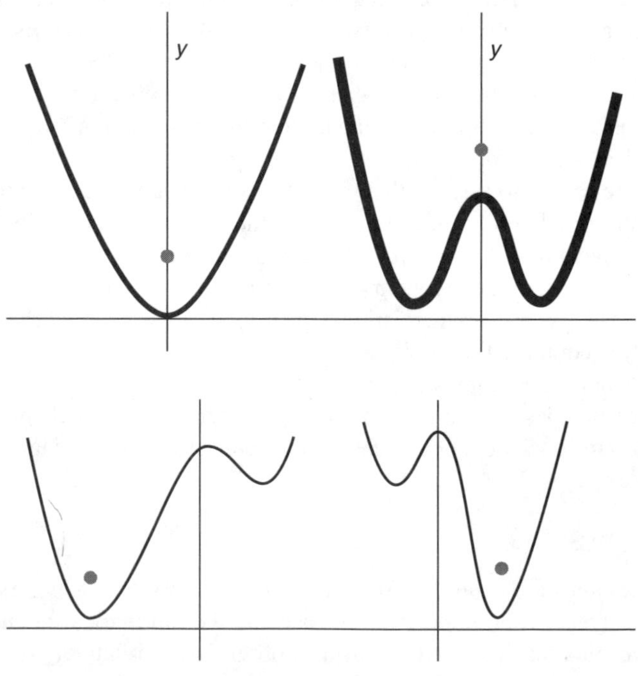

FIG. 2.13. General model for chemical phase transitions, showing distributions of potential energy as two control variables are allowed to vary.

The upper left panel of Fig. 2.13 is the condition where only one potential state exists ($b = 0$, $a = 0$); it becomes unstable as the bifurcation factor is allowed to increase. The upper right shows a system with two equipotential states ($b > 0$, $a = 0$). The control point could fall into either one. The lower panels of Fig. 2.13 show the control point falling toward one state or the other as the asymmetry parameter is allowed to deflect in one direction or the other. The valleys occupied by the control points in the lower panels reflect points of local stability, high probability density, and low potential energy for further system change.

Catalysts

A chemical catalyst is a reagent that accelerates the formation of compounds made from two or more other chemicals without being consumed in the process. Perhaps the all-time favorite catalyst was the presence of tetraethyl-lead in gasoline. Its presence lowered the ignition point for the octane–air mixture. The catalyst also facilitated a refinement process that required only half the amount of crude oil to make a quantity of gasoline compared to the unleaded gasoline currently in use. (Leaded gasoline produced unacceptable levels of air pollution, however. Thus, automobile engines are equipped with "catalytic converters," which allow the combustion of gasoline without tetraethyl-lead).

According to Kauffman (1995), the odds of life forming on earth would be very slim if life were to rely on the random slamming of protein soup molecules. It would have had to be the case that there were special biochemicals in the soup that acted as catalysts. Such catalysts would facilitate the recombination of certain protein compounds with certain others. The RNA–DNA system currently in fashion today maintains the integrity of the design of a species and keeps the so-called random variation contained.

The behavior of catalysts can be described mathematically as a system of typically three equations. As with the case of the Lorenz attractor mentioned earlier and the general self-organized model depicted in Fig. 2.12, variables x, y, and z are related such that $x = f(y, z)$, $y = f(x, z)$, and $z = f(x, y)$. Such an interrelated grouping of functions would be called *replicator equations*.

The Rugged Landscape

The rugged landscape model of self-organization describes changes in the adaptive behavior of species. The theoretical scenario (Kauffman, 1993, 1995) begins with a species that is well-adapted to its ecological niche. It is normally distributed along many variables that are *not yet* relevant to its survival. Eventually, a cataclysm of some sort hits, and the species must find a new source of food and a new place to live. The species disperses itself around the rugged landscape trying out new niches. Some niches work well so long as the species members that are trying to occupy it share some traits that facilitate their survival in that niche.

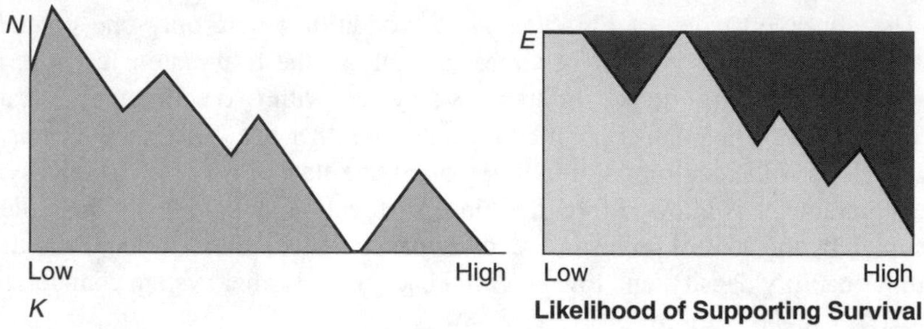

FIG. 2.14. The rugged landscape self-organization dynamic. *Left*: The plot of *N* survivors given *K* adaptation-relevant traits. *Right*: The same function expressed as entropy given environmental support for survival.

Different locally stable ecosystems require different adaptations. Kauffman (1993, 1995) refers to the locally stable ecosystems as *fitness peaks* in reference to the concentrated probabilities of organisms surviving in those locations. The fitness peaks are, for all intents and purposes, the low-entropy valleys of the Ginzberg–Landau phase transition. Figure 2.14, left panel, depicts the distribution of survivors as a function of the number of traits shared. This is the $N|K$ distribution. There is a large portion (N) of the original species that survives by sharing only one (K) trait. Progressively smaller numbers of organisms are found that share progressively more traits as might be required of an ecological niche. The distribution is lumpy, showing subgroups of organisms "living" on "fitness peaks." Figure 2.14, right panel, depicts an inversion of the $N|K$ distribution such that the fitness peaks shown on the left panel fit into low-entropy valleys of the landscape on the right. The distribution of organisms can be thus restated in terms of the landscape's properties. If the landscape is "rugged," selection forces must be strong in order to hold a species in a specific area. Under those conditions, the surviving species members will need to exhibit a relatively greater number of special characteristics that distinguish them from the general population. If the landscape is "smooth," selection forces are relatively weak. Under those conditions, the surviving species members are much less differentiated from the general population (Kauffman, 1995; McKelvey, 1999).

The landscape scenario also requires another parameter, C, to denote the complexity of an organism's interaction with other species in the environment. Some of the interactions may be competitive. In either case, there is a co-evolutionary process taking place whereby the species that occupy a location adapt to each other (Kauffman, 1995; McKelvey, 1999).

An important dynamic, therefore, is the potential movement of a species from one local niche to another. The previous scenario involved the differentiation of a species into subgroups, now the subgroups will try their luck at hopping niches. According to some contemporary ecologists, an organism that is well-suited to its niche becomes proportionately less likely to colonize another environmental "patch." If there is an invasion of their own territory, they do not colonize effectively in response; thus the phenomenon became known as *extinction debt* (Tilman, 1994; Tilman, May, Lehman, & Nowak, 1994). Good colonizers, on the other hand, do not have a lot of reasons to stay where they are; they are more or less compelled to use their colonization advantages to keep moving. Some possible dynamics of *N*, *K*, and *C* that could apply to business strategy decisions are discussed in Chapter 4.

Multiple Basin Model

A new mechanism of self-organization was recently developed by Crutchfield and van Nimwegen (1999). The multiple basin dynamic builds on the rugged landscape concept to describe how small changes in genetic structure can self-organize into new and different species. A schematic of the concept appears in Fig. 2.15. The basins represent subgroups of species members, which are in turn connected to each other through narrow portals.

Following the thinking in evolution theory over the past two decades, Crutchfield and van Nimwegen (1999) observed that the relationship between a genotype and a phenotype is subject to many sources of imperfection. There are similar imperfections between the relationship between the phenotype and actual fitness.

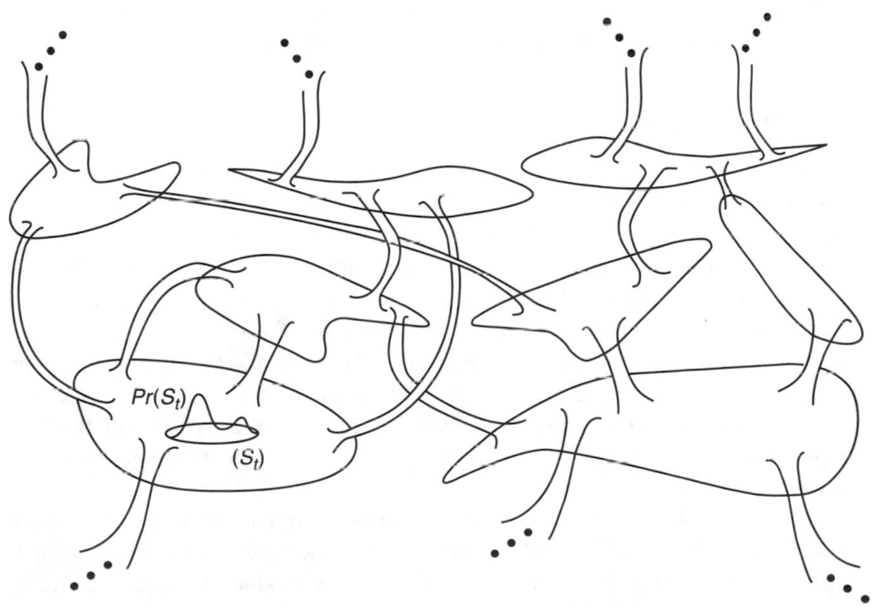

FIG. 2.15. The multiple basin self-organization dynamic by Crutchfield and van Nimwegen (1999). Reprinted with permission.

Furthermore, transitions between one dominant phenotype expressed by a species and a new phenotype later in time are not always gradual. Rather, they often occur in sudden dramatic shifts, or punctuated equilibria.

According to the multiple basin scenario of self-organization, an organism expresses variability on numerous and potentially adaptation-relevant traits. Trait combinations within certain ranges of values predispose the organism toward fitness in a particular attractor basin. Some combinations of traits, however, predispose the organism toward low fitness in one basin, but at the same time position the organism at the edge of a portal connecting it to a new basin where its fitness will be much greater. The sudden shift through a portal explains the sudden discontinuities in fitness inherent in punctuated equilibrium models for evolutionary processes.

The multiple basin mechanism of self-organization is reasonably consistent with the thinking in the field of ecology. For instance, one may think of fisheries in terms of their major oceanic basins (e.g., Guastello, 1997a; See chapter 11). At the same time an ocean is a very large place. There are many smaller ecological niches within any one of them that sustain some species groups and not others. Furthermore, others have observed that the predator–prey relationship between fish and their food supply (e.g., plankton) produces a patchiness within any one such niche (Medvinsky, Tikhov, Enderlein, Malchow, 2000). Subregions of the niche contain different densities of predators and prey, which are not continuous from one subregion to another. Echoes of the multiple basin dynamics also show up in the extinction debt dynamics mentioned earlier.

Sand Piles and Avalanches

The sand pile model of self-organization centers around a question that is common to all models of self-organization: Can a global structure emerge from local interaction among agents or subsystems? According to Bak (1996) who literally studied sand piles with his coworkers, the mechanism works as follows. We have a sand pile onto which we allow more sand to trickle. At first, the pile just gets a little taller. Then sand runs down the sides to increase the size of the pile overall. Eventually, however, enough sand has trickled onto the pile that the shape of the pile shifts dramatically. Here we observe an avalanche from the initial pile into several piles of different sizes. The frequency of small piles is greater than the frequency of large pile, according to the inverse power law. The general idea is shown in Fig. 2.16.

It is noteworthy, however, that the $1/f$ sandpile dynamics really only work for simulations of sandpiles under some circumscribed conditions (Vespignani & Zapperi, 1997). Some simulation strategies do not produce the self-organizing dynamics at all (Rushkin & Feng, 1997). Simulated sand is not real sand. Real sand isn't pure, it can be sticky or contain clay. Pouring or raining the sand onto a pile can induce different long-run effects (Weiss, 1999).

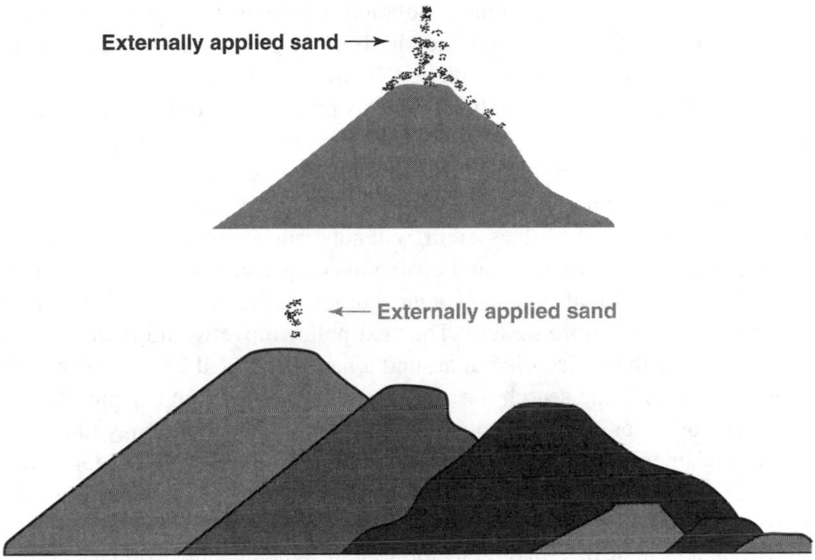

FIG. 2.16. The sand pile self-organization dynamic. *Upper*: Sand is applied to an existing pile. *Lower*: An avalanche occurs at a critical point that results in a distribution of piles of different sizes.

Systems at the Edge of Chaos

Systems at the edge of chaos are predominately living systems that slip in and out of a chaotic regime through self-organization (Waldrop, 1992). There is growing evidence to suggest (Freeman, 2000; Grigsby & Stevens, 2000) that organisms that are most capable of survival are those that can respond to potentially chaotic flows of information coming from the environment. Additionally, they can generate the variety of response elements that are as diversified as the states observed in mathematical chaos. Once patterns of stimuli have been detected and associated with responses, feedback loops form that maintain the stimulus–response connections. Behaviors and physical structures thus self-organize in a manner that resembles a phase transition (Vetter, Stadler, & Haynes, 1997). The organisms that would exhibit the best long-run survival are those that are continually poised at the edge of chaos. Meanwhile, those of us who study them from the other side of the looking glass would be looking for control variables that might explain when an organism's behavioral organization would slip from chaos to self-organization and back again.

In contemporary evolution theory, it now appears that selection principles operate on populations that have a high degree of diversity such that their numbers over time or space, or distributions of genetic qualities, are close to chaotic. Because genetic qualities are correlated, the genetic structure of a population is self-organized, and reorganizes when confronted with a selection dynamic. The self-organization ensures the future stability of that population. By contrast, populations that are isolated in stable niches and stable therein, become greatly destabilized when an environmental event disrupts their niche (Kauffman, 1993).

At a more general level of analysis, which would not be confined to population dynamics, complex systems coevolve with their environment and other species. A few generalizable principles emerge. An attempt to control a complex system, perhaps through natural selection or an organizational or political policy by operating on only one feature of the system, will not eradicate or otherwise nullify the system. The system will mutate and evolve to compensate for the environmental assault. The secret of real system change is to locate the dynamical key that supports or unravels the entire system. The next policy move would be to guide the reorganization of the entire system around a new dynamical key (Hubler, 1992). A problem involving the search for a dynamical key appears in Chapter 9.

The edge of chaos phenomenon as it is currently understood may indeed represent a fundamental principle of life, learning, psychology, and organizational behavior. On the other hand, it also suggests strongly that mathematical chaos may be difficult to find in social systems. Where it occurs it might not last a long time before the forces of self-organization set in. When we investigate a complex social structure we might be observing a system that is already self-organized to a great extent.

CATASTROPHE THEORY

A mathematical catastrophe involves a sudden change in a system's state. The sudden change is propelled by one or more (most often two) control parameters. Bifurcation functions are always involved, and they range from a single critical point to a complex manifold. Catastrophe functions do not require an underlying assumption of a self-organization mechanism. On the other hand, the sudden changes implied by self-organization mechanisms can be modeled as catastrophes. For instance, the shift in work performance from "adequate" to "excellent," or from "employed" to "turnover" would be examples of catastrophes that do not require an assumption about self-organization; that particular model is considered in Chapter 5. The shift of an organism, or organizational strategy, from one fitness peak of a rugged landscape to another would be a class of examples that does involve a self-organization mechanism, some of which appear in Chapter 4. Similarly, the differentiation of a species across a landscape would involve a self-organization mechanism; an application of those concepts to leadership emergence appears in Chapter 9.

The central proposition of catastrophe theory is the classification theorem (Thom, 1975), which states (with qualifications) that, given a maximum of four control parameters, all discontinuous changes of events can be modeled by one of seven elementary topological forms. The forms are hierarchical and vary in the complexity of the behavior spectrum they encompass. The models describe change between (or among) qualitatively distinct forms for behavior, such as remaining on a job versus quitting; they do not necessarily infer any notion of desirable or undesirable outcome.

Steady states and changes in behavior are governed by one to four *control parameters*, depending on the complexity of the behavior spectrum under consideration. In NDS, a control denotes an independent variable that has a particular function in the change process. In research, the investigator would identify one or more psychological measurements that would correspond to a particular function. I introduced the term *latent control parameter* (1987) to denote the underlying parameter in the topological model, which is distinguished from research variables that may, singly or in combination, *contribute to* the latent control parameter.

The elementary catastrophe models are classified into two groups: the cuspoids and the umbilics. The elementary cuspoids involve one dependent measure, have potential functions in three to six dimensions, and response surfaces in two to five dimensions. They are the fold, cusp, swallowtail, and butterfly. The names reflect fanciful interpretations of what parts of their geometry they resemble. The elementary umbilics involve two dependent outcome measures, three or four control parameters, and response surfaces in five or six codimensions. The umbilics are the wave crest (or hyperbolic umbilic), hair (or elliptic umbilic), and mushroom (or parabolic umbilic) models.

The term *codimension* has multiple meanings in topology, depending on where it is being used (Poston & Stewart, 1978). Option 1: It is an elision of "control dimension" meaning "number of control parameters." Option 2: It refers to the sum of control parameters and behavioral outcome (order) parameters. Option 3: It refers to the sum of geometric dimensions for the behavioral spectra, especially when systems are being compared that contain varying numbers of behavioral spectra. Throughout this book I will refer to control parameters as control parameters, and use the codimension of a model to mean Option 2 above. There is no contradiction between Options 2 and 3 if cuspoid models (one behavioral spectrum) are involved, but complications arise when umbilic models are involved. A mushroom model appears in Chapter 6, and I will be explicit there as to what behavioral spectra and control parameters are involved.

The descriptions of the elementary models and sundry others are considered next. Arnold (1974), Gilmore (1981), Poston and Stewart (1978), Thom (1975), Thompson (1982), Woodcock and Davis (1978), and Zeeman (1977) serve as general references for the structure of catastrophe models and provide numerous applications outside the social sciences. The full set of elementary catastrophes and many applications to organizational behavior appear in Guastello (1995a).

According to the *singularity rule*, which is a major result of the classification theorem (Thom, 1975), there is only one possible response surface for a bifurcation set with a given number of control parameters. The singularity rule actually holds true for catastrophe models with five control parameters, as well as for those models with four or fewer controls. There are four catastrophe models with five control parameters. One model, the *wigwam*, is a six-dimensional cuspoid. There are three umbilics with five control parameters, each of which has a model codimension of 7. Their names are the *second hyperbolic*, *second elliptic*, and *symbolic umbilic* models. They differ in the number of modulus terms they contain. For a glimpse at the complex geometry associated with some of those models, see Callahan (1980, 1982).

Catastrophe models of still-greater complexity exist, but they do not conform to the singularity rule. The simplest of those is the *double cusp*. The double cusp consists of two dependent measures and six control parameters. Each dependent outcome oscillates between two stable states of behavior. There are four eight-dimensional response surfaces associated with the double cusp potential function. The topology of the double cusp and other nonsingular catastrophe models can be found in Arnold (1974) and Zeeman (1977).

Fold Catastrophe Model

The coverage of catastrophe models in this chapter is largely limited to the first two elementary models only, which are the fold and cusp catastrophes. The cusp is the model that is used most. The fold is good for a warm-up exercise for understanding the cusp. Swallowtail, butterfly, and mushroom models do appear in this book, but it would be simpler to explain them at the points in the narrative where they occur. In any case, each model has a *potential function*, a *response surface*, and a *bifurcation set*. The response surface describes the change in behavioral state over time, and it is the most interesting aspect of the catastrophe models in the social science applications. The potential function is the integral of the response surface function. The bifurcation set is the pattern of instabilities underlying the catastrophe response surface; it is the derivative of the response surface, or the second derivative of the potential function.

The potential function for the fold catastrophe is

$$f(y) = y^3/3 - ay, \tag{2.22}$$

and its response surface is defined as the set of points where

$$\delta f(y)/\delta y = y^2 - a, \tag{2.23}$$

where y is the dependent measure and a is the control parameter. The fold model is the basic geometric building block of the seven elementary models and beyond. It describes a change in behavior from a stable steady state or attractor to an unstable state as a function of a. The relationship between a and y is a common threshold model. The behavior is observed to remain steady, even though a is changing. Once a hits a critical value, however, behavior changes abruptly. Because the change is in the direction of an instability, the trajectory of y leaves the basin of the attractor and flies outward, never to return. The equilibrium values of y are determined by setting Equation 2.23 equal to 0. The negative value is the center of the stable attractor, and the positive value is the unstable center.

Haslett, Moss, Osborne, and Ramm (2000) published an illustrative example of a fold catastrophe model that was based on self-organized work behavior. The situation involved postal workers in Australia who sorted mail. The pay rules under which they worked encouraged them to work either extra fast or extra slow. If the mail volume was light, they would work extra fast and thus be able to go home early and still get paid for the whole shift. If the mail volume looked like it was going to be medium-heavy or heavy, they would stretch the work out so they could qualify for some overtime pay and a meal allowance. The least attractive option for them was to do a normal day's work in a normal day's time. The analysis of the distribution of "fly days" and "mealies" indicated that there was an unstable attractor for fly days, and a stable attractor for mealies. The antimode (repellor) was the normal day's work. The one control parameter was the daily mail volume.

Cusp Catastrophe Model

The cusp surface is three-dimensional and features a two-dimensional manifold (unfolding). It describes two stable states of behavior. Change between the two states is a function of two controls: *asymmetry* (a) and *bifurcation* (b). At low values of b, change is smooth, and at high values of b it is potentially discontinuous, depending on the values of a. At low values of a when b is high, changes occur around the lower mode and are relatively small in size. At middle values of a, changes occur between modes and are relatively large, assuming b is also large. At high values of a, changes occur around the upper mode and are again small.

The cusp response surface is the set of points where

$$\delta f(y)/\delta y = y^3 - by - a. \tag{2.24}$$

The cusp surface appears in the upper portion of Fig. 2.17. Change in behavior is denoted by the path of a control point over time (dotted line). The point begins on the upper sheet denoting behavior of one type, and is observed in that behavioral modality for a period of time. During that time its coordinates on a and b are changing when suddenly it reaches a fold line and drops to the lower value of the behavior, which is qualitatively different where it remains. Reversing direction, the point is observed in the lower mode until coordinates change to a critical pair of values, at which moment the point jumps back to the upper mode. There are two thresholds for behavior change, one ascending, and one descending. The shaded area of the surface is the region of inaccessibility in which very few points fall. Statistically, one would observe an antimode between the two stable states that would correspond to the shaded region of the surface.

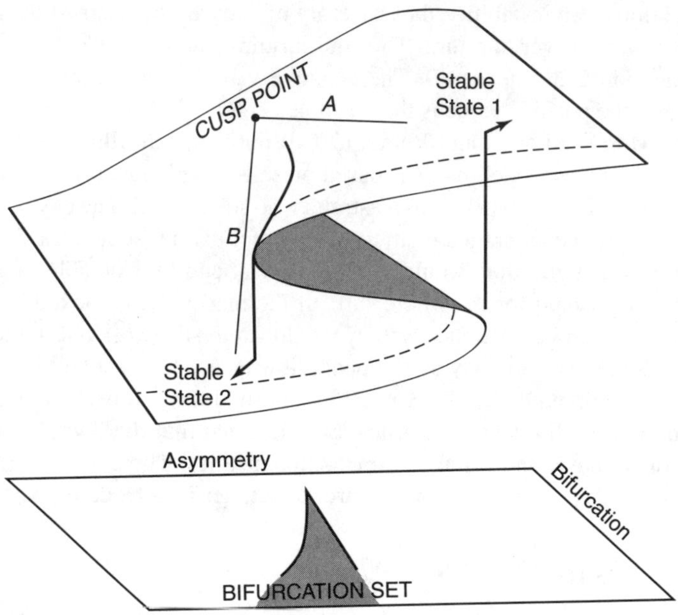

FIG. 2.17. The cusp catastrophe model.

The cusp and higher order models also have a control surface on which the bifurcation set is drawn, mapping the unfolding of the surface in (for the cusp) two dimensions. When highlighted on the response surface itself, the cusp bifurcation set induces two diverging response gradients, which are joined at a *cusp point*. The diverging gradients are labeled *A* and *B* on the cusp surface in Figure 2.17. Behavior at the cusp point is ambiguous. The cusp point is known as the point of degenerate singularity and is the most unstable point on the surface. Analogous points exist in other catastrophe models as well.

In a dynamical system, the behavioral variable (y) changes values. Static systems are not change oriented; rather the observed behavior takes a few qualitatively different forms, often with gradations. Static bifurcations are readily seen to underlie discontinuous or multimodal probability density functions (Chapter 3). Bifurcation structure may be less apparent by visual inspection of data for some dynamic applications, particularly where a distribution of points centers around one mode before a change process and around a second mode after the change. It should be noted, however, that the catastrophe functions are not inherently static or dynamic; it is the application and data that give a model a static or dynamic character.

The attractor centers of the response surface can be found by setting Equation 2.25 equal to 0. The solution will produce three roots. The two negative roots represent attractor centers, and the positive root represents the repellor center. Critical values of y where instability takes place can be found by taking the first derivative of Equation 2.25, setting it to 0 and solving. The same analytic principles apply to the other models below.

Classification

The elementary cuspoids, as well as other nonelementary models, vary in complexity. Complexity is signified by the highest exponent for the behavioral variable in the surface equation, for example, the quadratic term for the fold, the cubic for the cusp, and so forth. The leading exponent denotes the number of control parameters in the model, each with its own unique function, and the complexity of the behavioral array they perpetrate.

The taxonomy of models, together with the singularity rule, allows us to reduce the plethora of possible discontinuous change functions to a paltry few. Because topological models are rubberized rather than rigid, catastrophe models can withstand perturbations without changing their classification, so long as a tear in the surface is not introduced. This principle is known as *diffeomorphism up to transversality*.

Random Force

A *random force* occurs when a system is exposed to any entropy-inducing events, in which each element of the system (e.g., subjects in an experiment) has an equal probability of exposure (Agu, 1983). As elements increase in entropy, the probable location of each element in the space expands to the limits of its confinement. Bifurcations reduce the entropy of the system by partitioning energized elements into neighborhoods of relative stability or equilibrium (Thompson, 1982).

In the dynamics appearing since Agu and Thompson, a distinction is often made between an externally applied source of entropy and entropy that is indigenous to the system itself. The rugged landscape model is essentially assuming an indigenous source of entropy whereby the species distributes itself across a landscape. The sand pile model, however, is predicated on an externally applied source of sand. Similarly, the concept of information has shifted. In the Shannon (1948) framework, information is what an external observer needs to predict the state of the system. In the dynamics of Prigogine and Stengers (1984), however, information is *produced by* the system as it exhibits its complex (chaotic) deterministic behaviors.

One can next define situations where elements are not equally exposed to random force, but instead are systematically exposed. The level of exposure becomes the *b* parameter of a cusp model. Where there is more than one parameter of exposure, *c* is introduced, and the resulting behavioral spectrum becomes swallowtail (examples appear in Chapter 9). In a swallowtail, *b* and *c* can coact only additively or subtractively. If both can occur, then the butterfly factor *d* governs the degree to which *b* and *c* are additive or subtractive; and example of a butterfly catastrophe model appears in Chapter 5. In all cases, control *a* governs the proximity of the control point to the critical manifold.

Causality and Time Reversal

The traditional concept of causality holds that if we do *A* today and obtain *B* tomorrow, and obtain the same pattern on a few replications just to be sure, then *A* causes *B*. Some simplistic systems work that way, no doubt, but NDS theory shows that the causation of phenomena can be much more complex. In the case of the catastrophe models, when random force and bifurcation are considered jointly, the coaction of the two may be said to cause a phenomenon. The concept of *cause* is now replaced by a combination of *control*, which implies a bifurcation mechanism, entropy, and autonomous process.

An *autonomous process* is the sequence of behaviors that emanate from the underlying structure of a system. A system with a particular bifurcation set will exhibit a distinct pattern of behavior given a sufficient random force. Entropy itself is not sufficient, as other control parameters, notably asymmetry, affect the process. The nature of the attractors themselves is an important contributor to the end result. General NDS shows that there are several classic cases of attractors, each of which produces different patterns of behavior over time. Self-organized systems and coupled dynamics are essentially concatenation of elementary processes considered thus far.

Some catastrophe functions are, in principle, reversible. A cusp, for instance, describes the oscillation between two stable states where the oscillation involves two separate thresholds—one "ascending" and one "descending." Catastrophes with unstable attractors, however, may not be so reversible, although there appeared to be some reversibility in the case of the Australian mail rooms. The dynamics of a repellor shoot a control point into space, and the point can go anywhere, but not back to the repellor. If there is no attractor in the field to catch the flying point, the point will continue its course.

Self-organizing processes, like general biological evolution, are not reversible. Chaotic functions, to compare dynamics further on this point, have only a minuscule chance of reversibility because of both the nonrepeating nature of the forward-generating process and sensitivity to initial conditions. It is important, therefore, when choosing a model to represent the dynamics of a phenomenon, to choose a model that represents whether the process is thought to be reversible or not, and to what extent.

Global and Local Dynamics

So far the attractors within the catastrophe models themselves have only been characterized as stable and unstable. There were also unstable points that have been identified as repellors. The stable attractor points given are also known as "equilibria." The catastrophe models were developed as having smooth mappings in the neighborhood of the attractor. As such, the change in behavior in the close proximity of an attractor appears linear. It is only when the global, or total space of the model, is considered that the nonlinear functions become obvious.

Control points can approach catastrophe attractors asymptotically, in which case we have fixed-point attractors, or else orbit around the fixed point, in which case we have limit cycles. The width of the limit cycle is a matter of degree, and thus we can allow a continuity between fixed point and limit cycles in a generalized definition of an attractor in a catastrophe model.

Boundaries can introduce an attractor-like structure into a model also. For instance, if we were to crash automobiles into a very solid brick wall, the distribution of wreckage would be dense around the wall, and less dense away from the wall. This is an imperfect example, of course, but it makes the point that a boundary can produce a structure on the density of control points that can analyzed as if it were a stable state in global model. The presence of boundaries in a system, however, can also induce self-organization (Nicolis & Prigogine, 1989); thus phase transitions of different varieties may result from the presence or manipulation of boundaries.

Chaotic attractors are more problematical for catastrophe modeling because of the bifurcation structure that is thought to underlie each chaotic attractor. The catastrophe model might well define the global structure, but the goodness-of-fit associated with the mathematical or statistical analysis will be compromised by the presence of additional structures that could give the impression that the catastrophe model less is relevant than it might actually be. The alternative approach, of course, would be to plan for such contingencies in advance and to build a mathematical model for a phenomenon accordingly. Situations where chaotic attractors occur within catastrophes can be considered as special cases of synergetic coupled dynamics. Examples pertaining to fishing harvests and stock price dynamics are encountered in Chapter 11. Another example pertaining to infrastructure investments by the Soviet government was reported in Rosser, Rosser, Guastello, and Bond (2001).

One of the close points of contact between catastrophe and chaos theories is seen in the similarities between the cusp model and chaotic bifurcation in Period 2 of the logistic map. Although the two entities are not synonymous, the logistic function in Period 2 can be reasonably approximated by a cubic polynomial function (Thompson & Stewart, 1986). Thom (1983) viewed chaos theory as a generalization of catastrophe theory, while other writers might prefer to view catastrophe theory and chaos theory as close relatives within the domain of NDS theory.

The last point to make in this section is the distinction between global and local dynamics. This distinction extends beyond catastrophe models to virtually any other complex dynamical scheme; dynamic schemes are elaborated in Section 2.6.

A *globally stable* situation is one in which asymptotic stability occurs no matter how far from the equilibrium the control point is allowed to deflect. A *locally stable* situation is observed in a catastrophe model when the control point jumps from one attractor basin to another and remains in the latter basin. Changes in behavior along a catastrophe model surface are reversible. Hysteresis is the phenomenon by which behavior oscillates between stable states and also denotes the double threshold effect.

3

Structural Equations

Structural Equations for Testing Nonlinear Dynamics Hypotheses

As the old saying goes, "If it looks like a duck, walks like a duck, and quacks like a duck, it's probably a duck." The goal of this chapter is to determine whether we indeed have a dynamical data duck or just a wet and sloppy mess. More specifically, we'll be looking at the structural equations technique for testing NDS hypotheses. Because the vast majority of new applications of nonlinear dynamics to organizational behavior presented in this book involved the use of the structural equations technique, this chapter is necessary for clarifying the statistical reasoning that was involved throughout the applications. The structural equations methodology is an extension of analytic procedures that have been applied regularly to conventional problems in the social sciences.

Structural equations are used to (a) select a model that captures the conceptual dynamics of a system, (b) assess its degree of fit to the actual data, and (c) to compare the results against two alternative hypotheses, which are that a simple linear model provides an adequate description of the process, or that the data consists of only noise. By "noise" we mean that neither the hypothesized dynamical equation nor the linear model describes the data.

One might ask here: "There are so many possible nonlinear functions, how do we know which ones to test?" Fortunately, we have hierarchical sets of models to work with, and a theorem about singularity. Each model in the hierarchy subsumes properties of the simpler models. Each progressively complex model adds a new feature. There are two such hierarchies to consider: (a) the catastrophes for discontinuous change, and (b) the exponential series for other dynamical processes.

The models for catastrophes are the results of Thom's (1975) classification theorem, which is that all discontinuous changes of events can be described by one of ten elementary models. The models are hierarchical and involve one or two dependent measures (order parameters), and up to five control parameters. Beyond that point, we exceed the bounds of singularity, where there is only one response surface (or model) that will describe the configuration of events.

In the event that we have something other than a discontinuous change process, we would employ the exponential series of models (derived in Guastello, 1995a, Chapter 3). The simplest in that series is the Lyapunov function, which is an indicator of entropy and a test for chaos. The second in the series is the May–Oster bifurcation model, which is relative of the logistic map. Beyond those two models we have models with multiple order parameters or transfer functions or lag terms.

Arguably, the catastrophe models are dynamically more complex than those of the exponential series, but the computation is probably more familiar. The logic of hypothesis testing was also developed with catastrophe models and dates back to the early 1980s (Guastello, 1982a, 1982b). The hypothesis testing sequence procedure will be elaborated one step at a time as follows: (a) type of data and amounts that are required; (b) probability functions, location, and scale; (c) structure of behavioral measurements; (d) the catastrophe models, which can be tested through power polynomial regression; (e) the exponential series of models, which are tested through nonlinear regression; (f) catastrophes with static PDFs, and hypotheses about the control parameters; and (g) systems with more than one order parameter, phase space, and embedding.

DATA REQUIREMENTS

Because we are usually trying to test hypotheses about time-phased events, we have to use time series data of some sort. (Note: A spatial series can be substituted for a temporal series if one is testing a spatial hypothesis, but the arguments that follow are framed in time series terms.) Our set of observations can be one long time series, which would be taken on one person, object, or system repeatedly. Alternatively, we might study *ensembles* of shorter time series from several people, objects, or systems. Or, we could have many different people, objects, systems, each contributing no fewer than two observations in time.

How many observations do we need? Some of the nonstatistical computations require several thousand observations. For the statistical procedures considered here, 50 cases or less could be enough if the model is not too complex. The standard relationships between sample size, effect size, statistical power, alpha level, and the number of estimated parameters would apply here. In other words, more high-quality data is usually more valuable than less. More important than a huge sample, however, is that we have observed the full range of dynamics that is supposed to be part of the function under study.

PROBABILITY DENSITY, LOCATION, AND SCALE

In conventional linear analyses, we would assume a multivariate normal distribution. Here we do not: Rather, we will be working with exponential and complex-exponential distributions. A standard exponential distribution appears in the upper portion of Fig. 3.1, and an example of a complex one appears in the lower portion.

West and Deering (1995) identified many examples of exponential distributions associated with dynamic events. More generally, however, any differential function, f(z), can be staged as a probability density function (pdf) using the Ito–Wright formulation:

$$\mathrm{pdf}(z) = \xi \exp\left[-\int \mathrm{f}(z)\right], \tag{3.1}$$

(Cobb, 1981, Guastello, 1995a), where z is the order parameter, pdf(z) is the cumulative probability associated with a particular value of z, and ξ is a constant that is introduced to ensure unit density. In this general model, the Gaussian distribution (also known as the "normal distribution" or "bell curve") becomes a very special case.

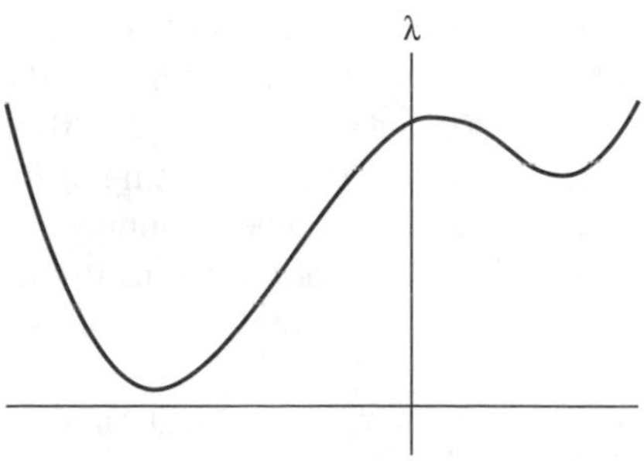

FIG. 3.1. A very misleading function would be obtained if we were only allowed to see the part of the curve to the right of λ.

We now arrive at the concepts of location and scale, such that

$$z = (y - \lambda)/\sigma_s, \tag{3.2}$$

where y is the raw observation of the order parameter, λ is the location parameter, and σ_s is the scale parameter. Location is commonly measured as the lowest value of the data series, although the mean of z might be used. Scale is variability around a mode, rather than about the mean, but is often estimated as variability around the mean. If we were to measure it as variability around modes, however, the calculation would be

$$\sigma_s = \left[\sqrt{\sum_{y=1} \sum_{m=1} \left(y_{m-}^{m+} - m_i\right)^2}\right] \Big/ N - M \tag{3.3}$$

(Guastello, 1992a, 1992b, 1995a; Guastello, Gershon, & Murphy, 1999). The calculation of scale in Equation 3.3 involves partitioning the frequency distribution of y into modes and antimodes. The N in the denominator of Equation 3.3 is the total number of observations. M represents the number of statistical modes around which points are actually observed to vary. For instance, M could equal 2 for many cusp applications if there were no points in the antimode. If there were points in the antimode, dispersion around the antimode should be included also; thus $M = 3$ (in a cusp). To continue, y is the raw score for behavior, and m_i is the modal value of y. Squared differences between y and m_i are summed over the range of y ($m-$ to $m+$) within the neighborhood of m_i, then the sums are summed over modal regions.

The resulting variable z_i is calibrated in moments. The location and scale transformations need to be made on the order parameter and the control variables prior to analysis with the structural equation. In ordinary (multiple) regression, location and scale, which would be the mean and standard deviation for normally distributed variables, do not make an impact on the regression weights, or R, the coefficient of multiple regression. Indeed the computations of R and the beta weights automatically convert raw observations to standard scores. If the model is nonlinear, however, the estimation of location and scale do make a different in the results that one could obtain. As mentioned above, the positioning of the location point fixes the lower limit of z. If we were to take a generic nonlinear function, such as the one shown in Fig. 3.2, and only analyze observations to the right of the location parameter, we could have some very different conclusions regarding the correct shape of the model.

The transformation of y to z, with regard to location, guards against false conclusions of linearity. This is especially important because many nonlinear functions are locally linear for short regions of y. For instance, in nonlinear dynamics, the trajectory of a point in the neighborhood of the epicenter of a fixed point attractor is linear, even though the full trajectory from the origin to the epicenter is globally

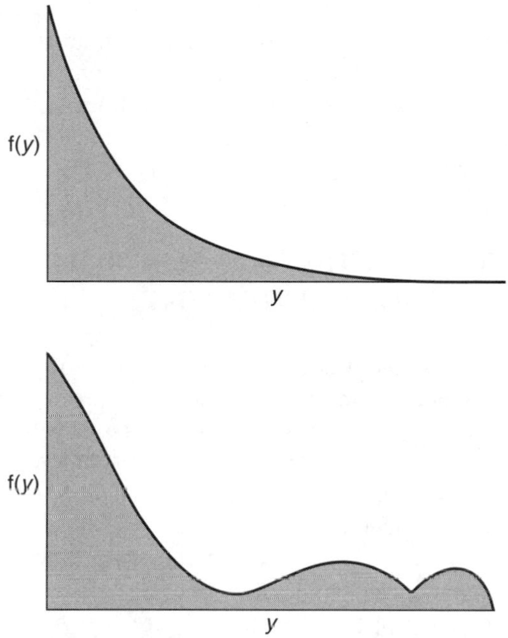

FIG. 3.2. Two exponential probability density functions. *Upper*: Simple example. *Lower*: A complex example that is actually a swallowtail catastrophe model.

nonlinear. This state of affairs also underscores the importance of sampling the entire spectrum of dynamics associated with the function.

The contribution of the scale parameter can be observed in one of the most elementary nonlinear relationships. Supposed we start with the general linear model

$$y = \beta_1 x_1 + \beta_2 x_2 + \beta_3 x_3, \tag{3.4}$$

and make the substitution

$$x_3 = x_1 x_2. \tag{3.5}$$

The multiplicative term, sometimes known as an interaction, or bilinear effect, has a nonlinear contribution on y. If x_1 and x_2 are not corrected for scale before multiplying, the variance of x_3 becomes biased by whichever one of x_1 or x_2 has the larger standard deviation. That bias in turn has a negative impact on the regression weight β_3, which, in the ordinary general linear model (GLM) computational procedure corrects for overlap with other regression weights. Thus, correction for scale improves the statistical power of the test on the nonlinear weight and removes bias simultaneously.

The corrections for location and scale together, furthermore, convert an interval scale y into a ratio scale z (if y wasn't initially a ratio-scaled variable). The resulting variable z is calibrated in standardized units, or moments. This principle takes on additional importance when estimating the fractal or Lyapunov dimension through nonlinear regression, where it is important that the conclusion about dimension is not an artifact of the unit of measurement.

STRUCTURE OF BEHAVIORAL MEASUREMENTS

Physical sciences and psychology have different approaches to data treatment. Both acknowledge the presence of "noise"; psychologists call it "error." The approach in the physical sciences, insofar as nonlinear dynamics are concerned, is to take the experimental data observations, apply a filtering technique, then make direct calculations of metrics such as the fractal dimension on the purified numbers (e.g., Abarbanel, 1996; Kanz & Schreiber, 1997). These procedures do not obviate any problems of undersampling and oversampling, the extent to which noise has been removed, and the effect of noise on calculations of fractal dimension, and so forth.

The structural equations approach described here does not extricate the noise function before analysis. Rather, the separation is inherent in the computational procedure itself. The logic begins with the standard psychometric assumption that a mental measurement, X, consists of a true score, T, and error, e:

$$X = T + e. \tag{3.6}$$

Errors in common psychometric theory are assumed to be normally distributed with a mean of 0.0. Furthermore, errors of measurement as assumed to be unrelated to other errors or to true scores. Note that this form of error, if it were observed in a time-series, would fit the definition of *independently and identically distributed* residuals, or IID.

For nonlinear structural equations, we continue the definition of the behavioral measurements to reflect a set of measurements such that the variance of X is the sum of true score variance and error score variance, such that

$$\sigma^2(X) = \sigma^2(T) + \sigma^2(e). \tag{3.7}$$

Next, we allow true score variance to consist of two components; one part is the variance accounted for by the nonlinear function, and the other part is associated with a linear function that is a subset of the nonlinear function.

Error is also allowed to contain two parts. One part is independent error, or IID error as described earlier. The other part is dependent error variance. Dependent errors occur when a random shock is introduced to a dynamical process that is sensitive to initial conditions (any affine transformation would fit this description). The error as well as the true score is iterated repeatedly through the nonlinear function. Furthermore, it has been shown that non-IID residuals are indicative of a nonlinear process (Brock, Hseih, & LeBaron, 1991; Guastello, 1995a).

The variance of a set of observations in a nonlinear dynamical process thus consists of four parts:

$$\sigma^2(\mathrm{X}) = \sigma^2(\mathrm{L}) + \sigma^2(\mathrm{NL} - \mathrm{L}) + \sigma^2(\mathrm{DE}) + \sigma^2(\mathrm{IIDE}). \tag{3.8}$$

They are, from left to right: the variance associated with the linear component, the nonlinear component, dependent error, and independent error. A well-specified nonlinear model will capture all the dependent error and treat it as variance accounted for by the nonlinear function. Occasionally, the removal of a nonlinear function may still result in non-IID residuals. It may then be possible to remove a second function from the residual variance.

POWER POLYNOMIAL REGRESSION METHOD

The power polynomial regression method is best illustrated using the cusp catastrophe as a hypothesized model. The cusp is one of the ten elementary models derived by Thom (1975) with the classification and singularity theorems mentioned earlier; see Chapter 2. The cusp model describes two stable states of behavior with a bifurcation manifold in between. Its *response surface* describes an accident as a discontinuous change of events that is the result of gradually changing underlying processes. There are two stable states of behavior; transition between them is governed by two control parameters. The criterion (or order parameter) in the application that follows is work performance at two points in time.

The cusp equation for the response surface is

$$\delta \mathrm{f}(y)/\delta y = y^3 - by - a. \tag{3.9}$$

Applying Equation 3.1 to Equation 3.9, its pdf would be, therefore

$$\mathrm{pdf}(z) = \xi \exp[-\theta_1 z^4/4 + \theta_2 b z^2/2 + \theta_3 a z]. \tag{3.10}$$

As a power polynomial regression equation over time, it would be stated as

$$\Delta z = \beta_0 + \beta_1 z_1^3 + \beta_2 z_1^2 + \beta_3 b z_1 + \beta_4 a. \tag{3.11}$$

Note that all we had to do was to convert y to z, insert regression weights, and we have a variation of the general linear model, where nonlinear terms have been substituted for one of the X's in Equation 4. (We also introduced a quadratic term, which is explained below.)

A network of hypotheses is contained in Equation 3.11. First, there is the overall statistical significance of the model, and size of the R^2. The R^2 coefficient from multiple regression, with variables specified by Equation 3.12, describes how well the data approximate a true cusp model. F (or t) tests on the regression weights denote the contribution of each term in the model. In optimal situations, each term in the model accounts for a unique portion of criterion variance. The power potential denotes and implies a particular bifurcation structure. Several experimental variables may be hypothesized as bifurcation ($\beta_3 b z_1$) or asymmetry ($\beta_4 a$) variables if desired. Under less than optimal conditions, bivariate correlations between the individual terms and the difference equation may be significant, but empirical weights may not all be significant in the multiple regression model. Here the validity of the structural model could still be upheld, but a cross-validation strategy is recommended to confirm the conclusion.

When a catastrophe (or other dynamical) model is tested, its R^2 coefficient is compared to one or more structural linear models containing the same control variables. In often happens that the *linear pre–post* model provides the strongest alternative:

$$y_2 = B_0 + B_1 y_1 + B_2 a + B_3 b. \tag{3.12}$$

Occasionally, however, the *linear difference* equation is more effective than the *linear pre–post* model, and thus makes a more challenging alternative hypothesis:

$$\Delta y = B_0 + B_1 a + B_2 b. \tag{3.13}$$

The dependent variable, y, needs no correction for location or scale because ordinary linear models are robust with respect to those transformations. The R^2 coefficient for the nonlinear model should exceed the R^2 for the linear alternative.

Note that the difference equation, Equation 3.14, is *not* a linear model even though the resemblance is strong:

$$\Delta y = B_0 + B_1 y_1 + B_2 a + B_3 b. \tag{3.14}$$

If we integrate both sides of the equation, we get a simple quadratic function

$$y_2 = B_0 + B_1 y_1^2. \tag{3.15}$$

Equation 3.15 is the kernel of many interesting nonlinear dynamics.

Illustrative examples of cusp catastrophe analyses with structural equations appear in this book in Chapters 5 (turnover among air force recruits) and 6 (organizational networks). For more examples, see (Guastello, 1995a), Clair (1998), and Byrne, Mazanov, and Gregson (2001).

EXPONENTIAL SERIES WITH NONLINEAR REGRESSION

This series of models was devised to answer questions about exponential expansion and contraction, the measurement of fractional dimensionality, the Lyapunov exponent test for chaos, and the presence of bifurcation structures. The objective for developing this series of models was to define a series of models that would be, like the catastrophes, hierarchical structures of elements. Rather than being restricted to integer dimensions, however, the series would have to accommodate noninteger dimensions.

That brings us to the curve shown in Fig. 3.3, which is well known as the "French Curve." It is used by apparel designers to cut curves. Depending on how the curve is turned, it can be used to model any curve in the human body; "one size fits all," as the saying goes. The curve is an exponential function of an exponential function.

The derivation of the exponential series began with the wave crest catastrophe (Guastello, 1995a). The wave crest model was chosen for this task because it was the closest of the catastrophe models to the logistic map in its structure. The wave crest contains two order parameters (dependent measures) and three control parameters. One of the control parameters, which we call c in Equation 3.16 et seq. is a bifurcation variable that works for both dependent measures. A Fourier transform was then applied to the wave crest, which turned it into an exponential function over time:

$$f(x + y) = \exp[cxt] + \exp[cyt]. \tag{3.16}$$

With just a few steps, we have a path between Equation 3.16 and the simplest models in the exponential series (see the original version for the details that

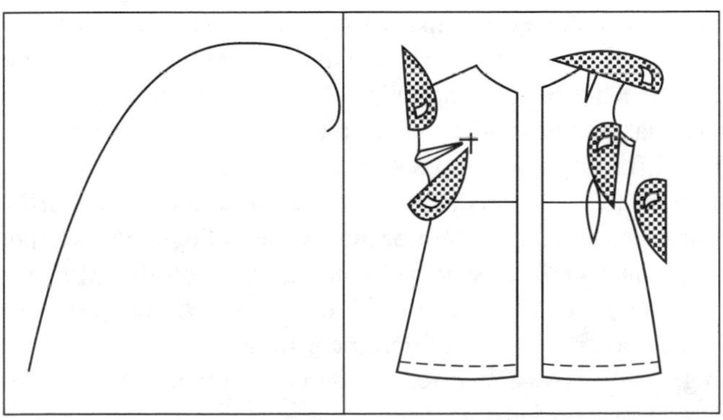

FIG. 3.3. The French Curve and its application in dress making. From the Dritz styling curve package. Reprinted with permission of the Rym–Dritz Corporation.

I am deliberately circumventing here). First, the second-order parameter can be substituted so that it is now just a lag function of the first dependent measure. Second, we can allow the second lag function to dissipate, so that the time between lags disappears. Third, we can rearrange terms by moving the bifurcation parameter; thus we arrive at the May–Oster bifurcation model. Fourth, we can drop the bifurcation effect altogether. Then we substitute a variable that is proportional to y_1, and we have the Lyapunov function. Fifth, we can simplify everything one more time, by letting all the time intervals be of equal length.

Now that the series of models has been defined, we can translate them into nonlinear regression models. The order parameter is once again corrected for location and scale, and regression weights are introduced. The simplest model in the exponential series then becomes

$$z_2 = e^{(\theta_1 z_1)}, \tag{3.17}$$

where θ_1 is a nonlinear regression parameter estimated empirically in the course of the analysis; θ_1 is also the Lyapunov number. If it is positive, then the function is expanding and chaotic. If it is negative, then the dynamics of the system are better characterized as fixed points or periodic functions, depending on their dimensionality. The Lyapunov dimension, D_L is

$$D_L = e^{\theta_1}. \tag{3.18}$$

Equation 3.17 can be embellished by adding additional regression parameters for fit such as θ_1 and θ_3 in Equation 3.19. The term θ_3 is an additive constant that is not proportional to z.

$$z_2 = \theta_1 e^{(\theta_2 z_1)} + \theta_3. \tag{3.19}$$

θ_3 is different from λ, however, in that λ fixes a lower limit to the entire distribution of z, while θ_3 describes a constant change in the conditional distribution of z with each iteration. If it is found on a preliminary analysis that θ_3 is not statistically significant, or that it shares variance with the exponent, θ_3 can be deleted from the model without affecting the interpretation of structure.

It is important to note a procedural distinction here between GLM regression and nonlinear regression. In GLM procedures (including the power polynomials), the regression constant B_0 is specified automatically by the GLM procedure. In nonlinear regression, constants such as θ_3 (and θ_1 for that matter) must be specified by the user. The potential range of nonlinear functions that can be handled from nonlinear regression is vast, and regression constants and fixed constants could legitimately appear anywhere.

The second model in the exponential series is the case where we have an unknown bifurcation variable. Here we test for the structure, but because we have neither an hypothesis as to what it could be or data to test it, we estimate the bifurcation variable θ_1 as a regression parameter:

$$z_2 = \theta_1 z_1 e^{\theta_2 z_1} + \theta_3. \tag{3.20}$$

In this case dimension is calculated as

$$D_L = e^{\theta_2} + 1. \tag{3.21}$$

If we had a hypothesis that a particular variable could be contributing to the bifurcation parameter, that variable would be slipped in between θ_1 and z_1 in Equation 3.20. Thus, we would have

$$z_2 = \theta_1 c z_1 e^{\theta_2 z_1} + \theta_3. \tag{3.22}$$

The R^2 coefficients associated with Equations 3.17, 3.19, 3.20, and 3.22 are measures of goodness-of-fit. The difference $(1 - R^2)$ is the variance associated with noise, error, or other deviations from the model. A comparison linear test is already built into the nonlinear regression model. If the regression parameter for the exponent (θ_1 in Equation 3.17 or θ_2 in Equations 3.19, 3.20, or 3.22) is not significant, i.e., zero, then the exponent of e is zero, and D_L is 1.0, which is a line. Note, however, that the size of an estimated nonlinear regression parameter is not dependent on the size of the R^2, or semipartial r, as it is in ordinary linear regression. Because the shape of the model is closely tied to the nonlinear regression weights, the significance tests on the weights are at least as important as the overall R^2.

It is still useful, nonetheless to compare R^2 for the nonlinear model against R^2 for a simple linear effect. Usually Equation 3.23,

$$y_2 = B_0 + B_1 y_1, \tag{3.23}$$

or Equation 3.24, where y is a function of the number of units of elapsed time, is adequate:

$$y_2 = B_0 + B_1 t \tag{3.24}$$

Illustrative examples of the exponential regression models appear in this book in Chapter 5 (motivational flow), Chapter 6 (creative problem solving groups at the edge of chaos), Chapter 8 (work group coordination experiments), Chapter 9 (hierarchical organization experiments), and Chapter 11 (attractor structures in unemployment and inflation economics, and oceanic fishing). Also see Guastello, 1995a, Chapter 9 (population dynamics), Chapter 11 (savings and loan institutions, production lines, problem solving groups), and Chapter 12 (polarization and war), and Guastello and Philippe (1997).

CATASTROPHE PDFS WITH NONLINEAR REGRESSION

Instead of using the dynamic difference equations for catastrophes, it is sometimes preferable to study catastrophe functions by examining how well they fit a characteristic pdf. The pdf method of testing hypotheses might be preferable because we have a multimodal distribution of data that is thought to be the result of a self-organizing process, and there are no individual differences in time-1 scores on the order parameter. We would need a distribution of time-1 scores of z_1, instead of a constant value of 0.0, if we were to use the dynamic difference equations.

As we saw earlier, the cusp pdf is three-dimensional. In the illustrative example that appears in Chapter 9, the goal is to fit a swallowtail catastrophe distribution, which is four-dimensional. The study involved 18 groups of people with seven to nine people in a group. The groups were given a creative problem-solving task that lasted approximately one hour. Although the groups were initially leaderless, they were alleged to have self-organized into leadership roles, secondary leadership roles, and nonleaders, which would be everyone else. At the end of the problem-solving session, participants were asked to rate each other with regard to who acted most like the leader, and who acted second-most like the leader. Individuals could collect 0 to 16 rating points in this fashion.

The distribution of ratings was thought to conform to a swallowtail catastrophe. The swallowtail model is shown in Fig. 3.4. Its response surface is

$$\delta f(y)/\delta y = y^4 - cy^2 - by - a, \tag{3.25}$$

where a, b, and c are the three control parameters. Its pdf would be, therefore,

$$\text{pdf}(z) = \xi \exp[-z^5/5 + z^4/4 + cz^3/3 + bz^2/2 + az]. \tag{3.26}$$

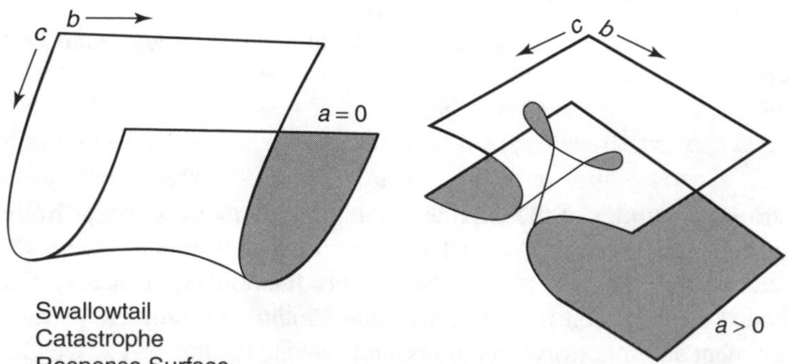

FIG. 3.4. Two three-dimensional sectionings of the swallowtail catastrophe response surface.

The interesting section of the swallowtail pdf was used in Fig. 3.1, by the way, as an example of a complex probability density function. The pdf then becomes a statistical expression by inserting nonlinear regression weights, θ_i, and absorbing the constants and negative signs into the weights:

$$\text{pdf}(z) = \xi \exp[-\theta_1 z^5 + \theta_2 z^4 - \theta_3 c z^3 - \theta_4 b z^2 - \theta_5 a z]; \qquad (3.27)$$

ξ is treated as a regression weight also.

Hypothesis testing concerning whether the data fit the swallowtail distribution was conducted in two steps. The first step was to determine whether the hills and valleys of the distribution were real, or just chance fluctuations. The question was answered by power polynomial regression where the number of observations associated with a leadership score was a nonlinear function of the leadership score:

$$\text{freq}(y) = \beta_0 + \beta_1 y + \beta_2 y^2 + \beta_3 y^3 + \beta_4 y^4. \qquad (3.28)$$

The term R^2 is then calculated for the polynomial fit. A significance tests on each of the regression weights would indicate whether the apparent bends in the curve are likely to have occurred by chance. The R^2 for Equation 3.28 is then compared with the R^2 for the linear component alone:

$$\text{freq}(y) = \beta_0 + \beta_1 y. \qquad (3.29)$$

In the event that statistical significance is obtained for the nonlinear elements in Equation 3.28, the plot of the resulting function will illustrate the critical points that correspond to points of high density (modes) and low density (antimodes).

The second analysis fits the data to the swallowtail pdf itself. The degree of fit is tested using nonlinear regression; the procedure is a slight variation of the nonlinear regression models demonstrated already. First, the leadership scores were transformed into z scores by correcting for location and scale; the z scores were used in the right side of the pdf equation in the usual manner. What is new, however, is that, for the left side of the equation, the leadership scores must be transformed into cumulative probability density values. Cumulative probability values (logit transformation) are readily obtained from an ordinary frequency distribution table made from the raw data.

Before proceeding further, some comment should be made about the importance of good control variables in the development of nonlinear models and the theories that should go along with them. So far we have focused most attention on the structure of the models themselves, and have been nonchalant about the control variables. The situations concerning polynomials for catastrophes, the exponential series, and exponential pdfs will be mentioned separately below.

The catastrophe models are particularly interesting because the control parameters that make up the bifurcation sets all have different functions. As we mentioned earlier, more than one experimental variable can contribute to a control parameter. It is thus important to have strong hypotheses about which experimental variables should behave as each control parameter. The catastrophe models need to be tested with control variables in place; otherwise we would just be testing a generic polynomial series. More importantly, it has been shown (Guastello, 1992a) that about half of the accuracy of a catastrophe model is associated with the correct specification of control parameters.

The situation is less clear with the exponential series of models. Some models contain control parameters that have bifurcation effects and others do not. It would follow, however, that models that have low to moderate degrees of fit might be improved by introducing more elements, such as control variables or transfer functions from other order parameters in the system.

When catastrophe pdfs (or other complex pdfs) are tested through nonlinear regression, the situation appears to be different again in that we can proceed in the direction of structure first, followed by structure with the control variables. This structure-first procedure appears advisable based on the few known applications. The degree of fit tends to be greater for structure only; fit is then *attenuated* by the introduction of control variables. Of course, the goal is to lose as little fit as possible in the course of the procedure. Equation 3.30 is the structure-first model, which is a simplification of the swallowtail pdf given in Equation 27:

$$\text{pdf}(z) = \xi \exp[-\theta_1 z^5 - \theta_2 z^4 \theta_3 z^3 - \theta_4 z^2 - \theta_5 z]. \tag{3.30}$$

If the weight for the z^4 term is not significant, it can be dropped also from the model because it is just another correction for location.

Controls variables can now be studied in two ways. One way is to place control variables in the respective positions a, b, and c, in Equation 3.27. Guastello, Craven, Zygowicz, and Bock (2001) adopted this approach in a continuation of the leadership studies, and found that indeed we could identify interesting control parameters. We also found that R^2 dropped from 0.995 to 0.700 when the control variables were introduced. We can understand this attenuation effect by looking more closely at the regression weights for any of the nonlinear regression models.

The weights θ_i that are produced in a nonlinear regression model are adopted when their significance tests show that the weights fell within a 95% confidence interval that did not contain 0.00. In other words, for each weight, there is actually a small distribution of weights. The distributions of weights occur when we try to bend the curve in such a way as to accommodate each point in the data set. Thus, in principle, we could generate parameter estimates for each and every observation in the data set. These individual parameter estimates indicate how the underlying curve would have to be bent in order to accommodate a particular point by passing through that point.

In the alternative test for a control variables using models such as Equation 3.30 (not used in the examples in this book, but see Cobb, Koppstein, and Chen, 1983), we would be correlating experimental variables with latent control parameter estimates. Because the correlations between variables and latent parameter estimates are all less than 1.0, the overall R^2 attenuates when the control variables are entered into the model directly. There is, therefore, some part of the latent control parameter variance that can be predicted by the experimental variables, and some part that is not predicted by them.

Parameter estimation does not have a counterpart in GLM analyses. In GLM R^2 describes the extent to which all points conform to a line. There is no bending of the line to accommodate individual points. If the line were to be bent, it would be a curve. (And thus the GLM would not be a GLM!)

SYSTEMS WITH MORE THAN ONE ORDER PARAMETER

So far we have confined our remarks to systems with only one order parameter. We did mention, however, that the catastrophe models can accommodate some systems with two order parameters, but beyond a certain point of complexity, the response surface becomes nonsingular. In the event we are working with one of the more manageable catastrophes with two order parameters, we would have partial differential equations for each order parameter. For instance, in the simplest case, which is the wave crest catastrophe, the two functions are

$$\delta f(x)/\delta x = 3x^2 + a + cy \tag{3.31}$$

$$\delta f(y)/\delta y = 3y^2 + b + cx. \tag{3.32}$$

These particular functions are interesting because the order parameter y is part of the equation for order parameter x and vice versa. We can turn them into regression equations as we did with the other catastrophe models.

Alternatively, we can test the two functions simultaneously using the polynomial transformations with canonical correlation analysis. The general statistical model would be

$$\gamma_1 \Delta u + \gamma_2 \Delta v = \beta_0 + \beta_1 u^2 + \beta_2 a + \beta_3 cv + \beta_4 v^2 + \beta_5 b + \beta_6 cu, \tag{3.33}$$

where u and v are x and y that have been corrected respectively for location and scale, γ_1 and γ_2 are weights on the two order parameters, β_i are regression weights for the elements on the predictor side of the equation as before, and a, b, and c are the control parameters. Two examples of this use of canonical correlation have involved accidental death versus other insurance claims (Guastello, 1995a, Chapter 7), and two types of responses generated in conversations of creative problem solving (Guastello, 1995a, Chapter 11).

In the exponential series, the simplest model with two order parameters is

$$u_2 + v_2 = e^{\theta_1 u_1} + e^{\theta_2 v_1}. \tag{3.34}$$

We can then introduce one or two bifurcation functions. If we add both bifurcation functions and a few convenient regression weights, the model becomes

$$u_2 + v_2 = \theta_1 u_1 e^{\theta_2 u_1} + \theta_3 v_1 e^{\theta_4 v_1} + \theta_5. \tag{3.35}$$

Nonlinear regression, unfortunately, does not have a counterpart to canonical correlation that will allow for unequal weighting of the two order parameters. If it is absolutely necessary to have unequally weighted order parameters, the two order parameters should be run in separate equations with u and v each appearing separately on the left side of the equation. Although it is possible to imagine a bolt-on canonical weighting scheme for u and v, it is also possible to imagine that Equation 3.43 would grow to a total of 11 estimated parameters in the process, which would put a severe drain on the cross-validity (generalizability) of model.

THE ROLE OF EMBEDDING DIMENSION AND ATTRACTOR RECONSTRUCTION

So far we managed to tear through a wide range of complex analyses without having to rely on any particular definitions of embedding dimension or heuristics about plotting points in phase space. The information that we have sought concerned (a) model structure, (b) the contribution of experimental variables, (c) dimensionality as an indicator of complexity or turbulence, (d) the relative amounts of determinism or noise, (e) the relative efficiency of one model over another, and (f) the dynamics we can infer from knowledge of all the foregoing indicators. All that information can be obtained from R^2, $1 - R^2$, e^{θ}, D_L, and the various significance tests.

New needs may arise, however, if we want to portray the data as projections in phase space. So far we can make two projections without introducing anything new. One is to plot the raw data, and just report the analyses of the functions. Alternatively, we might wish to plot the *predicted values* of z, based on the best function that we pulled out of the analysis. This choice would portray the determinism without the IID noise.

At this point, the choice of embedding dimension requires some reckoning. The ordinary habit is to portray the function in two dimensions, usually plotting Δz against z_1. If there are two order parameters, such as u and v in the previous example, a plot of Δu against Δv would be useful. The plots would lose their clarity, however, if each order parameter is actually embedded in more than two dimensions, and we did not know how many plotting dimensions would be required. For this purpose, Abarbanel (1996) introduced the principal components technique for finding the correct embedding dimension of a time series variable; the same technique also served the purpose, in principle, of separating determinism from noise. The principal components method is just one of several techniques that have been developed for the same purpose. For further examples, see Abraham (1997), and Kanz and Schreiber (1997).

The principal components technique is introduced next. The only published example in the social sciences to date (Guastello & Bock, 2001) is summarized in Chapter 10. Although it is an apparently new tool in the natural sciences, principal component analysis has a long history of development and use in the social sciences. In common usage, a principal component analysis will reduce a matrix of correlations among variables to a smaller set of common sources of variance. The first component of variance will contain the largest amount of variance, and subsequent components will represent sequentially less variance. Although the number of possible components is equal to the number of original variables, all but the largest components will contain trivial variance made up from unique sources of noise (Rummel, 1970; Tabachnick & Fidell, 1989).

The solution to a principal component analysis takes the form of a matrix of correlations between original variables and the underlying components. This correlation–component matrix is further subjected to a geometric rotation, which can be either a linear (orthogonal) or nonlinear (oblique) transformation. Rotations are used to enhance the interpretability of the component analysis and the contents of each component. In the oblique case it is possible to produce, furthermore, a matrix of correlations among the rotated factors.

Abarbanel's (1996) procedure for cleaning a time series starts with a covariance matrix of data points. The principal component analysis determines the correct embedding dimension for the time series. The number of components that result from the analysis signifies the embedding dimension.

The first step is to convert the raw scores of a time series to Z-scores in the standard statistical definition [$Z = (X - \mathrm{M})/\mathrm{SD}$]. A covariance matrix of all the data points is then created. The matrix entries would be the cross-products of the Z-scores. The covariance matrix is then component-analyzed. Statistical packages such as SPSS (used in the ensuing data analysis) can accept matrix input. The final [rotated] factor solution will look like a matrix of correlations between N variables and P components, where P is much less than N because only components of adequate size were retained. In actuality, it will be a set of coordinates wherein each of the N original observations in the time series is projected into P-dimensional space. The resulting P-dimensional points can then be plotted in phase space.

Principal component analysis usually involves an array of procedural heuristics, assumptions, and caveats; the application to cleaning a time series analysis would be no exception. The list involves, at minimum, the heuristics that might be used to determine the correct number of components, the choice of rotation strategy, the assumption of Gaussian residuals, and the sampling space of the time series.

Abarbanel (1996) did not review the issue of how to determine the number of components. The common practice of retaining components with eigenvalues greater than 1.00 is controversial because it has a tendency to retain too few factors. Other plausible criteria are the percentage of variance accounted for by the component structure or a scree test (Cattell, 1966).

A scree test consists of a plot of the serial order of a component and eigenvalue associated with it. The eigenvalue is in turn associated with the percent of variance accounted for by a component. The scree plot should show a precipitous decline in variance associated with the first few components. The decline is followed by a sharp bend in the curve, beyond which only very little variance is associated with a component. The breakpoint in the curve serves as the demarcation between components that are retained or discarded. Guastello and Bock was (2001) found that the scree test was useful, but the bend in the curve was not always as sharp as was hoped.

Abarbanel (1996) did not address the issue of what type of rotation strategy to use, or whether orthogonal or oblique rotation should be used. It would appear, however, that orthogonal rotation was intended, because that is the closest in meaning to an embedding dimension. He did mention in his later chapters that if there is synchronization between order parameters, points across dimensions are correlated and the embedding space becomes noninteger. The synchronization scenario implies oblique rotation.

The results of a conventional principal components analysis will depend on the quality of each of the correlations contributing to the initialization matrix. Pearson product–moment correlations are optimal to the extent that sampling range is maximal and that each variable is normally distributed. In a related fashion, it is also necessarily assumed that the residual differences between raw and components-filtered scores is also normally distributed. It is *not* likely that the Gaussian distribution requirements will be met because of the pervasive exponential distributions that underlie most dynamical variables.

The length of the time series is as important to the principal components filtering process as it is to other forms of dynamical computation. In conventional uses of principal components analysis, the omission of important variables that are connected to those being factored could change the resulting factor structure. The dynamical counterpart is the violation of the ergodicity assumption mentioned earlier.

The final heuristic problem in principal components analysis that is relevant here is that there is no fixed criterion for a quality of a solution. Several sources of differences in potential outcomes of components analysis were already mentioned. Interpretability of the solution is, for the most part, the final piece of evidence to consider in regard to whether a components analysis is "good" or "bad" (Tabachnick and Fidell, 1989). Fortunately, there are some statistical criteria germane to nonlinear dynamics that can be applied and compared between the raw and components-filtered data.

The data for the problem given in Chapter 11 were subjected to the principal components analysis outlined above. The SPSS computer package presented some unplanned challenges. Although SPSS is designed to accept a covariance matrix as input in some of its subprograms, the factor analysis subprogram (which has options for principal components analysis) can only accept correlation matrices. That problem was solved by "tricking" the program into thinking that it was encountering a correlation matrix. To do that the covariance entries were divided by 10, which produced entries all less than $|1.00|$. Then the diagonal entries of the matrix were replaced by the value 1.00. Arbarbanel (1996) has also written a computer program dedicated to the principal components analysis of phase space that should handle these data preparation procedures automatically.

A variation on the principal components procedure might be useful when the necessary data are available, whereby we could use an ensemble of time series observations rather than one time series. The ensemble would represent multiple observations from the same system. The covariance matrix would be replaced by a correlation matrix of observations from one time series with every other time series. Thus, if there were 10 such time series, each containing N observations, the matrix of correlations would be 10×10, rather than $N \times N$.

Principal components analysis would then be calculated on the 10 by 10 matrix. The final (rotated) set of loadings from the components analysis would be between one time series of observations and the underlying component. The phase portrait would be a plot of the weighted sum of observations from all the original time series that load on a component. A loading of $|.30|$ is the usual rule-of-thumb for determining whether a loading is large enough to include a variable with a component; criteria larger or smaller than $|.30|$ may be used if doing so will improve simple structure.

In Equation 3.36, $\mathbf{W}$ is a $1 \times t$ vector of original time series observations that is t observations long:

$$\mathbf{W} = \sum_{T=1}^{T} [r^2{}_{iT} S_T Z_{it}] + e. \tag{3.36}$$

It is expressed as a sum of T processed component values. The term Z_{it} is an observation i from the original time series that has been transformed with regard to location and scale. The term S_T is the proportion of variance of the original time series that is accounted for by the particular component. The $r^2{}_{iT}$ values are the squared component loadings. To obtain a processed score for one observation on one particular component, take the Z_{it} and multiply it by the $r^2{}_{iT}$.

SUMMARY

The main points of hypothesis testing with structural equations can be summarized as follows:

1. A differential function can be represented as a pdf by use of the Ito–Wright formula.

2. All behavioral measurements contain three sources of variance: true score, dependent error, and independent error.
3. The variance of a set of dynamical behavioral measurements consists of four sources of variance: determinism from a linear component, determinism from a nonlinear component, dependent error, and independent error.
4. A nonlinear model will become a better fit for data to the extent that dependent error can be restated as nonlinear determinism.
5. Begin the hypothesis testing process by transforming observed data into Z, with respect to location and scale.
6. Choose a nonlinear dynamical model from the hierarchical series that is the closest fit to the theoretical expectations. For discontinuous change processes, try one of the difference equations for the catastrophe hierarchical series. For the test for chaos and other dynamical structures, use the exponential regression series.
7. Test control variables in their respective positions in the models.
8. Choose one or more control equations for comparison. These will usually contain the control variables, but not the nonlinear effects, and will usually be run through ordinary GLM.
9. Evaluate R^2 coefficients for each model and compare. Use a simpler nonlinear model if necessary. Evaluatc rcsults for control variables.

Optional: Plot the phase portrait. Use principal components procedure to separate dimensions underlying what appears to be a single order parameter. Plot the time series that was produced by the principal components analysis. Calculate nonlinear regression models for each component.

4

Organizational Change and Development

Organizations differ in terms of their structure, social climate, culture, and—let's not forget the obvious—the products they make or the services they provide. Organizational *change* thus pertains to some combination of the foregoing groups of characteristics. Organizational *development* (OD) is an organized set of planned activities designed to transform an organization from one state of being into another. Although OD programs are often introduced to remedy a dysfunction of some sort, they could be applied just as readily as part of an organized strategy to adapt to changes in the market place, or to facilitate an organization's own initiatives for developing new products or markets. The essential common denominator in all true OD programs is that the organization recognize a need for change and take a concerted action to make the change (French & Bell, 1999).

The next section of this chapter summarizes some landmark developments in the understanding of organizational differences and their effects on the internal functioning of the organization. The second and subsequent sections of the chapter describe the NDS models of organizational change; some of the new contributions are subtle while others are blatant. In particular, the exposition emphasizes the continuity between individual consciousness and the organizational counterpart, which is a form of collective intelligence.

ORGANIZATIONAL STRUCTURE, CLIMATE, AND CULTURE

Structure

Organizational structure variables were first delineated in Weber's (1946) theory of bureaucracy. They include the organization's size, levels of hierarchy, centralization or decentralization, span of control, and division of labor. In earlier times (Porter & Lawler, 1965) there was no clear association between an organization's functionality and its levels of hierarchy or centralization. Rather, the optimal number of hierarchical levels and degree of centralization was relative to what the organization was trying to accomplish. In more recent times, computer-based technologies have facilitated a drop in the necessary levels of hierarchy. The new forms of technological support could condense middle management jobs that involved collating information and passing it onward and upward. The combination of new means for speeding communication and the demand for greater speed has resulted in initiatives for reducing communication bottlenecks. The hierarchical aspect of organizational life is expanded further in Chapter 10.

Larger organizations tend to have larger subunits and greater dysfunction in terms of lower job satisfaction and higher rates of absenteeism, turnover, and accidents (Guastello, 1988; Porter & Lawler, 1965). Group productivity rates tend to follow the general rule of optimal size, however. The dysfunction associated with larger organizations or subunits may be related to poor coordination (Comer, 1995; this topic is expanded in Chapter 8) or to the division of labor being cut too narrowly.

Historically, there have been two groups of responses to the division of labor problem. One is sociotechnical systems theory, which originated with Trist and Bamforth (1951), and the other is job characteristics theory, which originated with Hackman and Oldham (1976). The central idea behind sociotechnical systems theory is that work should be rationalized from the viewpoint of the people who do the work, rather than from the viewpoint of the work itself. Under this general theme, the best way to divide work among people is to put a group of people who have the necessary capabilities together with the work, and then let the natural process of self-organization take over (DeGreene, 1991). The optimal arrangement of people and tasks will ensue. DeGreene also noted that in a changing work environment, the self-organizing properties of the sociotechnical systems approach offer the flexibility that a group needs to make adaptive responses. He also found, however, that the capability to be flexible is not alwaysapparent in the upper levels of the organizational hierarchy.

A later product of sociotechnical systems thinking is the autonomous work group. In those situations, work that was once organized as a fixed sequence of specialized processes, as in an assembly line, is now given over to a group. The group establishes its own sequence of people and tasks, including the supervision or managing functions that used to be allocated to a supervisor. Although some type of supervision may be involved, a level of the organizational hierarchy may be deleted in some cases.

The focus of job characteristics theory is to improve the motivational content of jobs by increasing levels of skill variety, scope of the individual assignments (broad instead of narrow), importance of an individual's task to the work of others, autonomy, and feedback from the job itself (Hackman & Oldham, 1976). Although there was a precedent, dating back to Herzberg, Mausner, and Snyderman (1959) to expect positive outcomes for work performance and attitudes, the positive outcomes from job redesign did not always materialize, according to Hackman (1992). One poignant explanation for the lack of effective of job redesign was that organizations were not willing to wait through the transition period, during which time work output would drop while workers regrouped their tasks and acclimated to the new work flow. During the transition there was also an opportunity for workers to become discouraged, and those who naturally showed little tolerance for ambiguity were least likely to acclimate to the new work systems. Another source of frustration was located in the group level process by which the contributions of individuals were meant to connect to a whole outcome.

Later research on autonomous work groups sought to connect the best ideas of sociotechnical systems theory with job characteristics theory (Cohen, Ledford, & Spreitzer, 1996; Pearson, 1992). Sociotechnical systems theory addressed the group level process in a vague sort of way without clarifying the specific reasons for its success, and its success was not consistently observed by those who tried to do so (Cordery, Mueller, & Smith, 1991). Job characteristics theory needed some semblance of a group process.

Research now shows that positive attitudes toward autonomous work groups' quality of work life does depend on the attentiveness to job characteristics; the group task design is preferred to traditional divisions of labor (Cohen et al., 1996; Cordery et al., 1991). On the other hand, Pearson (1992) reported improvements in job satisfaction, but not for role ambiguity or role conflict (stress-related variables) over time for autonomous groups. Pearson did report increases in role ambiguity, conflict, and accidents, and a decline in motivation among the nonautonomous group counterparts in that study.

Cohen et al. (1996) found that ratings of productivity improved as a function of groups' ratings of their quality of work life and the use of group task designs. Management's ratings of group productivity were negatively correlated with the extent to which a group encouraged the use of supervisory behaviors such as self-evaluation, self-criticism, goal setting, and encouraging rehearsals of group activities before executing them. Pearson (1992) found, in a more straightforward result, that newly implemented autonomous work groups outperformed conventional work groups after four weeks of implementation.

Cohen et al. (1996) reported less absenteeism among autonomous work groups. Pearson (1992) found that absenteeism among autonomous work groups did not change during the experimental period although absenteeism increased among the traditional work groups. Cordery et al. (1991) found that absenteeism was greater among autonomous groups, as did Wall, Kemp, Jackson, and Clegg (1986), but the current thinking is that absenteeism is better explained by confounding organizational-level variables. A separate study by Ward (1997) suggested that the overall effectiveness or satisfaction with autonomous work groups could be predicated on the workers' trust in management.

Climate

An organization's *climate* is characterized in terms of the dynamics taking place among individuals and between the individual and the organization as a whole. The climate concept eventually gave way to an interest in an organization's culture.

Mead (1934) was a pioneer in the study of group and organizational differences; he defined concept of *group personality*. When individuals assemble into groups, the groups take on personalities that distinguish them from other groups, in much the same way that an individual's personality distinguishes him or her from other individuals. The group personality is a composite of individual traits, but the traits held most in common among group members become dominant features of the group personality. Furthermore, the leader's traits receive the most weight in the group personality composite.

Note that a self-organizing effect appears to be operating here, although it was not known as such back in the 1930s. The social process known today as *social facilitation* produces a group-level effect in a process similar to the synergetic mechanism put forth by Haken (1984). The group effect becomes a hierarchical effect that shapes future contributions by group members. If the group elects a leader that is truly a representative of its dominant traits, those traits would be expected to dominate further.

The group remains the basic building block for understanding and changing organizational behavior (French & Bell, 1999). However, as additional analysis has revealed, there appears to be as much variability in climate within organizations as there is between organizations; much of this variability can be traced to the psychological contributions of the organization's top-ranking people (Drexler, 1977). Meltzer (1942) offered the first major distinction between organizations by fusing contemporary politics with clinical psychology. A *humanistic* organization responds to human emotional needs and advocates democratic internal processes. An *inhuman* organization views its members as machines and adopts policies of exploitative and autocratic rule. Meltzer's field research indicated that the functionality of an organization could be improved by humanizing the interpersonal relations of key personnel.

According to McGregor (1960), behavior in organizations is the result of a set of beliefs about human nature. Organizations operating under Theory-X beliefs develop policies under the assumption that the individual has an inherent dislike for work, will avoid work or responsibility, is mainly seeking money and security, and is best motivated to work through coercion and punishment. Theory-Y beliefs hold that work is as natural play or rest, that people will seek responsibility and exercise self-directly and self-control in pursuit of organizational objectives, and that the ability to exercise imagination and creativity is widespread in the population generally underutilized by organizations. Based on this contrast, McGregor viewed organizations that operate under Theory-Y principles as more effective than Theory-X organizations.

Likert (1961) conceptualized four types of organizations: exploitative authoritarian (System 1), benevolent authoritarian (System 2), consultative (System 3), and participative (System 4). System 1 organizations are closely akin to Theory-X organizations. System 2 organizations are no more democratic than are System 1, but rather than exploiting the personnel, the emphasis is on "helping" or "taking care of the employee." In System 3, input from employees is sought on many decisions, and many discussions take place between management and employees. Nonetheless, the rank-and-file employees have no consistent opportunities to influence decisions, and their recommendations may or may not be followed. In System 4, employees are actively involved in making decisions. Likert's work represented yet another theory that advocated participative management for organizational effectiveness.

Organizational climate research conducted during the 1960s and 1970s focused on empirically derived traits and types. The most commonly found trait constructs were individual autonomy, rigid versus flexible division of labor, reward and achievement orientation, warmth and support, progressiveness or concern about development, degree of risk taking, and tight versus loose control (or supervision) of activities (Saal & Knight, 1988). When normal-range traits are bent out of shape, however, we obtain organizational pathologies. Kets de Vries and Miller (1986) identified five types of organizational pathology, based on commonly recognized clinical classifications: dramatic, schizoid, compulsive, depressed, and paranoid. Excessive risk taking and flamboyance characterize dramatic organizations. Although the assumption of risk often pays off, the organization is often unwise in its choices of risky ventures. Schizoid organizations have difficulty focusing on a business plan, resulting in senseless changes of policy that only serve to confuse the work force. Compulsive organizations place greater priority on bureaucratic procedures than they do on actually accomplishing needed tasks. Depressed organizations are characterized by poor morale and general lack of energy among employees. Paranoid organizations operate under the belief that entities within and outside the organizations are out to destroy them; work life is riddled with politics and secrecy. In all five pathologies, the symptoms indicate critical losses in efficiency.

Culture

The concept of culture entered the literature on organizational differences in two ways. The first invoked conventional notions of culture and nationality, and is typified by Theory Z (Ouchi, 1980), which compared American and Japanese organizations. Life in American organizations is typically characterized by individual rewards, tasks defined for individuals, concern with individual career advancement, concern with developing career specialization, rapid advancement within the company, frequent performance appraisals, and centralized control of decisions by management. Japanese organizations, by contrast, are characterized by group rewards, tasks designed for group efforts, concern with long-term commitment to the company, concern with the company as the focal point of one's career development, slow advancement through the corporate ranks, and infrequent individual reviews. Furthermore, in Japanese organizations, the largest possible decisions are pushed downward to the lowest possible person in the organizational hierarchy.

Ouchi (1980) traced differences in social and reinforcement structures to the preindustrial ecologies of Japanese and American farmers. The Americans who grew wheat in the vast flatlands of Kansas required individuality and self-reliance in order to survive. The Japanese who grew rice on paddies in mountainous terrain survived through teamwork and cooperation. In another view of history, however, the contrasts between American and Japanese work organizations began with Japan's acceptance of the Total Quality Management ideas put forth by the American management scientist W. Edward Deming in the late 1940s (Deming, 1986). Deming strongly emphasized the group nature of work; his ideas did not catch on in the U.S. engineering management community until much later.

The second and more widely used application of the culture concept describes organizational differences within a society. Lundberg (1985) found several available definitions of organizational culture. Some are more corporate centered, such as "the way we do things around here," or "a general constellation of beliefs, mores, values systems, behavioral norms and ways of doing business that are unique to each corporation" (pp. 170–171). Other definitions are anthropological, such as "the transmitted and created content and patterns of values, ideas, and other symbolic-meaningful systems as factors in shaping human behavior" (p. 170). Organizational cultures can be distinguished on the basis of their artifacts and legends, values and assumptions, climate, and structure.

Van Maanen and Barley (1985) noted that organizational cultures could contain subcultures. Subcultures are often defined in terms of job assignment, status, or equity. Because of the greater homogeneity of members at the top levels of organizations, descriptions of an organization's culture may not necessarily apply to the workers at lower echelons.

According to Schein (1990), there are three points of view on whether it is possible to change an organizational culture. The anthropological view is that culture cannot be changed effectively, nor should one try to do so. This view represents a belief in the inherent stability of the "attractor," or possibly it represents a euphemism for an organization that has too much psychological baggage to move effectively (Guastello, 1995a).

Schein's (1990) second viewpoint is that of business management, who would observe that organizational culture changes occur all the time. Perhaps that opinion is based on the vast assortment of OD efforts that occurred in the previous half-century; one can only surmise in retrospect how many of those OD efforts changed climate, how many changed culture, how many of them changed something else altogether, or changed nothing at all. In any case, Goldstein (1994) preferred to set up conditions that *allow* a culture to change, rather that creating conditions that force it to change in a particular manner.

The third viewpoint is that of the strategic leader, who capitalizes on chance occurrences and dramatic events that could have a cultural impact (Schein, 1990; Wheatley, 1992). The strategists would then follow up with the right messages and actions to promote continued change in the desired direction.

Stacey (1992) observed, however, that some cultures are more firmly ingrained than are others. For those that are firmly ingrained, change efforts are better spent developing creative potential and strategic managerial reactions to problem situations. Specific actions many have an impact on the culture, but that should not be a primary concern. When cultures are less well ingrained, however, capitalizing on chance could induce change, but the change in culture might not stabilize, and the culture might change again when surprise events occur. How would such an organization be distinguished from a schizoid organization?

THE DYNAMICS OF ORGANIZATIONAL CHANGE

2-D Force Field

Lewin (1947, 1951) conceptualized OD as a three-stage process consisting of *unfreezing*, *change*, and *refreezing*. During the unfreezing process, the organization is getting used to the idea of change, understanding why it is necessary, conducting an organized diagnosis of their situation, and setting objects for the change. In contemporary thinking, the diagnostic stage of the process is organized around the *action research model* (French & Bell, 1999). The core idea behind action research is that the rigor that is usually associated with scientific work in applied settings should be incorporated into an OD project. The consultant or change agent is both a social scientist and practitioner. At the same time, however, OD is a joint effort between the organization and the consultant. The change agent and the organization's members jointly produce diagnoses. Change procedures are mutually planned, and evaluations of activities mutually formulated opinions.

The consultant is not there to show off. The consultant is there to bring out the best in the people of the organization.

The action research phase of unfreezing begins with a commitment from the organization to the OD effort. The organization then identifies a team of its people to coordinate all the internal activities of the project. Next, after explaining the project's purpose and procedures to everyone, the consultant utilizes standard tools such as surveys, meetings and discussions, one-on-one interviews, and so forth. The effort produces a picture of how the organization behaves, the nature of the problems that the organization is experiencing, who feels that way, where the conflict are, and so forth.

The organization and OD consultant jointly identify programs, procedures, and patterns of social relationships that need improvement. They also identify any barriers to change. The process is replete with feedback meetings where the data are discussed, analyzed, interpreted, and argued. Eventually action planning occurs, which should be logically linked to the diagnostic findings. Throughout the process, the participants should discuss a simple-sounding question, "How will we know that what we've done is a success?" The answer serves as the basis of evaluation studies later on, where the data collection, interpretation, discussion, and argument meetings are frequent and involve every possible relevant person in the organization.

Possible barriers are attitudes and behaviors that are so entrenched in the organization that localized change efforts are not sufficient to permanently effect change. Some organizational members have vested interests in the old ways of doing things, and any threats to those interests meet with active resistance, if not sabotage of the change efforts. Other types of barriers may not be related to the willingness to change, but in conflicts with regard to what the organization should change into. What we now recognize as an "organizational culture" might be a euphemistic way of saying that there is too much old baggage to allow adaptive movement. Once again, vested interests could play insidious roles in the direction of change and the propagation of culture.

Lewin (1951) recognized that such conflicts arise in the course of an OD effort. He conceptualized those conflict dynamics as a force field. The force field is composed of two types of forces: the pressure to change, and the resistance to change. When pressure to change exceeds resistance, then the forces of change prevail. If resistance prevails, no one is going anywhere. The force field concept is commonly depicted in a two-dimensional display using simple linear dynamics, as in Fig. 4.1.

The repertoire of change techniques has grown since Lewin's first efforts. Initially there was the T-group, or sensitivity training group, in which participants learned something about themselves, human relations, and how they affect other people. Those elements of learning form a microlevel form of unfreezing. After the participants were thawed, the next part of the program was to learn new interpersonal skills, such as communication styles, person perception, and group

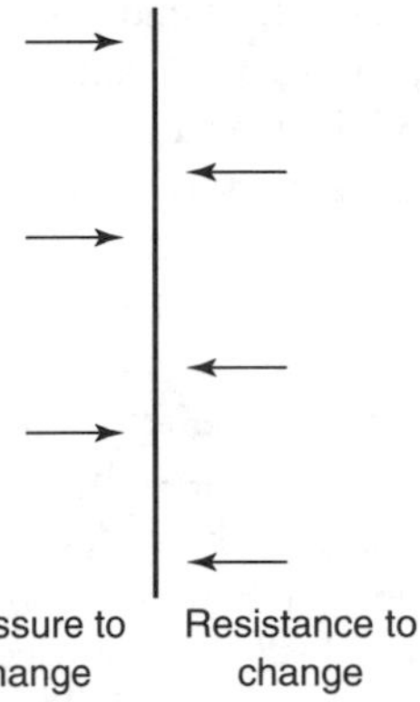

FIG. 4.1. Force field dynamics for organizational change in the conventional paradigm.

leadership to name a few. The final stage of sensitivity training was to reintegrate the new learning into one's permanent repertoire of social behaviors. Unfortunately, T-group training was not a smashing success most of the time, according to evaluation studies (Woodman & Sherman, 1980), because too often the T-group participants return to environments where people behave as they always did and supported the old, and usually deficient, social patterns.

Today's gamut of OD techniques includes team building approaches, conflict resolution strategies, communication and human relations training of all sorts, the action research model, job redesign, and process consultation, to name some broad categories (French & Bell, 1999). Although some success with each of those techniques has been reported, the trend appears to be that when the evaluation methods are more rigorous, the odds are smaller that a favorable result will be obtained (Woodman & Sherman, 1980; Terpstra, 1981). Kegan and Rubinstein (1973) reported that, at one point in history, there was a tendency for intervention techniques to be chosen on the basis of consultants' pet preferences, rather than on the basis of any well-known problem-solution linkages. Perhaps that finding was a result of the theory and knowledge base that practitioners have had to work.

Importantly, however, Kegan and Rubinstein (1973) also found that the reported success of OD was consistently tied to the level of trust among members of the organization. There is a substantial nexus of relationships among the constructs of trust, utility and vested interests, cooperation, and competition. The relationships involve a strong representation of NDS concepts. The NDS contributions to the understanding of trust and cooperation are unpacked in the next and subsequent chapters in the context of game theory and its applications.

Process consultation (Schein, 1988) is a technique whereby the consultant observes the processes that the organization exercises when it conducts its business, solves problems, and arrives at critical choices. Based on those observations, the consultant makes recommendations for changing those processes. The consultant is thus implicitly assuming particular cause and effect linkages exist between process variables and organizational performance, and that by tweaking the process, performance will be proportionately tweaked as well. The thrust of the evaluation evidence is, however, that process consultation strategies are generally unsuccessful (Hackman, 1992).

To return to the broader theme, the refreezing part of the OD process is the phase where the newly formed patterns of behavior and social learning have become crystallized permanently, or stabilized, in the organization's behavior strategy. The organization is now capable of solving its own problems and no longer needs the consultant. The social science knowledge that it has been acquired by the organization throughout the OD process has now been harnessed. The organization is now capable of solving its own problems self-sufficiently. The consultant then disengages, makes a graceful exit, and cashes the check before it bounces.

3-D Force Field

The first model for describing organizational change processes through NDS theory was based on a contrast between evolutionary and revolutionary change as depicted by a cusp catastrophe model. The cusp model for organizational change appears in Fig. 4.2 and reflects updates and modifications to the original idea based on new progress in NDS theory for organizational change (Bigelow, 1982; Gresov, Haveman, & Oliva, 1993; Guastello, 1995a, 1997b; Guastello, Dooley & Goldstein, 1995; Lange, Oliva, & McDade, 2000).

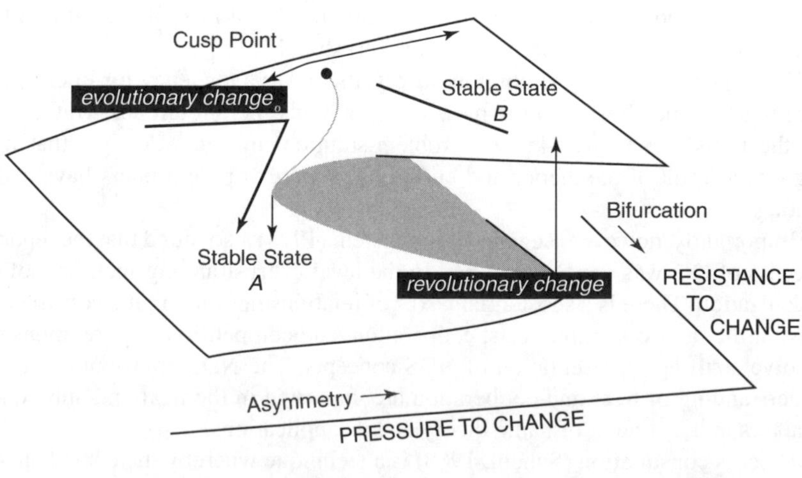

FIG. 4.2. Cusp catastrophe model for organizational change.

Classical biological evolutionary processes are relatively slow and progressive, and evolutionary change in organizations is no different. Each step in the change process is a logical outgrowth of the organization's state of development at a prior step in the change process. Examples of evolutionary change would include the use of new or improved personnel selection procedures or training programs, or growth in the organization's size in response to a steadily increasing demand for the organization's products.

A revolutionary change, by contrast, is relatively sudden. More importantly, however, the end result of change is qualitatively distinct from the starting situation. Revolutionary changes might involve a drastic change in the organization's structure from tall to flat, or centralized to decentralized. Other examples might occur in the course of mergers and acquisitions where roles and cultures are reconstructed or amalgamated. Some changes in business strategy might qualify as revolutionary change, depending on how distinct the new ideas were from the prior state of the organization.

Ramaprasad (1982) observed that the distinction between evolutionary and revolutionary change may not be especially obvious. A long sequence of evolutionary changes could lead up to a large and dramatic change in the way an organization does business and in its profitability. A dramatic cultural intervention, perhaps one that tries to transform a traditional American firm to Theory Z management, could indeed be revolutionary or could make no impact at all. Revolutionary changes, he conjectured, were rare in the long run. His reasoning was based on an analogy with biological evolution, which, in his interpretation, showed that long-lasting biological mutations were rare.

On the other hand, the cusp model and other NDS processes make particular note of critical points: The right intervention at the critical moment could have dramatic results even if the intervention is relatively small in scope. In a related fashion, evolutionary progress in a number of the organizations subsystems can simultaneously reach a critical point in the respective developments. At that time, according to synergetics theory, a *blow-up regime* (e.g., Knyazeva & Haken, 1999) occurs in which a revolutionary change takes place of its own accord.

Another case of slow revolution is the result of a negative feedback loop that may be built somehow into the organization's structure. While a deliberate intervention is taking place, the negative feedback loop slows down the pace of change. Doing so allows the organization to assess the impact of what had been accomplished and to direct the change process as necessary. Human factors engineers who might be trying to guide the introduction of a new technology into an organizational process of some sort have observed examples of this phenomenon over the years. The *active user syndrome* reflects the conflict facing someone who is trying to go to work every day and meet production goals and who, as a consequence, does not have the adequate time to explore new technologies or new potentials of those technologies. By the same token, once a critical point in the group's needs has been reached, the utility of investing time in exploring other options decreases greatly.

Cusp models contain two control parameters, which Bigelow (1982) defined as pressure to change (asymmetry) and resistance to change (bifurcation). Pressure to change will have a different effect on organizational behavior depending on the level of resistance. At low levels of resistance, pressure to change promotes a smooth and regular progression from one course of action to another. At high levels of resistance, however, the amount of pressure that would have otherwise resulted in change would probably not be enough. When pressure reaches a critical threshold, however, change is sudden. The result is a qualitative and discontinuous shift in organizational strategy.

Cusp functions are reversible. Organizational change, once it has occurred, may reverse itself if there is a substantial drop in the pressure that precipitated its change in the first place. The double-threshold function on the cusp surface indicates, however, that the critical point for changing back to the original form is located at a lower level of pressure that the critical point for making the change.

Resistance does not simply mean that forces exist that counteract efforts toward change as in Lewin's model, although Lewin's dynamic represents one way for events to turn out. Rather greater levels of resistance predispose the organization to greater discontinuities of change, if the pressure to change is sufficiently strong. The resistance concept is closely analogous to the modulus of elasticity parameter in the Euler buckling model for structural beams and human performance under load (Guastello, 1985, 1995a). The "stiffer" the organization, the more likely it will be to "snap" when pressure becomes too great.

Often the pressures to change originates, at least in part, from environmental sources. The "stiff" response could easily translate into a significant financial failure, which a good many organizations would regard as a convincing form of pressure. The model does not specify the origins of all forms of pressure, only that they aggregate into one control parameter. The resulting pressure parameter, together with resistance, are the two control parameters most proximally related to actual change.

Gradients on the cusp response surface are trajectories running between the bifurcation point and the attractor centers. Gradients represent transformations of the latent independent control parameters. One type of gradient dynamic in the organizational change model occurs where resistance to change could lead first to financial impairment, which in turn would lead to increased pressure to change, as just discussed. At a more general level of analysis, Lewin's (1951) vectorfield of opposing forces is now replaced by a field of diverging vectors which support the change or no-change attractor (DeGreene, 1978).

Another gradient behavior is shown in Fig. 4.2 as part of the slow revolution dynamic. Once a revolutionary effort has built up sufficient momentum it could then encounter belated resistance, which would occur too late in the process to have much effect. Alternatively, the revolutionary change initiative might not meet with ideological resistance, but there might be some temporary challenges as the revolutionary forces dismantle the organizational machinery of the old system and institute the machinery of the new.

The slow revolution and rising economic pressure constitute two types of gradient dynamic favoring change to a particular attractor. The *Maxwell convention* in catastrophe dynamics (Zeeman, 1977), however, favors a gradient move back toward the more *probable* state, which is usually the previous state. If the dynamics of change involve a collision with a boundary condition, a special case of the Maxwell convention, which Greeley (1986) identified as a *bumper dynamic* could occur (Guastello, 1995a). A version of the bumper dynamic was also independently identified by Argyris and Schon (1978) in their concept of single- and double-loop learning, both of which are considered next. Both the bumper dynamic and double-loop concepts could promote much more than a dampening of change initiatives; they would challenge any particular change goal and possible suggest improved goal definitions. The dynamics of improving objectives are considered subsequently.

Single-loop learning, according to Argyris and Schon (1978), describes a sequence of events that connect a set of goals and objectives, an action plan, and results of those actions. The set of goals and objectives rests on a set of assumptions concerning cause and effect relationships among actions and events in the environments plus organizational values and other aspects of its culture. The single loop is a feedback between results and action that serves the purpose of reinforcing a current action plan or precipitating its modification to produce better results. The limitation of single-loop learning is that the underlying assumptions and premises of the action plan are never questioned. *Double-loop learning* contains a second feedback loop from results to the set of goals, assumptions, and values. Not only can results of actions modify the action, but also they can modify an entire strategy for action, goals, and perhaps some aspects of a culture that promotes dysfunctional strategies.

Adaptive Responses from Savings and Loan Institutions

Gresov et al. (1993) tested a new application of the cusp model as Bigelow (1982) initially defined it. The organization they studied was a savings and loan institution in California. The organizational change behavior that formed the dependent measure was *response to competitive pressure*. Response was measured by four variances: growth rate as measured in dollar assets, percentage of assets invested in residential mortgages, percentage of brokered deposits, and sales volume of mortgages on the secondary market (Gresov et al., 1993, p. 197). The two control parameters were organizational design and competitive pressure.

Pressure was measured as the number of savings and loan institutions operating in California during a given time period. The three organizational design measures were chosen to reflect the potential for facilitating change or inflexibility toward change: organizational size as measured in dollar assets, years since the organization was incorporated, and its number of branch offices (Gresov et al., 1993, p. 197). Dollar values were corrected for inflation.

The measurements just described were taken at 26 repeated intervals over a 10-year period. Some observations were spaced semi-annually, while others were spaced at quarterly intervals. No correction for time interval appeared to have been made. The GEMCAT method of latent variable extraction (Oliva, Desarbo, Day, & Jedidi, 1987) was used to extract weighted combinations of the control variables and competitive response.

Because the version of GEMCAT in use at the time did not provide a measure of fit between the latent control variables and the latent response surface, the connection between the controls variables and competitive response was accomplished by graphical analysis. Plots of competitive pressure versus design in two dimensions (cusp bifurcation set) showed the greatest point density (of control parameter coordinates, not behavioral response) in the neighborhood of the no-change attractor. For Time Frames 1 through 9, pressure was low, and design (resistance) was increasing. For Time Frames 9 through 12, pressure increased, such that the design-pressure coordinates blipped across the bifurcation set to the neighborhood of the change attractor. Pressure subsided in Time Frames 14–26; response reversed direction (Gresov et al., 1993, p. 200).

The trajectory of control parameter coordinates did not appear to show the same amount of stability around the change attractor as there was around the no-change attractor. Gresov et al. (1993) also presented a three-dimensional plot of their control parameters with their latent behavioral outcome measure, which, in my opinion was curvilinear, but not easily identified as a cusp (p. 204). Fortunately, Gresov et al. published their latent data points in a table, which facilitated my reanalysis of their data (Guastello, 1995a) using structural equations for both the cusp dynamic difference equation and the exponential series.

The principal findings from the analysis were as follows: (a) The linear pre–post model was a better-fitting model ($R^2 = .58$) than the cusp ($R^2 = .40$). Although there was some evidence of cusp-like structure, an ordinary linear interpretation was more true; (b) the best-fitting model was the exponential structure ($R^2 = .64$):

$$z_2 = \theta_1^* e^{(\theta_2^* design^* Z_1)}. \tag{4.1}$$

Attempts to include pressure in the model in Equation 4.1 were not successful. (c) Further examination of the Lyapunov exponent indicated that the function was chaotic with a dimensionality of 1.86. The phase portrait is shown in Fig. 4.3.

The conclusions that were drawn from of all the analyses were as follows: (a) The cusp theory was broader than the actual dynamics taking place in the particular savings and loan company in the study. The actual dynamics were a little less than quadratic order. (b) Design was a decent indicator of bifurcation. Within

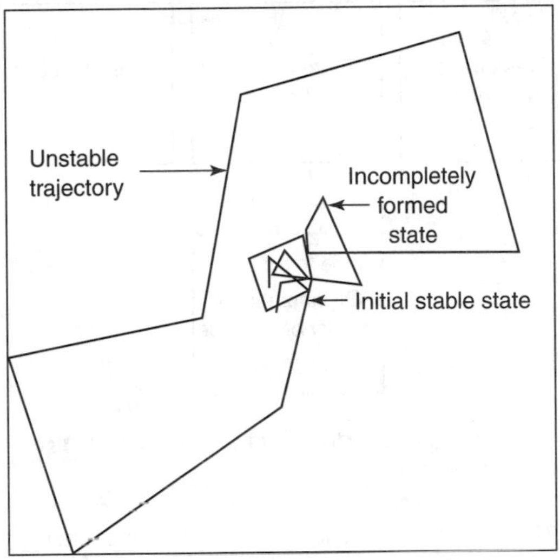

FIG. 4.3. Phase portrait of organizational change for a savings and loan institution.

the context of the theory in use, Design controlled Resistance to Change, where change took the form of Competitive Response. (c) An approximately quadratic form should have one control parameter, and one was found; the pressure variable did not do much good in the model. (d) The dynamics of organizational change for the savings and loan institutions could be characterized as a sequence of initial stability, an excursion into instability, and a return to original form. Change had not stabilized. (e) Because the Competitive Response function was chaotic, in addition, it was conjectured that function might be a relative of the Rossler attractor. (In the years that have elapsed, no one has pursued this point any further, to my knowledge.)

The Role of Technology

The examples of organizational change that have been expressed in dynamics so far have regarded change as a global entity. Two recent studies have given attention to the role of technology. The first concerns the possible cases where technology is produced by the organization. More specifically, Staudenmeyer and Lawless (1999) addressed a situation where an organization's rate of innovation out-paced the decline of older technologies. As new features of the technology (e.g., a telephone system) are added, new links have to be made among parts of the system. As new features are requested by users, the technology becomes "brittle," meaning that a small change requires extensive relinking to many parts of the system so that the system can stay internally coordinated.

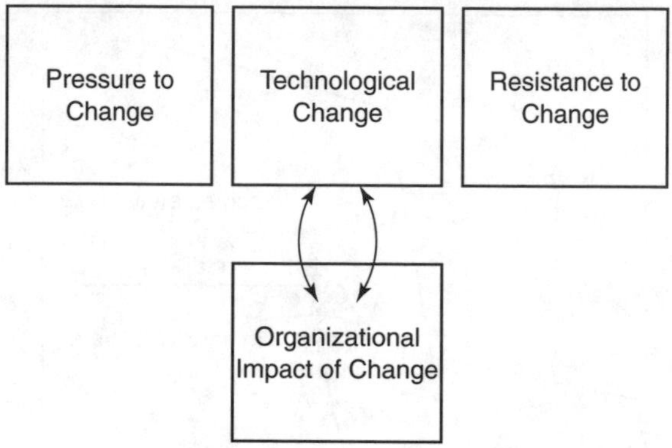

FIG. 4.4. Technologically driven change complicates the force field within an organization.

At some point the technology reaches a crisis point where it becomes more sensible to rewrite the Big Program from scratch. The demands on the humans for doing so can be extensive. At the same time, the pressure to change the system from scratch is closely tied to the organization's dwindling knowledge about how the product was initially assembled. Fortunately for their client, there were still a few people left in the organization who still remembered how to manipulate the original program code, all 15 million lines of it, after 20 years. There still remained the problem of how to shut down the existing system while the new system was being installed.

A model for the situation is given in Fig. 4.4 (after what I heard and saw at the conference presentation). Technological change in this model is the result of two-opposing forces: pressure to change and resistance to change. Pressure to change may come from new governmental regulations, competitors' initiatives, and customer sources. Resistance to change comes from the product size and the complexity of the product structure, the need to keep the present version of the product available, and the knowledge problem mentioned earlier. Staudenmeyer and Lawless (1999) named this form of resistance, *sociotechnical embeddedness*.

The second model for technology and organizational change concerns the case of a technology that is competing with related technologies (Lange et al., 2000). The model shown in Fig. 4.5 depicts product adoptions favoring one of two competitors in the first seven time periods of the series, with an abrupt shift to competitor's offering in the eighth time period and beyond. The asymmetry control parameter is composed of variables depicting product awareness and opinions about the product. The bifurcation control parameter contained indications of whether a competing piece of software had companion products to go with it and the number of organizations that had adopted either platform in the current quarter of the year. The adoption of either platform indicated a growth in the market size.

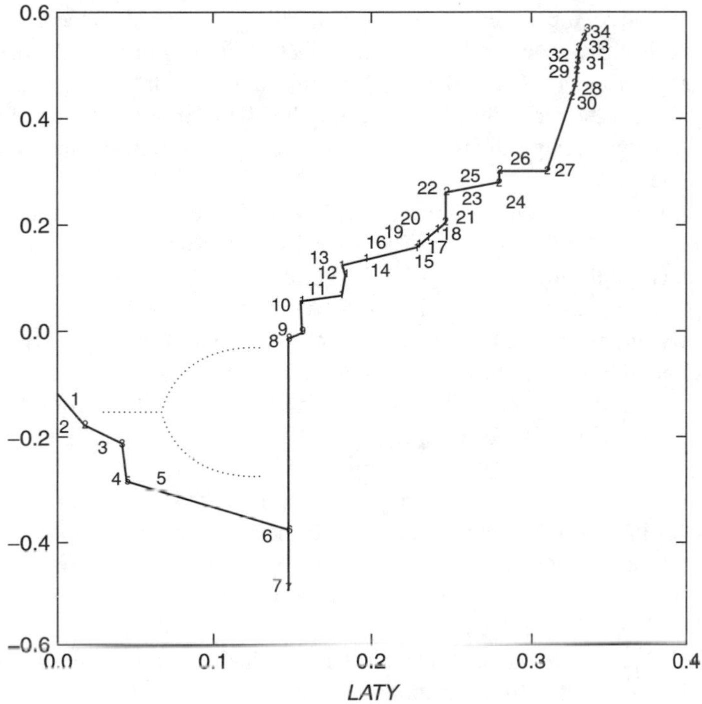

FIG. 4.5. Two-dimensional view of the cusp catastrophe model for the adoption of competing technologies, by Lange et al. (2000). Here *LATZ* reflects both the adoption choice and the number of accessories available for the product for 34 quarters; Latent Installed Base (*LATY*) reflects the total amount of familiarity with either product. Reprinted with permission.

The data were analyzed with the newest version of the GEMCAT program. Lange et al. (2000) concluded that the dynamics were described very well by a cusp catastrophe model; the control variables defined above were identified empirically. In the early phases of the market for the products they studied, adoptions of either product were growing simultaneously. After a period of time, however, there was a rapid shift in favor of one of the products. The strong shift in the markets would reflect a strong impetus for both organizations to make internal changes. One competitor had to make some drastic improvements in order to stay in the market. The other competitor had to cope (crying all the way to the bank, I'm sure) with the demand for greater production volume.

The product adoption story that Lange et al. (2000) portrayed is not too different from the "lock-in" phenomenon (Arthur, 1989). In Arthur's (often-retold) saga, the VHS and Beta formats for videorecorders competed for adoption. The two formats were not compatible with each other. The makers of VHS were generous with format licenses to other organizations that wanted to make videorecorders and videotape products. The makers of Beta rejected offers to license and tried to vertically control the technology. As a result, the VHS format was adopted faster and more widely. VHS products and rental outlets proliferated, and the interest in Beta dwindled.

Having lived through those times, I have a version of the story that includes a third competitor—the laser disk. The laser disk technology was essentially the same as the digital video disk (DVD) format today, only it was formatted for a 12-inch platter instead of a 5-inch disk. It delivered a great digital picture but competed poorly against the analog videotapes. Why? Because laser disk only allowed playback, and the user could not record favorite TV shows or plug in a camera. The growing popularity of VHS created a lockout of laser disks from the rental stores, and laser disks disappeared. By 1984, RCA Corporation gave up and sold the laser disk technology. The technology suddenly came back at us in pieces. Compact disks (CD) began to replace phonograph records for the new generation of people buying audio equipment; this replacement was timed, curiously enough, right around the time any patents on stereo phonograph equipment were beginning to expire. CD technology has now installed itself in desktop computers, and the digital videodisk (DVD) is back in a smaller size, now that all the digital technologies are relatively compatible. Finally, what ever happened to digital audio tape (DAT)? My guess is that has been preempted by the burnable CD.

There are several points to these audio-visual stories. (a) Lock-in happens. It has been called the Law of Increasing Returns (Arthur, 1989), which is in turn a relative of the principle of sensitivity to initial conditions. Two products may start out at relatively equal market shares, but with different deployment "functions" could end up in very different places. (b) Competition landscapes often involve a lot more than two competitors. (c) Good technological ideas are necessary but not sufficient. Organizations' strategies for production, promotion, and linkages with other products are essential parts of the process and require creative ideas as well. Let's unpack those ideas. It's a big suitcase.

Logistic Map Dynamics

So far we have considered organizational change as a global outcome, as in the case of the savings and loans institutions. Complex organizations such as RCA mentioned above (now a part of General Electric) are involved in multiple product–market combinations, each of which could be confronting a profound pressure to change in some way. If we look *within* any organizational subunit that is confronting change, we can see the additional dynamics of sociotechnical embeddedness. Various models of self-organization all point to the notion that it is the local interaction among elementary work groups that gives rise to the global phenomenon that the external viewer would recognize as The Change.

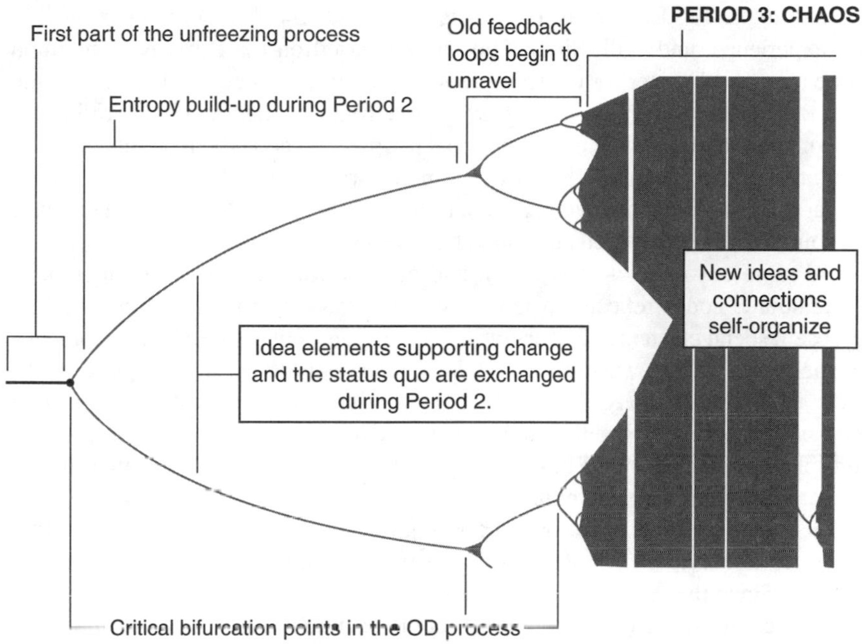

FIG. 4.6. Logistic map dynamics for organizational change.

Organizational theorists and practitioners have suggested in different ways that the logistic map function is a decent model of the OD process (Goldstein, 1994; Guastello, 1995a, 1997b; Guastello et al., 1995; Kiel, 1994; McClure, 1998; Michaels, 1989, 1991; Stacey, 1992; Zimmerman, Lindberg, & Plsek, 1998). Different writers emphasize different aspects of the process, as one can imagine. Figure 4.6 brings the phenomenon up to date and takes into consideration my predecessors' best shots and my own interpretations.

Period 1 of the map is the unfreezing stage of OD. The organization needs to build critical levels of entropy in order move the change process forward. The activities of the unfreezing stage mentioned earlier contribute to entropy build-up. The nuance here is that there is a critical bifurcation point that must be reached before the organization is capable of meaningful change.

According to Bailey (1994), there are several sources of entropy in social systems. Population dynamics can be a source of entropy. Does the organization have sufficient numbers to carry out its functions? Does the internal population have the needed skills? The population that lives outside the organization readily generates new ideas and demands for products and segmentation of markets.

Populations can contribute entropy by virtue of their diversity. Although "diversity" is often used by organizations to denote group composition by gender or ethnicity, the underlying concept, which dates back to Lewin's human relations training in the 1930s, extends to all sorts of individual differences in personality, life experience, and skill. Simulation studies based on the Prisoner's Dilemma game (see next chapter) or the spin-glass method of self-organization show some pertinent illustrations (Guastello, 1995a; Huberman & Glance, 1993; Trofimova, 1996). If we take a sample of hypothetical people, and code them on their relative similarity to each other by virtue of personality traits or past histories of cooperation and competition (or anything else), they eventually form little aggregations. If the source codes were based on cooperation and competition, then the aggregations would represent internal cooperation and competition with out-group members. If the source codes reflected personality trait similarity, the aggregations might represent social clusters and cooperative interactions, but not necessarily competitive behavior. Global catastrophes of widespread cooperation and competition can occur in situations where internal diversity is high and the overall group is large (Guastello, 1995a). If population members actively exert influence on each other and select each other on the basis of some common preferences, the opportunities for coalition formation and polarization increase (Frank & Fahrbach, 1999).

Technology generates entropy, according to Bailey (1994), who made specific reference to the sociotechnical systems aspects of technology and product production. Since that time, however, computer communications technologies have accelerated the speed of communication among individuals within organizations and between organizations. The new technologies can preempt long and frequent airplane rides and even the 10-day airmail delay between continents. At the same time, the need for training new people increases with respect to the use of the new systems, the business habits that surround them, and the construction of messages that will be interpreted properly by the receiving parties. Organizational structures are changing in accordance with their communication patterns (Boland & Tenkasi, 1995; Fulk & DeSanctis, 1995; Hinds & Kiesler, 1995; Kiesler, 1997; Lea, O'Shea, & Fung, 1995; Orlikowsky, Yates, Okamura, & Fugimoto, 1995; Pickering & King, 1995; Zack & McKenney, 1995).

The availability of energy and materials also produces entropy. Food manufacturers may make low-profile shifts between cane, beet, and corn sugar. After acquiring some experience in the utilization of all three sources, and timing the shift between the different sources, the entropy level associated with the shift in sugar sources is usually low. On the other hand, the so-called "oil crisis" of the late 1970s had a dramatic impact on the textile industry when the latter suddenly needed to shift from polyester production (petroleum based) to cotton and wool. ("The fashion for this year will be *all natural fibers!*")

Information is another source of entropy. Information is the basis of both new ideas generated from within the organization and turbulence in the environment. The role of information in economics is considered in Chapter 11. As a preview, however, it should be mentioned that the role of information has shifted along with the transition to an "information economy." Information used to provide a support function within markets for products or securities. In the new economy, information itself is a product; as such it does not follow the same rules as ordinary markets (Boisot, 1995; Boisot & Child, 1999). If a unit of information is actually *interesting and relevant* to some organizational members, new dynamics form whereby people with the new information share it with others and use it to shape the sentiments and behaviors of others (Frank & Fahrbach, 1999). Thus, there is a linkage between the information flow patterns and influence patterns within an organization.

Given all these sources of entropy, it becomes the change agent's task to move the organization to far-from-equilibrium conditions and to allow the self-organization process to occur on its own. The central features of self-organization, as experienced by organizations are "spontaneous and radical reorganizing, activating nonlinearity, interrupting equilibrium-seeking tendencies, using departures from equilibrium, . . . establishing firm but permeable boundaries, [and] generating unpredictable outcomes" (Goldstein, 1994, p. 51).

Goldstein (1994) described several techniques for generating far-from-equilibrium conditions. *Difference questioning*, for instance, seeks the opposite of consensus; the variability of the incumbents' perceptions is more important than their average responses. Other techniques include *purpose contrasting*, challenging self-fulfilling prophecies and assumptions about the organization's culture, taking advantage of chance and serendipity, and using absurdity creatively. Purpose contrasting, like difference questioning, encourages people to discuss how they are different from each other, how their work objectives are different, and how those differences affect other things that they do. As the simulation work suggests, amplifying differences among people will increase the social entropy and balkanize the social networks. This is a necessary step toward reassembling the social networks.

Self-fulfilling prophesies were observed in organizations as far back as McGregor's (1960) Theory X-Y. If you treat people according to the Theory-X belief system (e.g., "they are lazy and irresponsible"), they will behave in that fashion (e.g., lazy and irresponsible). Thus, management would report, if asked to do so: "Of course we treat them like they are lazy and irresponsible. Look at how lazy and irresponsible they are." On the other hand, if the same people should be treated as if they were valuable participants in the organization, consistent with the Theory-Y belief system, they will behave like Theory-Y people. They would probably need a little time, however, to get over the shock and disbelief that management changed so drastically. The point of the matter here, however, is that self-fulfilling prophesies exist because they hold certain behavior patterns—which inevitably favor the status quo—in place. Those patterns need to be disrupted in the course of the OD process.

Self-fulfilling prophesies are simple examples of twisted logic that is sometimes more complicated. For instance, a hypothetical unnamed university (HUU) claims,

"We do not give cost of living increases here; we only give merit increases." When the bag of raise money reaches an academic department, however, it is only trivially different from the cost of living. After some obtuse calculations involving seniority and percentages, the department chairs determine how much of a raise each member of the department should receive; again, those amounts do not differ by much. The performance ratings, meanwhile according to HUU policy, are based on 45% allocation to research, 45% allocation to teaching, and 10% allocation to service activities both within and outside of HUU. The chair then fine-tunes the performance ratings so that they are consistent with the raises. Note that the chair's job is actually easier when there are poor performers in the group. In that case, one or two poor slobs can get the monetary shaft, thus saving more for the others. In the feedback interview, the ratings are presented to the faculty members as if they were no unbelievable components to them. Imagine the surprise of a faculty member who is told that he or she should take time out of teaching or research to spend more time "being visible" so he or she could be appointed to more committees.

Goldstein (1994) gives an example of the creative use of absurdity. A vice president of a subdivision of a large organization was having difficulty gaining control over his board meetings. The consultant, who attended one of those meetings, started talking to the VP in loud whispers. The room suddenly quieted down so everyone could hear the "secrets." In the next meeting, and several thereafter, the consultant required the VP to wear a crown, carry a scepter, and cant three times at the beginning of each meeting, "I do so love to be the king!" (pp. 35–36).

The dynamics of Period 2 indicate that oscillations take place between two states. In the original application of the Verhulst–May–Oster equations it was the population of a species that went up and down. In organizations there may indeed be populations of people fluctuating, where the populations are defined in terms of an attitude set, business strategy preference, or skill set. More importantly, however, the real fluctuation occurs between new and old *ideas*. A related principle is tested empirically in Chapter 6 in the context of creative problem-solving group activities.

The OD change process continues past Period 2 and into the period-doubling phase of the map. There the connections among organizational subsystems, or pieces of logic are beginning to unravel. They become fully unraveled in Period 3, which is still known as chaos. At that point, it is possible for the self-organization to take place, wherein new interrelationships are formed among people, tasks, groups, and the environment. The feedback loops that once sustained the pre-change state are now rewired to permit greater adaptation to environmental pressure, from both within and outside the organization. Refreezing in Lewin's perspective is now interpreted as self-organization, which restores the organization to state of lower entropy. The new changes need to be embedded in the system in such a way as to prevent relapse. Effort should be allocated to the self-replication of new ideas and work patterns where possible.

Boundaries affect the self-organization of systems within. In organizations, boundaries may form along the lines of physical space, division of work, or the social network patterns mentioned earlier. Boundaries may be distinct or indistinct, permeable or semi-permeable. It is important to choose the right boundary for the right purposes. Conflicts among coworkers or suppliers and clients have been known to arise when the nature of a boundary went from firm to fuzzy and when the parties to the agreement had no clue that the transition had taken place (Eoyang, 1997).

Evolutionary Bifurcations

Theorists have expressed interest in the network of bifurcations inherent in an evolutionary process (e.g., Guastello, 1995a; Puu, 2000b; Stacey, 1992). A pattern of branches may have the symmetric regularity of the logistic map, but without the transition to chaos. Alternatively, a fractal branching pattern, such as the one shown in Fig. 4.7 captures the idea: The initial state of the organization could be depicted as a stable state. Entropy in this case would be a combined result of inflowing information from the environment that induces pressure to change plus some of the dynamics of resistance. As entropy increases, change eventually moves to an attractor that has been sighted on one or the other branches of the map in Fig. 4.7. One simple form of resistance event may not be a disagreement that change is needed, but it may be a reaction of "we don't want to do anything until we know what we're doing and considered our options," which is a fair enough initial response. Once action has been taken toward one attractor, feedback from the environment can sustain that initiative or not.

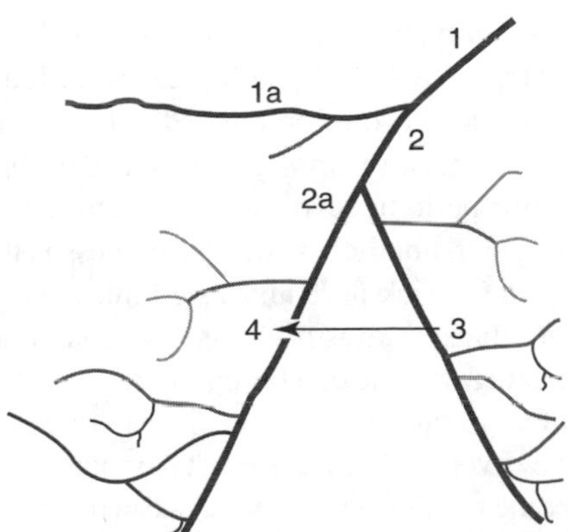

FIG. 4.7. Bifurcations in a decision path could reflect an underlying fractal structure.

In the event a path is not sustained, the organization may turn back before it is gripped in the attractor basin, or it may change its direction. Sometimes change is not reversible, as we have seen in many evolutionary dynamics, in which case entropy continues to increase until the organization reaches the next bifurcation point, where additional changes are made. For instance some critical points in an organization's decision path are given on Fig. 4.7. The paths might represent opportunities to introduce an innovation to a product line, attempt to open a new market, or change some other strategy of operation. At Point 1, the organization is following a path where it encounters a bifurcation opportunity, whereupon the organization could follow Path 1a or Path 2. It chooses Path 2 and soon encounters another opportunity to choose between Paths 2a and 3. Note that the option of choosing 1a is no longer available. The organization chooses the path to 3, but decides that it would rather be on the other side of the bifurcation at Point 4. The organization makes a sudden jump; unlike the previous evolutionary changes, this jump is a catastrophic, or revolutionary change.

Punctuated Equilibria

The experience of an OD effort is long story, and it takes quite a bit of effort to do the job once. It is easy, therefore, to forget about new OD efforts that await the organization in the future. One idea that the "freezing" metaphor does not convey well is actually the opposite of what we would expect from "ice." As the result of an OD effort, the organization should be prepared to make change more readily, accept unpredictability, and interpret the potential for future change more effectively. This adaptive stance should be institutionalized along with the specific changes such as sociotechnical workflow, performance appraisals, and so forth.

Contemporary evolutionary theorists (e.g., Gould, 1983; Laszlo, 1991) now recognize that the so-called missing links in biological evolution are not missing at all. Darwin's gradualist concept of evolution posited only slow mutation and gradual adaptation. A hierarchical structure among genetic codes apparently exists, which has the effect of generating periodic revolutionary change. Thus, an organism leaps from one equilibrium state to another. A similar process is thought to occur in organizations, according to Gersick (1991). Vested interests keep the system from mutating too much until the system is no longer capable of assimilating demands for change into its existing structure. The dynamics around the manifold in the cusp model shown in Fig. 4.2 describe the evolutionary containment process.

The nuance here, however, is that we are not stopping the theory at one revolutionary change. Rather the revolutionary changes can occur repeatedly at relatively long intervals. The net result is not especially different from the stage theories of individual psychological development. The general model appears in Fig. 4.8 (from Guastello, 1995a, p. 388). Stage theories reflect a discontinuous qualitative change

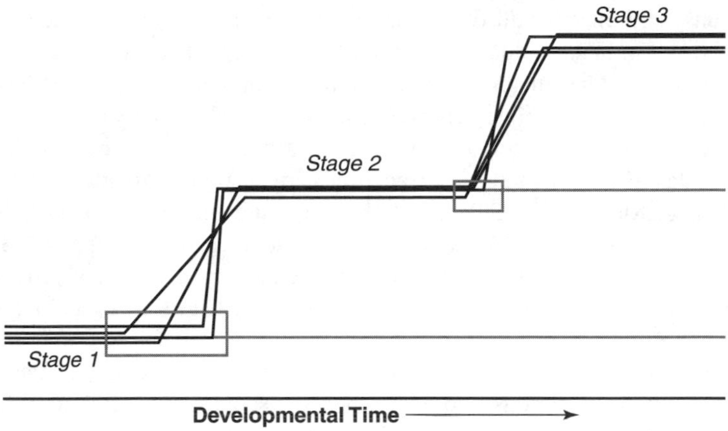

FIG. 4.8. A stage theory of development reflects a punctuated equilibrium phenomenon.

from one stage to another. Each person or entity progresses through an invariant sequence of stages, meaning that the order of the stages does not change. Each stage is progressively more complex than the preceding stage, and subsumes all the cognitive and social structures of previous stages. The stage sequences for human psychological development are quasi-reversible, meaning that a person at a later stage of development has access to schemata found at an earlier stage.

The transition between stages is the result of an assimilation and accommodation dynamic. Assimilation reflects the system's drive toward stability. The system maintains its current structure, or level of complexity, for as long as circumstances will allow. When too many situations arise that are too complex to be handled adequately by an existing structure, an accommodation response takes place and the person transits to the next stage of development.

In NDS theory, the stair-step arrangement of developmental stages is essentially a punctuated equilibrium model. When events occur that seriously challenge the capabilities of the system, the system is increasing in entropy and reaching a far-from-equilibrium condition. Eventually, the system reaches a bifurcation point, which is a point of maximum instability, at which time the system either accedes quickly to its next stage of development, or retrenches to its former stage. Retrenchment often means not solving one's problems and paying the consequences for not doing so. But even there, a qualitative shift has taken place from immaturity to arrested development.

The sequence of stages in Fig. 4.8 are drawn as a cord of several trajectories to indicate that broadly defined developmental stages are actually the result of several subprocesses, and that it is likely for development within each subprocess to be unsynchronized with development in other subprocesses (Thelen, 1992; Metzger, 1997). In individual development, subprocesses would include cognitive complexity, emotional maturity, moral judgment, and social interactions. The exact outcome is a result of the interaction among those psychic components (van Geert, 2000). Developmental theorists arrived at the same conclusion as organizational theorists that developmental stage transitions are cusp-catastrophic in nature (van der Maas & Molenaar, 1998). Similarly, we could make an extension by way of living systems theory (Miller, 1978 et seq.) to societal development. Societal subprocesses would include agriculture and technology, economics, government, transportation and communication, social services, health care, and ecological consciousness (Guastello, 1995a).

Whereas Gould emphasized the role of hierarchical structures in the organization of genetic mutations into evolutionary discontinuities, Bak and Sneppen (1993) interpreted the punctuated equilibrium phenomenon as an example of the self-organized criticality inherent in the sandpile situation. There is an inverse relationship between the size of an evolutionary movement and frequency of evolutionary movements. Smaller morphological changes are proportionately more common in a manner consistent with the $1/f$ power law function. The presence of the power law function suggests two points (at least): (a) The larger, more dramatic evolutionary changes are the result of self-organized criticality that is traceable to the local interactions among micro-level evolutionary drifts. (b) The underlying structure of the evolving living shapes is fractal.

The potential importance of fractals as descriptions of living forms is well known (Bunde & Havlin, 1996). The more exciting development in this area, however, is in the development of algorithms that track gradual shifts in shape along a small number of parameters that could be the result of an evolutionary mutation process (Kocic, 2001). At the present time, however, this branch of mathematical pursuit has not reached the point where discontinuous punctuated equilibria can be observed through a combination of parameter values.

Of closer relevance to matters at hand, however, Morel and Ramanujam (1999) explored the dynamics of self-organized criticality in organizational structures. They pointed out that most changes in organizations affect the smallest "branches" of the "tree." Proportionately fewer affect larger systemic subunits. When enough small changes accumulate, however, then the potential for widespread organizational change is possible. Larger organizations, furthermore, are have greater potential for broad morphological change because there have greater numbers of nodes or network ties. Nodes are places where sections of the organization can join other sections creating an intersection of communication. Dooley and Ven de Ven (1999) continued the metaphor: One piece of information does not generate a report. If enough information is generated, i.e., a critical threshold has been crossed, a report is generated. If enough reports are generated, then a functionality in the organization needs to develop that will assimilate, process, and file the reports in an advantageous manner.

Rugged Landscape Dynamics

The rugged landscape model of self-organization has also gripped the imagination of the latest wave of organizational theorists. McKelvey (1999) reported a group of simulations that were constructed around questions of how to combine internal complexity, *K*, with external complexity, *C*, given that competitor firms are also present and that different fitness peaks exist in the economic ecosystem. There were several important findings. First, given that two or more firms are competing for a particular niche with complexity *C*, low-*K* firms will have an advantage over high-*K* firms. On the other hand, if a particular competitor is already functioning in a particular niche with complexity *C*, it would be advantageous for the new firm to adjust its level of *K* to match the competitor's *C* (p. 312).

Second, there is a co-evolutionary tendency for organizations occupying a fitness peak (or pocket) to gravitate toward common levels of *C* and *K*. If $C > K$ overall, an innovation by one firm will give that firm a competitive advantage. On the other hand, the innovation will diffuse throughout the pocket giving all incumbent organizations an increase in fitness (McKelvey, 1999, p. 312). I observe here that the practice of swapping "benchmark methods" is an example of co-evolutionary fitness improvement. Although many examples of benchmark exchange among systems engineers pertain to nodes on the lesser branches of big trees, we already know by now that those small-looking innovations can combine into substantial and desirable mutations of organizational life.

The third major point that McKelvey (1999) made was predicated on the complexity of the value chain, which is the number of organizations that contribute to the making of a product by providing subassemblies, raw materials, information resources, and so forth. If the complexity of the value chain, *N*, is large, then organizations will have an advantage over competitors to the extent that they keep their own internal complexity small.

Systems can evolve toward greater complexity, but in doing so they run the risk of hitting a threshold beyond which they cannot function. Kauffman (1995) called this phenomenon a *complexity catastrophe*. McKelvey (1999) interpreted this point as meaning that small innovations are better than large ones, or many innovations at once. Barnett and Freeman (1999) studied an organization that made semiconductors over a couple of decades. Efficiency, or profitability, went up when a small number of innovations were introduced in a given year. But the year in which the organization introduced eight different new product ideas resulted in serious financial distress. The sociotechnical system was not able to adapt to the coordination demands of all the innovations it was trying to produce.

McKelvey (1999) and Levinthal and Warglien (1999) both noted that the shape of the competitive landscape and options available to any particular actor are distorted by the presence of actors who arrived there first. For instance, product positioning involves some recognition of the positions of other products. This observation led Levinthal and Warglien to consider whether organizations can design their own landscapes. They observed that a landscape that is too smooth will be "slippery" and thus not permit fitness peaks or pockets. A landscape that is too rugged may promote a high degree of adaptability, but only to a small space. According to Tilman's (1994) extinction debt principle, a species that has become highly adapted to one niche has a proportionately more difficult time colonizing other niches. Good colonizers are not the most locally adaptive entities.

Simulations by Levinthal and Warglien (1999) showed that interdependencies among actors on a landscape will promote some behavioral variety and non-incremental search, while low interdependency promotes predictability and stable attractors. Thus, an organization can increase its interdependencies with other organizations as a way of increasing its colonization potential. Local adaptation, on the other hand, requires both autonomy and low interdependence. Coupled landscapes, however, involve a different challenge. There, the *N* contains networks of suppliers and customers, for whom cooperation and coordination are critical.

CONSCIOUSNESS IN ORGANIZATIONS

If organizations make decisions and generate creative and adaptive ideas, then something akin to consciousness is occurring. Furthermore, because the organization is made up of people, there is some relationship between the individuals' consciousness and the collective unconsciousness. Indeed, a related idea came up in Mead's (1934) concept of the group personality. In contemporary thinking, where the organization is a complex adaptive system (Dooley, 1997; Levinthal & Warglien, 1999; Stacey 1992, 1996), the creative thinking processes are of central importance to an organization's survival. Therefore, in this final section of the chapter we explore the nature of individual consciousness and its relationship to the collective organizational unconsciousness; the latter is closely related to the organization's culture. Those ideas are expanded and developed in the subsequent chapters in this book.

Individual Consciousness

One of the longest-lasting contributions of analytic psychology is the distinction between the conscious and unconscious mind. Consciousness is usually regarded as a moment-to-moment stream of experience. In my case right now, consciousness consists of my attempts to decipher the scribbles in my notebook, the response of the word processor to the grammar and spelling, and the CD playing in the background. The stream is interrupted by another flow that begins with the klunk of the door bell, the dog barking, my voice muttering, "I've got to fix the handle on this screen door," the man behind the door saying, "Sign here please," and that voice saying again, "My new books from Erlbaum just arrived."

Ideas that are located in the preconscious are those that are not immediately conscious, but can be called into consciousness if the right cue is presented. For instance, I can go for weeks on end not thinking about the screen door, but suddenly the whole story of its disrepair comes to consciousness again when I struggle to get it open.

Cognitive psychology has been rooted in the experimental scientific tradition, which is quite different from the analytic method of operation. In the early decades it was convenient for cognitive psychologists to parse processes into separate functions of psychophysics, perception, sensation, cognition, memory, and psychomotor response. "Controlled" experiments were designed in such a way as to obviate certain cognitive processes while manipulating others. Perhaps the division of scientific labor is a remnant of Newtonian thinking, "If we can understand how each of the parts function we can understand the whole process." On the other hand, the division of labor can be interpreted as another example of the rugged landscape phenomenon. There were plenty of unanswered scientific questions and a small number of people to respond. Each new entrant to the scientific landscape picked a topic and produced something of interest. Ecological niches, or fitness peaks, formed around the centers of scientific productivity. The next wave of scientists then chose a location among the productive centers or found new territory altogether. There was some coordination between university faculty and graduate students.

In recent years, however, there is a growing awareness of the artificial nature of the boundaries among cognitive processes. The integrated nature of the cognitive process is particularly poignant in contemporary studies of memory using functional magnetic resonance imaging (FMRI). There we find different *combinations* of spatial locations of brain activation, depending on whether the memory task involves memory for words, pictures, or events (Gabrieli et al., 1996). Similarly, the cognition and action combinations have melted into units now known as autonomous agents (Tschacher & Dauwalder, 1999).

A diagram of the integrated cognitive process appears in Fig. 4.9. Virtually all the cognitive processes represented in the figure, and combinations thereof, have been studied through NDS concepts (Clayton & Frey, 1996, 1997; Davids,

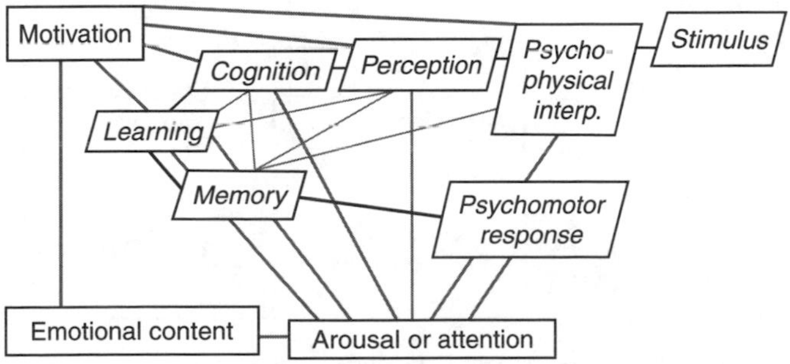

FIG. 4.9. The network of relationships among cognitive functions.

Button, & Bennett, 1999; Gregson 1992, 1995, 1998, 1999; Guastello, 1995a; Kelso, 1995; Kohonen, 1989; MacCormac & Stamenov, 1996; Orsucci, 1998; Pressing, 1999; Tschacher & Dauwalder, 1999; Ward & West, 1998). It is only a small matter to integrate the social content of motivation into cognitive processes, as suggested in Fig. 4.9, or other aspects of personhood such as personality, temperament, genetics, and so forth. The result would eventually become a tangled array of boxes and arrows.

Unconsciousness

While a network of cognitive and brain functions are at work to produce what we experience as consciousness, the cognitive processes themselves are largely hidden from view; i.e., they are part of the *unconscious*, along with a wide range of thoughts, attitudes, and emotions. Some unconscious material is accessible with modest effort. For instance, numerous interpersonal learning exercises are based on the Johari Window, which is based on the following ideas: All information about ourselves is divided into two categories—that of which we are aware, and that of which we are not aware. Furthermore, the same information can be redivided into two categories—that which other can see and that which they cannot see. The result appears in Fig. 4.10.

The information about ourselves that is visible to us and to others is not especially interesting from an interpersonal learning point of view. Similarly the information that neither we nor others can see is not going to do us much good either. On the other hand, information about us that we know, but which others do not know, is something we would want to consider disclosing—or not, depending on what it is and whether we are trying to build intimacy or negotiate the sale of small countries. Information that others can see about us, but which we cannot

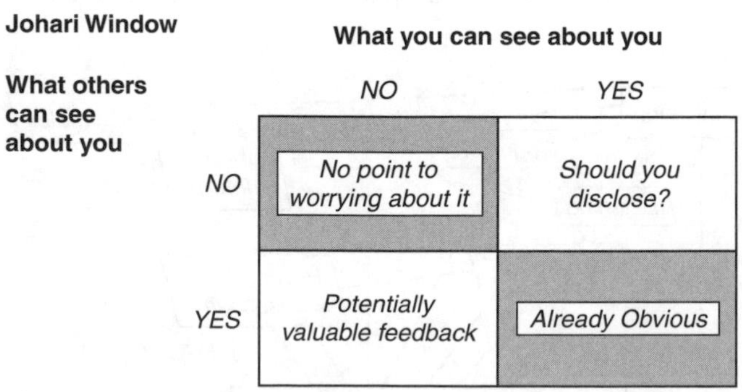

FIG. 4.10. The Johari Window that appears in many interpersonal learning exercises.

see, can sometimes be a source of constructive feedback. Actually, the role of the psychoanalyst is to target that sort of information and present it to the client in a constructive and accurate manner.

According to Jung, the portion of our personality that we do not readily see is a structure that he calls the *shadow*. We usually prefer to keep the contents of the shadow hidden from view, especially our own. The fewer nightmares we share on a day-to-day basis the better we feel, and the more friends we keep.

Jung expanded the shadow idea further by saying that the contents of a person's unconscious could be segmented into a *personal unconscious* and a *collective unconscious*. The personal unconscious contains pictures, ideas, symbols, and emotional connections that are all derived from an individual's unique experience. The collective unconscious contains a storehouse of ideas and symbols that occur frequently in the culture. Symbols involving suns, moons, stars, kings, queens, fish, serpents, can be found in the mythologies of distinctive cultures, and these symbols show up in individual dreams. Indeed, some noted theosophists of the early 20th century made detailed studies of the extensive use of certain symbol groups, especially those that spanned different cultures and epochs of history. Jung was partial to the writings of 17th-century alchemists.

Because of the trans-generational and trans-cultural pervasiveness of these symbolic *archetypes of the unconscious*, Jung concluded that the contents of the collective unconscious were genetically transmitted. It was certainly a provocative thought in its day, but professional psychology today does not take the idea of genetically transmitted symbols (or *racial memory*) seriously. The simpler explanation prevails: We learn ideas of all sorts from our culture, and that learning is a powerful explanation for many behaviors. Furthermore, social institutions play a major role in keeping a good deal of social symbolism alive. The concept of an archetype, as opposed to idiosyncratic mental trash, is a close relative of the cognitive concept of a *prototype*, which is an idealized notion of an object. We use prototypes on a regular basis when we classify objects into categories; a prototype is a "good" example of what belongs in a category.

Collective Consciousness

Next, let's take a bunch of those agile minds, together with their deep thoughts and personal trash, and give them all computers with Internet accounts. Suddenly we have a form of *collective intelligence*. Technology does more than play a big role in what we do for a living, or how we do it, or how we draw it on an organizational chart. It shapes our notion of *who we are* (Terkle, 1984).

The idea of collective intelligence originated with studies of social insects, such as ants. An ant colony self-organizes into jobs such as foraging for food and nest maintenance. If there is a labor shortage in one of those areas, ant personnel are diverted from another task. Food foraging follows a pattern whereby the foraging patrol heads out in one direction on the first foray, then systematically adjusts its course by a few degrees for the next successive forays. No one ant actually knows the entire plan, but the collective executes it well (Sulis, 1997).

Humans, meanwhile, invent tools to enhance their capabilities. Some tools channel energy. Other tools replace some human energy and time with a nonliving system's energy and time. Some tools extend our psychomotor precision, while other tools extend the capabilities of our minds. Tools for communication or transportation allow us to stretch or break barriers of time and space. When we use them we experience feedback from our tasks that tell us what we are capable of doing. When enough people receive the same sorts of feedback, then a segment of the population has something special in common.

Our newfound abilities to communicate globally and work asynchronously led Kelley (1994) to suggest that future work will more often resemble a hive mentality. The centralized control that is typically found in conventional work organizations is dissolving into distributed local control by individual actors. Organizational boundaries no longer contain information flow as rigidly as they once did. People can still be discrete about company business, but a good deal of communication across the boundary that was not probable years ago is commonplace now. The hive mentality suggests that we are not controlling tasks in the conventional sense any longer, but rather, the collective knows the big picture even where the individual does not. The modicum of control that used to be the domain of humans (management or otherwise) is distributed between the people and their machines.

At some point, however, the forces of self-organization will kick in. It then behooves the people who are responsible for the functioning of the system to know how to guide those processes. I will return to the topic of controlling chaos and self-organization in Chapter 12.

Organizational Shadow

If we have a collective intelligence, then we might just as well have a collective unconscious that bears some similarity to the hive phenomenon. In fact, Stacey (1996) posited the existence of an organizational shadow, which is for all intents and purposes an extrapolation from Jung's ideas of a shadow structure and a collective unconscious. The shadow is the place in organization life where elementary ideas combine to form what we recognize as the organization's culture. It is also the facility where new ideas for business products and adaptation to the external environment are formed. The organization's shadow is not readily visible to the management, although some will report having an "intuitive understanding" of "how people think here." Those who have such a tacit knowledge of the organization's consciousness are more communicative than most people with the contents of the organization's shadow. To understand the shadow further, it is necessary to introduce the concepts of memes and autopoiesis.

The concept of a *meme* was introduced by Dawkins (1976), according to Tracey (1996) who catalogued the thinking on this subject. A meme is a unit of social information that circulates throughout a culture (in the usual broad sense) or a more localized social sphere. A meme resembles a gene in biology in the sense that it is an elementary information-containing structure. Memes combine somehow with other memes to produce more memes. An *idea* is a pattern of information, which can be also conceptualized as a pattern of memes. A particular pattern, should it be able to keep itself together, can be regarded as a meme by itself.

The content of a meme can include cultural iconography such the Statue of Liberty in the United States, the maple leaf in Canada, Mt. Fuji in Japan, the Sphinx and pyramids in Egypt, and indigenous animals and national flags everywhere. Memes can include icons of lesser stature such as the tailfins on automobiles of the 1957–1962 period, the typography of pop art and advertisements of the art deco period, the shapes of beverage bottles, the way the crowd gasps "Ooooh" and "Ahhhh" when the fireworks explode on the Fourth of July, and the curious habit that some people have of throwing money into any body of water that resembles a fountain. Memes include the ideas that are inherent in our governmental Constitution, Declaration of Independence, Magna Carta, and analogous declarations elsewhere. The entire contents of the golden phonograph record that was sent into deep space by the Voyager space probe represents some of civilization's favorite memes.

Memes do not replicate by the same physical and chemical mechanism as genes. Rather, they transmit, diffuse, and replicate by communication. Societies develop methods, such as school systems, for transmitting memes in a systematic fashion. Popular and fine art entertainment, specialized publications, libraries, and computer networks are all media for the transmission of memes. Societies promote the transmission of memes that it believes are good for its survival. At the same time, society develops methods of not-transmitting memes of which it does not approve. Occasionally society backs the wrong horse whereupon, after a cataclysm of suitable proportions, the once-preferred memes are extricated, and what was once censorship reverses itself.

Sometimes the transmission of memes is subtle and passive, and we don't feel a thing immediately. A friend once commented, "When I first took the job at [censored corporation] in New York, I was only there a week before I was assuming the posture. I started walking at a 45-degree angle, with my head downward so I couldn't see anybody, and my arms pumping at my sides. I had to stop myself. I put in for a transfer."

Sometimes the transmission of a meme halts with an affable culture clash. Two academics tell a story: "When [*W*] first joined our department, he used to run up and down the halls everywhere he went. We asked him why he ran so much and he explained that, in his previous university in Japan, all junior faculty members were expected to run through the halls. Normal walking was only allowed for senior faculty." *W*'s new colleagues told him it was okay to walk, and so he did without hesitation.

Autopoiesis is a mechanism by which systems replicate themselves. The concept was first introduced by Maturana & Varela (1980), expanded for social systems by Luhmann (1986), and for cognitive dynamics by Kampis (1991). At the cellular level, cells utilize the genetic mechanism to replicate themselves exactly, thus reinforcing the assumption of an ultrastable and homeostatic system (Maturana & Varela, 1980). The assumption of ultrastability in cognitive and social systems is not so well founded, however (Scheper & Scheper, 1996). The difficulty in identifying the actual mechanism responsible for meme transmission in social systems also presented a challenge to the scientific efficacy of the concept, according to Scheper and Scheper. My opinion on the ultrastability assumption is that autopoietic mechanisms, should we be successful in locating them, serve to enhance the stability of systems through self-referential feedback loops. The "refreezing" and local stability in the cusp model of organizational change are essentially trying to accomplish the establishment of an autopoietic mechanisms within the organization.

The social and cognitive work on the autopoietic construct indicates that the difficulty with identifying the transmission mechanism was only a temporary annoyance. According to Luhmann (1986), Bailey's (1997) interpretation thereof, and my interpretation of Bailey, the self-referential component of a social autopoietic mechanism indicates that the system has a modicum of self-awareness. Certain feedback loops exist for the purpose of reflecting back to the system information about its current nature. Other aspects of the same information source indicate what the system *is not*. (Recall the Johari Window concept for interpersonal understanding in Fig. 4.10.) The transfer of information takes place through communication. Communication begins with the formation of utterances, the use of words, grammatical structures, and norms of politeness. Communication often involves the use of additional complex mechanisms such as printing, publishing, television, or the World Wide Web. The nonliving storage takes the form of printed paper, magnetic tape or disk, engraved vinyl, perforated metal, and so on.

At the cognitive level of analysis, Kampis (1991) emphasized that an important part of the process involves recognizing patterns, finding new patterns, communicating those patterns, and utilizing those patterns in consistent ways. The medium of storage appears to be biochemical and involves an entity we call our memory, but the neural circuitry has not been mapped out except in the simplest fashion (Abduleav & Posner, 1997; Gabrieli, et al. 1996). The mathematics of symbolic dynamics appear to be an appropriate means for describing how a system might capture an emergent pattern of information and then proceed to replicate it, according to Kampis (1991). To date, three studies have been conducted to my knowledge in which actual human conversations were analyzed through symbolic dynamics for patterns of communication behavior (Guastello, 2000a; Guastello, Hyde et al., 1998; Pincus, 2001). A broader program of organizational process research that is based on the analysis of conversations is now underway, however (Poole, Van de Ven, Dooley, & Holmes, 2001).

Patterns in the *movement* of communication content within an individual brain have not been assessed from an NDS perspective, to my knowledge. If we are interested in information movement patterns among people, however, there is a 50-year history of social network research to rely upon. A network exists because some information is passed among its members. If information is being passed, the patterns of transmission constitute a network. Some networks have firmer boundaries than others, but that is an issue we will save for Chapter 7.

To return to organizations again, organizations are mid-range structures between individual brains and entire societies (Bailey, 1997). Organizations have means of replicating ideas and communicating them that involve versions of the individual cognitive processes and the societal storage and transmission mechanisms. As memes float freely, members of the organization look for patterns. Patterns are recognized to the extent that they have *meaning*, or connectivity with patterns already stored. An organizational culture, according to Weick (1996), is continually in the process of being made, as memes diffuse, and members of the organization try patterns of meaning for size. Note the use of meaning as a construct implies that new patterns will be recognized and retained to the extent that prior frameworks can accommodate them. In other words, society prefers new memes that are consistent with those for which it has already given its approval. A similar mechanism is revisited in Chapter 6 where we explore the dynamics of creative thought.

At the same time, organizations have boundaries between their subunits, which can be rigid, permeable, or fuzzy, as mentioned earlier. Boundaries restrict the flow of memes. They also promote the self-organization of basins into local repertoires of memes. Once the boundaries are opened, however, opportunities suddenly arise for culture clash, conflict, and mutual growth of the adjacent subunits.

Technology in Vision and Shadow

It is difficult to talk about icons of an organization's culture without referring to ideas that are idiosyncratic to an organization and thus do not have too much relevance to the general reader. The general notion of cultural memes, however, applies to a much broader cross section of society, including the organizations that make their living by tapping into the flow of memes. Thus, it is appropriate to consider the role of technology itself as a huge source of memes relevant to the culture and development of business organizations.

"Science" represents our knowledge of how the world around us works. As imperfect as they may be, we still manage to isolate patterns and make new and useful objects, as well as enchanting artifacts that we enjoy looking at or listening to. We call the practical patterns "technology." Ever since the first mammoth bone was sharpened into a knife, technology has always played some role in the improvement of our collective standard of living. The transformation was widespread at the beginning of the Industrial Revolution, which of capitalized on the science and scientific thinking of Galileo, Newton, Euler, and many others.

The advent of machine tools and numerous other inventions pertaining to communication, transportation, and information storage in the period 1865–1920 led to many new expectations of what technology could deliver in the future and how it could improve life in the present. Simultaneously, the composition of the economy was changing drastically as people left the farms to work in organizations. Life in organizations changed as organizations grew and individuals became increasingly alienated from the means of production. They too were cogs in a big wheel, or "sociotechnical system" as we now call it, whereas once before, most of them were the hubs of little systems. Mass production technologies, nonetheless, made economies of scale possible, technology products available to more people, and work extremely inhuman if you were on the wrong end of the food chain.

The economic system in the United States buckled and snapped in 1929. Economic historians would point to the economic hardships in Europe, the uncontrolled nature of the stock market, deficits in the banking system, and asymmetric distribution of wealth as contributing causes. Contemporaries might emphasize the complex systems nature of that nexus of problems. Unemployment hit 50% in the early 1930s, which ushered in what is now remembered as the worst financial epoch in U.S. history. The reforms of 1933 and later almost seemed to work, until fear of the national debt in 1937 propelled a redirection of government funds toward paying off the banks (Brouwer, 1998). The depression relapsed. Labor protests and strikes drew orchestrated violent reactions from management (Sexton, 1991).

Against the background of hardship, technology marched on with progress in transportation and communications, new ideas for household appliances, harnessing of electric power, and architecture. The *Wizard of Oz* appeared in color, and television became functional. Flash Gordon took science fiction from Jules Verne and H. G. Wells into outer space. The public once again saw technology as a way out of its plight. The electric high tension wires that we consider eyesores today were icons of technological advancement in the 1930s.

Technology and architecture were the themes of the 1939 World's Fair in New York. People waited in line for hours to gain admission to the GM Futurama exhibit, and the long lines persisted throughout the many months of the Fair (Gelernter, 1995). Some of the visual images from the Fair appear in Fig. 4.11, which is composed from a group of post cards I picked up at an antique shop. The picture at the top is the Trylon and Perisphere, which was the icon of the entire fair. The legend on the back of the post card says, "The 200-foot Perisphere within which visitors view from a revolving platform suspended in mid-air a dramatization of the World of Tomorrow. Clusters of fountains screen the piers supporting the Sphere so that the great ball appears to be poised on jets of water. The 700-foot triangular Trylon at the left, a unique architectural form, serves as a Fair beacon. Architects: Harrison and Fouilboux."

Many of the exceptional architects of the Fair disappeared during or after the War, along with many of the ideas they portrayed, according to Gelernter (1995). Technology, nonetheless, was already making a lot of promises at the 1939 World's Fair, and after the War, it *delivered.*

FIG. 4.11. Scenes from the 1939 World's Fair in New York *Top*: Trylon and Perisphere. *Center left*: GE Building. *Center right*: Appliance Building. *Bottom left*: Westinghouse Building. *Bottom right*: Cosmetics Building.

SUMMARY

Chapter 2 explained the basic principles of NDS—attractors, bifurcations, chaos, fractals and dimensions, self-organization, catastrophes, and their interrelationships. Chapter 3 explained how the statistical footprints of the dynamical structures can be observed through the method of structural equations. A set of direct connections among the dynamics, qualitative theory, and data analysis is an essential part of any empirically grounded science of organizations. Indeed, many of the early attempts to write dynamical theories of psychology or of organizations have been limited by the lack of empirical support with real (as opposed to simulated) data. On the other hand, if one looks hard enough, the first signs of empirical realism in nonlinear organizational theory are dated to the early 1980s.

This chapter starts the nonlinear dynamical theory of organizations by making the first set of connections between dynamics and organizational phenomena, beginning with global, or organization-level change phenomena. Organizations differ with respect to structure, climate, and culture. Those three groups of characteristics are either targeted explicitly for organizational change, or they are often observed to change as a result of some other planned change process.

Next we moved on to the dynamics of change, beginning with Lewin's classic paradigm. Five nonlinear dynamical processes were then introduced. One nonlinear process involved the cusp catastrophe model that described the continuity between evolutionary and revolutionary change between two stable and qualitatively different states. The empirical example, which involved a group of savings and loan institutions, showed signs of cusp structure using one form of data analysis (GEMCAT); the savings and loan data shown an incomplete behavior transition and chaotic behavior (positive Lyapunov exponent) using the method of structural equations.

Technology, and the social system that surrounds it, can be a driver of organizational change. Here we might observe the product adoption cusp, as in the second empirical example. When the sociotechnical system becomes brittle enough, however, a revolutionary change is going to be needed. Here we can expect the logistic map dynamics (second nonlinear process) to play out in a sequence of entropy producing instability, chaos, and self-organization. Empirical examples of chaos and self-organization can be found in many specific instances that appear in subsequent chapters.

Change in organizations is not restricted to only one dramatic episode. It may reoccur at aperiodic intervals. Hence, the concept of punctuated equilibrium (third nonlinear process) was introduced to organizations from evolutionary biology. Other evolutionary phenomena, such as branching patterns in strategic planning (fourth nonlinear process), and the dynamics of locating an ecological niche in a so-called rugged landscape (fifth nonlinear process), might be observed also.

Organizational changes of either the evolutionary or revolutionary varieties require ideas for change on the part of the organizational members. The last section of this chapter drew a parallel between individual consciousness and unconsciousness and the collective consciousness of organizations. This theme is developed in subsequent chapters in their subthemes concerning group creativity, evolutionary games, virtual organizations, and group coordination.

5

Nonlinear Motivation Theory

This chapter expands the butterfly catastrophe model of motivation in organizations that was developed in previous works (Guastello, 1981, 1987, 1995a). In the last installment, a running start to the NDS concepts was provided by summarizing the conventional theories of motivation that showed historical importance. Each of the main principles from general motivation theory was represented in the comprehensive nonlinear model. Because that part of the story has not changed appreciably, I will not repeat it here. Rather, the first two sections of this chapter summarize the main elements of the butterfly model and provide the necessary groundwork for the expansion of the nonlinear motivation theory.

One new element is the theme of utilities, which are inherent in the expectancy theory of work motivation, game theory, and personnel selection. The third section thus explains game theory, its nonlinear properties, and its role in organizational behavior. The fourth section contains an empirical study of turnover in the U.S. Air Force. The application involves a subset of the general motivation model, and provides an example of the role of utilities in personnel selection when nonlinear models are used. It becomes apparent, furthermore, that the variables that have the greatest impact on the retention of recruits shift during the first term of enlistment.

Another new element that appears in the last section of the chapter is the concept of motivational flow. Flow is the experience of intrinsic motivation and total task involvement. Similarly, the nonlinear dynamics of motivation have an experiential component as well.

SOME BASIC CONCEPTS

Intrinsic Work Motivation

The distinction between intrinsic and extrinsic motivation was initially based on animal learning theory (Premack, 1971). Animals will perform a behavior, Task A, in order to receive permission to perform a Task B, if the probability of performing B is low. If the rules for the same animal were reversed, such that performing Task A was rare, the animals would perform B in order to have an opportunity to perform A. In other words, rare behaviors can reward common behaviors, and it really did not matter what the tasks were (at least from the point of view of a rodent in a cage). People, meanwhile, would find also find their jobs "rewarding" if the opportunity to do that sort of work was relatively rare (Mawhinney, 1979). Similarly, the forms of participation in decision making that have been advocated ever since Herzberg et al. (1959) can be regarded as sources of intrinsic motivation because such opportunities are infrequent.

Deci's (1972) definition of intrinsic and extrinsic rewards centers around the principle of where the rewards came from. Extrinsic rewards are those that require an outside party to deliver, such as the paycheck from one's employer. Intrinsic rewards do not require an outside party to deliver; rather, the intrinsic rewards came from the task itself. Intrinsically motivated people are, for example, those who obtain their principal motivation from the opportunity to achieve, wield power, or doing something that reflect some sort of personal values. Extrinsicly motivated people think of the money first, if not also last and foremost.

According to social motivation theory, there is only one type of motivation, and that is arousal. All social motivations can be placed in one of three categories: achievement, affiliation, and power (McClelland, Atkinson, Clark, & Lowell, 1953), which are, in turn, all forms of intrinsic motivation. Achievement motivation is the concern with standards of excellence, or unique accomplishments and long-term goals (McClelland, 1961). Achievement-motivated people like to set goals, make plans to reach them, and take action; the process of effective goal setting is an important aspect of motivation itself (Locke & Latham, 1990). Affiliation is the interest in establishing or maintaining positive emotional relationships with other people. It tends to be low among entrepreneurs and managers in organizations (McClelland & Boyatsis, 1982). Power is the concern about getting or maintaining control of the means for influencing people (McClelland, 1975). Power motivation is an important motivation for entrepreneurs, and the dominant motivation for executives in organizations.

Power motivation can take the form of *personalized power* whereby the person directs the goals of power toward the self; it is sometimes expressed by concerns for one's reputation, winning an argument with another person, or other types of interpersonal competition. A manager whose power motive is directed primarily toward personal goals will be seen a manipulative, exploitive, and having a win–lose attitude toward subordinates. A *socialized power motivation*, on the other hand, directs the goals of power toward other people, and is sometimes expressed by giving help to people who need it but do not request it, and taking action to mobilize people around a worthwhile activity. A manager whose power motive is directed primarily toward other people is concerned with making others feel more powerful and in control of their behavior and outcomes.

Intrinsic and extrinsic rewards interact in an odd way. In studies of both humans and monkeys, if an extrinsic reward is introduced to a task situation where the worker was already intrinsically motivated, the result was in a decrease in output, rather than an increase. (Pritchard, Campbell, & Campbell, 1977; Enzle & Ross, 1978). The obvious problem here is that if humans who go to work every day do not receive their raisins and bananas every so often, they will find a job where they do.

Four explanations for the contrast between experimental results and real world observations have been proposed. If we put them together, they make some sense. First, the introduction of extrinsic rewards causes a *temporary primitivization* of one's motivation, whereby the extrinsic reward creates a shift of attention away from the intrinsic qualities of the task to the more obvious, and primitive, extrinsic reward (McCullers, Fabes, & Moran, 1987). Second, people who go to work every day have basic human existence needs to fulfill, and a job that does not fulfill those needs is unacceptable. In more general terms, if the first basic premise of a relationship is an extrinsic exchange, the extrinsic exchange will be critical to the survival of the relationship (Eisenberger, 1992; Guastello, 1981). Third, there is some truth to the experimental findings: People who seek to develop their careers, denoting a concern with the interest value of their tasks, are sometimes willing to take major cuts in salary to change from dull jobs to something more exciting. The fourth view is that money, even though it has extrinsic reward properties, has considerable symbolic value, as do most other aspects of reward in organizations. The culture of the organization shapes the relative importance of intrinsic and extrinsic features of the rewards. The manipulation of the relative importance of intrinsic and extrinsic features of the rewards is under the control of management (Maehr & Braskamp, 1986).

Cognitive Theory

Equity theory (Adams, 1965) is a concept of motivation that centers on the idea that equity and inequity underlie the stability or instability of personal and employment relationships. A (relatively stable) state of equity implies is a situation where Person A's ratio of outcomes to inputs is equal to that of Person B (or a collective

"Other"). If inequity is perceived by Person A, A will take action to restore equity, such as putting less into a relationship, putting something new into the relationship, or terminating the relationship.

Deviations in the input–output ratios are tolerated to some extent. The threshold of inequity for Person A to respond to an overpayment is usually larger than the threshold of inequity for Person A to respond to a shortage (Adams, 1965). In many situations, Person B is making decisions about the relationship also. Persons A and B may make several adjustments in order to reach stability. If "Person B" actually represents multiple others, and the relationships are in a state of flux, a chaotic network of relationships is likely to ensue. Networks are considered in Chapter 7.

According to Vroom (1964), motivation is the amount of effort, or force (F) a person will expend on the job:

$$F = \sum (E_{ij} \times V_j), \tag{5.1}$$

where E_{ij} is the *expected probability* of the behavior i being followed by an outcome of a given type, and V_j is the *valence* of the outcome, that is, its potential satisfaction value. According to Wahba and House (1974), Equation 1 was at least the eleventh of its kind, where the first dated back to 17th century economics. In psychology, the concept can be traced back to Tolman (1932), who claimed that

$$Behavior = Drive \times Habit\ Strength, \tag{5.2}$$

and perhaps more importantly, that the rat knew where the cheese was located. A rat would thus run to the branch of a radial maze that had a higher E_{ij} of containing cheese, rather than follow a sequence of turns that were learned through operant conditioning.

Expectancy theory continued with additional propositions. First, valence V_j, is itself a product of instrumentalities, I_{jk}, which are beliefs that outcome j leads to other outcomes k; and V_k is the valence associated with those additional outcomes:

$$V_j = \sum (I_{jk} \times V_k) \tag{5.3}$$

(Vroom, 1964). Textbooks now commonly condense Equations 5.1 and 5.3 to

$$F = \sum (E \times V \times I), \tag{5.4}$$

with no loss of meaning. Valences are understood as both extrinsic and intrinsic outcomes (Wahba & House, 1974). Furthermore,

$$P = f(F \times A), \tag{5.5}$$

where A is ability (Vroom, 1964). Equation 5.5 states that motivation moderates the relationship between ability and performance.

BUTTERFLY CATASTROPHE MODEL OF MOTIVATION

Surface

There are three distinct modes of performance: high, good enough to get by, and poor enough to warrant termination. A butterfly surface (Fig. 5.1) would be required to describe change in behavior, or the distribution of behavior among the three modes. The butterfly also allows for voluntary turnover from good performers. A control point, which denotes the behavior that is taking place, can slide off the cliff that separates the top and bottom sheet of the surface. The control point can also slide through the hole, or pocket, in the middle of the surface and come to rest at the middle stable mode. When studying change in behavior among the two work modalities and turnover, turnover would be scored 0.00 on a performance scale ranging from 0.00 to some positive value.

Absenteeism can be regarded as a hysteresis between staying on the job and quitting. Frequent absences can become a stable mode of behavior in its own right. Three modes of absenteeism can be typically identified from personnel

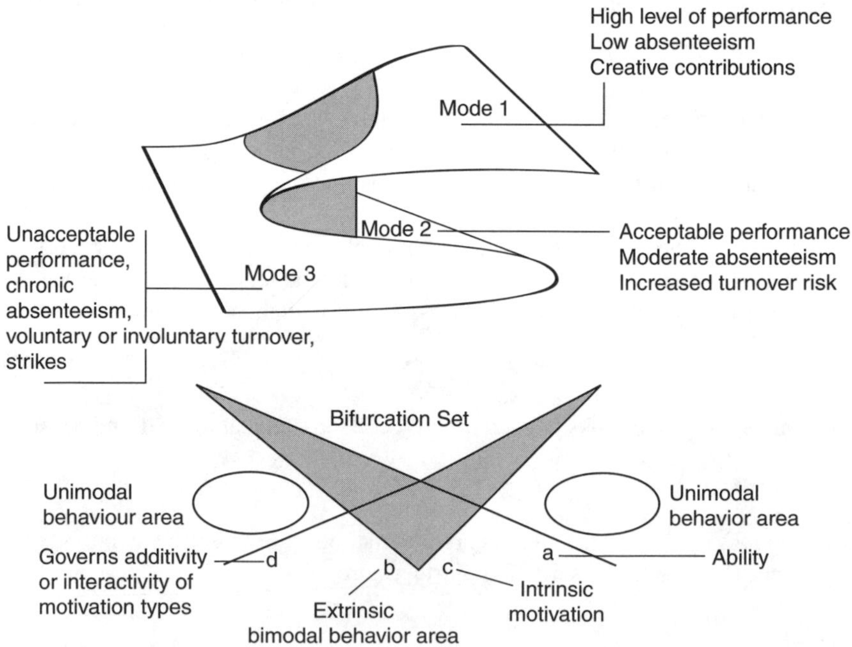

FIG. 5.1. The butterfly catastrophe model of motivation in organizations.

records: those persons who gravitate toward no absences at all, those who gravitate toward what they perceive as an average level, and the chronic absentees. The modalities for absenteeism, performance, and turnover can be organized into a butterfly surface as follows.

On the upper sheet of the surface, subjects would show self-directed, internally committed behavior: high output and high quality work. Innovation, which would be partially based on prerequisite abilities (and considered at great length in Chapter 6), would occur at the extreme end of this subdivision; an important preview, however, is that creative work thrives on intrinsic motivation. Absenteeism rates would gravitate toward virtually none, although, conceivably, internally directed and competent people might organize their work to permit an occasional day off. Some people in the neighborhood of this attractor would harbor a strong intent to leave the organization, while others would harbor none. No discernible difference in the work behavior between the two groups would be expected, however.

The attractor on the middle sheet of the response surface is characterized by externally motivated behavior at low levels of commitment. Innovation would not be forthcoming from high ability employees. Quantity and quality of work would be merely adequate. Absenteeism would occur at the average level for the organization or work group. Turnover intentions would be greater than what would be expected from the upper sheet. Unlike the upper sheet, there would be less disparity among employees on turnover intentions.

The lower mode would describe people who leave the organization voluntarily or are fired for chronic absenteeism or poor performance. In organizations that do not have an organized absenteeism policy, chronic absentees would be noted at this level. Strikes and riots are expected in extreme conditions. Turnover is the asymmetric reverse of organizational entry, as explained earlier.

The mathematical statement of the butterfly catastrophe response surface is the set of points where

$$df(y)/dy = z^5 - dz^3 - cz^2 - bz - a, \tag{5.6}$$

in which y is the behavior spectrum and a, b, c, and d are control parameters.

Control Parameters

Control parameters in the hypothesized model are a = ability, b = extrinsic motivation, c = intrinsic motivation, and d = organizational climate. Ability is broadly defined, and may consist of cognitive measures of ability, job-specific personality measures or social skills, or ability to attend work as defined in the Steers and Rhodes (1978) process model for absenteeism. Extrinsic and intrinsic motivation are defined as they appear in the conventional motivation theories. Additionally, demographic variables, otherwise known as moderators of ability, would contribute to parameter b.

Relative to motivation, however, the general rule is that *d* governs the coaction of intrinsic and extrinsic motivation; the culture that management propels determines what is a motivator and what the salient motivational conditions of an organization happen to be (Maehr & Braskamp, 1986). Parameter *d* may vary across gross types of organizations, (e.g., work, volunteer, academic), across organizations with type, or across subunits within an organization. Climate may be manifest in social conditions, social perceptions, or objective features of an organization's structure such as its size. An organization's climate may emphasize particular motivations such as achievement; achievement may be salient in a broader form such as a preoccupation with product quality.

For (arbitrarily) "low" values of *d*, intrinsic and extrinsic motivation are additive, and a relatively greater number of behavior changes would occur between adjacent attractor states on the response surface. For higher values of *d*, intrinsic and extrinsic motivation are interactive, and a relatively greater number of behavior changes would occur between the extreme attractor states on the response surface. Because *d* is continuously defined, it would follow that the additivity or interactivity of intrinsic and extrinsic motivation is actually a matter of degree. Leadership style and organizational policies and practices would determine the specific relative contributions of intrinsic and extrinsic motivation to the behavior spectrum.

Gradients

The surface gradients of the butterfly surface describe changes in behavior from an ambiguous (unstable) state to one of the stable modalities. The pocket of the butterfly surface is the point of greatest instability. Gradients often illustrate interesting theoretical properties. In the motivation model they describe satisfaction, equity, tension, and commitment constructs. In the case of equity perception, a person may have a reasonably clear notion of what constitutes fair or unfair exchanges, although some deviation is tolerated. This approximating process occurs in a single exchange, but more so in repeated exchanges. Equity judgments are made relative to something, and involve a social comparison process. If a person's outcome-to-input ratio exceeds that of a comparison person or other reference point, a relative reward is experienced. If the ratio is less than the reference, a relative cost is experienced.

In a work relationship, the repeated exchanges integrate into a long continuous pattern of exchange. The exchange itself can become quite complex, consisting of numerous intrinsic and extrinsic facets, some of which are inevitably valued by some people more than other quantities. The processes of social comparison and judgment are thought to apply to each important facet of the exchange. Each facet is perceived and judged in approximately the same way as a signal is detected relative to noise in a psychophysical process. According to most motivation theories (cf. Guastello, 1995a), people process intrinsic and extrinsic rewards (or promises of rewards) differently. Thus, intrinsic and extrinsic rewards occupy separate control parameters in the butterfly model. In a job relationship, therefore, the individual is judging four varieties of signal that comprise the surface gradients: extrinsic rewards, extrinsic costs, intrinsic rewards, and intrinsic costs.

Some exchanges involve higher stakes than others, in which case they would be represented on the part of the surface that shows comparably greater unfolding. High stakes situations are those where large potential outcomes are paired with large inputs, and larger potential losses exist as well. According to the butterfly mechanism, the stakes need to be sufficiently high for the individual to reach the basin of one of the performance attractors. Low stakes exchanges, by contrast, occur around the butterfly point and are inherently unstable. There is not much exchanged, so there is little to gain or to lose. Performance would reflect mid-range output on the average, but would be unstable and susceptible to strong signals coming in from another source, such as a better job. On the other hand, should the motivation to work be suddenly enhanced by a new approach to management, a trajectory to a middle- or high-performance attractor would be observed.

Tension and commitment were initially identified (Sheridan & Abelson, 1983) as part of a cusp model for turnover. Tension and commitment represent positive and negative aspects of intrinsic motivation. Tension arises from a job that is interesting, arousing, and novel in an unpleasant way. Commitment is the positive side and is a hybrid composed of the interest value of the task, job involvement, and the motivational qualities of the employee and the surrounding work environment.

Approach–avoidance

If one were to view the cusp surface divergence gradients in two dimensions, they would be equal in length, but different in their slopes. The downward gradient is steeper. This relationship describes the differential approach and avoidance gradients that have long been observed in animal and human social behavior. The subject avoids a negative stimulus faster than it approaches a positive one (Brown, 1948). The approach–avoidance gradients are implicit in all motivation-performance subspaces, and account for the differential impact of positive and negative utilities in expectancy and financial decision making (Kahneman & Tversky, 1979; Leon, 1981). To give a simple example, suppose we were to present an unseasoned investor with a set of possible business transactions, all with varying probabilities of gaining and earning varying amounts of money. Our investors would avoid the possibility of losing $500 considerably faster than they would accept a possibility of earning $500; in others words, $500 lost is bigger than $500 gained.

Approach–avoidance gradients are inherent in the butterfly model also. Of course, the dynamical field is a bit more complex because of the presence of a third behavioral state. In psychological terms, the middle sheet of the butterfly surface functions as a compromise solution between the extreme states of approach and avoidance. There are two approach gradients and two avoidance gradients in this case; there is a pair of gradients associated with the intrinsic valences and extrinsic valences.

In other decision environments, the dynamical field is norestricted to just three states. In some cases, there are multiple goals, which have the power to attract, but there is no particular state that requires avoidance. In other cases, the system of goals contains feedback loops such that if enough time is spent in one goal condition, the attractiveness of another goal condition is enhanced (Abraham, 1995). Game theory, considered next in this chapter, provides a framework for interpreting multiple strategic responses that a decision maker can adopt, especially where the attractiveness of a strategy depends on the actions of another decision maker. If the attractor states comprise associations with other people or organizations, then we have a *social network*; the formation and reorganization of networks are addressed in Chapter 7. Asymmetries in a network of relationships produce the emergence of leaders (Chapter 9) and other hierarchical structures (Chapter 10).

GAME THEORY

Game theory is a formal mathematical approach to economic behavior where two or more economic agents are involved (von Neumann & Morgenstern, 1953; Zagare, 1984). A game consists of a set of strategic options, each of which delivers utilities to a player. The utilities associated with each option, however, depend on the actions taken by one or more other players. A brief taxonomy of games would be useful here.

Strictly Competitive Games

The first distinction is between the zero-sum, or noncooperative game, and cooperative games. In a noncooperative game, the values of the possible outcomes for one player are opposite the values of those same outcomes for the competitor. One player's winnings are the other player's losses. Optimal decision making is thus one where one's outcomes are maximized and the others' outcomes are minimized; this is the *maximin principle*. Players do not typically share information in a noncooperative game, and binding agreements are not possible. For competitive games, there is at least one strategic condition that is a stable expression of the maximin outcome (Nash, 1951), known as a *Nash equilibrium*.

Although it is possible to conceptualize a one-person game, where one player works against the environment, or a slot machine, the more interesting games are interactive and require at least two players. Thus, game theory considers two-person, three-person, and n-person games. The simplest games for two players are the 2X2 games, where each player has two options.

Of the many ways of configuring 2X2 games, some games have *trivial* outcomes. Trivial in this case means that the best option for one player is always the same option, no matter what the other player does. For practical applications, it is valuable not to underestimate the importance of a so-called trivial game or to fail to recognize one; they might not be so trivial. The received wisdom of the past few thousand years is "not to underestimate one's opponent," which is generally good advice. On the other hand it is important not to overestimate the opponent's capabilities. In a game of bluff, the power of one player resides in the perception of that power, rather than in the substance of that player's capabilities. When such games are in effect, it helps to simply go through the lists of options: If A does *this*, what is the best option for B? If A does *something else*, is the best option for B still the same? Is there anything A could do that would change the best option for B?

Mixed Strategy Games

A cooperative game is structured in such a way that outcomes could exist that provide maximum returns to both players if certain joint plays are made. In those cases, information sharing is strategic, and binding agreements are possible (Zagare, 1984). The Prisoner's Dilemma game has become particularly dominant in the game literature because of its capability of producing both competitive and cooperative results. A Prisoners' Dilemma game matrix appears in Table 5.1. In the classical scenario, two players are hypothetically arrested for armed robbery. The district attorney is trying to make a case against them but needs the cooperation and confession of at least one player in order to prosecute successfully. Thus, a deal is offered to the players, each separately: If one confesses, or *defects*, before the other, the one who confesses gets off with a light sentence, while the one who does not confess receives the heavy sentence. If both players *cooperate* with each

TABLE 5.1
Utility Matrix for Prisoner's Dilemma Game

		Player B C	Player B D
Player A	C	3,3	4,1
	D	1,4	2,2

other by not confessing, they stand a good chance of being found not guilty. If both players confess, their outcomes are only a little better than the worst possible sentence.

The values in the table are values of the outcomes to each player, expressed as ranks. In any noncooperative game, the rational player will prefer the one option out of the four that will maximize gains and minimize losses. If there is a play that satisfies this maximin principle, then an *equilibrium* occurs, which represents the play that both players will select. When the game is played repeatedly, players will choose one option more often than another; that choice becomes their *dominant strategy*. If one player knows another player's dominant strategy, then strategic moves are made accordingly (von Neumann & Morganstern, 1953). For instance, the cooperation strategy may work in the beginning of a series of games, but if a player learns that the odds of an opponent defecting are high, then a defect strategy will occur.

Alternatively, in a finite game series where the end of the series is known to the players, the optimal strategy is to cooperate until the second to last round, then defect. We return to the topic of continual, or iterative, gaming following a brief discussion of strictly cooperative games.

Strictly Cooperative Games

Some gaming strategies involve options where each player can take an action that contributes to the good of the group, or does not take any such action. Three strictly cooperative games are important to group dynamics; they are the stag hunt, intersection, and bandwagon. Brief descriptions of those scenarios follow below, and specific applications are developed in Chapters 7 and 8.

In the stag hunt scenario, a group of hunters are trying to surround and capture a beast. If each hunter contributes maximum effort to the task, the stag will not be able to get through the circle of hunters, the stag will be captured, and the reward of the capture is shared by all. If one of the hunters is a little slow to react one day, or decides to go hunt rabbits by himself, it might not matter so long as another hunter nearby can adapt and pick up the slack. Or, the stag might not try to escape by the slow hunter. On the other hand, if the number of hung-over or indifferent hunters is too great, the stag has many chances to get away and will be likely to do so. The outcome for the group is no shared reward. In other words, the outcome for the group is reduced to that of the least effective person (Crawford, 1991).

The intersection game is modeled after the four-way stop intersection. If each car approaching the intersection takes its turn in the correct order, then all cars proceed through the intersection without a problem (Crawford, 1991). On the other hand, if one car tries to go through out of turn, we have a screeching of brakes, or the ominous "boom" and sound of shattered glass, not to mention a new level of confusion as to which car should go through the intersection next if that is possible. The trick to the successful navigation of a four-way stop intersection is to figure out what rule is actually in place. There could be several possibilities: (a) The car on the right goes first, as prescribed by the local driver's manual. (b) Big truck intimidates small car. (c) East-west traffic alternates with north-south. (d) Cars proceed in the order in which they arrived at the intersection.

In the bandwagon situation, the utilities to the group increase as the number of group members increase. At the same time, the cost of participation goes down. Hence, the ratio of rewards to costs increases as more people join the group. According to Glance and Huberman (1994), the bandwagon dynamic explains the mass action of citizens that resulting in the destruction of the Berlin Wall in (former) East Germany. The first people to protest the wall ran the greatest risk of arrest. But as more people joined the protest, the risk of retaliation to any one person declined.

Iterative Games and Evolutionarily Stable Strategies

Sometimes games are played, or studied, in a finite series, where the game is played only once or played in a finite series. In some of the more interesting situations, the game is played an infinite number of times. When real humans are playing, "infinite" simply means that the game is played many times, but the players do not know when the series will end. In computerized simulations of the game, several hundred iterations can be played tirelessly.

Players do not always maintain the same strategy throughout a series of games. Examples were presented earlier where there was one clear shift in a player's dominant strategy throughout a game series. Alternatively, however, players may use a *mixed strategy*, in which they switch strategies back and forth depending on the game matrix values or recent past experiences with other players. In cases of mixed strategies, the game matrix values for each player are not simply the values of payoffs such as in Table 5.1; rather, the values are expected odds of a strategy taking place multiplied by the valence of a particular outcome. The probabilistic interpretation of game values is most apparent when the game is played by multiple players simultaneously in an infinite series. The infinite series of games characterizes societal processes more so than the one-shot game or a series for two players in a single continuous relationship.

Tit-for-tat (TFT) is a particular mixed strategy in which the player begins with cooperation and sustains cooperation until an opponent defects. A single defection is tolerable, but the TFT strategist will shift to defection in response to subsequent defections. TFT strategists may revert to cooperation with new players or in response to strategy changes toward cooperation from other parties. TFT is a relatively successful strategy in terms of a player being able to maximize outcomes over repeated plays (Axelrod, 1984; Casti, 1989, 1995). On the other hand, TFT is more complex than all-cooperation (all-C) or all-defection (all-D), and there may be a cost of complexity associated with operating a TFT policy (Hirshleiffer & Coll, 1988).

Other complex response functions might include a policing action whereby the policing agent cooperates with those who cooperate, and defect on players who have accumulated a history of defection (Hirshleiffer & Coll, 1988). Another strategy occurs when a player's reputation for cooperation or competition spreads among the network of players. As a result, the players can select or avoid gaming partners. These complex and hierarchical strategies are collectively known as *ogliarchic reaction functions* (ORFs). An ORF will assign changes in utilities to deviations from cooperative behavior, and trigger functions whereby the changes to utilities are enacted (Friedman & Samuelson, 1994).

Not all games have equilibria, which are also known as *saddle points*. In NDS, saddles are not structurally stable. They attract players in some iterations of the game but may push them away after the play is made and the results are known. Saddles can be easily upset by changing the values of the game outcomes for the players. In more complex games involving two players and more than two options, or n-players and n-options, there may be more than one saddle point. Furthermore, there could be a saddle point among the saddle points, but there is never any guarantee that a real world game will have such attractive solutions (Zagare, 1984). In the event that there are multiple Nash equilibria in a game, one or more saddle points will emerge as *evolutionarily* stable, meaning stable in the long run. Although there is no guarantee of evolutionary stability from a set of gaming utilities, it is closely tied to the Nash equilibria when it exists (Crawford, 1991; Maynard Smith, 1982).

Is Loyalty Dead?

A reporter from the Denver Post (Booth, 1996) pondered whether loyalty as a social value was dead. He had several sources of loyalty in mind: Were the large corporate layoffs that were common at that time contributing to a loyalty crisis of some sort? What are the implications for consumer behavior, or for professional contracts? My response to the main question made three points: (a) The loyalty problem as the reporter defined it is part of a broader problem of societal cynicism. (b) The employment practices related to the widespread downsizing efforts were, in all likelihood, making the problem worse. (c) There are additional implications from NDS and the economic theory of games.

Cynicism is an entire outlook on life, although it is expressed as a work attitude. It is characterized as distrust in other people, particularly authority figures. For instance, cynical people would agree with the idea that the economic and political system exploits the masses and serves those who already hold power. They would agree that conforming to the rules or "playing the game" is more important than working hard, that nice guys finish last, and that politicians by and large do not care about their constituencies. One important trend is that confidence in business and leadership among working Americans fell from approximately 76% in the late 1960s to about 15% by 1989 (Kanter & Mirvis, 1989). Comparable values for later years are not available, but our research showed (Guastello, Rieke, Guastello, & Billings, 1992) that 98% of college students in a small Midwestern sample would endorse cynical survey statements to some extent, and would at least be regarded as "skeptical realists" in this regard. (On a 1–5 scale ranging from disagree to agree, a skeptical realist would agree at least to the level of 3 to a cynical statement.)

Cynicism takes on several garden varieties, but cynical types can be placed in two broad categories. One group, by virtue of their warped views of human nature and sufficient position power, continually exploits and deceives the less powerful. The other group of cynics adopts a defensive posture. They often experience psychic conflict between their own better judgment and the messages they receive from society. The history of labor relations in the United States, disappointing political figures, and advertising that stretches the truth beyond all recognition would contribute to the disturbing messages from society (Kanter & Mirvis, 1989). The same problems and perception of authority figures make it far more difficult for would-be leaders to lead than ever before (Bennis, 1988). Today, I would include much of the rhetoric of policy makers and "spin doctors" as further examples of where truth is stretched beyond recognition.

Cynicism is not related to personality traits in the sense that it is an attribute of a "type of person." It could happen to anyone. Those who are affected by it the most, however, show symptoms of depersonalization, estrangement, and lower self-esteem. Ironically, the students who endorsed the cynical statements on the survey more often scored higher on the Work Ethic scale (Guastello, Rieke, et al., 1992). A possible explanation for that correlation is that the people who are committed to working the hardest are the ones most likely to run up against the boundaries and limitations of the systems in which they work.

As a general rule (there are exceptions), downsizing has done little to enhance the functionality of the firm; this topic is expanded in Chapter 10. This trend is of course a contrast to what was at the time the stock market reaction to the downsizing efforts. Consider this cynical scenario: An executive group wants a spike in income, so they downsize, thereby showing a short-term profit on the books by reducing payroll. Much of the downsizing is targeted at the senior employees who both know more and earn more. The executives collect a bonus. Wall Street reacts favorably, so the executives exercise their stock options, sell their holdings, and collect another bonus. Then, chop-chop, they write down on their resumes how they increased the profitability of the firm and apply for another high-paying job where they do the same thing before anyone catches up with them.

Meanwhile, back at the ranch, the remaining employees discover that their coworkers are gone, but the work is not. Everyone is expected to do more. Colleagues who are regularly involved in screening and hiring corporate executives have reported to me that the average candidate they see reports working 55–60 hours per week. Another reported that he was informed that he was taking over the functions of a downsized coworker in addition to his own. "Will there be a pay increase to go with that?" he asked. "We can give you 3%," was the response. (That percentage was slightly more than the inflation rate at the time.) At the other end of the food chain, the "assistant managers" of retail stores in shopping malls have a similar experience; because they are exempt from the wage and hour law, their salaries often work out to subminimum wage levels.

Corporate downsizing efforts occur in an economic environment that is characterized by the lowest purchasing power of the minimum wage in the last 20 years, a downward pressure on wages generally, and globalized capital. According to Cunningham (1995), in the 1989–1994 period, corporate profits rose 62%, executives' pay increased 55%, while others' wages have only risen 15%; the latter was less than the accumulated rate of inflation (19%) over the same period. Globalized capital means that it is less likely than ever before that corporate profits are going to be reinvested in the communities, or countries, from which they were derived.

The game that is relevant to the loyalty question is the iterated version of Prisoner's Dilemma. In Hirshleiffer and Coll's (1988) computer simulations, players start a relationship off in good faith, and are likely to do so if their partners behave accordingly. If the players expect their partners to defect, however, the rational choice is to defect early in the game series. As a result of thousands of people playing thousands of times in this fashion, the rate of defection eventually overtakes the rate of cooperation by a long shot. Fortunately, however, defection levels eventually bottom out, and they could be forestalled with the introduction of ORFs.

Where the bottom is located in real terms is uncertain. One plausible mechanism, which could occur in insecure economic times, would activate a basic economic rule whereby people hoard cash, spend less, and seriously slow the economy (this topic is expanded in Chapter 11). The displaced people and their displaced loyalties will self-organize into new economic and policy units. Some of those units will reorganize labor against management, reorganize new goods and services production systems, and erect more governmental controls against predatory behaviors of the power elite. In other words, it is possible to set the stage for a class war.

Of course, there is no requirement that the bottom must be reached before any positive change can occur. In better economic times, labor has some leverage over management and can bargain, either explicitly or by defecting on their jobs, for a better standard of living and job security.

3-Person Games

A competitive game with three players is called a *truel*. An example shows up in the graveyard shoot-out scene toward the end of the movie, *The Good, The Bad, and the Ugly*. The three main characters were suddenly faced with the opportunity to take one shot at each other. Each character wanted to walk away alive carrying the hitherto buried gold. Thus, each player had one way to "score" and two ways to die. Clint Eastwood's character (Good) had removed Ugly's bullets the night before, thus disarming him. Good kills Bad. To keep matters complicated, there was a torn bag of gold among the intact ones, and only one horse. Good takes the horse and the intact bags, leaving Ugly to walk and figure out how to carry his gold out of the desert.

Corporate decisions are usually not so flashy, but the logic of the truel occurs often enough. According to Borges (1997; Borges & Guastello, 1998), organizations often rethink their investment strategies into activities or programs that facilitate production quantity, product quality, and human resources. Each investment area can be regarded as an attractor of investment. If too much investment goes into quality without regard for other requirements, the price of the product exceeds the limits tolerated by the marketplace. If too much priority is given to quantity without regard to quality, then the price of the product goes down or the profit margin increases; the consumer demand for quality will counteract the low cost, however, and the demand will shift to a more expensive but higher quality product.

Leaps forward in production quality or quality would be limited without an investment in human resources. We saw earlier, that equity of pay will affect quality of input, assuming the necessary training is available. After enough investment in training and attractive renumeration, however, the organization should expect a return on that investment. Some types of quality or quantity investment do require simultaneous investments in human resources. Some investments in quantity also positively affect quality objectives. In these coupled circumstances we have, in essence, coalitions between two or more competing demands.

We simulated investment shifts using a set of (computerized) magnets, as shown in Fig. 5.2. Human resources, production quantity, and quality are shown as the

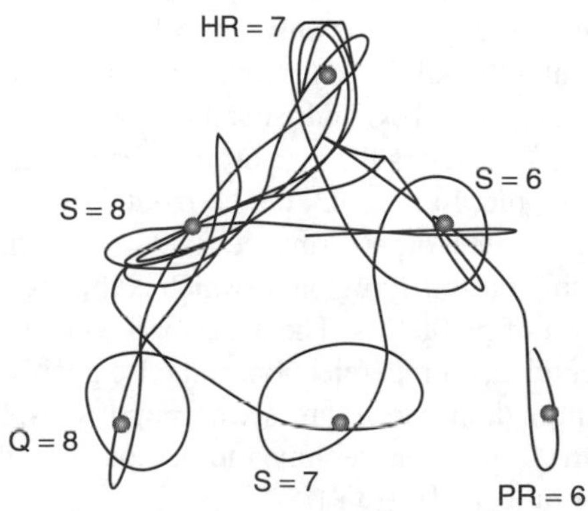

FIG. 5.2. Magnet simulation of a three-attractor decision problem showing chaotic trajectories. Attractor and saddle charges are based on data from Borges and Guastello (1998) and are calibrated in pixel radii. HR = Human resources, PR = Production quantity, Q = Product quality, S = saddle; Central pull strength = 8.

vertices of the triangular arrangement. Between two vertices are saddles where the spheres of influence from two vertices intersect. In the center of the arrangement is a three-way saddle, or central pull, which is one that avoids investment in any of the three areas. We can set the relative strengths of the vertices and central pull to any level we please. Then we inject a point into the dynamical field to represent a decision outcome. What is important, however, is that once a point is injected into the field, it is likely to rest on a saddle for a period of time, then zap to another location in the field, then move again over time.

UTILITY OF SELECTION TO THE EMPLOYER

Here it is useful to introduce a bit more basic theory regarding the utility of a personnel selection scheme to the employer who intends to use it. Taylor and Russell (1939) first articulated the basic concepts of selection utility. In their definition of the utility question, successful employment was a dichotomous outcome that was based on the employer's judgment and criteria of "success." Utility was then the extent to which the proportion of successful employees increased with the use of a particular selection devise.

Taylor and Russell (1939) found that utility depended on three quantities. The *selection ratio* (SR) is the ratio of the number of job openings to the number of applicants. The *base rate of success* (BR) is the percentage of people who would be considered successful if the selection procedure were not used. Usually we are inclined to say that the BR is the proportion of people who would be successful if people were selected at random, but in real life there is always some sort of selection device in effect, even if it is only self-selection.

The third ingredient is the validity coefficient, *r*, which is the correlation between the test and performance. SR, BR, and *r* combine to produce values of selection efficiency. Selection efficiency is the proportion of successful people to the total number of selected people. In Fig. 5.3, the horizontal division bar represents the minimum acceptable predicted performance level, *Y*, and the vertical bar represents the corresponding cut-off score on *X*, which is the predictor of success, or a weighted combination of predictors. The areas marked I, II, III, and IV represent correct hits, false negative, correct rejection, and false positive decision outcomes, respectively; all four quadrants are expressed as proportions. In the Taylor–Russell utility function, both *X* and *Y* are assumed to be normally distributed. *Selection efficiency* is then the ratio **I** / [**I** + **IV**].

The Taylor–Russell system requires a discrete payoff function, which is fixed at the cutoff score on *X*. Instead, if we were to select from the top of the available distribution, the highest *X* hires would be worth more than the middle-X, even though both were considered good enough to select. Jarrett's (1948) method of figuring utility improved on these rough spots in the basic theory.

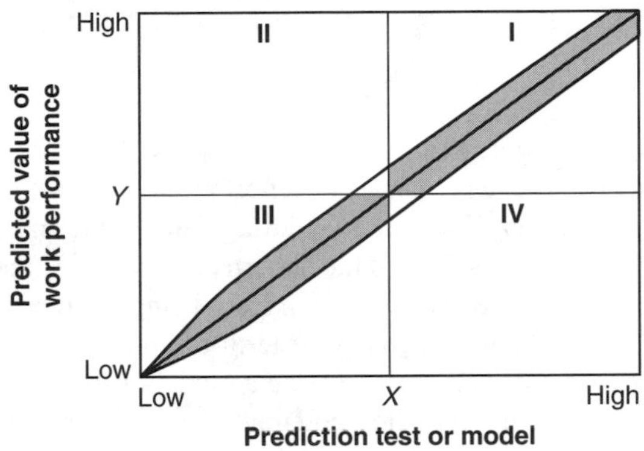

FIG. 5.3. Schematic for the Taylor–Russell utility function.

Jarrett's method drew on Taylor–Russell concepts, but it took into consideration the performance range, which is thought to be a continuous value, which the Taylor–Russell model does not consider. If the range of possible performance levels is small, great selection methods are only going to have a small impact on collective efficiency. If the range of possible performance levels is large, however, a modest selection method can have a substantial impact on collective efficiency.

In Jarrett's definition of utility, a selection system can be evaluated in terms of the ratio of a mean work performance of a group that is selected by the system to the mean work performance of an "unselected" group (or "utility ratio"). Jarrett's utility ratio can be estimated from validation data by the formula:

$$E' = r\,v(h/p), \tag{5.7}$$

where E' is the utility ratio, r is the validity coefficient, v is the coefficient of variability in the criterion (ratio of the work performance standard deviation, to the work performance mean in the sample), h is the height of the normal curve at the point of truncation in the criterion variable, and p is the selection ratio. If multiplied by 100, E' becomes the percentage of improvement in production. Note that this method requires a real zero point in the measurement of work performance. This value is the now-familiar location parameter. The height of the normal curve at given values of z (standard score of Y) can be obtained from a table found in a mathematics and statistics handbook.

In the NDS application that follows, we are still interested in using the basic concepts that apply to figuring utility of selection. We run into a new challenge, however, in that we cannot assume a normal distribution. Instead, the utility of the selection model will be figured in more primitive form. The preview is that the selection model that is based on discontinuous change produces an utility function that is also discontinuous.

TURNOVER AMONG AIR FORCE RECRUITS

The objective of this project was to determine the possible merits of the cusp catastrophe model for two-stage personnel selection when applied to the prediction of performance and turnover among airmen during their first term of enlistment. The cusp catastrophe model is a subset of the butterfly catastrophe model of motivation in organizations. The USAF is currently experiencing an elevated drop out rate of new airmen before their first four-year term of enlistment is completed. The purpose of the study, therefore, was to build a model of the turnover process that would predict drop-out and retention potential. The cusp catastrophe model was targeted for use in this situation because of its specific purpose of describing and predicting discontinuous change processes, and because of its growing number of successful uses in personnel-related applications.

The cusp catastrophe model for work performance and turnover is shown in Fig. 5.4. The behavioral outcome is depicted as having two stable states, where attrition from the Air Force is one stable, although undesirable, outcome. Successful performance in the Air Force is the other stable state. Between the two extremes is a low-density region comprising people who have not left the Air Force before the end of their term, but who are not performing successfully either.

The transition between acceptable performance and turnover is inherently discontinuous, according to the model. The transition between the two states is governed by two control parameters, which have different impacts on the change in work performance over time. The *asymmetry* parameter governs the proximity of

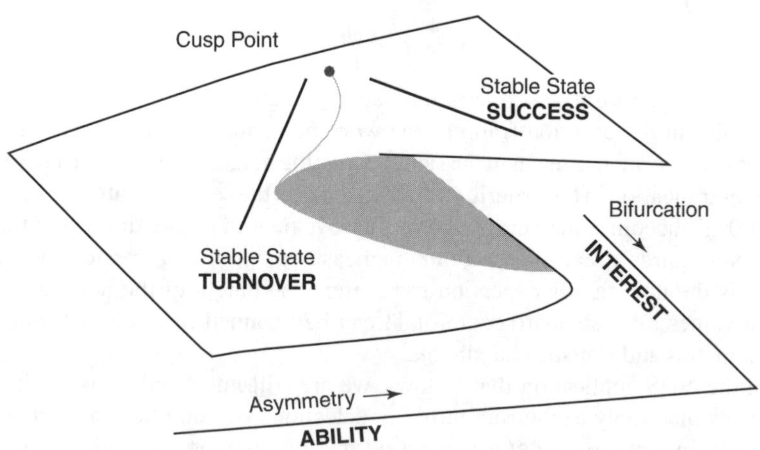

FIG. 5.4. Cusp catastrophe model for two-stage personnel selection, Air Force application.

the employee to a critical threshold at which behavior changes suddenly. Either the individual is capable of "catching on" and doing well, or the individual terminates involuntarily for unsuccessful performance or voluntarily in search of employment that is more compatible with one's skills. In the theoretical performance-turnover model, a spectrum of relevant ability measures contributes to the (latent) asymmetry parameter.

The bifurcation parameter governs the degree of discontinuity between the two modes of behavior. In an ideal cusp probability distribution, the bifurcation parameter regulates the transition (splitting) from a homogenous, unstable behavioral state to two locally stable states. In the theoretical performance-turnover model, motivation variables make substantial contributions to the bifurcation parameter. Highly motivated people will engage their abilities and will either succeed or fail decisively. Less motivated people may still be observed to do well, however, but their performance is carried by strong abilities and may not be stable over time, particularly if they lose interest in what they are doing.

Motivation can be operationalized in several possible ways, just as there are several theories of work motivation that have all been regarded as useful and successful in empirical studies of work situations over the past 40 years. Both extrinsic and intrinsic motivation constructs should be taken into account here. Examples would include pay in the extrinsic category, and vocational interest in the intrinsic category. "Intrinsic" in the latter instance refers to the interest value of the work to the employee. The VOICE battery of interest measures used by the Air Force served this purpose adequately. Ideally, people whose interests are compatible with their work in the Air Force would be motivated to perform well and to complete their term of enlistment.

The cusp model for personnel selection and turnover makes two special requirements from the data set. The first is that the work performance data be collected at two or more points in time. This is a routine procedure in many organizations, although conventional selection models do not make use of all the available performance data.

The second special requirement is that the performance scale be coded such that the turnover condition is part of the performance scale. This objective is achieved by using the lowest value of the performance scale, numeric zero in this situation, as the value where the employee is not longer present, i.e., is performing at the zero output level ad infinitum.

Performance measurements are ratings given annually to airmen on a 1 to 5 scale such that values of 4 and 5 are considered successful, and values of 1, 2, and 3 are not successful such that termination would be recommended by the Air Force. Turnover for purposes of this study can be voluntary or involuntary, and its measurement would not be affected by the voluntary nature of the termination. For those persons who had terminated before the time of a particular performance evaluation, a performance value of 0 would be scored for the later performance

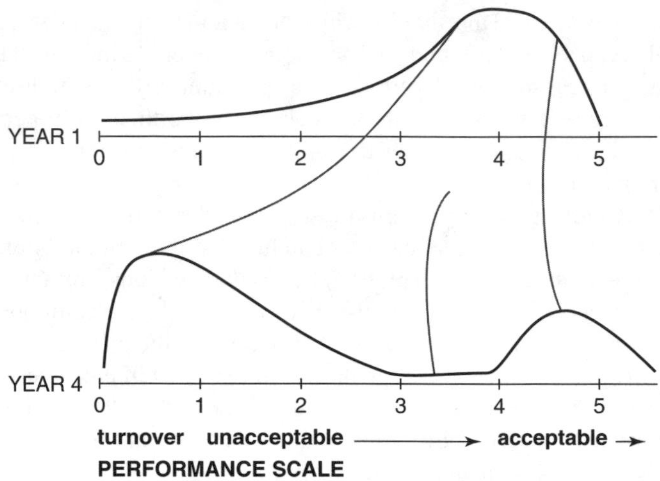

FIG. 5.5. Hypothetical distribution of Airmen's performance ratings as they progress through a term of enlistment.

measure. Thus, one may observe a growing proportion of 0 values from the first to the fourth performance evaluation.

The cusp probability density function is three-dimensional. Figure 5.5 shows a hypothetical cusp distribution for the performance-turnover problem where there is a unimodal distribution of performance scores that is centered around the cusp point at Year 1. The cusp point is the point of greatest instability. By Year 4, however, the distribution has separated, showing a greater proportion of cases in the turnover mode, while the successful cases have stabilized at performance scores of 4 or 5.

Participants and Variables

Participants were 59,397 Air Force enlisted personnel who entered the Air Force after 1990, and for whom a sufficiently long performance and data history had become available. From this database, a sample of 5,038 cases were randomly selected for purposes of calibrating the cusp and alternative linear prediction models. Cross-validations of the models were conducted by resampling 10 data sets of approximately 1,000 cases each. The participants were 80% male.

Ability and vocational interest data were collected around the time of initial enlistment. Performance ratings, rank and pay grade, and number of dependents was collected at 6-month intervals beginning after 6 months tenure, and at 6-month intervals thereafter.

TABLE 5.2
Descriptive Statistics for Ability and Interest Measures for the Calibration Sample

ABILITY	*Mean*	*Std. Dev*	*INTEREST*	*Mean*	*Std. Dev*
General	54.068	8.546	Administr	67.785	20.417
Arith	54.556	8.333	General	64.954	17.011
Word	53.715	7.435	Elec	66.055	17.220
Paragraph	54.227	7.729	Mech	64.102	20.840
Numerical	54.925	8.594			
Coding	54.524	9.152			
Auto & Shop	52.770	9.868			
Math	55.141	9.161			
Mechanic	54.833	9.518			
Elec	52.625	9.615			

Ability measures were scales from the Armed Forces Vocational Aptitude Battery (ASVAB). ASVAB contained 10 scales, which were used separately in this application: General Ability, Arithmetic, Word, Paragraph, Numerical, Coding Speed, Auto & Shop, Math, Mechanical Aptitude, and Electronic Aptitude. Descriptive statistics for the ability measures in the calibration sample appear in Table 5.2.

Vocational interest was measured with an instrument developed by the Air Force (VOICE), which contained for scales: Mechanical, Administration, General, and Electronic interests (Watson, Alley, & Southern, 1979). Descriptive statistics for the interest measures in the calibration sample appear in Table 5.2.

Performance was usually measured by two raters using the 1–5 scale mentioned above. At the first 6-month rating period, there was a substantial quantity of airmen who had not been rated, and often only one rating was available at other time intervals. For that reason, the ratings designated as "First Rater" in the database were used for the present purposes, although Second Raters were used to assess the reliability of the rating data itself.

The 1–5 scale was amended, as described earlier as a 0–5 scale, such that persons who had quit the Air Force before the rating activity took place were designed as 0, and persons who were not rated at all (but were in the database later on) were scored as 3. The resulting 0–5 scale took on the following interpretation: 5 = acceptable to the AF; 4 also acceptable to the AF, but less than a 5; 3 = future with the AF is highly uncertain; 2 unacceptable to the AF; 1 = very unacceptable to the AF; and 0 = has left the AF.

The reliability for the performance-turnover criterion was defined as the correlation between the two raters' ratings. Because of the irregular distributions of scores on this measure (see below), the correlation was captured using the lambda statistic for the concordance of frequency distributions. Lambda was calculated in symmetry form (neither the first or second rater was regarded as a dependent

TABLE 5.3
Reliability and Scale Coefficients for the Performance-Turnover Criterion

Time	*Symmetric λ,*	*Second Rating is Dependent*	*GK λ Second Rating is Dependent*	*Scale*[a]
1	1.00	1.00	1.00	0.644
2	1.00	1.00	1.00	0.850
3	0.96	1.00	1.00	0.979
4	0.46	0.96	0.95	1.444
5	0.46	0.71	0.67	1.727

[a] Ordinary standard deviation was used.

measure), and in asymmetric form where the second rating was considered dependent, and the first independent. Goodman and Kruskal's (1963) Lambda was also calculated with the second set of ratings dependent.

Lambda coefficients appear in Table 5.3 for the first five time periods. Reliability was perfect for the first three time periods; these values were probably supported by the large number of "3" and unrated airmen in those periods. By time period 4, it was clear that the first set of ratings was much better than the second, and that the ratings were still quite satisfactory. By time period 5, reliability had dropped to around .70, but these values still reflected a very usable criterion.

Figure 5.6 shows a 3-D plot of the frequency distributions for the performance-turnover criterion at six successive points in time. The 0 group increased from

Cusp Distribution of Airmen Performance Rating

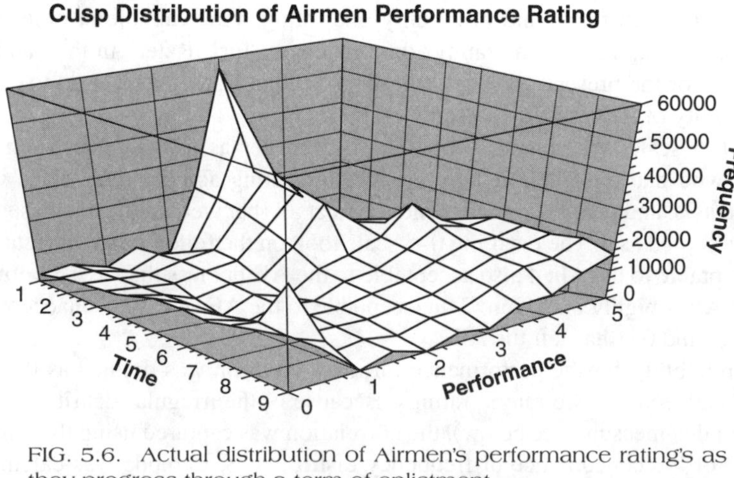

FIG. 5.6. Actual distribution of Airmen's performance ratings as they progress through a term of enlistment.

4.7% of the sample at Time 1 to 15.3% at Time 4, to 23.0% of the sample by Time 6. The "3" group dispersed from 95.3% of the sample at Time 1 to 49.7% at Time 4, to 12.3% at Time 6. By Time 6, 63.4% of the sample was rated as acceptable to the Air Force. For reasons external to any control by the airmen themselves, the Air Force could not retain and offer reenlistment to all qualified people. Thus, the focus of this the modeling, detailed below, was on airmen performance and retention during the first two years of service.

For better visualization, the contour in Fig. 5.6 was carried out through Time 9, and was based on data from all 59,397 airmen. It is possible to see the cusp probability density function take form over time. Note that a comparison of two time slices of approximately the same shape (e.g., close together in time, near the rear of the surface) would register as a linear effect, while a shift across the curvatures of the response surface manifold would register as a cusp effect.

The rank and pay grade variable was scored as follows: 31 = Airman Basic; 32 = Airman; 33 = Airman First Class; 34 = Senior Airman; 35 = AF Staff Sergeant; 36 = AF Technical Sergeant. Airmen who had left the Air Force at any time interval were scored 0 on this variable. The number of dependents at each time interval was available only for airmen who were still in the Air Force. Therefore, this information was reduced to a dichotomous variable such that 1 = has two or more dependents while still with the AF; 0 = all others.

Nonlinear Modeling

The cusp catastrophe model is tested as a polynomial regression model:

$$\Delta z = \beta_0 + \beta_1 z_1^3 + \beta_2 z_1^2 + \beta_3 b z_1 + \beta_4 a, \tag{5.8}$$

where z is the behavioral outcome, Δz is a change in the behavioral outcome, and a and b represent control parameters for asymmetry and bifurcation, respectively. In the proposed turnover model, indicators of ability would be inserted where the asymmetry parameter is specified. Interest variables would appear where the bifurcation parameter is specified. The term $\beta_3 b z_1$ would be expanded to include several possible interest variables. Similarly, the term $\beta_4 a$ would be expanded to include several possible ability variables. The behavior outcome is corrected for location (λ) and scale (σ_s) as defined in Chapter 3, and measured at two points in time; the raw score for the behavior criterion was the 0–5 performance-turnover scale.

Cusp models for the turnover process were calculated over the following time horizon: Time 1 versus Times 2, 3, 4, and 5; Time 2 versus Times 3, 4 and 5; Time 3 versus Times 4 and 5; and Time 4 versus Time 5. The ability measures, number of dependents, and pay grade were tested as asymmetry variables. Pay grade and the interest measures were tested as bifurcation variables. This assignment of variables to control parameters was based on the catastrophe model of motivation in organizations. The stepwise regression procedure was used because the primary goal of the analysis was to produce models that could be used for straightforward prediction. All variables that were tested in a model were allowed to compete to produce a model that accounted for the largest amount of criterion variance with the smallest number of predictor variables.

When a catastrophe model is tested, its R^2 coefficient is compared to one or more structural linear models containing the same control variables. In this type of application, the *linear pre–post* model provided a strong alternative:

$$y_2 = B_0 + B_1 y_1 + B_2 a + B_3 b. \tag{5.9}$$

The special linear comparison models defined in Equation 5.9 were expected to benefit indirectly from the underlying cusp theory. The benefit comes from the use of the performance-turnover measure at two points in time plus the definition of the criterion itself to include the turnover cases as zero-level performance. Thus, another comparison relevant to this project is the conventional general linear model that would ordinarily be used for predicting turnover.

In the convention approach, each airman would be designated as a 1 if they still remained with the Air Force at a given point in time, and 0 if they left the Air Force at that particular point in time. The statistical model would be set up as a two-group discriminant analysis, which simplifies to a multiple regression model with a dichotomous criterion; the latter model provided the most comparable comparison of R^2 coefficients for this purpose. The predictor set would include all the ability and interest measurements that were used in the cusp models. Pay grade would not be included because it had the same scaling problem as performance, in that there is no pay grade assigned to attrition cases. Attrition cases would register as "missing data" on the pay grade variable.

Because the model was intended for practical prediction purposes, a cross-validation strategy was employed to assess the stability of results. Ideally, the model developed for one group of airmen should be tested against an independent sample of airmen to determine the limits of generalizability. Split sample cross-validation, although commonly used, would only show that the two subsamples are composed of people who were collected in the same fashion. A better strategy would be a repeated sampling procedure whereby one or more of the best cusp models would be tested on repeated random samples taken from a larger database. Resampling techniques would allow a better assessment of sampling variability and the stability of regression weights given the number of variables that happen to be in the model.

The larger database in this instance provided 10 independent random samples of 1,000 cases. The most important model(s) were tested on each of the 10 samples, and the mean and standard error of R^2 (or R) was calculated.

Utility Analysis and Cutoff Scores

The goal of the analysis was to determine the actual numbers of correct predictions of turnover and satisfactory performance that could be made by using the cusp catastrophe model and its alternatives. Standard utility methods assume, somewhere in the calculation process, that the performance criterion the predictor variables are normally distributed. According to analyses conducted thus far, such an assumption could produce grossly misleading results. Therefore, the utility of the prediction model alternatives was assessed in terms of actual hit rates, false positive rates, and so forth, under identical conditions.

The calibration data set of 5,038 cases was used for utility analysis. There were two steps in the process. The first was the comparison of the three models where the predicted values of performance-turnover were taken literally, i.e., where the output numbers were interpreted according to the original scale. The second step was to refine the cutoff point for cusp model to maximize its hit rate, reduce errors of prediction, and otherwise take advantage of its prediction capabilities.

Some base rate information is necessary for interpreting the results. According to the population data base of 59,327 cases, the base rate of attrition at six months of enlistment (designated Time 1 in this study) is 4.72,% which would translate to 237 cases out of 5,038. The attrition rate in the sample was 19.4% at 2.5 years of enlistment (designated Time 5), or 975 cases.

Modeling Results

We can cut to the chase here by comparing R^2 coefficients for the cusp model, the linear pre–post comparison, and the standard Air Force model for all five time intervals, as shown in Fig. 5.7. As the time interval increased from 6 months between the first and second ratings to 30 months, the standard model did not improve appreciably. The linear pre–post model was the strongest model for the shortest time periods, but its R^2 dropped precipitously at 24 months. The R^2 for the cusp model improved as the time factor increased, such that it overtook the pre–post model when the Time 2 ratings reached 24 months, and improved again at 30 months.

The regression results for the models ending at 24 months and 30 months are given in Table 5.4. The reason for providing both sets of results is to show that the active variables did change over time.

Conventional linear models were built to predict the dichotomous turnover criterion at Times 1 through 5 based on ability and interest variables only. The model for turnover at Time 1 accounted for only 0.9% of the criterion variance. There were four contributing variables: math ability, mechanical interest, general ability, and auto-shop ability. The latter two variables were negatively weighted, and appeared to represent suppressor effects. Successful people in the first 6 months were those who showed greater math ability that was over and above their relative

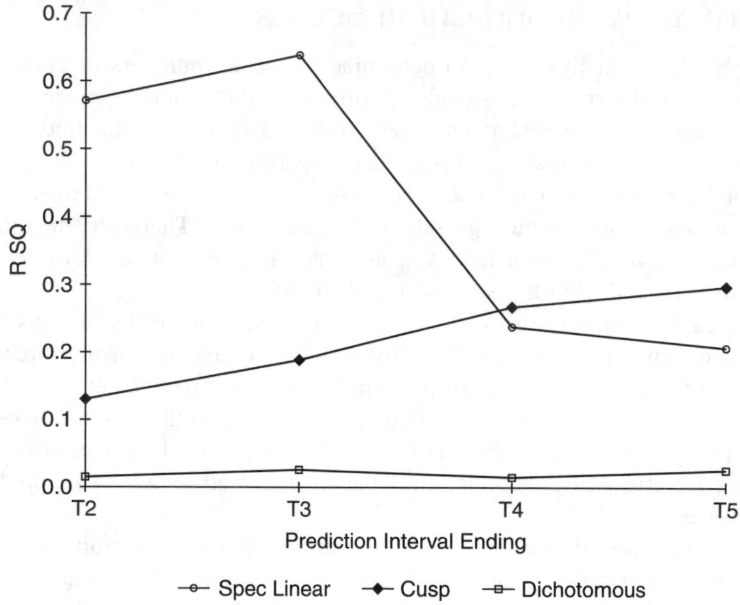

FIG. 5.7. Plot of R^2 coefficients for Air Force performance and turnover models as the time lapse increase from time-2 = 12 months, to time-2 = 30 months.

general ability, and interest in mechanical work over and above their existing knowledge in that area.

The conventional linear model for the dichotomous criterion at Time 2 = 24 months accounted for 1.3% of the turnover variance. The three predictors in the model were electronic interest, more than two dependents at Time 3, and general ability (negative). The conventional linear model for the dichotomous criterion at Time 5 accounted for 2.5% of the turnover variance. The five predictors in the model were more than two dependents at Time 4, math ability, word ability (negative), mechanical interest, and arithmetic ability (negative). Statistical details of the conventional linear models, linear pre–post models, and cusps that end at Time 2 = 24 and 30 months, appear in Table 5.4.

The predictive accuracy for the linear model predicting the performance-turnover criterion at Time 2 = 24, dropped to 24.0% of the criterion variance, down from 40.7% at Time 2 = 18 months. There were three contributing variables at 24 months, which were, in order of importance: pay grade at Time 1, interest in electronics, and Word (verbal) ability. Thus, the same motivation pattern showed through, with the exception that Word ability replaced general ability as the suppressor effect.

TABLE 5.4
Summary of Regression Models at Time 2 = 24 and 30 months
(Stepwise Solutions, N = 5038)

Time 2 = 24 months		*Time 2 = 30 months*	
Variable	*t*	*Variable*	*t*
Standard Model			
Electronics interest	6.02[c]	Dependent at T = 24	8.44[c]
Dependent at T = 18 mo	4.92[c]	Math ability	6.46[c]
General intellectual ability	−3.07[b]	Word ability	−2.96[b]
$R^2 = 0.013$		Mechanical interest	2.65[b]
		Arithmetic	−2.33[a]
		$R^2 = 0.025$	
Linear Pre–Post			
Grade at T = 6 mo	2.82[b]	Grade at T = 6 mo	7.24[c]
Electronics interest	4.83[c]	Performance at T = 6	−3.95[c]
General intellectual ability	−2.26[a]	Word ability	−4.00[c]
Performance at T = 6 mo.	2.65[b]	Coding speed	2.00[a]
Arithmetic ability	−2.15[a]	Mechanical interest	4.55[c]
$R^2 = 0.407$		Math ability	3.71[c]
		$R^2 = 0.209$	
Cusp			
z_1^3	9.40[c]	z_1^3	−11.80[c]
z_1 *Grade T = 6 mo.	4.88[c]	Grade T = 6 mo	7.23[c]
z_1 *Electronics interest	5.08[c]	Word ability	−4.01[c]
Word ability	−2.54[c]	Coding speed	1.98[a]
$R^2 = 0.267$		z_1^* Mechanical int.	4.66[c]
		Math ability	3.72[c]
		$R^2 = 0.296$	

$^a p < .05, ^b p < .01, ^c p < .001.$

The predictive accuracy dropped further for the linear model predicting the performance-turnover criterion at Time 5, although it did account for 20.8% of the criterion variance. There were six contributing variables, three of which were not found in the previous linear models. They were, in order of importance: pay grade at Time 1, performance at Time 1, word (verbal) ability, coding speed, interest in mechanics, and math ability. Word ability, once again, acted as a suppressor effect.

The cusp model for the interval ending with Time 2 = 24 months accounted for 26.7% of the criterion variance. The four components of the model were the cubic potential, pay grade, and electronic interest as bifurcation variables, and word ability as an asymmetry variable. Once again the Word ability variable was negatively weighted.

The cusp model for the interval ending with Time 2 = 30 months accounted for 29.6% of the criterion variance, and was also more accurate that its linear counterpart. The contributing qualitative variables that were part of its linear counterpart

TABLE 5.5
Summary of Cross-validation Coefficients for the Prediction Models

Sample	*Linear*	*Cusp*
1	.4277	.5024
2	.3726	.4519
3	.4433	.5298
4	.4156	.4854
5	.4527	.5364
6	.4548	.5406
7	.4122	.5233
8	.4611	.5237
9	.4409	.5180
10	.4104	.4934
average	.4291	.5105
std. dev.	.0271	.0274
std. error	.008	.009
average r^2	.1841	.2606

were statistically significant here also. The six components of the model were the cubic potential; pay grade, word ability (negativcly weighted), coding speed, and math ability as asymmetry variables; and mechanical interest as a bifurcation variable.

Cross-Validation Analysis

The objective for prediction purposes was to predict behavior as far into the future as possible based on data available as soon as possible. With these constraints in mind, two models were selected for further cross-validation study, which were the cusp model and its linear counterpart predicting Time 5 behavior based on Time 1 data and test scores. Ten samples of 1,000 cases were taken, and a summary of the cross-validation coefficients (Pearson product–moment correlation between the predicted and actual value of the criterion), their standard errors, and values and their standard errors appears in Table 5.5.

The average r^2 coefficient for the special linear comparison model was .18, and the average r^2 coefficient for the cusp was .26. The cusp model represented a ratio of 1.4 : 1 in predictive accuracy compared to the linear counterpart, and a 10-fold improvement in predictive accuracy compared to the conventional method of defining and analyzing the problem.

Utility Analysis

Predicted values of performance-turnover at Time 5 were calculated using the cross-validated regression models discussed above plus the prediction equation for the dichotomous criterion. Predicted values were then multichotomized into integer values 0 to 5 for comparison with actual values at Time 5 in a contingency table format. Predicted values less than 0.5 were recoded to 0, predicted scores in the range of 0.5 to 1.5 as 1, and so on until scores greater than 4.5 were recoded to 5.

The conventional dichotomous model produced predicted values of Time 5 performance that were all in the range of 0.5 to 1.5. As a result, there were no correct predictions of turnover. The contingency table for the special linear comparison produced predicted performance values of 0 and 1 only; the 0 cases were literally interpreted as turnover cases. The hit rate for turnover was 260 cases, which represented 26.7% of the actual cases. There were no false positives. (Note: Because the objective of the study was to predict attrition, the correct identification of a turnover case was designated as "hit," and the incorrect identification of a turnover case was designated as a "false positive.")

The final step in the process was to set the cutoff point for greatest advantage. In doing so there would be some trade-off between correct hits and a nonzero false positive rate. It is also understood that the Air Force does not offer reenlistment to all its qualified airmen at the end of their first term. The reasons for not offering reenlistment are partially related to skill needs and overall budget. Thus, a small number of false positives in the early stages of enlistment would save the job of training and then refusing to reenlist the airmen later on.

The contingency charts in Table 5.6 show the predicted and actual outcomes for the cusp model at different cutoff points on the predicted value of performance at 30 months of enlisted service, beginning with a cutoff placed at the 50th percentile value of 4.075. (Note: These decimal values, which were carried out to at least two places, are critical.) When the cutoff is placed at 4.075, 67.4% of the turnover cases vanish. If we consider further that airmen with performance scores of 1, 2, or 3 are also undesirable at 30 months, 1,143 undesirable cases are excluded at this point. The advantage of selection then becomes 906 cases or 1,812 salary years for the sample, or 359.7 salary years per thousand recruits. This figure would be an underestimate to the extent that airmen rated 1, 2, or 3 continue their term of enlistment beyond 2.5 years. The advantage must be considered, however, alongside a false positive rate (airmen rated 4 or 5) of 27.2%.

The false positive rate can be abetted by dropping the cutoff score, as shown in the other scenarios given in Table 6. If the cutoff score is dropped to 4.00, 38.9% of attrition cases vanish, along with 164 other poor performers. The advantage of selection becomes 283 cases, or 112.3 salary years per thousand recruits. The associated false positive rate is 6.0%. On the other hand, if the false positives would eventually be refused reenlistment by the Air Force, the saving would actually be increased by 304 people times 3.5 salary years, or 211.2 salary years per thousand recruits. The total savings would be 323.5 salary years per thousand recruits.

TABLE 5.6

Comparison of Utilities for the Cusp Model with Varying Cutoff Points

Cutoff at Predicted Value = 4.057 (50th Percentile)

PERF5 (Actual)

CUSP5B	Count / Row Pct / Col Pct	.00	1.00	2.00	3.00	4.00	5.00	Row Total
Reject .00	Count	657	2	40	444	959	410	2512
	Row Pct	26.2	.1	1.6	17.7	38.2	16.3	49.9
	Col Pct	67.4	50.0	52.6	51.7	47.7	36.8	
Accept 1.00	Count	318	2	36	415	1052	703	2526
	Row Pct	12.6	.1	1.4	16.4	41.6	27.8	50.1
	Col Pct	32.6	50.0	47.4	48.3	52.3	63.2	
Column Total		975	4	76	859	2011	1113	5038
		19.4	.1	1.5	17.1	39.9	22.1	100.0

Cutoff at Predicted Value = 4.000

PERF5 (Actual)

CUSP5B	Count / Row Pct / Col Pct	.00	1.00	2.00	3.00	4.00	5.00	Row Total
Reject .00	Count	379	2	13	149	273	101	917
	Row Pct	41.3	.2	1.4	16.2	29.8	11.0	18.2
	Col Pct	38.9	50.0	17.1	17.3	13.6	9.1	
Accept 1.00	Count	596	2	63	710	1738	1012	4121
	Row Pct	14.5	.0	1.5	17.2	42.2	24.6	81.8
	Col Pct	61.1	50.0	82.9	82.7	86.4	90.9	
Column Total		975	4	76	859	2011	1113	5038
		19.4	.1	1.5	17.1	39.9	22.1	100.0

(Continued)

TABLE 5.6
Continued

Cutoff at Predicted Value = 3.98

PERF5 (Actual)

CUSP5B	Count / Row Pct / Col Pct	.00	1.00	2.00	3.00	4.00	5.00	Row Total
Reject	.00	326	1	9	79	131	52	598
		54.5	.2	1.5	13.2	21.9	8.7	11.9
		33.4	25.0	11.8	9.2	6.5	4.7	
Accept	1.00	649	3	67	780	1880	1061	4440
		14.6	.1	1.5	17.6	42.3	23.9	88.1
		66.6	75.0	88.2	90.8	93.5	95.3	
	Column Total	975	4	76	859	2011	1113	5038
		19.4	.1	1.5	17.1	39.9	22.1	100.0

Cutoff at Predicted Value = 3.95

PERF5 (Actual)

CUSP5B	Count / Row Pct / Col Pct	.00	1.00	2.00	3.00	4.00	5.00	Row Total
Reject	.00	270		1	15	36	16	338
		79.9		.3	4.4	10.7	4.7	6.7
		27.7		1.3	1.7	1.8	1.4	
Accept	1.00	705	4	75	844	1975	1097	4700
		15.0	.1	1.6	18.0	42.0	23.3	93.3
		72.3	100.0	98.7	98.3	98.2	98.6	
	Column Total	975	4	76	859	2011	1113	5038
		19.4	.1	1.5	17.1	39.9	22.1	100.0

If the cutoff score is dropped to 3.98, 33.4% of attrition cases vanish, along with 89 other poor performers. The advantage of selection becomes 178 cases, or 70.7 salary years per thousand recruits. The associated false positive rate is 3.6% of total. If the false positives would eventually be refused reenlistment by the Air Force, the savings would be increased by another 127.1 salary years per thousand recruits. Thus, the total savings would be 197.8 salary years per thousand recruits.

If the cutoff score is dropped to 3.95, 27.7% of attrition cases vanish, along with 16 other poor performers. The advantage of selection becomes 49 cases, or

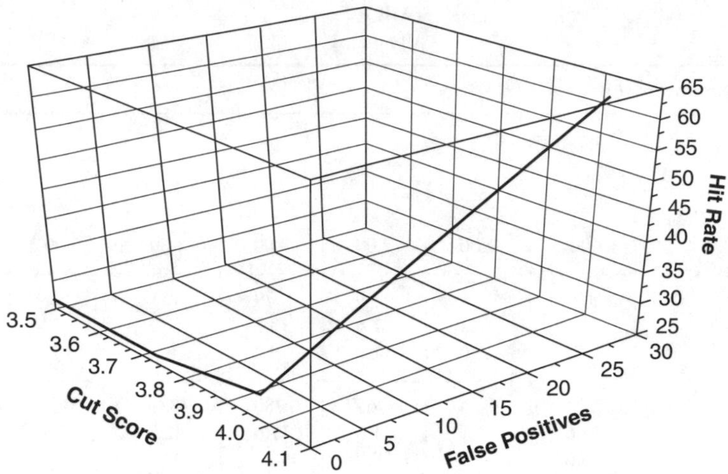

FIG. 5.8. Utility function for the cusp model at time-2 = 30 months showing the proportion of correctly identified turnover cases (hit rate) and false positives, as a function of the cutoff score on the predicted value of performance.

19.4 salary years per thousand recruits. The associated false positive rate is 1.0% of total. If the false positive would eventually be refused reenlistment by the Air Force, the savings would be increased by another 36.1 salary years per thousand recruits. Thus, the total savings would be 55.5 salary years per thousand recruits.

If the cutoff score is dropped to 3.75, the utilities are the same as those attained with the cutoff at 3.50. Figure 5.8 shows a plot of the hit and false positive rates associated with the cutoff scores tested above.

Discussion

The analyses provided a sequence of predictions of airmen's performance and turnover at several points during their first two years of enlistment. There were several important findings. First, the roles of particular ability and interest variables changed over time. Second, some of the most accurate models were cusp catastrophes; as predicted by the theory, ability variables contributed to the asymmetry parameter and interest variables contributed to the bifurcation parameter. Third, a cusp catastrophe model was isolated from the set, which would deliver the longest possible prediction into the future as early as possible; that catastrophe model would predict the performance-turnover criterion through 2.5 years of enlistment based on information available at 6 months of enlistment. Elaboration on these points follows.

In the ability group of variables there was a consistent pattern showing up whereby quantitative and mechanical abilities forecast success and general and word (verbal) ability showed the opposite effect in the multiple regression models. This is a classic suppressor system that indicates that the successful airmen are those who excel in the quantitative and mechanical ability and those abilities are particularly greater than their overall general ability. In other words, successful airmen show particular "best" abilities.

In the early stages of enlistment, general ability played the suppressor role. Later, general ability was replaced with word ability. Also in the early stages, the simpler quantitative abilities predicted success, but later, more complex math was necessary.

Interest in electronics was the prominent interest variable during the early stages of enlistment. Later on, however, mechanical and administrative interest became more relevant.

Three other qualitative variables were consistently part of the prediction models: pay grade at a previous point in time, prior performance, and the number of dependents. Pay grade represented both pay and rank. Those who did not progress through the sequence as quickly as the others were more likely to drop out of the Air Force.

Prior performance was a predictor of later performance. This was not a surprise given that the criterion was defined as a combination of performance and turnover, and the cases of turnover were retained in the data set. On the other hand, drops in performance were in the 3–5 score range were possible, but did not appear to occur frequently.

The number of dependents did show up as an important variable. Airmen with two or more dependents were more inclined to stay with the Air Force than airmen with less than two dependents. This effect was very small, however, and it only showed up in the conventional (dichotomous criterion) discriminant model.

The cusp model increased in predictive accuracy compared to its linear comparison model to the extent that the time interval between the z_1 and z_2 increased. Linear-looking change over relatively short time intervals is not uncommon. Greater time (or spatial movement) is required before the full nature of the nonlinear effect can be observed. Nevertheless, the cusp model was the best description for the performance-turnover criterion at furthest point into the future with the earliest possible data.

The cusp model that was selected for use as an actual prediction model contained five variables in addition to the cubic potential. Mechanical interest was the bifurcation variable; stronger interests were associated with a greater propensity to stay with the Air Force and somewhat better performance overall. Thus, there was a greater gap between the turnover and the level of performance for those who remained. The asymmetry parameter was composed of a set of four variables: pay grade at Time 1, coding speed, math ability, and word ability; the latter was negatively weighted.

The R^2 associated with the cusp model was .30, which compared favorably to the values of .21 and .02. These values were obtained for the special linear comparison and conventional linear dichotomous models, respectively. These three values readily transform to R values of .54, .46, and .16, respectively. The cross-validation analysis showed that the validity coefficients for both the cusp and its next best alternative were robust over 10 new samples with Rs of .51 and .43 for the cusp and its alternative, respectively.

The utility of the cusp model varied depending on where the cutoff score on the predicted values of performance was placed. At the low end of the range of values tested, a cutoff of 3.5 would render a prediction advantage of five turnover cases per thousand recruits, or 9.1 salary years per thousand, with no false positives (incorrectly identified turnover cases). At the other end of the spectrum, if the cutoff were placed at the 50th percentile, or a predicted performance score of 4.057, the model would render a prediction advantage of 179.8 turnover cases and poor performers per thousand recruits, with a cost savings of 359.7 salary years per thousand. There was a 27.2% false positive rate, however.

Two additional points about utility were important here. First, the utility associated with any cutoff point was very sensitive to the exact level at which the cutoff point was set. Second, the Air Force could probably tolerate a model false positive rate because of its program of offering reenlistment to only a portion of airmen who completed their first term. Thus, a small false positive rate would, in this case, translate into a cost advantage for the Air Force. Given these points and the utility function itself, the suggested cutoff score would be 3.98. This choice would render a prediction advantage of 35.3 turnover cases and poor performers per thousand recruits, for a cost savings of 70.7 salary years per thousand. The modest false positive rate of 3.6% would actually increase the savings to 197.8 salary years per thousand recruits.

MOTIVATIONAL FLOW

Flow is the experience of complete involvement of an individual within an activity (Csikszentmihalyi, 1988, 1990, 1996). It is the subjective experience of intrinsic motivation and a useful construct for explaining individuals' involvement in work and leisure activities. Creative work is especially influenced by flow. The core elements of flow are the challenge of an activity and the involvement of a person's skills in that activity. Flow is greatest when skill involvement and challenge are high, and lower otherwise. When flow is high, an individual perceives full control of the environment, has focused attention and reduced anxiety, and experiences enjoyment. The pleasurable experience of flow is intrinsically rewarding, might be remembered more completely, and sought more often. To the extent that the environment allows them to do so, people will spend more time in high-flow activities before switching to another task than they would in low-flow activities.

Mannell, Zuzanek, and Larson (1988) examined this assumed relationship between intrinsic motivation and the flow experience. They found that activities that were more freely chosen were more pleasurable, produced a decrease in tension, and more frequently produced flow experiences than activities that were not freely chosen. Surprisingly, the highest level of flow experience occurred when activities were freely chosen, but chosen for the benefit of others or long-term benefit to oneself. It was suggested that a sense of obligation or commitment may be required for an individual to choose activities requiring more effort, which in turn provide an opportunity for flow experiences.

Csikszentmihalyi and LeFevre (1989) showed that flow experiences offered a higher quality of experience than nonflow activities. Flow experiences were rated much higher in feelings of creativity, satisfaction, and positive affect. Contrary to expectation, the majority of those experiences occurred while people were at work, not in leisure activities. Interestingly, while leisure was more likely to be reported as intrinsically motivated (wanting to do something), work provided more experiences of flow while being reported as more extrinsically motivated (wanting to do something else). This creates a paradoxical situation in which people are experiencing more enjoyable flow activities while at work, while they are reporting that they wish to be doing something else.

In light of the dynamical history of motivation and the temporal nature of flow, it would follow the flow experience would fluctuate over time in a nonlinear dynamical fashion. Inasmuch as a normal person's life could easily accommodate three or more interesting and flow-generating activity sequences per week, it would follow that the potential for chaos is strong. A summary of the daily log study (Guastello, Johnson, & Rieke, 1999) follows next. Further details of the methodology and analysis appear in the original article.

Daily Log Method and Analysis

The participants in the study were 24 university students who ranged in age from 19 to 55 years. Most of them held part-time or full-time jobs. The average number of hours worked during the 1-week data collection period was 17.3 hours, with a range from 0.0 to 45.9 hours. All participants completed a 7-day log of what activities they were doing, how long the activity lasted, and how they rated the level of skills and challenges inherent in the task. Every time they changed activity they recorded a new entry. A list of 22 categories of activity was provided.

Participants rated the level of skills and challenges for each activity on a 0 to 9 point scale, with 0 being low and 9 representing high skill or challenge used or required. The measurement of flow for each task logged by each person was the cross-product of their skill and challenge levels recorded for each task divided by the cross-product of the within-person standard deviations for skill and challenge. The use of the cross-product measurement was based on definitions given by previous researchers.

The first phase of the analysis was to compute, for each person, the correlations among skill, challenge, flow, and skill challenge and flow at a lag of one log entry. In the second phase, data sets for logbook entries were transformed into a time series for each person such that each frame of data pertained to a 15-minute interval; an activity that persisted for an hour thus required four such frames. This second data set was used to calculate nonlinear regression models for exponential expansion, Lyapunov dimensionality and the test for chaos, and the linear model counterparts using the method of structural equations.

Results

Preliminary analysis showed that the correlation between time spent in a task and the flow level was considerably greater when data frames involving sleep were not included in the analysis. Thus, we skipped over the sleep entries. The mean time-flow correlation was .28 across the sample of participants. Structural equation models were based on time lags of 1 hour; preliminary analysis showed that 15-minute intervals were too short to ascertain dynamic patterns. The simple exponential model turned out to be a better representation of the data than the bifurcation model.

The R^2 coefficients for the nonlinear models (average $= .26$) exceeded their linear counterparts (average $= .05$) in all cases. The mean D_L was $+1.16$ with a range between 1.06 and 1.26. The positive Lyapunov exponent denoted chaotic shifts in levels of motivational flow.

In the final analysis, linear correlations were computed between key distribution parameters and the amount of time spent working for pay and sleeping. The work hypotheses were based on previous research that showed greater levels of flow for work time. Here the finding was that R^2 for the nonlinear model was indeed significantly correlated with the amount of time spent working ($r = .42$, $p < .05$). In other words, there was less noise in the flow trajectory for people who divided their time between work and other aspects of life.

The term D_L, which denoted the complexity of the time series, was not significantly related to the amount of time spent working for pay. The sample size was small, and the observed value of r was moderate, and the lack of significance may be related in part to the small sample size. On the other hand, D_L was also strongly related ($r = .70$, $p < .01$) to the R^2 for the nonlinear model. Because the two values are independently estimated (and are not the same by definition as in linear regression), this finding was potentially important.

As a further attempt to explain individual differences in the dynamics of motivational flows, a contour plot was created for individuals' time-flow correlations, R^2 associated with their linear models, and R^2 associated with their nonlinear exponential models. The three-dimensional plot is shown in Fig. 5.9.

Three clusters of people became apparent. One group showed slightly negative time-flow correlations, low temporal stability (low R^2 for the linear model), and low nonlinearity (low R^2 for the nonlinear model). Low R^2 for both linear and nonlinear models indicate a great deal of noise in the data. This group was designated Flow

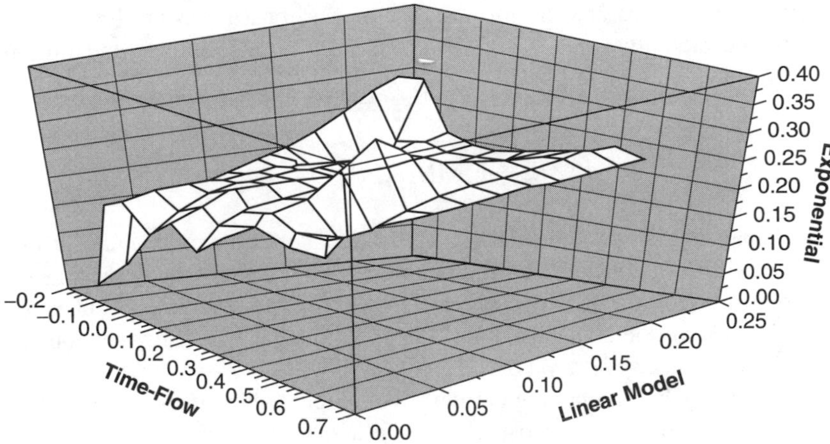

FIG. 5.9. Distribution of results for motivational flow, showing size of the exponent, R^2 for the linear model, and time-flow correlation for each participant in the study. From Guastello et al. (1999, p. 269); reprinted with permission of Human Sciences Press and Kluwer Academic Publishers.

Type A. Flow Type A appears to change tasks in short cycles with little regard to flow. Such a person would appear to be caught in a lifestyle where task selection is externally governed or motivated. Alternatively, Flow Type A individuals might simply have short attention spans.

The second group also showed slightly negative time-flow correlations, relatively high temporal stability, and relatively high nonlinearity. This group was designated Flow Type B. Type B appears to share the externally governed task selection, perhaps because of work or academic scheduling demands, but also reflect high differential flow associated with tasks; hence the strong nonlinear effect.

The third group displayed high time-flow correlations, low temporal stability, and high nonlinearity. This group was designated Flow Type C. Type C, in contrast with Type B, shares the differential flow with tasks, but involvement periods are relatively long and dependent on the flow level for that activity.

The study produced several new findings about motivational flow. Its dynamics were chaotic over time for all participants. This finding is consistent with an interpretation of the flow experience as one where the individuals are organizing their activities throughout a week in a manner that maintains flow on the one hand, and meetings externally imposed task and time demands on the other. This combination of forces produced irregular periods of high and low flow. The database did not permit any further analysis of the origins of these types. Future research might investigate control parameters in the process. Two possible control parameters appear to be internally versus externally governed activity schedules, and different flow levels for different tasks.

SUMMARY

This chapter began with some basic motivation concepts concerning intrinsic versus extrinsic motivation, and the cognitive dynamics of utility seeking. We then moved on to the butterfly catastrophe model of motivation in organizations and proceeded to extend the dynamical theory with regard to utility functions and changes in intrinsic motivation over time.

The butterfly catastrophe model describes three stable states of behavior in organization where accelerated performance and turnover are found at the extreme ends of the behavioral spectrum. The four control parameters are ability, extrinsic motivation, intrinsic motivation, and a management factor that governs the relative contribution of intrinsic and extrinsic motivation in an organization. The butterfly model, by virtue of its topological structure, contains a cusp subset model for personnel selection and turnover. The empirical example illustrated four main points: (a) The validity of the cusp exceeds that of conventional linear models to an increasing extent as the time horizon for prediction increases. (b) The variables that are important in predicting future performance can change over time, and depend on the particular endpoint for which an employer wants a prediction. (c) The empirical selection model is stable under repeated sampling. (d) It is possible to realize improved utility of selection to the employer using the nonlinear model.

Game theory offers a different approach to understanding utility and motivation, and it addresses strategic decisions by individual rational actors. Games, which are abstractions of real-world strategic situations, can be strictly competitive, strictly cooperative, or mixed strategy games. In all cases except the so-called trivial games, one player's utilities are affected by other players' action selections. Games in real life are often played iteratively, and players' utility selections grope toward evolutionarily stable states. In this chapter, we considered the case of three groups of players within an organization that were competing for resources and forming coalitions. According to the simulation, the formation and restructuring of coalitions over time is chaotic. Examples of strictly cooperative games are considered in Chapters 7 and 8.

Communities of iterated game players often evolve new rules known as ogliarchic reaction functions. Theorists have thus pondered when and how individual strategic decisions could self-organize into community-level effects. We will consider the validity of this conjecture in Chapter 10 in conjunction with hierarchical organizations.

Finally in this chapter, we considered how a person's level of intrinsic motivation ebbs and flows over a week's worth of activities. Overall, the flow is chaotic, as expected from the work on the flow of fluids and gases. Participants in the study could be grouped into three types based on three numerical indicators: (a) their correlations between flow level and time spent in an activity; (b) strength of the linear model, which denoted consistency of activity over time; and (c) the complexity of their nonlinear turbulence in intrinsic motivation level over time, as measured by their Lyapunov exponents.

6

Dynamical Theory of Creativity

The objective of this chapter is to examine relationships between NDS concepts and creative thinking at the individual and group levels of analysis. Dynamics that occur at the organizational and societal levels of analysis will be involved to some extent. A new theory emerges that involves NDS concepts of chaos, bifurcation, catastrophe, and self-organization. In doing so, it incorporates existing theory and addresses issues that have not been fully explored by conventional theory.

Several questions become parenthetically important: (a) What are the relationships between individual, group, organizational, and societal processes? (b) How do the relationships between system levels contribute to the understanding of creative processes at any of the levels of analysis? (c) Do any new rules emerge to explain how ideas are generated or how idea elements assembled into other new ideas? (d) What insights does it give to the group productivity problem, whereby the intellectual productivity of groups is only about half the time better than the production of the most competent individual? (e) Does NDS suggest whether creative ability is widely or narrowly distributed in the population? (f) Can an idea ever be original, or is "originality" a flattering but vacant construct?

The exposition begins with some basic and recent themes in creativity research. Themes involve general definitions, principles of divergent thinking, personality, cognitive style, environment, motivation, and the investment theory of creativity, along with a growing awareness of exponential effects in creative production. Next, ideas will rush in through the nearest window in a chaotic flurry, then self-organize into something resembling the solution to a problem. The speed of the flurry and self-organizing process vary a bit depending on whether one problem solver or a problem solving group is involved.

CREATIVITY BASICS

It is a challenge to choose the one best definition of creativity given all the varieties that have emerged over the last century. There is some common ground among them, however: original ideas, but "very rare" ideas are often close enough; a unique synthesis of idea elements into something new; the definition of new problems or the redefinition of problems already known, previously unknown solutions to problems; or improvements to existing solutions. One solution to a problem may improve on another by simplifying problem or solution elements without losing any essential functionality or meaning, or by fulfilling the intended purpose more often (Parkhurst, 1999). The literal roles of "problems," "solutions," or the realism often associated with them typically break down when works of art (e.g., surrealism) are considered.

A creative product is not devoid of context. It has a purpose, an audience, and a medium. The purpose may often be the "problem" to which I alluded earlier. The "audience" may be the entities that posed the problem to the creative thinker in the first place. A better-quality creative output begins with a thorough understanding of the problem; the "audience" or comparable entities set the criteria for a solution. Psychological studies of creativity focus on the characteristics of the problem-solving process and the problem solvers.

Divergent Thinking

Many, if not most, cognitive functions are not creative, and were never meant to be. Instead the frequent objective is to find the one correct answer, or the best answer of the options available. Optimal responses can take the form of numerical computation; memory for ideas, sights, sounds, and events; word choices and interpretation; interpretation of a set of logical propositions; or the conversion of one set of symbols into another set. These mental operations are collectively known as *convergent thinking* processes, and are characteristic of the thinking that occurs in common IQ tests.

Divergent thinking, on the other hand, characterizes creative thinking processes, in which the goal is to come up with many possible solutions, answers, or options. Often the more unique or aesthetically pleasing responses are given preference. Divergent thinking can take several forms also, such as producing many possible adjectives that could be used to describe a given object, organizing and reorganizing a set of objects into categories, producing novel uses for common objects, drawing analogies between one relationship and another, and suggesting possible consequences of an unusual but significant event (Guilford, 1967).

The type of thinking inherent in the Consequences test (Christensen, Merrifield, & Guilford, 1958) is one of my personal favorites because it compels a person to think through the implications of an event on a complex system. A typical question might take the form: "What would happen if global warming caused the seas to rise and the state of Florida suddenly fell below sea level?" (This is not an actual test question.) The possible responses generated in a 5-minute period would depict both immediate consequences and remote consequences that were contingent on one or more immediate consequences. An example of an immediate consequence would be,"People couldn't drive their cars very well." An example of a remote consequence would be, "The disproportionate number of deaths among the elderly would disrupt the life insurance industry's actuarial tables."

Not long ago it was controversial as to whether the cognitive and other predisposition to creative behavior were specific to a domain of endeavor (e.g., visual art, music, literature, stage performance, science and engineering, business) or whether they generalized across domains. The controversy was based on the generally low correlations among specific measures of divergent thinking, personality characteristics associated with creative people (see below), and the various means of rating creative behavior, such as awards, teachers' ratings of students' work, and experienced judges' ratings of creative works (Baer, 1993; Hocevar, 1981; Storfer, 1990). It was eventually discovered, however, that people who are productive in one creative domain are proportionately more productive in other domains. Patterns of creative productity fall into two common factors that place the art forms into one common group. Science, engineering, and business comprise the other group, and, most importantly, there is a correlation between productivity in the two groups of domains of about .32 (Guastello, Bzdawka, Guastello, & Rieke, 1992; Guastello & Shissler, 1994; Sternberg & Lubart, 1995).

Personality

People who are making, or have made, their careers in the creative professions tend to share some personality traits. The profile, which was initially based on the Sixteen Personality Factors Questionnaire (16PF; Cattell, Eber, & Tatsuoka, 1970; Cattell, Cattell, & Cattell, 1994) has been fairly stable over the past half century. Creative people tend to be aloof rather than warm and participative, abstract thinkers rather than concrete thinkers, dominant or assertive, serious as opposed to cheerful, nonconforming, socially bold rather than timid or shy, sensitive, imaginative, open-minded to new ideas and experiences, and self-sufficient in that they prefer to work alone rather than in groups (Cattell & Drevdahl, 1955; Cattell et al., 1970; Guastello & Shissler, 1994; Rieke, Guastello, & Conn,

1994). Creative people whose work spans multiple domains tend to be more self-controlled and perfectionist than those who are primarily centered in one domain.

The typical creative professional shares some similarities with the typical business leader-manager, and exhibits some notable differences as well. They tend to be similar with regard to assertiveness and social boldness. They conflict, however on rule-following behavior, openness to new ideas, imagination, and self-sufficiency. What the Creative would call "closed-mindedness," the Business Manager would call "respect for tradition." What the Creative would call "lack of imagination," the Business Manager would call "pragmatism." The opposite of self-sufficiency on the 16PF is "group dependency." Here the Business Manager would mutter something about "achieving consensus," while the Creative would wonder how old the managers were when their mothers first let them cross the street alone.

The clash probably originated from the Creatives living in a world where ideas collide and conflict in the natural course of events. There it is necessary to define points of view and probable scenarios of future payoffs that would result from the ideas in play. Eventually, one must commit to a point of view even if it not universally shared. The deliberations typically occur before those who are not privy to the deliberations have a chance to examine the ideas for themselves. Thus, one group appears to the other to be slow to catch on, while the other group might be mistaken for narcissistic.

It is probably evident from the foregoing remarks that any organization that requires creative thinking from time to time has a built-in formula for a personality clash. In organizations where the incumbents have gotten used to these differences, the conflicts are not so great. It is noteworthy, however, that the most recent thinking in leadership theory puts a greater premium on creativity on the part of the leader, and in the facilitation of creativity in the work force. The leadership aspect of these developments are considered in Chapter 8, while the other group dynamics pertaining to creativity are presented here first.

In the few studies that exist on personality traits and creative problem-solving groups, the active personality traits are somewhat different. Hogan and Hogan (1993) reported a study of creative problem-solving groups where some of the experimentally contrived groups contained members who all scored above average on rule-following behavior, while other groups contained one person who scored low on that trait. Rule-following behavior in this context was measured as a broader trait called Conscientiousness. The results showed that the groups contained one non-rule-following person delivered better solutions to the experimental problem. This finding is not uncanny in light of the many creativity specialists who encourage "out of the box" thinking; we return to this particular matter in the subsection on cognitive style below.

In a second study of creative problem-solving and personality (Guastello, 1995a), the groups were not composed on the basis of personality, but all members completed the 16PF before the problem solving activity began. The 1-hour activity was videotaped, and each verbal response by each participant was coded for one of nine types of contribution to the conversation. A factor analysis of the individuals' contributions showed that there were two patterns of response. One was a *General Participation* consisting of information seeking, information giving, clarifying remarks, gatekeeping, initiating lines of discussion, and following. The other was an *Especially Creative Contribution* that consisted of tension reducing (wisecracking or otherwise breaking uncomfortable silences), initiating, clarifying, harmonizing (usually conflict resolution of some sort), and unclassified responses (which were often unintelligible on the videotape).

Three traits were associated with greater amounts of general participation: warmth and participativeness, social boldness, and unpretentiousness. Warmth is the opposite of the trait appearing in the standard profile. Boldness is also a standard element. Unpretentiousness is a new variable in the profile. Greater amounts of the especially creative contributions were correlated with the same three traits plus one more, which was assertiveness. The results indicate that effective participation in a creative problem-solving discussion requires the development of traits that promote frequent positive interaction with the other participants (warmth and unpretentiousness), and traits that help one get a creative word in edgewise (assertiveness and boldness).

Motivation

Creative productivity is, for the most part, intrinsically motivated (Amabile, 1983; Feldhusen, 1995). This is not to imply that Creatives are unresponsive to tangible rewards, but the primary impetus is internally driven. The negative contribution of extrinsic rewards shows up in experiments that manipulate the use of evaluations and feedback of the creative works. Explicit evaluations inhibit creative content or quantity of artworks and writing.

The investment theory of creativity (Sternberg & Lubart, 1991, 1995) reflects the motivations for achievement and power. According to the theory, people who work in creative settings choose their projects based on their estimation of the odds of each possible project paying off. The R & D laboratory shares a common task with the commodity investors: They "buy low" and "sell high." Some ideas can be "bought low" either because they are new and untested but promising, or because they do not work well. Unlike the commodities trader, however, creative workers must take into account their own abilities to add value to their source material and must assess their personal odds of doing so compared to other workers' odds.

Each person has a different notion of payoff, and both intrinsic and extrinsic reward structures could play a role as a general rule. Higher risks could have higher payoffs, but a lower likelihood of any payoff. Creative persons must navigate the trade-off between total reward size, project costs, and uncertainty. Noncognitive variables, such as personality traits or cognitive styles, are relevant insofar as they explain a person's agility at buying low and selling high.

Cognitive Style

Cognitive style is a mixture of personality and mental ability concepts. Style describes how people use their mental abilities rather than how much of any abilities they have. Six taxonomies of cognitive style were selected for examination here: the Creatrix (Byrd, 1986), the Whack Pack (von Oech, 1992a, 1992b), the Six Thinking Hats (DeBono, 1985), mental governance (Sternberg & Lubart, 1991, 1995), the adaptor–innovator continuum (Kirton, 1976; Kirton & DeCiantis, 1986), and chaotic cognition (Finke & Bettle, 1996). They were chosen because their core concepts appear in several taxonomies of style particularly where creativity has been involved. A taxonomy of the eight styles that are part of the Creatrix appears in Fig. 6.1 along with cross-references to similar style concepts drawn from other theories.

The Creatrix

Starting at the lower left of Fig. 6.1, low motivation and low risk-taking produce a work style that does not amount to much more than copying ideas from other sources (*copycat*). Moving to the right, low risk-taking with a high motivation to be creative results in the *dreamer*. The individual produces new ideas in substantial quantities and may value them, but does not take the risks required to finish them

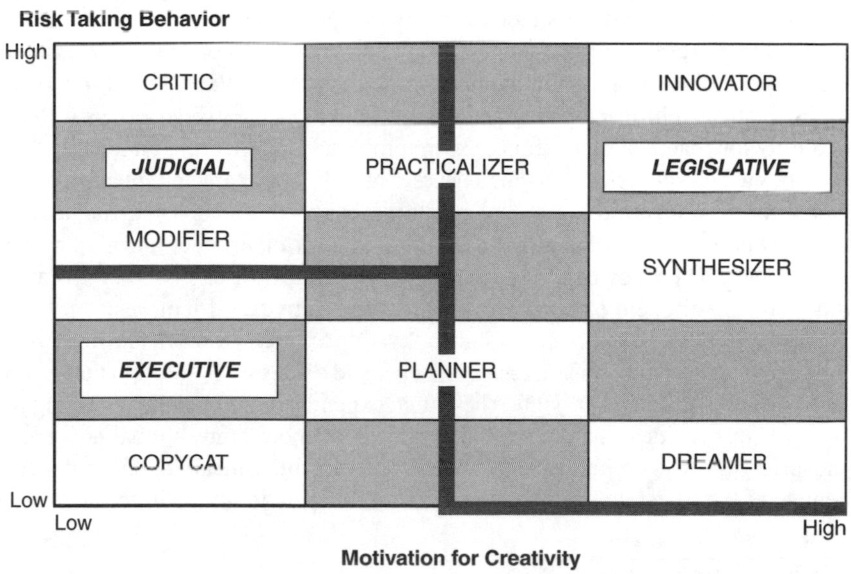

FIG. 6.1. Taxonomy of cognitive styles based on the Creatrix and theory of mental governance. From Guastello et al. (1998, p. 79). Reprinted with permission of the Creative Education Foundation.

and bring them to an audience or market. (Perhaps some elements of persistence and task motivation are also responsible here.) One would expect that both the copycat and dreamer styles would be low productivity styles, and less productive than most who engage in creative activity. The shaded areas of Fig. 6.1 are transition regions where two adjacent styles would be mixed; this is an implication for the continuous nature of the two underlying variables, motivation for creativity and risk taking.

The *planner* has a moderate motivation for creative work, but takes a greater number of risks than the copycat or dreamer. The planner will try alternative ideas, mentally experiment with options, but is not likely to become committed to one viewpoint or another. Empirical research suggests, however, that the more productive research and development teams were those whose supervisors who helped groups to explore many alternative ways of formulating a problem or solution strategy early in a research project (Redmond, Mumford, & Teach, 1993). The process of continually redesigning and replanning a project throughout its development is thought to be critical to developing exceptional creative products.

Modifiers take more risks than planners and dreamers, but they report low motivation to do anything especially creative. According to Byrd (1986), their idea of an innovation is to move two machines closer together for a better performance result. The *synthesizer* on the other hand, is no more risky than the modifier, but succeeds in taking diverse ideas and putting them together in a new way.

Practicalizers are willing to assume a fair amount of risk. They are motivated by the possibility of making an idea a reality more than by creating the idea from the beginning. Their preferred contribution to a collective project is to do what it takes to get an idea from the drawing board to the market place. To do so would require a fairly well-developed sense of what is a viable creative effort, as well as the ability for practical innovation to solve problems in delivering an idea.

Critics will assume relatively high degrees of risk, but, characteristically, do not display much motivation to produce creative ideas themselves. Their risk-taking translates into a special talent for critiquing an idea or product and finding its hidden flaws. Their coworkers, according to Byrd (1986), can become irritated with their temperament of negativity and lack of positive contributions.

Innovators are characterized by high motivation for creative work and high risk-taking propensity. They seek the new, original, and different. A solution that is too conventional is not good enough. They often expend exceptional efforts trying to bring a high-risk idea to fruition at the expense of more conventional concerns. Innovative products do not usually flow on a predictable timetable, thus the management of the truest innovation becomes very difficult and often unwanted.

Whack Pack

A Whack Pack (von Oech, 1992a) is a deck of cards each containing a cute picture and a briefly stated suggestion for how to approach a situation more creatively.

The Whack Pack and its companion book (von Oech, 1992b) comprise a training technique more so than a theory, but they do codify some important points about cognitive styles from the vast literature on creativity. The intention is to contrive exercises, which can be as simple as "Pick a card, any card!", where the random and spontaneously selected suggestion is used as a springboard to explore some feature or limitation of the problem and solutions with which a person could be wrestling. According to the back of the package, "It will 'whack' you out of your habitual thought patterns and allow you to look at what you're doing in a fresh way."

The cards are organized into four "suits," and are labeled as creative styles: the *explorer*, the *judge*, the *artist*, and the *warrior*. The judge is essentially the critic in the Creatrix scheme. The artist turns resources into ideas, and puts ideas together in new and different ways, and thus could characterize the synthesizer, the dreamer, and the innovator. The warrior is closely akin to the practicalizer, and manifests a combination of risk-taking and motivation, whereas the artist engages primarily in divergent thinking. The explorer is creative about finding new sources of ideas; this style does not have a direct analog in the Creatrix scheme.

Creatrix critics can be warriors too, however, because they allegedly share the risk-taking tendency. In works of science for instance, a certain element of criticism is fundamental to generating new ideas as the scientist looks at a set of experiments, data, and conclusions and asks, "What's wrong with this picture?" The answer often leads to new approaches to the problems. Reflective criticism would be more effective than "gonzo" criticism.

Von Oech (1992a) began with the premise that each person has a dominating style, but the training process is predicated on fostering greater innovation through use of a combination of styles during the creative process. Note that the cognitive aspects of creative thinking are interwoven with the style concept. Divergent thinking needs to be deliberately engaged on occasion, hence the need for a Whack. Mental sets do not always break spontaneously, and a good Whack is bound to help.

Mental Governance

The investment theory of creativity (Sternberg & Lubart, 1991, 1995) goes beyond "buying low and selling high" to include a theory of cognitive style known as the theory of mental governance. There are three categories of styles that are analogous to the *executive*, *legislative*, and *judicial* branches of government. The legislative style creates the raw material in a fashion akin to the dreamer, synthesizer, and innovator styles of the Creatrix. The judicial style is akin to the Creatrix critic or Whacking judge. The executive style occupies the lower left quadrant of the Creatrix. Even when creative ability is present, the executive prefers structured and unambiguous tasks and roles in group projects.

The three main forms of mental self-governance can be characterized by their form, level, scope, and orientation. Forms may be monarchic, hierarchical, ogliarchic, or anarchic. Levels may be global or local. Scope may involve working alone or in groups. Orientation could be progressive or conservative. There are, therefore, 96 possible combinations of attributes for cognitive style or mental self-governance. The 96 varieties do not register on the constructs in Fig. 6.1, however; thus it is necessary to defer expanded explanations to the original sources. It is noteworthy, however, that the empirical studies on mental self-governance showed that elementary and secondary school students received more favorable ratings of their work from their teachers if their cognitive style was more closely matched to the teacher's style. Furthermore, teachers tended to overestimate the similarity that did exists between themselves and their students (Sternberg & Lubart, 1995). This similar-to-me effect would appear to undermine many possible ways of studying the relationship between creative styles and creative products where ratings were used as a criterion.

Six Thinking Hats

DeBono (1985) identified six cognitive styles, which he called "thinking hats." Although a person might have a dominant style, the goal for creativity enhancement is to develop some flexibility among all the possible styles. A thinker should become a fluent user of all six differently colored hats.

The *white hat* style is centered upon pure facts and information. Thinking is stripped of any opinion, commentary or elaboration; it utilizes the power of objective observation. The *red hat* style is centered upon the emotional content of the idea or message and utilizes intuition as its primary mental capability. The white and red styles do not appear to be localized to any one specific style in Fig. 6.1. The white hat might legitimately characterize all styles in Fig. 6.1, however, insofar as factual thinking helps all other styles to produce results. The red hat, meanwhile, denotes a motivation and verve that might reasonably characterize all but the lower left quadrant of Fig. 6.1.

The *black hat* style is the critic and is similar to the critic in other taxonomies. The *yellow hat* style is characterized by optimism and a positive outlook on what can be done with an idea or project; this style would characterize the practicalizer in the Creatrix, but could readily splash over to successful synthesizers and innovators.

The *green hat* style is the one most heavily loaded with divergent thinking, resource utilization, and idea combination activities. It would reasonably describe the right half of Fig. 6.1. The *blue hat* style is characterized by thoughtfulness and attention to the process of creation. Blue hats remain aware of their own thought processes and how well they might be handling a situation.

Adaptor–Innovator Continuum

The Adaptor–Innovator continuum (Kirton, 1976) represents polarity in cognitive style. The *innovator* pole is occupied by people who, by habit, redefine problems and break mental sets regularly, produce many ideas in response to a problem situation, accept greater risks associated with unstructured situations, and who may be seen as shocking, impractical, or abrasive by the adaptors. The *adaptor* pole, by contrast, is occupied by people who accept existing definitions of problems, generate a limited and selected range of ideas in response to a problem situation, and gravitate toward traditional approaches to problems and solutions. They might be seen as backward, intolerant of ambiguity, and relatively uninspired by the innovators. The two constellations are the result of three independent variables: sufficiency of originality, efficiency, and rule/group conformity. According to a review of the construct by Mudd (1995), these three constructs have been empirically associated with productivity in research and development teams. The Adaptor–Innovator continuum can be traced as a rough diagonal across Fig. 6.1 from lower left to upper right.

The Adaptor–Innovator continuum is closely related to the processes of assimilation and accommodation identified by Piaget (1952). In Piaget's theory of intellectual development, the individual will assimilate new ideas into existing structures until the old structures can no longer manage. Accommodation results in new mental structures, which are then capable of assimilating large amounts of new material. Eventually the process must recur again. It now appears that among adults, there can be a tendency to lock into existing structures or a tendency to experiment with new ones. Although both processes were necessary for the individual to reach intellectual adulthood, there is a greater role of motivation, personality, and perhaps situational demands in determining whether the process of making new mental structures continues further.

Empirical Study

My coworkers and I investigated whether there are differences in the quantities of creative output associated with the cognitive styles described thus far (Guastello, Shissler, Driscoll, & Hyde, 1998). In the first of two studies, 626 adults from a range of creative occupations (industrial and academic scientists, engineers, social scientists, artists, musicians, hair stylists, and sundry others including undergraduates), completed the Artistic and Scientific Activities Inventory (ASAS; Guastello, 1991; also see Guastello et al., 1998). The ASAS measured their quantity of creative output in several domains (various arts, science, business) and their dominant cognitive style out of eight options. In the second study, the measurement of styles was changed to allow for continuous measurement of each style separately; there were 277 undergraduates who also completed the ASAS.

The results showed substantial positive correlations between innovator, synthesizer, and planner styles with productivity, with negative or null relationships for other styles. Furthermore, creative output was highest for people who engaged in a wide repertoire of cognitive styles. We recommended, therefore, that creativity training or enhancement programs continue to allocate time to repertoire development.

Chaotic Cognition

When I came home from my last trip to Switzerland, I was totally impressed with the pinpoint timing of the Swiss train system. I had to make six connections between Zurich and Gstaad. One of the rides lasted only about three minutes, and the time to change to the next train was only two minutes. If the trains had not been scheduled so well, or if I did not keep my focus with the luggage, I would still be walking through the snow right now.

Of course I was in Gstaad for a chaos conference. The scheduled presentations were as creative, well-planned, well-timed, and clearly delivered as one could ever hope for. A few creative flurries broke out as the conference warmed up. It was fascinating to hear and watch some of the luminaries of nonlinear dynamics zap between dripping honey sticks, category formation, the deep principles of collective intelligence, and the mathematical modeling thereof, in a 5-minute span. It was not as though I had never seen creativity in action before, but the stark contrast between the two types of thinking was especially poignant. (I was also running a fever of 104°F, which probably affected the experience.) In any case, the experience made a lot more sense when a copy of *Chaotic Cognition* (Finke & Bettle, 1996) crawled into my hand.

Finke and Bettle (1996) identified two contrasting types of thinking, which they call orderly thinking and chaotic thinking. Although they noted an association between orderly thinking and convergent thinking, and between chaotic thinking and divergent thinking, they emphasized that the cognitive styles go beyond simply having strong abilities in those areas. Orderly thinkers are typically goal-oriented, prefer simple explanations to not-so-simple situations, but are likely to miss out on anything that could happen spontaneously in life. Chaotic thinkers put a premium on play and exploration and living for the moment, but may become disenchanted with life when they must function in an orderly fashion.

Even within a group of eminent creative writers, tendencies toward order or chaos can be observed. Finke and Bettle (1996) categorized Sigmund Freud, Plato, Franz Kafka, and Charles Dickens as essentially orderly. On the other hand, Carl Jung, Socrates, James Joyce, and John Keats qualified as chaotic.

Chaotic thinking, when turned on at the right time, can produce strategic advantages against someone who is relentlessly orderly and nasty besides. For instance, Finke and Bettle (1996) observe that orderly thinkers can become overly critical and pompous when they have attained positions of power and authority. They find scapegoats convenient. Now imagine that you have been an efficient, reliable, and energetic employee, but now it is your turn to become the boss' scapegoat. Suggested responses would be those that complicate the boss' reality. You could respond to an unfair criticism by reporting that unspecified others are doing whatever it is to a much worse extent than you are. You could advise the boss at a moment unrelated to the evaluation context that unspecified others are doing things to undermine the boss' position, authority, or credibility on some issue. You could try a three-step maneuver: (a) Get the boss to commit to a position on a controversial issue. (b) Support the boss' position publicly with embellishments and exaggerations of the boss' intent. (c) When the boss objects, you then apologize publicly adding that he really said quite the opposite (pp. 138–139).

In the relationships between competing organizations, strategic management can benefit from the dumping of a little chaos on the competitor. Stacey (1992) recounted several uses of what amounts to chaotic reasoning. I'll retell one of them. At one point in history, Kodak had a virtual monopoly on camera film in the United States. A new competitor, Fuji, suddenly entered the U.S. market with the usual array of advertising and promotion, and more importantly a strong growth in sales. Kodak could have responded with predictable countermeasures such as introducing new products, new advertising campaigns, and price competition, but they did something very different instead. The painted up a blimp with the Kodak logo, and flew it to Tokyo where it hovered over Fuji building for a few weeks. The stunt attracted enough attention so that it generated a sizable increase in sales for Kodak products in Japan, and Fuji had to divert $30 million from their U.S. advertising budget to counteract the lossest home.

The orderly thinker would have reacted to Fuji in a predictable way, which would have generated a predictable response. The chaotic solution, however, was a success because it defied others' notions of what is logical, and it probably appealed to the amusement-seeking tendencies of other chaotic thinkers with cameras. On the other side of the relationship, a strategic response to a chaotic stimulus would be one that restores the system to predictability. The known strategies for controlling chaos in physical systems and decision environments are elaborated in Chapter 12.

Another counterpoint between orderly and chaotic thinkers pertains to the use of goal-setting, which sometimes takes the form of vision and mission statements. This counterpoint is better left until Chapter 9. Instead, the topic now turns to chaos and self-organization in the creative thinking process itself.

CHAOTIC FLOWS AND INDIVIDUAL CREATIVITY

This section compiles current knowledge about the dynamics of creative processes. The exposition begins with chance-configuration theory, which, in its original form, involved the following components: the role of the environment, the apparent randomness that is involved when mental elements are combined into a new idea, the self-organization of mental elements into the new idea. In doing so, we examine the chance component as consider whether it is really chaos instead.

The Environment

The creative person's psychological environment is an important factor that influences creative output (Campbell, 1960). Creative ideas are regarded as configurations of mental elements. Large numbers of mental elements are the result of an enriched home environment in a person's formative years and an enriched professional life later on. Enrichment would include access to a variety of intellectual and artistic experiences, resources, objects, and people with whom to discuss ideas. For adult professionals, a well-stocked library, laboratory equipment (or comparable resources), competent colleagues, and a travel budget for conferences would be important aspects of enrichment.

Later research has highlighted the importance of the social environment. Management support for creative behavior and an organizational climate or culture are highly influential as well. The social environment should value creativity, tolerate ambiguity, and tolerate individual differences, and emphasize the intrinsic rewards of work (Isen, Daubman, & Nowicki, 1987; Siegel & Kaemmerer, 1978). As such it would be the opposite of an authoritarian environment (Billings, Guastello, & Rieke, 1993). Similar principles can be observed at the societal level as well. Societies tend go through oscillating periods of creative pushes, followed by less profound creativity and greater routine exploitation of the new intellectual resources (Baba & Ziegler, 1985; Csikszentmihalyi & Getzels, 1973; Guastello, 1995a; Haustein, 1981).

Throughout the studies of the contributions of the intellectual and social environments, one may get the impression that the environment is a static force over time, even though environments can be different. The cultural studies indicate that, in the very long run, the environment is anything but static. Others have addressed the shorter run phenomena as well. If we imagine that economic and market forces have self-organized according to several pertinent sets of rules, and the strategies of economic actors are based somewhat on rationality, then it follows that the economic and social environment could be complex but hardly a matter of pure noise. An individual or organization, both of which we regard as complex adaptive systems, thus makes further strategic responses, including those that are imaginative and creative.

It follows, therefore, that the social system propels a complex, rule-governed, or deterministic state. The presence of stochastic noise may make the situation all the more interesting, but it does not negate the underlying deterministic processes. The environment is thus a chaotic process if no directional dynamics are active. Directional dynamics would be observed as self-organizing processes, usually rapid ones, in one or more social or economic sectors. The subject now turns to creative responses by individuals, and the extent to which they are better described as stochastic or deterministic events.

Chance and Determinism

The early environmentally centered research suggested a hard-line view that the process of creative behavior is random across individuals insofar as the individuals are all exposed to sufficiently enriched environments. This notion gave rise to the chance aspect of chance-configuration theory (Simonton, 1988). Substantial attention was thus directed at understanding the stochastic process that applies to creative behavior. Contemporary NDS theory, however, illustrates that interesting stochastic processes are associated with creative behavior. The first earmark of a dynamical process is the presence of exponential distributions of key behaviors (Bak, 1996; West & Deering, 1995). Although the presence of those distributions, or inverse power functions, does not prove the existence of fractal structure or chaos, it is a necessary condition to begin the exploration. The exposition continues with chance-configuration theory, at the heart of which is the debate as to whether process is really random, or an example of deterministic chaos.

Exponential functions in creative work trace back to Lotka (1926) who first discovered that the distribution of creative works among Washington Academy of Science members was not normally distributed, but highly skewed with a long positive tail. When he plotted the relationship between the number of publications per author (N in Equation 6.1) against the number of authors with a specific number of publications (F), there was a close, straight-line correlation ($-a$; b is a regression constant) between the natural logarithms of the two variables:

$$\log F(N) = -a \log N + b, \tag{6.1}$$

(West & Deering, 1995, p. 87).

Simonton (1988) studied many data sets drawn from creative professionals in different domains, and concluded that the core distribution function was exponential. If we assume that there are N mental elements (which could be elementary source ideas or mental operations on them) that give rise to a creative work, then the number of permutations is e^N, which is definitely not normally distributed over individuals. Furthermore, if N is the number of contributions in a field, than about 50% of the contributions are made by $N^{0.5}$ people.

The distribution of creative output over a lifespan is also interesting. According to Simonton (1989), there are two exponential functions involved, such that

$$p_t = c(e^{-at} - e^{-bt}); \quad c = \mathrm{f}(a, b, m), \tag{6.2}$$

where p_t is cumulative creative productivity at one point in time, a is the ideation rate, b is the elaboration rate, and m is lifetime creative potential. Early careers are characterized by the generation of fundamentally new ideas. Later works are characterized by greater elaborations of ideas proposed in earlier times. Creative potential overall does not dissipate over a lifetime. Rather, because the rates of decay slow down considerably over time, a person in his or her final professional decade can produce as much as a person in the first decade of professional life.

Rinaldi, Cordone, and Casagrandi (2000) examined the temporal output of famous musicians and scientists over a life span. The trends in creative production ebbed and flowed over time. The mathematical analysis showed that the temporal trends were consistent with the mathematical properties of intrinsic motivation and dissipation such as those discussed in the previous chapter, and those of Simonton (1988).

Huber (1998) studied the temporal patterns of patents obtained by inventors in one U.S. organization for the 1960–1995 period. He found that runs of patents produced by each scientist over the years in which that scientist produced patents followed a poisson distribution in 65% of cases. Huber characterized this result as indicating that a random process was operating, and that the process supported the chance-configuration principle.

Bak (1996) and West and Deering (1995) observed that Lotka's distribution fit the inverse power law, thus it is possible to conclude that a modicum of determinism was inherent in the distribution of creative works. This interpretation contrasts sharply the "random" explanation the was offered in the past. The possible presence of "something fractal going on" does not yet tell us what the processes are, however.

If we were to examine the probability density functions of creative works accumulated by people over shorter time horizons, the simple distribution with the long tail is more complex. It contains irregularities that indicate more complex dynamics. The ASAS mentioned earlier inventories creative works in two temporal categories. One category is the rate of creative output in various domains over a 3-year period. The other is the cumulative log of works on a person's "permanent record." For instance, the number of short stories written or attempted during the 3-year period would count as a contribution in the former category. The number of short stories published, however, would count in the latter category. The total score begins at 0, and 99.9 percentile is a score of 100. The distribution is shown in Fig. 6.2, and is based on data collected by Guastello, et al. (1998).

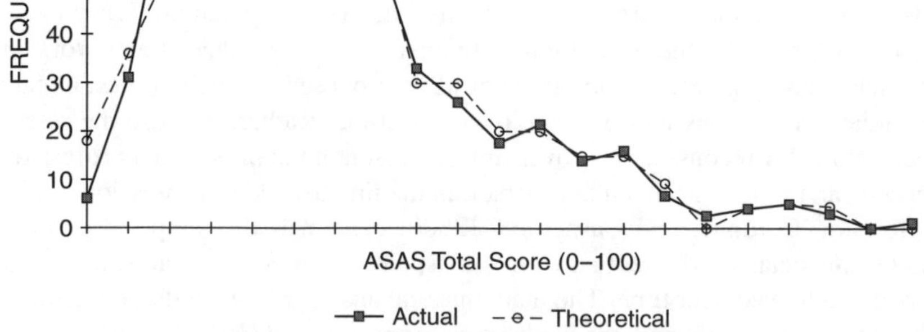

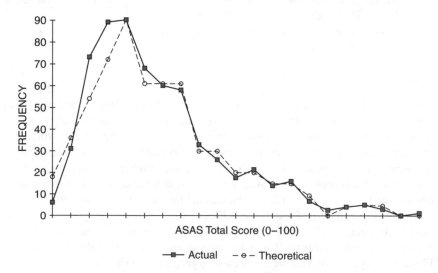

FIG. 6.2. Distribution of scores on the ASAS for rates of creative output.

The shape of the distribution had been identified previously as that of the mushroom catastrophe (Guastello, 1995a), which is also known as the parabolic umbilic catastrophe model. The distribution is characterized by a sequence of elements, which are (reading from left to right): a *blast, cascade, plateau, antimode*, and *aftershock*. The shape was first identified in a study of accidental and nonaccidental death rate in various occupational categories as they appeared in life insurance data. The shape was observed in several types of creative behavior data sets. The blast is a sharply ascending high density region near the low-scoring end of the distribution. That is followed by in irregular decline (cascade). The plateau is a flat nonzero area, which is followed by an antimode. The antimode is an expanse of scores with zero frequency. The aftershock is a new pocket of nonzero density at the high end of the distribution. It is important to note that the aftershock is part of the distribution, and not a disjointed subset taken from a different distribution.

The example given in Fig. 6.2 shows the idealized distribution superimposed over the actual distribution of ASAS scores. The other known examples (see Guastello, 1995a) sometimes show longer plateaus, longer antimodes, or stronger aftershocks. Discontinuous change occurs among a complex of states of two interacting order parameters, with change in states governed by four control parameters. The response surface is summarized by two polynomial partial differential equations. The twin function characteristic is consistent with the twin functions that characterize lifetime creative output, although the specific content of the functions is somewhat different in situations that involve observations over short time horizons.

The mushroom catastrophe was found to explain the dynamics of creative problem-solving in groups who were working together in real-time in an experimental situation (Guastello, 1995a). The participants played the Island Commission game (Gillan, 1979), which is reprinted in Appendix B. The groups' interactions were videotaped and each statement made by any member was scored as one of nine possible types of contribution, which, when factor analyzed, produced the two factors, General Participation and Especially Creative Contributions, as mentioned earlier.

The mushroom catastrophe response surface for creative production in problem-solving groups is shown in Fig. 6.3. The model requires four control parameters. Two of the four system control parameters, both of which were asymmetry variables, were occupied by personality traits. One cluster of traits distinguish high-production participants from low-production participants on the factor for general contributions. A fourth trait, assertiveness, distinguished those who most often gave especially creative responses from other participants. The two bifurcation control parameters were overall group activity level (there were seven groups of eight people involved in the study), which captured the influence of the immediate social environment, and the effect of "news bulletins," which captured an environmental contribution of a different sort. The news bulletins were introduced

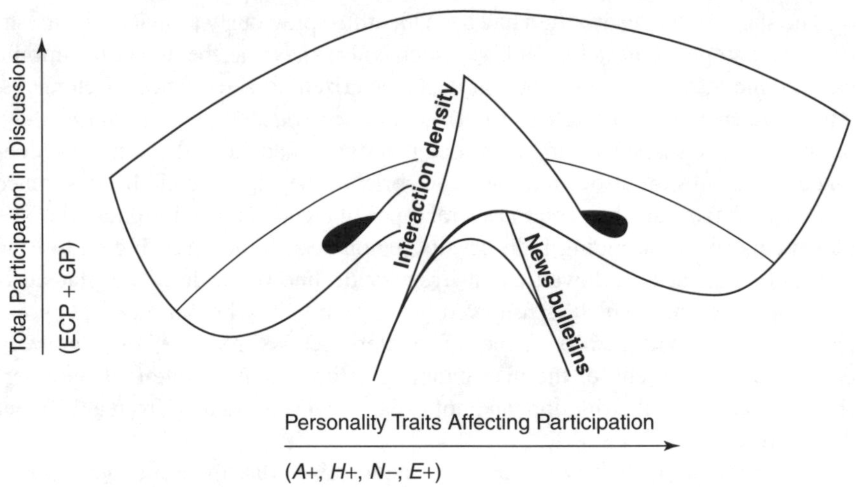

FIG. 6.3. The mushroom catastrophe model for responses in live problem-solving groups discussions.

periodically as part of the game; they contained unexpected changes in the problem situation that should provoke an adaptive response from the players.

The analysis of the creative process just described involved chaotic processes as well. The mushroom structure itself was verified through a polynomial regression technique. In this case, the nonlinear regression technique decribed in Chapter 3 was also used for estimating the Lyapunov dimension for the two flows together, which was determined to be +5.46. This high dimensionality, which is also fractal, was an important observation. According to the emerging theory, chaos leads to self-organization, and as creative self-organized systems engender more instability, it would follow that creative problem-solving groups are systems operating at the edge of chaos. The results of the experiment showed the positive Lyapunov exponents, which signify chaos and a relatively high dimensionality, which in turn indicated a greater level of complexity than most other social systems studied to date. A system that operates at the edge of chaos is one that toggles between chaos and self-organization. The self-organization dynamics of creativity are elaborated subsequently in this chapter.

Individual Cognitive Inflow

It is now possible to assemble the main principles that have been identified thus far into Fig. 6.4. The environment generates stimuli for identifying new problems and source material for new ideas. Stimuli are generated chaotically over time. A so-called enriched environment is one that contains greater amounts of information that is relevant to creative problem solving. This information can take the form of

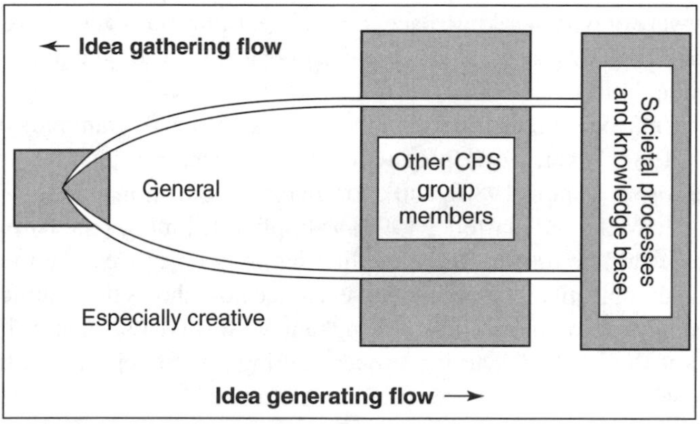

FIG. 6.4. Schematic for the flow of ideas during the creative problem-solving process.

physical objects (e.g., software, tools, publications) or flows that are stimulated by other people in the problem solver's environment. The amount of information and the energy that is applied to moving it around produces a particular level of entropy for the situation. Some studies that directly assessed the topological entropy inherent in a creative problem-solving environment are described later in this chapter when group phenomena are considered.

When the individual "plugs into" an information flow, the flow is experienced along two dimensions. One dimension is the content-specific information and the organization of that information. In creative problem-solving groups, contributions of this type became known as *general participation*. The other dimension is akin to the *especially creative contribution* in groups; here it is the particular operation of starting a new line of thinking, elaborating a line of thought, or rectifying some apparent conflict.

Once the information has arrived in the problem solver's experience, a series of cognitive operations take place whereby the individual combines the incoming flow with information that is already stored. A new nugget of information can be associated with existing information and stored with it. The new nugget can also act as a retrieval cue for items of stored information ("That gives me an idea!"). For instance, if an incoming unit of information contains elements {A, B, C}, and a particular stored unit contains elements {B, D, E}, an association would occur on the basis of element B (Kohonen, 1989). Associations can be made on the basis of multiple elements as well.

The learning phenomenon is thought to consist of two simultaneous processes: explicit learning and implicit learning. Explicit learning is the common form in which the person or animal emits a deliberate behavior, receives an obvious review or infomative feedback, and the reward or feedback strengthens or modifies the foregoing behavior. In explicit learning we assume that the person or animal is aware of what is taking place. Implicit learning, however, is an essentially unconscious thinking process that is typically occurring in conjunction with an explicit learning objective.

Experiments on implicit learning have used artificial grammars (Berry & Broadbent, 1988; Seger, 1994), production management in a sugar factory (Reber, Kassin, Lewis, & Cantor, 1980), and coordination acquisition among work group members (Guastello & Guastello, 1998) as implicit learning sets. Participants in the studies would be trained in the explicit learning objectives, then tested later on the implicit objectives. Experimental evidence now shows that implicit and explicit learning develop in parallel (Willingham & Goedert-Eschmann, 1999). The formation of the implicit learning process during an explicit task is thought to explain how behaviors that are regarded as "automatic" occur.

In addition to the extraction of grammatical patterns, implicit processes can involve the formation of categories. If we were to present human subjects with a list of randomly sorted animals, plants, and nonliving objects, and then ask our people to recite the items on the list in any order that comes to mind, we would obtain a nonrandom organization of animals, plants, and nonliving objects. The process of category formation would have started. On the one hand, the formation of categories is intrinsic to the command of any knowledge domain where the goal is to produce (covertly) some correct answers. On the other hand, the fluidity with which a person can combine and recombine objects into meaningful categories is an important form of divergent thinking (Hakstian & Cattell, 1978).

At a more general level of organization, the network of mental elements is known as a *semantic lattice*. A semantic lattice, furthermore, is thought to be organized into modules, which Hardy (1998) calls *semantic constellations*. For example, if we were to produce the statement "John shot Mary at Luigi's Restaurant," perhaps along with a purpose such as "Write a television scene on the subject of," we might elicit the semantic lattice that appears in Fig. 6.5. For each key word in the sentence, we can invoke a semantic constellation such as everything we know about John, his likes and dislikes, job, hang-ups, and what he thinks about Mary. We could build similar constellations for Mary, the restaurant, Luigi the proprietor, and the street where it happened. (And who is *Wally*?)

The content of one's existing lattices depends on one's prior history of information gathering and the variety of places from which one chooses to gather it. Here we can speak of lattice structures associated with the content domain, the *context* in which the information gathering took place, and the *depth of processing* that one applied to the incoming flow. Context may be socially driven. One's social habits are shaped by personality, and at the same time, social experiences shape the personality. Marks–Tarlow (1999) examined the process by which the personality traits, personality development, social roles, and unconscious conflict are shaped by immediate and long-term social interactions, or by the culture more broadly, to produce the psychological structure known as the *self.* The self, furthermore, shapes the content of lattices, the direction of new growth, and the reorganization

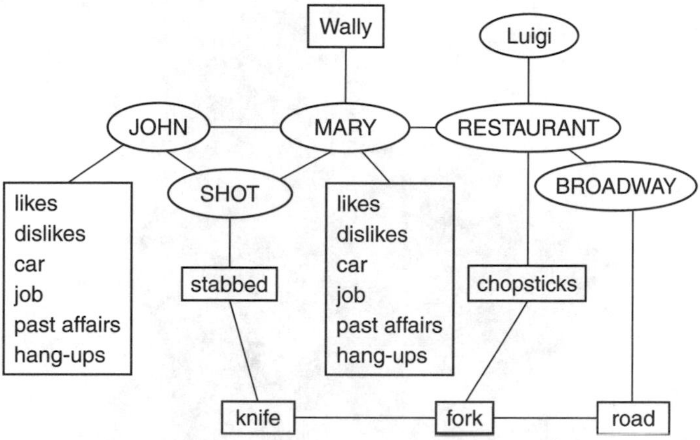

FIG. 6.5. Semantic lattice for "John shot Mary at Luigi's Restaurant."

of the lattice structures (Feldman, Csikszentmihalyi, & Gardner, 1994; Goertzel, 1997; Hardy, 1998; Marks–Tarlow, 1999).

The contribution of context is actually more broad than just its social aspect. It can be domain-specific as well, and driven to a great extent by implicit learning processes. According to Feldman et al., "The creative individual is marked by one or more asynchronies: an unusual configuration of talents, and an initial lack of fit among abilities, the domains in which the individual seeks to work, and the prejudices and tastes of the current field. Of course, in the end, it is the conquering of these asymmetries that leads to the establishment of work that comes to be cherished" (1994, p. 72).

The evolution of semantic lattice structures has not yet been studied empirically for their underlying dynamical properties. There is some reason to suspect, however, that the evolution of semantic lattices may bear some resemblance to the evolution of lattices in chemical systems. Figure 6.6 shows an idealized cubic lattice from Bunde & Havlin, (1996, p. 75). The dark blocks represent core structural elements. The gray sections are areas that are still "percolating," which is to say that they are growing. The structure overall is fractal. Growth requires, at minimum, the presence of new elemental units, sufficient entropy to move the pieces around, and an appropriate hook structure to connect the pieces (inert gasses have a difficulty here). The reaction requires an energy differential that makes connecting more efficient than remaining separated.

An assault from the environment can produce a crack in a structure if it is sufficiently strong, concentrated, and positioned. The formation of a crack will follow an internal pattern within the lattice, and its diffusion across the structure is fractal; an example appears in Fig. 6.7 from Herrmann (1996, p. 228). In the case of a semantic lattice, a structural crack may correspond to the formation of new categories and constellations of idea elements.

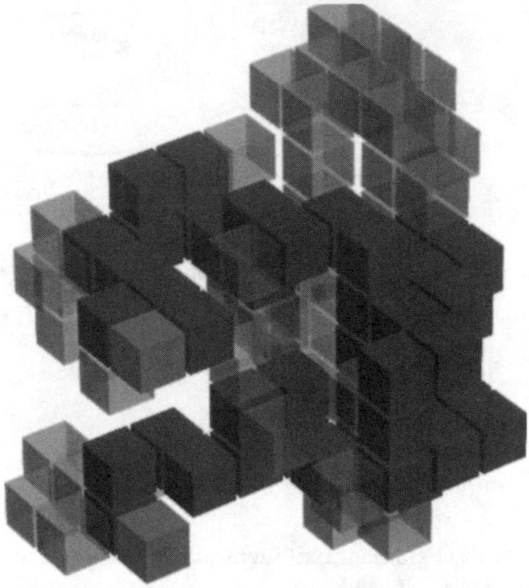

FIG. 6.6. The percolation of a fractal lattice; from Bunde and Havlin (1996, p. 75). Reprinted by permission of Springer-Verlag.

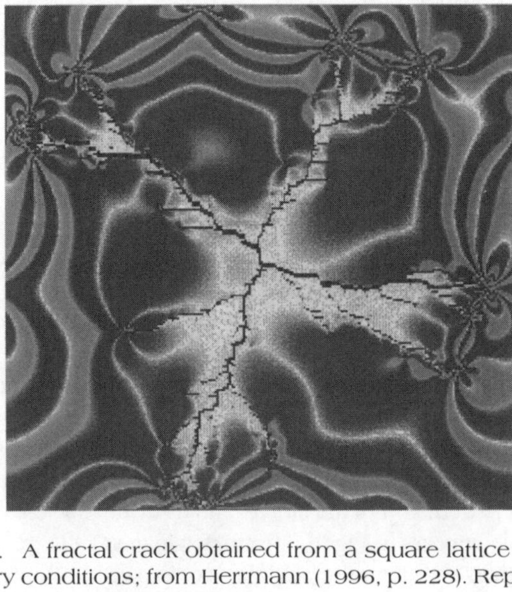

FIG. 6.7. A fractal crack obtained from a square lattice with free boundary conditions; from Herrmann (1996, p. 228). Reprinted by permission of Springer-Verlag.

FIG. 6.8. "Let your mind wander," from von Oech (1992b). Illustration by George Willett. Reprinted by permission.

Idea Production: Outflow

Sometimes we are looking for an idea that solves a problem, and sometimes we want to solve the problem better, or with originality, sparkle, and flair. Sometimes the originality, sparkle, and flair come more naturally than at other times. In any case, the production of new ideas requires a scan of one's semantic lattices. In Fig. 6.8, von Oech (1992a, card 15) advises us to let our minds wander. In doing so, we should look for new connections and contrasts based on common properties, uses of the objects, something that rhymes, and so on. Perhaps the Mad Hatter had the process nailed down when he asked Alice, "Why is a raven like a writing-desk?" After a couple pages of totally digressionary conversation, he continues, "Have you guessed the riddle yet?" "No, I give up," Alice replied. "What's the answer?" "I haven't the slightest idea," said the Hatter (Carroll, 1865/1988, pp. 59–60).

Novel ideas require unusual pathways and circuitous routes of pathway scanning, especially when we need to avoid the popular but failed lines of reasoning. Imagine that a logical set exists within a broader problem space, and that the logical set that is irritating us to no end is represented by one of the blocks in Fig. 6.8. A creative solution is one that will get us out of the box, as the saying goes—perhaps a long way out of the box. For example, von Oech (1992a, 1992b) tells a story that I see as especially relevant here. A shaman, somewhere Out West, is often called upon for advice by the hunters of his tribe when they are having unusual difficulty finding lunch. In response, the shaman would take a piece of deerskin, crumble it up, tie it so it stays that way, and soak it in water. After it has soaked a while, the shaman would dry it in the sun, and untie it. All the creases in the deerskin where the skin had been folded would appear clearly. Then he would point to a random spot on the skin and instruct the hunters, "This is a map and we are here. The lines are trails. Follow them on your next hunt." And sure enough, the hunters would find game. Why? Not because of any magical events, but because they would have looked in places where they did not look before.

The processes of idea outflow impinge on the broader question of whether any idea can be really original. Campbell (1960) argued against such a possibility with the reasoning that all the necessary idea elements are floating around the culture and only need to be scooped up by an interested party. The argument favoring the possibility of originality is predicated on Piaget's (1952) processes of accommodation and assimilation, which were introduced earlier in the context of the Adaptor–Innovator continuum. Each individual has a personal history of acquiring new ideas, and responding by assimilating or accommodating when a particular new idea is introduced. The storehouse of existing structures is about as unique as an individual personality.

Feldman et al. (1994) added that a process of *reflective abstraction* exists between the assimilation and accommodation processes. The mind is doing some work on the idea elements to force-fit them into existing schemata. Alternatively, the actual method of accommodation depends on what else happened to need accommodating at the same point in time in the individual's experience. A particular idea element may be accommodated by some, but assimilated by others. The more unusual is the host mind, the more novel the idea that can be processed and retained. "Chaos and disorder are perhaps the wrong terms for that indeterminate fullness and activity of the inner life. For it is organic, dynamic, full of tension and tendency. What is absent from it, except in the decisive act of creative, is determination, ficity, and the commitment to one resolution or another of the whole complex of its tensions" (pp. 125–126).

Self-organization

We are now prepared to unpack the alleged self-organization themes in idea production. Figure 6.9 depicts the organization of idea elements into a stable and regular pattern. The geometry that is implied by the figure should be regarded as symbolic rather than literal. In any case, theorists have uncovered at least three processes of self-organization that occur when ideas take form. They occur in the thinker's sphere of consciousness, in the organization of idea elements from the content domain, and the interactions with the environment (Abraham, 1996; Csikszentmihalyi, 1993; Gardner, 1993; Simonton, 1988; Zausner, 1996). Each area may be seen as more than one dynamic process taking place.

Within the thinker's sphere of consciousness there is the reorganization of semantic lattices, as mentioned earlier, when new information is received or produced. The lattices themselves represent both the content domain and personality or self; Abraham (1996) observed this distinction as a bifurcation in the

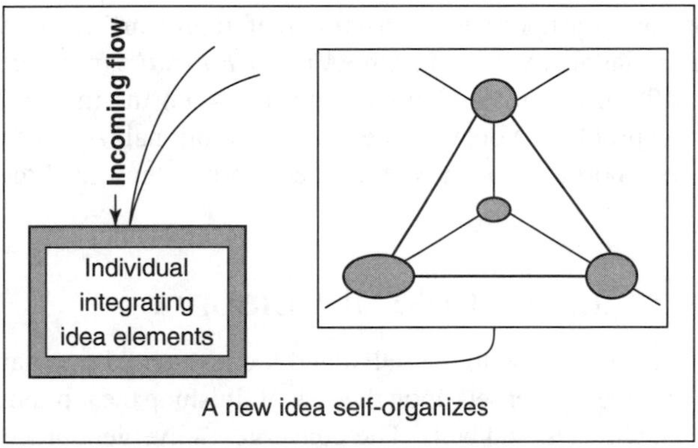

FIG. 6.9. Schematic for the self-organization of idea elements.

thought process and internal structure. A substantial reorganization of some component of the lattice structure may be responsible for one type of *insight*, whereby the thinker sees something new in the problem domain that was not seen before. The other type of insight is described next.

The internal flow of idea elements involves both convergent and divergent thinking, which Abraham (1996) noted were literally similar to the dynamics of a chaotic attractor. Objects that reach the center are propelled outward, and objects that veer toward the edge of the basin are pulled inward again. We experience this duality in thinking when we try some new combinations of ideas (divergent) and then compare the result against the requirements of the problem that we are trying to solve (convergent). For instance, we might ask ourselves whether the new idea meets the requirements or even exceeds them. Will it work for technical reasons? If so, how do we explain the idea to other interested parties. If not, what can we do to remedy the situation? The last question takes us back to another round of divergent processing.

In the case of artwork production, there seems to be a similar iterative process taking place, but it appears to be more similar to a process of channeling, rather than one of hypothesis testing. According to Zausner (1996), the artist is engaged in an iterative rapport between the ideal image the artist is trying to convey and the image that actually appears on the canvas. Personal and emotion expression is often involved in ways that other types of problem solvers try to hold in check. The mental operation, as she describes it, is similar to the Planner's cognitive style described earlier in this chapter. Not everyone engages in that or any other particular cognitive style.

The other people in the environment may act as useful or inhibitory sounding boards for the ideas we are trying to produce. Brainstorming groups as a whole go through similar patterns of convergent and divergent thinking (Torre, 1995a, 1995b). The second form of insight occurs at some time between the first idea that the thinker can converge upon and the last round of improvements or "tweaks." This is the one that is classically known as the *Aha!* or *Eureka!* experience. According to Simonton (1988), this form of insight occurs when the thinker has found a metaphor for the problem. Not everyone gets the emotional *zing* of *Eureka!* Often enough thinkers report the demands of all the iterative steps that brought the idea to fruition.

The Self-organizing Role of Metaphor

Once the Eureka has faded into the halls, and the household pets have recovered from the outburst, the thinker sets upon the task of finishing the job and applying the embellishments, whistles, and bells. The convergent–divergent process described above takes place again, but a new element is involved, which is the *metaphor*. A metaphor should be distinguished from an analogy; the latter has a longer history of psychological history in that it can be measured by tests of analogy making. A metaphor is a literary construction whereby a target object (or event or situation) is represented by a second object; the second object captures a few, but not all, the salient characteristics of the target object. A perfect analogy will capture all the salient features of the target object.

A metaphor acts as a filter for new ideas. New ideas that are brought into the scope of the problem space only insofar as they bear on the parts of the problem not yet solved, or those subproblems that are newly uncovered in the process of getting an idea from its initial form to its final destination. The metaphor also constructs a reality that attracts more ideas that are consistent with itself (Albritton, 1995; Smith, 1998).

One might observe that the construction of a metaphor is the first step in finishing an analogy. Equally true perhaps is that incomplete analogies, or metaphors, lend themselves to overly reductionist definitions of problem statements. One may make the counterpoint that science, specifically, has to be conducted that way or else nothing would ever be accomplished. I will leave that debate to the philosophers of science. For present purposes, however, the metaphor plays a pivotal role in the creative process, particularly where self-organizing dynamics are involved.

A locking-in process takes place once the metaphor is formed. If a new idea should suddenly enter at this stage in the thought process that is based on a totally different set of premises, or that would necessitate doing substantial amounts of work over again from scratch, that new idea would be "saved for much later on." The locking-in process might be observed more clearly when a collection of thinkers is involved rather than just one thinker. Consider the experience of an organization that I think of as one of my "pets." There we had a research and development department, which was itself bifurcated by function, and a management group that, shall we say, tended to have a different worldview depending on how close a manager was to the R & D process. The organization embarked on a noble project of converting an old-style ASCII computer interface for one of its Famous Products into something user-friendly, point-and-click-operable, and generally more advanced than the predecessor product and competitive with what The Competitors were already doing.

The R & D department had many parts to its job. The selection of programming environments depended on the capabilities they needed, which depended on the users' requirements, operation habits, and preferences. They summoned psychologists with ergonomics backgrounds, of which I was one, to figure out how to figure out what the user information should be and to actually acquire the information. Then management paid a product development firm three times as much as they paid the psychologists to read the user information, say things like, "This is great stuff," and draw hypothetical interfaces with colored markers. (In one version of the story, crayons were used instead of markers.) After a year of high-speed tinkering, the R & D department locked onto a design plan and proceeded with its work, with management funding the necessaries. After two years and two million dollars, the job was not finished. Then suddenly, the R & D group figured out a completely different interface system that would solve the outstanding problems but would otherwise look pretty different from Plan A. Management's response was that they had already spent two million on Plan A, and that was the plan they wanted.

Plan A went into production with only small modifications and, fortunately, it was well received by the users. Sometimes a little locking-in is good. At those times we would call it "decisiveness" or "commitment to a point of view." Johnson-Laird (1993) suggested that creative eminence is not solely tied to openness to new ideas at every opportunity. Sometimes it is a conservative adherence to one's already radical point of view that promotes excellence.

The Boundaries

If self-organization is going to take place, there must be boundaries that are strong enough to prevent willy-nilly dissipation of (mental) energies. Boundaries can be observed in at least two sources: the problem definition and the social judgment process. The iterative process between the ideal creative product and the product in production is essentially a negative feedback loop, which Greeley (1986) called the *bumper dynamic*. The bumper dynamic alters the problem solution if the line of thought is straying from its goal, or otherwise not working. Apparently, many great thinkers since the Renaissance have reported the existence of such a mechanism operating in their thoughts. The boundary conditions were often rooted in the thinkers' aesthetic values. Some thinkers reported clear internal messages about the suitability of an end product, whereas others may have experienced a struggle with themselves over the judgment. Some thinkers had a strong feeling of physical effort when they have resolved the bumper dynamics conflict during the creative process, but others have not.

The bumper boundaries can originate from the problem statement itself. New products are often produced with a specific function or market in mind. There could just as easily be requirements for particular capabilities of the product, aesthetics (e.g. "cool car" versus "professormobile"), energy efficiency, production deadlines, and interim target dates. Lund (1995) reported a demonstration of the bumper or boundary principle in which he gave three groups of engineering students a different writing assignment. Group 1 was asked to write something creative on any topic they pleased during the class period. Group 2 was told to write something creative on a specific topic. Group 3 was given a topic by picking a number from X to Y; the number corresponded to a story title. They were then asked to pick an occupation randomly from a list, along with an unusual activity. Lund reported that Group 1 hated the assignment and turned in minimal material. Group 2 did not like the assignment much either, but the writing was better. Group 3 loved the assignment and turned in several pages of material.

Lund's boundary conditions might just as readily be considered "launching pads," rather than "boundaries" which have a restrictive connotation. On the other hand, if someone plans on doing some "out-of-the-box" thinking, it is important to know where the box is located.

Knyazeva and Haken (1999) observed that one type of boundary may be inherent in the work itself. That boundary is the end of a story, conclusion of a drama, or similar ending for scientific works. By knowing the ending it becomes possible to organize the preceding material. Writers operate at their preferred levels of complexity to arrive at the expected result. During the process, the writer engages a selection process to ideas that could be included. Some of the ideas are retained from those that were dredged up from the activation of semantic lattices; other ideas were left behind.

Knyazeva and Haken (1999) also observed that idea groups are subject to a trial and error process. Ideas compete for feedback from the thinker or the outside world. Positive feedback sustains the idea group and the new idea elements that it accumulates. Multiple sources of positive feedback predispose the thinker's thought system toward a blow-up regime, which is a sudden increase in potential energy. It is experienced as insight, or the "Aha!" described earlier.

GROUP PROBLEM-SOLVING DYNAMICS

So far, we have left group processes as a part of "the environment." As Fig. 6.4 suggests, however, the environment contains social contributions at different levels of activity, with the highest activity found in the social group that immediately surrounds the thinker. Group-centered studies of creativity are discussed next. The groups have been observed in real-time face-to-face conversations and in computer-assisted environments such as LISTSERV discussions and conferencing software. The computer-assisted environments are convenient because they provide a medium that records each contribution to a discussion with precise time indicators. They also represent an increasingly common medium for creative problem solving. The special phenomena associated with computer-assisted environments are considered next along with the chronicle of nonlinear dynamical contributions to the understanding of creative problem-solving groups.

Real-Time versus Asynchronous Problem Solving

The comparative study of real-time and electronic problem solving media has uncovered four new group phenomena. One is the *unblocking effect*: In real-time brainstorming groups, some participants have difficulty getting a word in edgewise, particularly if the flow of ideas is heading in another direction. Electronic media, in which communication is asynchronous, give individuals the time they need to consolidate and phrase their thoughts and post them to the group.

Another special effect is the *critical mass*. A review of group productivity studies showed that group brainstorming sessions produce more ideas than are produced by the most competent individuals in about half the occasions where such comparisons were reported. At other times, the group is not more productive that the most productive individual. Some of the disappointing behavior of groups can be explained by whether tasks and rewards were defined for groups or for individuals; social loafing was another explanation (Shepperd, 1993). Dennis and Valacich (1993) found, however, that a critical number of group members is needed to gain an advantage for groups using computer media.

A variation on the critical mass hypothesis is the *group knowledge hypothesis*. The group knowledge hypothesis is that the group's performance level is determined in part by the combined knowledge level of group members, and that this relationship is moderated by a group's conflict management approach, and resource composition (Zornoza, Prieto, Marti, & Peiro, 1993). Resource composition in this context referred to whether the group members could produce a majority or plurality decision. A majority decision would be one that is preferred by 50% or more of the decision makers. A plurality decision would be an option that is preferred by more decision makers than any other option, but no option has 50% of decision makers' preference. Zornoza et al. tested these hypotheses with a series of 34 groups who performed a complex optimizing decision task in which there was a "best" answer. The groups worked either face to face, through synchronous time e-mail, or through video-conferencing. Support was found for the group knowledge hypothesis; r^2 for the effect varied between .22 for face-to-face, .18 for e-mail, and .14 for video-conferencing. Thus, the communication method was an important moderator, and thought to be the result of the different numbers of communications channels operating in each of the experimental conditions. There was a little support, however, for the hypothesis that participants' conflict management skills would moderate the resource-performance relationship.

The third major phenomenon pertains to *channels of communication and filtering*. The moderating effect of channels on the resource-performance relationship was noted above. Walther (1996) noted, however, that the *filtering* process that takes place in virtual group (real people whose communication and work products occurs solely through a computer network) communication has an advantage. According to Walther, the filtering of social content was overstated in several earlier studies, because friendships and romances do form in virtual media. Rather, the anticipation of continued interaction predisposes individuals to act in a friendly and cooperative manner. Unlike what often occurs in contrived experiments, participants can prepare outgoing messages without the stress of interpersonal interaction (p. 24), and because of the time asynchrony, task and interpersonal messages can become disentrained. It is also noteworthy, however, that the social remarks increase in cases where there is no limit to amount of participants' communication time (Walther, Anderson, & Park, 1994).

The fourth special effect pertains to the *natural formation of large discussion groups* on the Internet. That phenomenon is discussed in Chapter 7.

Group Members Generate Feedback Loops

It has been suggested that electronic media are catalyzing the self-organization of a collective intelligence (Guastello, 1998a; Guastello & Philippe, 1997; Mayer-Kress, 1994; Smith, 1994). If that were true, it should be possible to locate chaos dynamics prior to such self-organization. Indeed, Contractor and Siebold (1993) used simulation techniques to determine "boundary conditions under which groups reproduce, sustain, and change existing structures" (p. 535). They noted further that such structures apparently change in a punctuated equilibrium fashion. Structures would be produced in part by the group's expertise in the use of the decision support system, and the group's perception and awareness of norms. "Structures" implied conversational behaviors of very general varieties. Some common examples of "norms" were the quality of the thought product, quantity of production or apparent effort, civility of social interaction, and use of gatekeeping initiatives when participants' behaviors exceed a desired norm.

Their simulations were based on the quadratic logistic map function such that change in the time spent contributing (order parameter) was a function of the expertise contributed by the other participants and the norms. The quadratic function was capable of producing constant, cyclic, and chaotic activity clusters. The simulation results showed different phase portraits for participation time depending on prior expertise with the decision support system, presence of prior norms, and intensity of training between the sessions of activity.

Contractor and Siebold's (1993) findings were corroborated to a great extent by a separate line of research that involved actual problem-solving behavior. My analysis of a LISTSERV conversation (Guastello, 1995a, Chapter 10) showed that the quantity of individuals' output did change over time throughout a discussion according to a logistic map function:

$$\Delta z = \mathrm{f}[cx_1(1 - x_1)] = \beta_0 + \beta_1 C z_1 + \beta_2 C z_1^2 + \beta_3 P z_1 + \beta_4 P z_1^2, \quad (6.3)$$

where the function between the brackets is the standard representation of the logistic map, z is the length of a person's response in a conversation (statistically corrected for location and scale), and C and P are control variables (Guastello, 1995a, p. 323). C is *cumulative elapsed response*, which is the quantity of contribution by others that occurred in between consecutive responses by a single person. P was personal response style, which was essentially a "garbage can variable" containing individual differences in output levels that were not otherwise accounted for. Both C and P were responsible for the bifurcation effect. There was, furthermore, a global linear trend whereby C at Time 1 predicts a participant increasing output at Time 2.

Equation 6.3 deviates from the usual logistic map in that the criterion is Δz instead of z_2; the first attempt to test model used z_2, but it did not work out. The implication of the substitution is that the potential function for this creative process is a cubic rather than a quadratic. A new interpretation of my previous results has recently come to the foreground. It now appears that the underlying process is more similar to the biotic equation that Kauffman and Sabelli (1998) described. The bifurcation variable (cumulative elapsed responses) actually works backwards compared to the usual expectation from the logistic map: As the elapsed responses become greater, the bifurcation *closes* instead or opens. This phenomenon appears to be unifurcation that is generated for critical regions of the biotic function. Figure 6.10 is another example of the unifurcation that was observed in a similar new LISTSERV discussion (Guastello, in press).

In another effort, conversations among three small groups of problem solvers (with real, rather than simulated problem objectives) were studied over a period of approximately 100 days (Guastello, 1998a). The medium was electronic with ASCII communication through some specialized conferencing software. The amount of total output from each group per day was recorded, and fluctuations over time were analyzed for dynamic content. Figure 6.11 shows the density for each of the conferences; *density* was defined as the number of responses generated by the participants in a 4-day time period. Group 1 contained three discussants, Group 2 contained seven, and Group 3 contained eight.

It was determined that the groups' production over time was chaotic, and simultaneously driven by a second periodic dynamic. Equation 6.4 was obtained for density over time:

$$Z_2 = e^{(0.25 z_1)} + 0.43A - 0.26C - 0.34, \quad (6.4)$$

where, z_i is density at two consecutive observations in time, A is the number of active threads during the time interval of z_1, and C represents conference differences

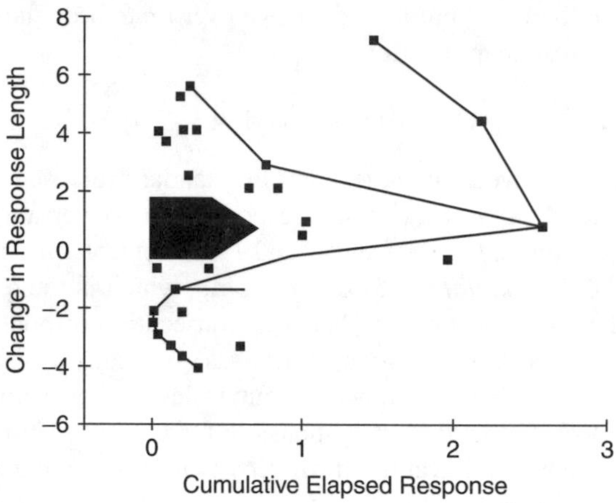

FIG. 6.10. Scatterplot of changes in response length in Experiment 1 as a function of the cumulative elapsed responses between two successive contributions of one participant. The solid dark area represents a very high density of points. Contours are hand-drawn to represent the possible location of the underlying bifurcation set.

($R^2 = .57$). The exponent to e was positive, indicating chaotic behavior and a dimensionality of 1.28. Conference differences were measured as a three-value effect-coded variable indicating the overall quantity of response from each conference; some discussion forums, which are combinations of topics and people, generate greater quantities of discussion than others.

The periodic function was the number of discussion threads, A, that were operating on a given day. The greater the number of threads, the greater was the total group output. Plots of the active numbers of discussion threads for each conference appear in Fig. 6.11. Equation 6.5 was obtained for the change in the number of threads over time:

$$A_2 = 0.75 A_1 e^{(-0.36 A_1)} + 0.33. \tag{6.5}$$

The exponent to e was negative, indicating that the function was not chaotic; the dimensionality of the time series was 1.70 ($R^2 = .73$).

Orbital Decomposition of Conversation Patterns

The latest frontier of creativity dynamics research has focused on the content of the messages in a conversation for purposes of isolating the social characteristics of the creative problem-solving process. Examples of social characteristics were the General Participation and Especially Creative Participation that were discussed

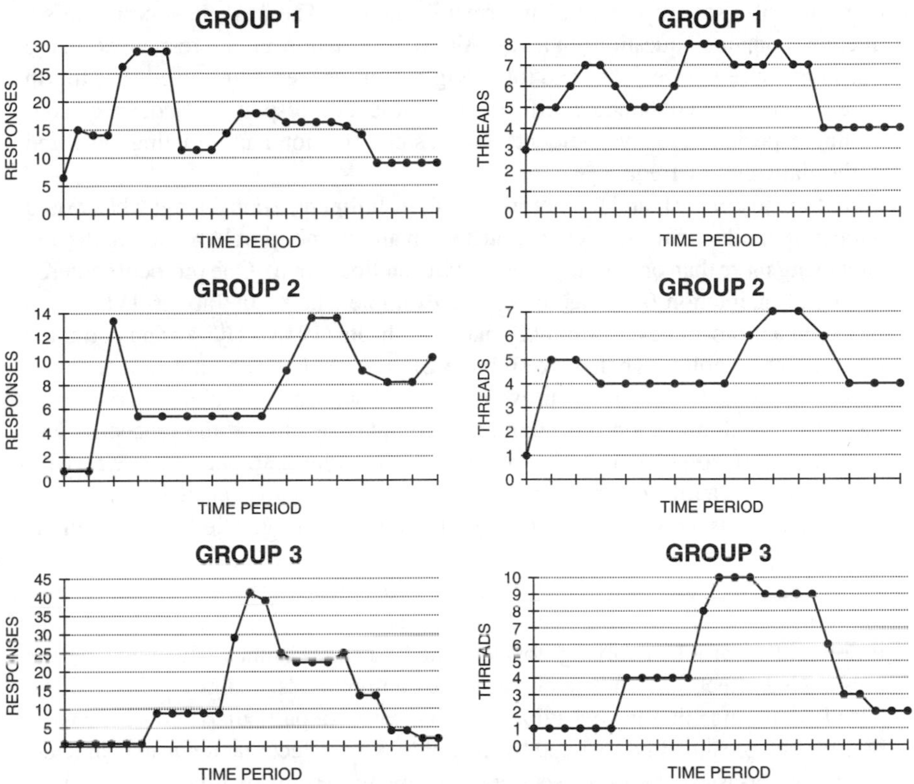

FIG. 6.11. Data from creative problem-solving groups at the edge of chaos. *Left panels*: Time series of group response density for each of three conferences. *Right panels*: Number of active threads for three conferences. From Guastello (1998a, pp. 50–51); reprinted by permission of the Creative Education Foundation.

earlier in the context of Fig. 6.3. Guastello, Hyde et al. (1998) analyzed a string of over 500 responses in one of the real-time problem-solving sessions (a game of Island Commission). Participants' responses were coded in one of nine possible types of input: requesting information, giving information, tension reduction, clarifying responses and ideas, gatekeeping, initiating, following, harmonizing, and unclassified responses. The response series was analyzed by the orbital composition technique, which captures the topological entropy of a series and its Lyapunov exponent for response strings of varying length, along with a statistical indicator of fit.

We found that sequences of four responses emerged that could not be reduced to the simple effects of combinatorial probabilities. The 528 observed four-item sequences could be reduced to 79 sequences that appeared more than once, and reduced again to four major conceptual categories. The most common sequence consisted of a steady stream of information giving. The next most common sequences contained questions in a 1:3 ratio to information-giving responses. In the third type of sequence, jokes and following responses were introduced. The fourth type of sequence contained clarification requests and responses. Sequences containing especially creative elements, such as clarification and initiating, occurred with relatively low frequency.

In the most recent, and temporarily final, installment, I considered what would happen if similar analyses were conducted on an Internet problem-solving discussion using more than one coding scheme (Guastello, 2000a). One protocol centered on social interaction (same as the earlier example, shown in Table 6.1) and was based on a protocol developed by Benne and Sheats (1948). The second pertained to problem completion behavior (Table 6.2) and was based on a protocol developed by Hirokawa (1983). Data were analyzed with a hierarchical variation of the orbital decomposition procedure; this complexification of the procedure was necessary to accommodate each response having more than one possible conversation code. As a rule, contributions to an Internet discussion can be longer than in real-time, and as a result, the opportunity to hit more conversational contributions increases.

The principal findings were as follows. First, there was a greater prevalence of clarification and initiating (particularly creative) behaviors compared to a real-time creative problem-solving episode; they were presumably liberated by the unblocking effect that tends to characterize computer-assisted group discussions. Clarification and initiating behaviors were indicative of particularly creative contributions and presumably liberated by the unblocking effect that tends to characterize computer-assisted group discussions. There were some qualitative similarities and differences between the results, for example, of the electronic group and the real-time group studied by Guastello, Hyde et al. (1998). For the electronic group, the string length was shorter, however, with two Social Interaction elements per string compared to four in the real time conversation.

Second, there were complex responses containing up to five conversational elements in the case of Social Interaction scoring system. These vectors of responses presumably resulted, in part, from the unrestricted length of an electronic group participant's posting to the discussion. An attempted monologue, even if fascinating in content, would likely be interrupted during its delivery to a real-time group, if only by other participants asking questions. Again, the extensiveness of the finding concerning the complexity of responses has yet to be determined.

Third, the two different scoring protocols produced different indicators of string length and entropy. The problem solution protocol data resulted in sequences of three responses instead of two responses for the Social Interaction protocol. Thus, the generalizability of these structures and the content of specific response strings are uncertain at the present time, but they are certainly the topic of future research on conversation patterns, creative and otherwise.

TABLE 6.1
Types of Social Interactions

Nominal Value	*Description*
1	**Requesting information**. An ordinary question or a statement that information of some type is needed.
2	**Giving information**. Statements of facts that were often of a technical nature.
3	**Tension reduction**. A supportive or morale-boosting statement or a joke.
4	**Clarifying responses and ideas**. A statement clearly intending to give further meaning in statement made by another participant or by the same participant.
5	**Gatekeeping**. Statements about what topics or approaches will be used by the participants or what topics will not be included in the conversation.
6	**Initiating**. A participant initiates a stream of discussion or appears to have started on a solution to one part of the problem. Initiating is often followed by a following response.
7	**Following**. Statements either made explicit reference to an idea given by another participant, or quoted passages were shown with cascaded passages from statements made by another participant.
8	**Harmonizing**. One form of harmonizing is an attempt to defuse a conflict between two other participants. Another form is for a player to state positive feelings about the group or its progress.
9	**Unclassified Responses**. Responses that do not fit any of the above categories or that were uninterpretable from the transcript.

Futuring

Futuring is a concept given to the activity of "creating new visions of the future." It is a gainful occupation of creative spirits in some scientific and philosophical circles. The development of future visions is critical to the future evolution of an organization, a group of people. Like the more specific group discussions described hitherto, future vision involves realities and semantic lattice structures that are shared by a great many people (Hardy, 1998).

For instance, the Foundation for the Future summoned a group of scientists with known futuristic proclivities to a real-time conference to discuss possible scenarios for human civilization in the year 3000 (Inayatullah, 1999). The group discussed the possibilities of a more diverse living system on the planets that would include chimeras, cyborgs, robots, and biologically created slaves. The philosophers cautioned that ethical thinking needs to evolve alongside scientific thinking if we want to prevent the future from being dictated by "Saturday Night Laboratories" that operate without regulation. Other scenarios of the future they considered involved space travel, contact with extraterrestrial intelligence, and new and different boundaries between the human and silicon aspects of collective intelligence.

A shared reality has the potential for selecting ideas that are consistent with it in much the same manner as a metaphor does for the individual thought process. At

TABLE 6.2
Types of Problem Completion Behaviors

Nominal Value	*Description*
1	**Orientation.** Comments and questions for understanding the problem, the purpose of the problem solving activity, or what qualifies as an acceptable solution. If an orientation remark occurs in the middle or later portion of the discussion, it could reflect a partial redefinition of the problem.
2	**Problem solving.** Information giving and requests for information, elaborations, or clarifications of earlier statements or contributions. Requests for clarifications without critical comments. Does not mean the same as giving a [new] argument to defend a position that was challenged by one or more of the other participants.
3	**Conflict.** Contrasts of point of view concerning solutions or approaches to solutions. Critique and evaluation of ideas that have been proposed. Includes remarks that "[something] does not make sense." Can include critique or second thoughts about one's own ideas.
4	**Decision emergence**. Expression of support or agreement for concluding ideas that have been expressed (as opposed to agreement about an approach). Support needs to be more specific than "interesting;" should say more about the correctness or viability of an idea.
5	**Social remark**. A social pleasantry often occurring in conjunction with task-oriented remark. Jokes and wisecracks are included here even if they are not accompanied by any other form of contribution during the utterance.
6	**Gatekeeping.** Remarks about what is pertinent to the discussion, agreements, or disagreements about pertinence.

the collective level, however, a collective metaphor is likely to shape the thinking of a great many individuals simultaneously. There is no guarantee that a concocted vision is futurism grounded in realism, futurism grounded in wishful thinking, or a return to the past portrayed as a wishful future.

The Foundation group, according to reports, was trying to consider as many viable alternatives and options as possible from the vantage point of the present point in history. It would be counterproductive to foreclose on (lock in) any particular scenario too soon. Too many of the unknowns are unidentified. In any case, the "critical" impact of the vision is neither good nor bad for a work group or organization, but it is critical to what could happen next. We return to the construction of future visions in Chapter 12.

SUMMARY

This chapter built a nonlinear dynamical theory of creativity that began with the sources of idea elements, traced dynamical processes by which thinkers rearrange and combine the elements with which they are working, and ends with creative work products. A simple subset of processes applies to individuals, and processes of greater complexity arise when the creative work is a group effort. The dynamical theory builds on the current state of knowledge concerning creativity and its relationship to divergent versus convergent thinking, personality, and cognitive styles; the style constructs include a process known as chaotic cognition. The nonlinear dynamics build on chance-configuration theory.

Chance-configuration theory initially explained how idea elements flow from enriched environmental sources to a thinker's mental space. It relied heavily on chance occurrences and did not allow much of a role for individual originality. Idea elements self-organize somehow the basis of a creative end product. Nonlinear dynamics research has later found, however, that nonlinear deterministic process account for what used to be called "chance," and that "chaos" more accurately characterizes the flows of idea elements through the creative process; $1/f$ distributions can be observed in some situations as well.

The aspect of the theory that describes what happens between the thinker's ears is based on the development of semantic lattices, verbal cognition research pertaining to lattices, and mathematical simulations on the percolation of fractal lattices. Idea elements are organized into lattice structures. Lattices are formed though conventional learning, implicit or incidental learning, and the broader mechanisms of assimilation and accommodation. Although people share some significant chunks of lattice structure, lattices are ultimately individualistic in their constructions. Idea elements are combined as the thinker moves flexibly around his or her lattice structures, thus forming new associations among idea elements. It is during this process that the originality of a creative product is introduced.

Self-organization dynamics occur in several ways. (a) The accommodation of new ideas promotes a reorganization of the lattices. (b) During the early phases of thinking process, the pursuit of several lines of thought converges into a target idea in a manner similar to a blow-up regime. (c) A metaphor is constructed by which a partial analogy is observed between the problem that the thinker is trying to solve and a new configuration of idea elements. (d) There is a self-selection of new ideas that are, on the one hand, consistent with the operating metaphor, and which provide some elaboration or missing details. (e) The problem constraints create boundary effects, which govern the criteria of a "good" solution and shape the completion of the creative work.

The last section of the chapter considered the role of groups in creative problem solving. The concept of an enriched environment now includes other capable problem solvers. Brainstorming among the group members is facilitated by computer-based media. Effects such as unblocking, critical mass, and channels of communication and filtering were identified and discussed.

The logistic map was thought to be a model for change in individual output as a function of contributions by other people. As such, a greater likelihood of chaotic idea flow would be expected as more contributions from other problem-solving participants are received. The latest work on the topic, however, suggests that, although individuals produce more output if they receive more input from other participants, the dynamic trend is toward unifurcation, rather than chaos; a biotic equation might be a better model.

If we were to make observations on an entire group over an extended period of time, different dynamics come to the foreground. Group output is chaotic, and driven by the number of threads or subtopics active in a conversation. We can also examine patterns of conversation style over time and extract patterns of social interaction or patterns by which a group moves from problem definition to problem solution. Future studies could consider how patterns from different groups would exhibit volatile or rigid patterns of interaction, and why.

7

Social Networks

This chapter explores the dynamics that underlie social networks, where individuals are the elementary components. Basic network concepts are presented first, which are then followed by a summary of recent thinking about the dynamics related to the formation and growth of a social network, its size, and its stability. In one example, we consider the case of networks that form on the Internet for purposes of information exchange and sporadic creative problem solving. The population dynamics that were inherent within formation of the network were the most poignant feature of the phenomenon.

Although most of the basic psychological research on networks pertains to networks of individuals, networks of organizations can be studied from the same framework. It appears that organizational networks can be easier to study because change does not occur as quickly as it does among individuals, and there are often objective indicators of network alliances to work from, such as the production of patents jointly held by two or more organizations. Thus, the first dynamical study of organizational networks appears in this chapter for the first time. The chapter begins by backing up a few paces to consider some important dynamics for dyadic relationships.

THE NATURE OF SOCIAL NETWORKS

A social network is a set of individuals, or possibly groups or organizations, that communicate with each other in some fashion. The limits of some networks may range in firmness from rigid boundaries to permeable and diffuse ones. The concept of social networks was first introduced by Bevales (1948), and the study of networks, or sociometric analysis, was augmented greatly by the graph-theoretical contributions of Harary, Norman, and Cartwright (1965). Networks themselves are represented as geometric configurations, or geodesics, that show the placement of each communicator relative to others in the network with connections drawn among those members of the network who communicate directly.

Two of the classic configurations, which have historically appeared in numerous organizational behavior texts, appear in Fig. 7.1. The star configuration shows one central person with others radially distributed. The pentangle shows the same number of people who are capable of N-way communication. These and other configurations, when taken in combination, represent the formal and informal communication patterns in organizations and any hierarchies that are involved. Efficient nonhierarchical organizations can be composed as well (O'Neill, 1984; this point is expanded in Chapter 10).

Network information is valuable for understanding sources and destinations of messages and elements of distortion that might occur along the way, such as those that might occur in social or work group processes. They might also serve as the basis for the engineering of industrial work processes, telecommunications equipment design, or the location of transportation hubs (Freeman, 1979; Kantowitz & Sorkin, 1983). They have had some value for uncovering "organized crime" activities (Kantowitz & Sorkin, 1983), understanding communities, markets, social change (Wellman & Berkowitz, 1988), job mobility (Levine & Spedaro, 1998), and the transactions within and between discussion groups on the Internet (Wellman, 1997) as well.

The content of communication could be as important for understanding emerging networks as the raw quantity of communication. For instance, Bales and Cohen

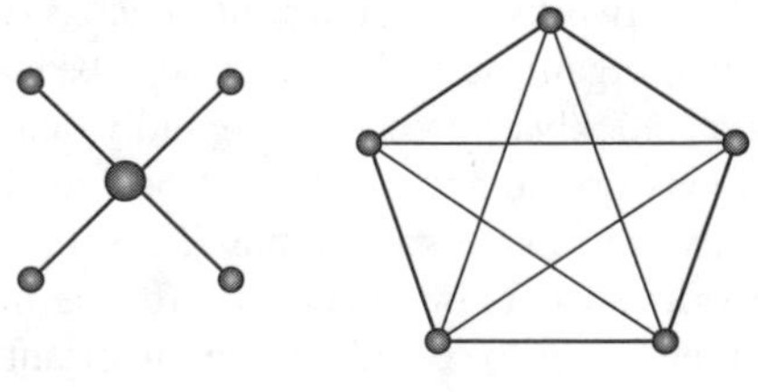

FIG. 7.1. Communication patterns for five people arranged for minimum (*left*) and maximum (*right*) interaction among group members.

(1979) classified communications within a three-dimensional taxonomy of dominant versus submissive, friendly versus unfriendly, and emotionally expressive versus controlled. These parameters of communication, in combination, could lead to cohesive (and probably cooperative) or polarized (and probably competitive) groups (Axelrod & Hamilton, 1981; Flache & Macy, 1997).

Some points in a network are more central in the communication flow within the network, while other are more peripheral. Such a distinction is perhaps most clear in the star network configuration in Fig. 7.1. Concepts of centrality are of particular interest in this study, and three varieties of centrality are explicated in this chapter.

Indices of Centrality

Freeman (1979) noted that many mathematical models for the centrality of a point within a network had been offered in the previous 20 years. After eliminating redundant and overly complex varieties, three concepts of centrality emerged that were based on principles of degree, betweenness, and closeness.

Degree is the depth to which a point is interwoven with other points in the network. It is a function of the number of adjacent points to any particular point, or $a(p_i, p_k)$, which is relative to the total number of possible links that an organization could have given the size of the network (n). Thus, centrality degree, *CD*, for a point (p_k), is (Freeman, 1979, p. 221):

$$CD = \left[\sum_{i=1} a(p_i, p_k)\right] \Big/ (n-1), \tag{7.1}$$

where n is the total number of organizations in the network.

Betweenness is the extent to which a point gets in between any two other communicating points. A betweenness indicator, *CB*, for a point, p_k, is (Freeman, 1979, p. 223):

$$CB = \sum_{i<j}\sum (g_{ij}(p_k)/g_{ij}), \tag{7.2}$$

where $g_{ij}(p_k)$ is the number of geodesics linking p_i and p_j that contain p_k, and g_{ij} is the total number of geodesics in the network.

Closeness is the extent to which a point enjoys the minimum number of points between itself and each other point in the network. It is actually an inverse function of decentrality, such that $d(p_i, p_k)$ is the number of edges between a point p_k and all other points. The closeness indicator, *CC*, for p_k, is (Freeman, 1979, p. 225):

$$CC = (n-1) \Big/ \sum d(p_i, p_k). \tag{7.3}$$

NONLINEAR DYNAMICS FOR NETWORKS

Systems that are in a state of chaos eventually self-organize into structures that are more stable. There are several mechanisms of self-organization, but common to all of them is the flow of information among subsystems (Haken, 1984, 1988; Kauffman, 1993, 1995). These flows are responsible for the development of positive and negative feedback channels, emergence of hierarchies, and driver-slave relationships. The nature and type of information flow has received a good deal of attention in social psychology and elsewhere, and theories of social exchange, games, and networks have all addressed one or more aspects of information flow.

The theory of social networks progressed substantially in the last two decades through its integration with theories of social exchange (Blau, 1967) and game theory (Axelrod & Hamilton, 1981). In the case of social exchange, each link in a network graph represents a form of exchange between two actors. The exchange may consist of similar or different psychological commodities. In task groups, the exchange might consists of approval for approval, or perhaps approval for task compliance (Flache & Macy, 1997). In friendship ties, however, a bit of time is required for a link to fully establish. A link will form if the friendship initiation attempt of one actor is reciprocated by the other (Zeggelink, Stokman, & van de Bunt, 1997).

Smith and Stevens (1997) introduced a motivational component to network formation among individuals. Motivation to affiliate takes the form of arousal, according to 1950s social-psychological theorists (Atkinson 1964, Cartwright & Zander, 1960; McClelland et al., 1953; Schacter, 1959). When two people affiliate there is an arousal reduction, which is mediated by the endorphin mechanism. Biological roots of this process can be traced back to mother-infant attachment and bonding. Once an affiliative link has been established, a set of four feedback loops form for arousal and arousal reduction within and across the two participants.

How do linkages form in an organized, or perhaps a chaotic, social milieu? According to Galam (1996), people interact a bit like atoms. Galam noted that although the metaphor is only partial, there are a couple of elements of similarity. Something akin to temperature occurs in the social environment that causes the people within to bounce around faster as molecules would do within a container. Random contacts occur until a drop in entropy occurs when the right pairwise combinations of people or atoms are found.

Smith and Stevens (1997) observed furthermore that, unlike the molecule analogy, additional people can join the aggregate until a group is formed. The extent to which the human aggregate grows might depend on context variables such as the complexity of the task or activities involved, the type of relationship between individuals and the groups, and whether competitive exclusion is part of the ground rules of the relationship. Additionally, individual differences in the *desired* number of friends can affect the growth of networks in terms of size or density (Zeggelink et al., 1997).

Dyadic Relationships

Once two people find that they have something in common, the forces of approach–avoidance and cooperation–competition then ensue. In the particular case of romantic relationships, the time evolution of the relationship can be volatile or not, depending on the strength of the attraction and propensity toward avoidance. Figure 7.2 portrays a time-evolution of dyadic relationships developed by Levinger (1980). The couple first goes through a phase of increasing exchange with each other. At some point they reach an unstable saddle, at which they rethink whether they want to continue the relationship or separate.

In Fig 7.3, Rinaldi and Gragnani (1998) model the phase portrait of the mutual attraction for robust and fragile couples. For robust couples, there are simple rather than multiple saddle points. Rinaldi and Gragnani's model was based on a historical and well-documented relationship between Petrach, a 14th century Italian poet and Laura, a beautiful but married woman. The relationship had numerous ups and downs—enough to generate many years of poetry. When he became too demanding, she fended him off to protect her marriage. Hence, the lower panel of Fig. 7.3 reflects a dynamical zone that characterizes normal stable relationships, as in the upper panel, and a lower saddle region reflecting the times of their relationship when they keep a much greater distance from each other.

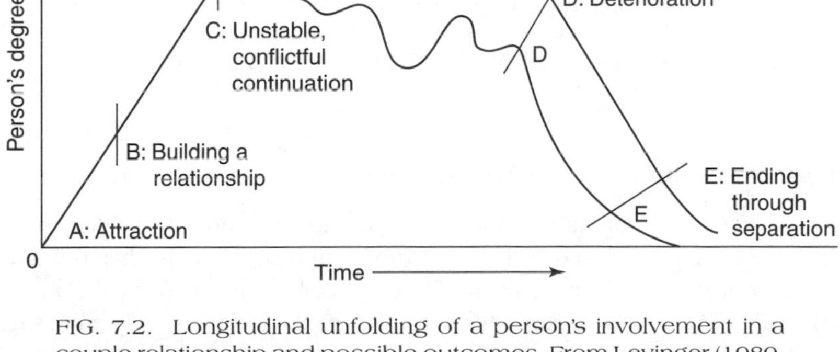

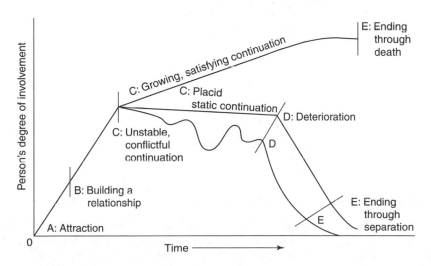

FIG. 7.2. Longitudinal unfolding of a person's involvement in a couple relationship and possible outcomes. From Levinger (1980, p. 522); reprinted by permission of Academic Press.

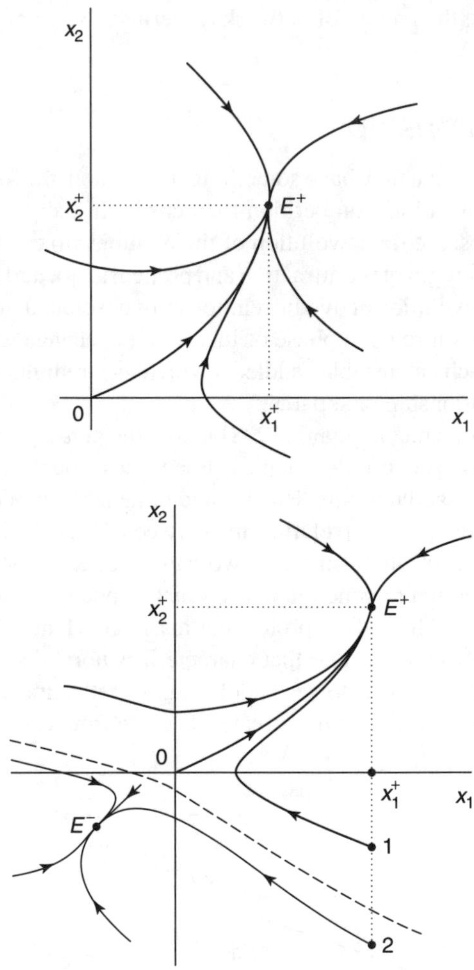

FIG. 7.3. Evolution of the feelings in a robust couple (upper) and in a fragile couple (lower) for different initial conditions. From Rinaldi and Gragnani (1998, p. 291); reprinted with permission of Human Sciences Press and Kluwer Academic Publishers.

Large Problem-Solving Groups

Computer-mediated communication can facilitate the work of problem solvers within one organization, and at the same time, unite people with shared interests from many organizations in the form of "virtual communities." Virtual communities now appear to grow in a pattern consistent with the bandwagon dynamics from game theory and population growth functions. A recent comparative study evaluated several models that were thought to be applicable to virtual community growth data: the fractal dimension extracted from the inverse power law, the Lyapunov dimension extracted from the exponential nonlinear regression modeling technique; two approaches to the identification of a fixed point attractor; population dynamics containing a bifurcation effect; and the analysis of critical points. The results showed that the population growth trend was clearly an application of May–Oster dynamics. The R^2 for that nonlinear regression model was .99. It was substantially higher than the R^2 indicator for other models, although there was some support for the other interpretations (Guastello & Philippe, 1997).

Two critical points in the growth of the virtual community were discovered. The first was a saddle located in the neighborhood of 546 subscribers. The second was an asymptotic fixed point in the neighborhood of 725 subscribers. Critical points were determined by plotting expected changes in population as a function of initial population, using the empirically derived population dynamics function; see Fig. 7.4. The data points shown in Fig. 7.4 are scaled in statistical moments and scaled such that negative change (Δz) scores represent population growth, rather than decline. Growth crossed the 0 point on Δz in two places corresponding to $z = 1.0$ and 1.2. The z scores are corrected back for location and scale to raw values of 725 and 546 subscribers, respectively. Growth was relatively swift up to the saddle. Afterwards it slowed as it continued its way toward the fixed-point attractor. Growth then hovered in the 725 region, although population size did start to edge beyond 800 when the data collection ceased.

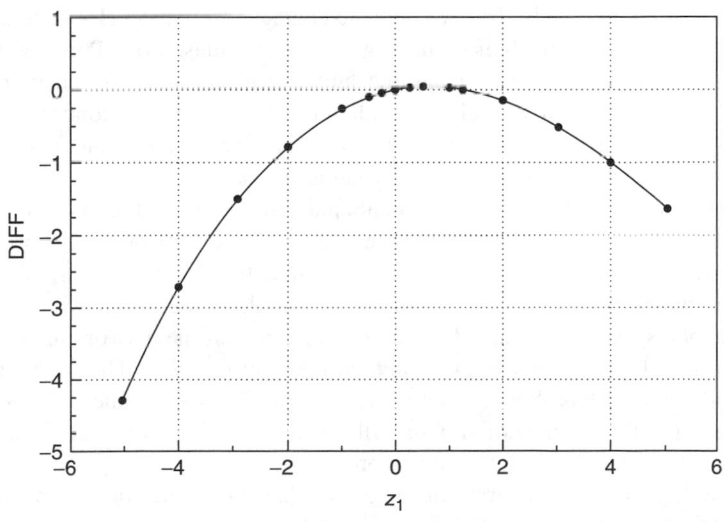

FIG. 7.4. Plot of change in population (DIFF) of a virtual community as a function of initial population. From Guastello and Philippe (1997, p. 144); reprinted with permission of Human Sciences Press and Kluwer Academic Publishers.

ORGANIZATIONAL NETWORKS

Organizations can form networks also, and their purpose may take the form of supplier chains or product–market collusion. It has been suggested that a dynamical self-organizing process underlies the formation of organizational networks (Borges & Guastello, 1996; Kauffman, 1995) although an explicit empirical analysis of an actual process has not been generated yet. That, indeed, is the subject of this study. More specifically, the goal of the following study was to examine the nonlinear dynamical processes in the formation of a network of organizations.

The following study proceeds from a study of the linkages among organizations within the telecommunication, computer, and semiconductor industries operating in Europe (Duysters, 1996). Duysters charted the growth and density of the three industry networks over three epochs: 1970–1977, 1978–1985, and 1986–1993. The linkages were based on the number of patents jointly held by two or more organizations during a time epoch. The goals of the present study were as follows.

The first goal was to examine social network generally, and the networks of innovating organizations specifically, for the possible sources and roles of information and entropy. The principles of information and topological entropy are useful for formulating hypotheses that involve the literal application of self-organization concepts to the formation of networks, communities, and other interacting social aggregates such as creative problem-solving activities; the highlights of that work were presented in the previous chapter.

The second goal was to express the growth of the networks as a nonlinear dynamical function that is already known to characterize the development of population sizes and the growth of virtual organizations (Guastello & Philippe, 1997). More highlights of that work appear in a subsequent section of this chapter.

The third goal was to examine the relationship between the concepts of centrality, which emerged in the context of social network analysis and exponential growth of networks in the population dynamics sense.

The fourth goal was to develop a mathematical model for the development of networks that accounts for the principles stated above plus one other principle, which is the joining, or dropping out, of an organization from a network. Classical network studies have been largely confined to bounded situations in which the roster of actors is fixed, or bounded, during the life span of the network under study. Real world networks, however, vary in their boundary rigidity. The cusp catastrophe model, which has shown some value for describing personnel selection and turnover within an organization (Guastello, 1982b, 1987, 1995a, and Chapter 5), was considered here as a plausible outcome.

The fifth goal was to illustrate an integration that is forming among three critical social theories: social network analysis, game theory, and social exchange theory. Nonlinear dynamics and self-organization theory, particularly as they apply to evolutionary processes, are common to those social processes already. One would expect, therefore, that nonlinear dynamics would introduce the final catalyst for theoretical integration. The broad theoretical linkages are considered below after an exposition of the more specific principles of centrality in social networks.

The basic concepts for networks can be extrapolated to networks of organizations. The active participants in an industry often make it their business to learn of each other's presence even if business relationships are not imminent or immediately sought. Informal contacts among people with common interests in independent interaction venues can increase such mutual knowledge and possibilities for formal business transactions. The growth of virtual communities on the Internet has been cited (Pickering & King, 1995) as an important catalyst for such interactions, which are not controllable from the vantage point of the formal internal mechanisms of any one business.

Indeed, extensive networks of weak linkages are often the best sources of news and technical information (Constant, Sproull, & Kiesler, 1997). They can expand more easily that dense networks because the threshold between "in" and "out" is relatively low. Guastello and Philippe (1997) argued, furthermore, that the dynamics for joining a network can be expressed as a bandwagon game. As a general rule, a bandwagon occurs when the cost of joining an activity decreases as more players join the activity. In the case of network growth, the two players are a particular person who is contemplating joining the group (or network) and the group itself as a unitary player. Participation by either the individual or collective may be low, moderate, or intense. The extent to which the information flow is positive for an individual, relative to the cost of involvement, predicts increases in network members. Information flow, assuming that it is relevant to individuals' needs, is greatest and more varied when networks are larger.

Banks and Carley (1997) noted that several mathematical models for network formation have been advanced over the years, but they share common assets and limitations. "[I]n order to test theories of change . . ., the researcher must generally capture data before the group reaches equilibrium. . . . [E]xperience suggests that external factors often intervene well before the simplicity of asymptopia is attained. Nonetheless, our analysis suggests that the closer the group is to this final state, the more indistinguishable key models become" (pp. 228–229). Several questions may be posed to nonlinear dynamics: How can the growth of a network of organizations be represented within a lexicon of dynamical structures known to pertain to similar situations? What is the essence of entropy? How are dynamical properties of organizational networks related to notions of centrality?

The medium for an empirical study centered on networks of organizations in the telecommunications, computer, and semiconductor industries. Linkages were determined by the presence of joint patent ownership; thus the network under study is concerned with innovation linkages. Although joint patent ownership is not representative of all possible types of links, they are important in their own right. Patent linkages show how organizations cooperate to produce technical items of mutual economic interest. Several factors probably contribute to the formation of links: the organizations are interested in similar products or problems, have comparable technical innovative competence, or make complimentary contributions to a joint effort. In the latter case, collusion is easier than making the object oneself, or collusion could be a move to forestall a competitive product.

The method for orbital decomposition (Guastello, 2000a; Guastello, Hyde et al., 1998) is an ideal place to begin modeling the formation of networks in light of its emphasis on linkages and communication. Consider a network of linkages among N organizations. Transform (mentally) to a matrix of $N \times N$ organizations where each cell entry is binary representing the presence or absence of any joint patents between organizations. The entire diagonal would be empty unless an organization was allowed to link to itself, meaning that it would generate patents without collusion with other organizations. Topological entropy (equivalent to information level) would be the base-2 log of the sum of diagonal entries. Thus, the initial entropy of an organizational network is a direct function of the number of individual organizations holding patents.

The foregoing only specifies a level of entropy at a given point in time, although in the empirical analysis that follows a "point" in time is an interval of 5 years. Thus, the volatility of a network is only partially related to the number of patent-holding organizations. A system of N^2 linkages contains diagonal entries whereby an organization links with itself. This situation is easily satisfied by an organization with a solo patent. Solo patents are interesting in their own way, but they are not contributing to a network. Thus, the concept must continue further so that the linkages themselves become the axes of the matrix of N^2 linkages at Time 2 versus Time 1. Persistent linkages would show up on the diagonal, and topological entropy would be again be a direct function of the sum of binary diagonal entries. Topological entropy computed in this fashion would be equivalent to the (largest) Lyapunov exponent (Guastello, Hyde et al., 1998; Lathrop & Kostelich, 1989).

A problem arises, however, when the process of composing matrices is continued over time. The time horizons for collecting linkage data require years instead of minutes or days. The number of linkage matrices that would be required to show any patterns that could be extracted from the orbital decomposition procedure would require an impossible length of time. A desirable solution would be, therefore, to redefine the function in terms of a more tractable process. At the same time it would be good to use the information about the *number* of linkages associated with any one organization. Information about the number of linkages per organization can be lost in the binary symbolic dynamics analysis; it might be reintroduced as a set of binary codes corresponding to an essentially continuous variable.

Thus, the measure of topological entropy associated with the changes in a network of organizations (or any other elements) as they occur over time would be defined as follows. Equation 3.19 is a nonlinear regression model that captures the Lyapunov exponent as a function of the number of links in the networks:

$$z_2 = \theta_1 \exp[\theta_2 z_1] + \theta_3, \tag{3.19}$$

where z_i is the number of links associated with an organization taken at two points in time, and corrected for location and scale. The expressions θ_1 and θ_3 are constants introduced to enhance the goodness-of-fit, and θ_2 is the Lyapunov exponent. If it is a positive value, the system is undergoing a chaotic expansion. If it is a negative value, the system is gravitating toward to a stable, saturated population size and linkage density.

Equation 3.19 is the simplest model in the series of exponential regression models for ascertaining Lyapunov exponents and dimensionality and other dynamical structures in data. The bifurcation Equation 3.20, allows some organizations to enter the network and not grow links to other organizations, while others could drop out of the network because of ordinary failure or by virtue of being absorbed by a larger organization:

$$z_2 = \theta_1 z_1 \exp[\theta_2 z_1] + \theta_3; \tag{7.20}$$

the strength of a bifurcation effect is denoted by the size of θ_1. Equation 3.20 is essentially a May–Oster population model; it was shown to be a close fit for the development of a virtual organization composed of individual members (Guastello & Philippe, 1997). Within this structure it is possible for a network of organizations to reach an asymptotically stable level of size and saturation of linkages or dissipate and die out.

A third model of potential relevance to the growth of organizational networks is the cusp catastrophe. Its mathematical origins (Thom, 1975) are separate from those underlying topological entropy, but similar concepts are involved, nonetheless. Equation 2.24 is a polynomial function for discontinuous change between two stable states; a repellor, or separatrix separates the two stable states:

$$df(y)/dy = y^3 - by - a, \tag{2.24}$$

where y is once again the number of links between an organization and another other organization in the set, b is the bifurcation parameter, and a is an asymmetry parameter. The application of the cusp model to organizational networks is analogous to the application of the cusp for personnel selection and turnover. The two stable states would be whether the organization stabilizes within the network or drops out of it. The response surface would be defined by the statistical equation:

$$z_2 - z_1 = \beta_0 + \beta_1 z_1^3 + \beta_2 z_1^2 + \beta_3 b z_1 + \beta_4 a. \tag{3.11}$$

The bifurcation and asymmetry parameters could be composed of more than one variable. Bifurcation and asymmetry variables would describe some of the properties of the network itself, differences among industries or markets, and differences among the organizations themselves.

In this study, it was of particular interest to study the extent to which these three indicators of centrality were related within a network of organizations and the extent to which the centrality indicators might be governed over time by the dynamics of network change and development. Thus, the first two hypotheses were:

1. There would be substantial correlations among the three indicators of centrality for a given network of organizations.

2. There would be substantial correlations between the three indicators of centrality and the raw number of links emanating from one network member. The raw number of links would form the basis of measurement for network growth.

The next three hypotheses concerned the dynamical structure of the networks. Verification of these hypotheses would be a matter of degree as determined by the R^2 associated with the statistical models, and the significance tests on the particular elements in the models.

3. Because the formation of a network was thought to be a process of self-organization from a chaotic state, the degree of entropy associated with the network would be represented by a positive Lyapunov exponent and a dimensionality of approximately 3.0. The degree of fit for the model in Equation 3.19 would be greater than that associated with a linear relationship between the number of links at two points in time.

4. Because of the potential for structural instability associated with organizations growing into the network and leaving the network, it should be possible to determine the presence of a bifurcating structure in the growth of links. Thus, the degree of fit for the model in Equation 3.20 would be greater than those associated with Equation 3.19 or a linear relationship between the number of links at two points in time.

5. If the inclusion or exclusion of an organization in a network is actually bi-stable, as suggested by the personnel selection concept, the cusp catastrophe model should show a good fit to the linkage data. The cusp model is a cubic polynomial, which is consistent with the expectations from Hypothesis 3, and contains a bifurcation structure, which is consistent with the expectations from Hypothesis 4. Thus, the degree of fit for the cusp model in Equation 3.11 would be greater than those associated with Equations 3.19 and 3.20, or a linear relationship between the number of links at two points in time.

In order to conclude some generalizability of the results of the foregoing hypotheses beyond one network, the hypotheses were tested on data comprised of networks of three related industries: computer manufacturing, telecommunications, and semiconductor manufacturing. Industry can be used as a categorical (nominally scaled) variable with two degrees of freedom.

6. If the control variables affecting the cusp process were related to the specific dynamics of an industry (one of the three studied here), dummy coded variables representing industry should make significant contributions to the cusp control parameters in Hypothesis 5.

Data

Network data for this study was initially published in Duysters (1996, pp. 167–182) for three European industry networks: computer manufacturing, telecommunications, and semiconductor manufacturing. Network data showed the number of organizations, linkages, and for three points in time. A linkage in this context represented the presence of a patent that was jointly owned by two organizations. Although Duysters' network analyses did show the presence of multiple link between two organization, only one link per pair of organizations was considered in the computations used here. Network diagrams for the computer industry are shown in Fig. 7.5 as an example.

The three time intervals were 1970–1977, 1978–1985, and 1986–1993. An organization was considered as part of its industry network for all three periods of time if it appeared at least once in the network diagrams. The distributions of subsample sizes and linkages are shown in Table 7.1. The total number of organizations appearing in any of the three temporal epochs in the three industries was 196. The overall standard deviation of links was used as the estimate of the scale parameter in the nonlinear analyses. The location parameter for links was 0.00 in all three time periods.

The three measures of centrality (*CD*, *CB*, and *CC*) for these networks were provided by Duysters (1996). Hypotheses concerning linkages were tested at Time 3, where the variability among organizations was greatest.

Results for Linear Correlations

Bivariate correlations among the three measures of centrality, number of linkages at time 3, and the number of linkages at Times 1 and 2 appear in Table 7.2. Calculations were made for all 196 organizations together, and for the subset of 88 organizations that showed nonzero links at Time 3. The results showed, when all organizations were considered together, that there was a substantial correlation between the simple number of links associated with an organization and the *CD* indicator of centrality. The relationships between the simple number of links and *CB* and *CC* were also strong but not as large. The correlation between links at Time 2 and Time 3 ($R^2 = .04$) served as the comparison benchmark for the linear model against which to compare the nonlinear models. These correlations all dropped when only the subset of 88 organizations was considered. The correlation between *CD* and links at Time 3 was the most buoyant, however.

A multiple regression analysis was calculated to determine the combined relationships between the measures of centrality and links among organizations at Time 3. The R^2 for the three independent variables was .79 ($F_{3,192} = 246.57$, $p < .001$). Weights for all three measures of centrality (CB: $t = -2.33$, $p < .05$; CC: $t = 3.40$, $p < .001$; CD: $t = 16.60$, $p < .001$) were significant when all three variables were forced into the equation. These results showed that *CD* and

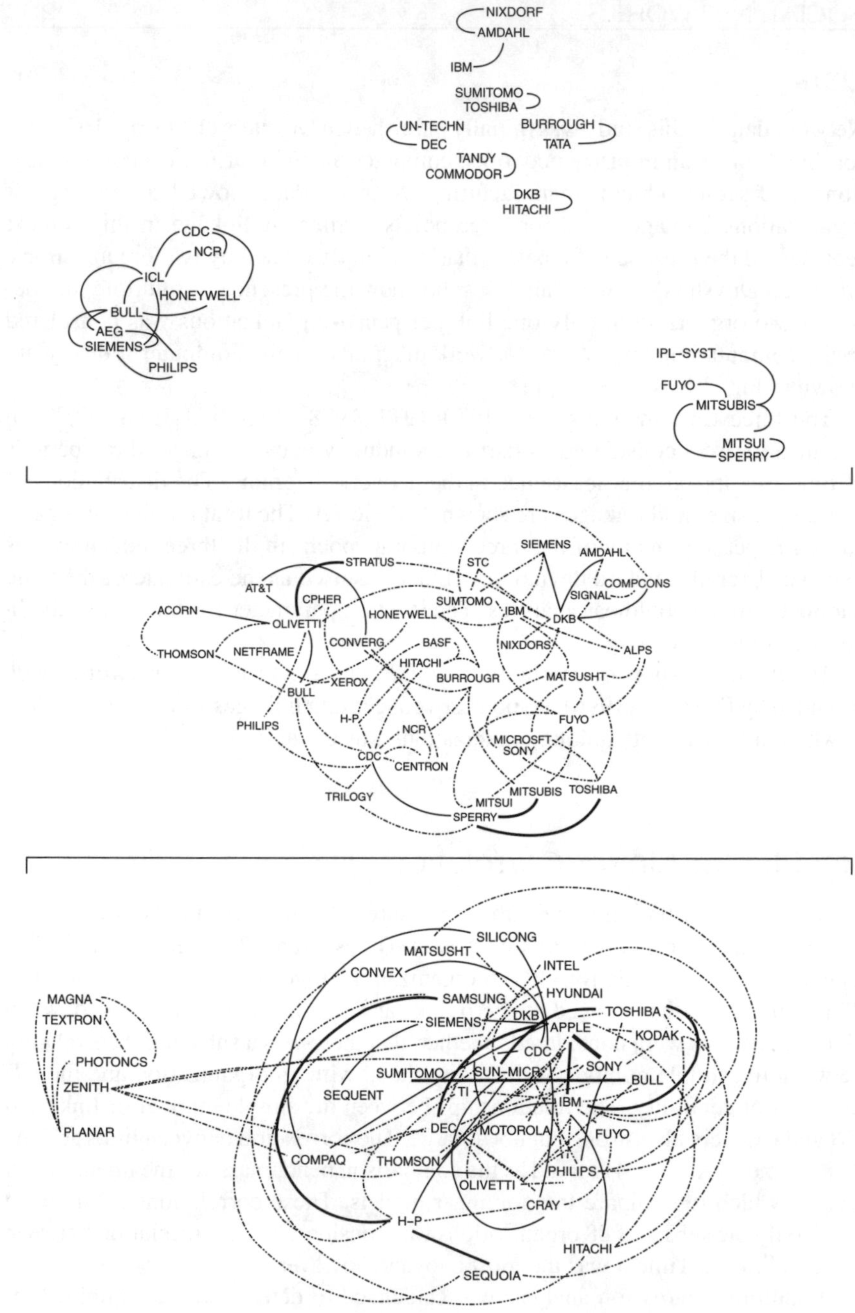

FIG. 7.5. Evolution of alliances in the computer industry 1970–1977 (top), 1978–1985 (center), and 1986–1993 (lower). From Duysters (1996, p. 167, 170, 171); reprinted with permission of Edward Elgar Publishing Limited.

TABLE 7.1
Raw Numbers of Organizations, Mean and SD of Links in all Three Time Epochs

Organizations	*Time 1*	*Time 2*	*Time 3*
Computer, number	26	38	34
Telecommunications, number	15	39	39
Semiconductor, number	16	37	38
Mean number of links	0.55	2.90	3.70
SD of links (scale)	1.04	3.15	4.13

TABLE 7.2
Bivariate Correlations Among Critical Variables

	Link-3	*CD*	*CC*
N = 196 organizations			
Links at Time 1	−.07		
Links at Time 2	.20**		
CD	.88**		
CC	.63**	.62**	
CB	.63**	.76**	.60**
N = 88 cases that showed nonzero links at Time 3			
CD	.76**		
CC	.01	.06	
CB	.42**	.61**	.24*

Note: CD = Degree, CC = Closeness, CB = Betweenness.
$^{*}p < .05$, $^{**}p < .01$.

CC increased as the number of links increased, but the growth in *CB* tended to lag behind the growth in *CD* and *CC*.

The additional of *CB* and *CC* into the regression model did not extend R^2 beyond what was obtained for *CD* alone, however. Thus, it was possible to say that the number of links was adequately represented by the Degree indicator alone.

Results for Nonlinear Models

The nonlinear regression analysis for Equations 3.19 and 3.20 produced R^2 values that were less that .01 for Time 1 links predicting links at Time 2. Thus, there was virtually no prediction of the network evolution based on the first time frame. The results were better, however, for Time 2 link predicting links at Time 3. The following results were obtained for Equation 3.19 with $R^2 = .12$:

$$z_3 = 0.24 \exp[1.15\, z_2] + 0.73. \tag{7.4}$$

Weights for θ_2 and θ_3 (but not θ_1) were significant at $p < .05$. The dimensionality, D_L, associated with a Lyapunov exponent of $+1.15$ is $= \exp[\theta_2] = 3.16$.

The results for Equation 3.20 were only nominally better, however. The same value of R^2 was obtained, although the weights for all three regression coefficients were significant at $p < .05$:

$$z_3 = -3.82\, z_2 \exp[-0.74 z_2] + 3.43. \tag{7.5}$$

The cusp catastrophe model (Equation 3.11) was defined to test the hypotheses that the underlying control parameters were dependent on the dynamics of a particular industry. Two dummy coded variables represented the computer manufacturing and semiconductor industries. Both of them were tested as bifurcation and asymmetry variables. The regression equation for the cusp showed a significant t test on all four combinations. The overall R^2 of .70 was substantially higher than those obtained for other models of network growth that were tested here ($F_{6,189} = 73.05$, $p < .0001$); the detail of significance tests appears in Table 7.3.

Discussion

The foregoing analyses produced some interesting findings, which are interpreted next in terms of the original hypotheses. As anticipated in Hypothesis 1, there were substantial correlations among the three indicators of centrality. They shared 36 to 58% of variance indicating that they were all approximating a common underlying principle. On the other hand, 42 to 64% of variance was in disagreement.

As anticipated in Hypothesis 2, there were substantial correlations between each of the three measures of centrality and the number of links associated with an organization. Thus, all three centrality measures were somehow the result of, or predecessors to, the density of an organization's linkage. *CD* was the most closely associated indicator, and interestingly, *CC* and *CB* did not contribute any additional prediction to the number of links.

The simple correlations between organization's links at two points in time were relatively low. There was no prediction at all between an organization's link from

TABLE 7.3
Significance Tests for the Cusp Model
of Organizational Network Formation

Element of the Model	t
Links, cubic	9.41***
Links, quadratic	−13.52***
Bifurcation, computer	−2.24*
Bifurcation, semiconductor	3.67*
Asymmetry, computer	2.22*
Bifurcation, computer	−1.98*

*$p < .05$, **$p < .001$, ***$p < .0001$.

the time of the earliest epoch of the network's development to the Time 2 period. Once the network had formed somewhat at Time 2, however, it was possible to obtain some prediction of an organization's link with a linear model. The strength of the linear model was $R^2 = .04$, which did not compare favorably to the nonlinear models.

The remaining hypotheses concentrated on the number of links rather than measures of centrality, although it is understood that link density and centrality are related. Hypothesis 3 concerning the exponential model and the D_L was supported. The simple exponential model was more accurate ($R^2 = .12$) than its linear alternative. The D_L value of $+3.16$ indicated that the system trajectories were chaotic, and of a complexity similar to the cusp catastrophe. The exponential model containing the bifurcation factor, which was tested in Hypothesis 4, offered no predictive advantage with respect to the number of links, compared to the simple exponential model.

The cusp model, which also contains a bifurcation structure fared substantially better than the two exponential models ($R^2 = .70$) in Hypothesis 5. The efficacy of a cusp hypotheses depends to a great extent on the quality of control variables that are tested as part of the model's control parameters. In this case, the two industrial group membership variables were associated with both control parameters; Hypothesis 6 was thus supported. A strong bifurcation effect for an industry would indicate that it was subject to greater growing and dropping of links over time, compared to the industry represented by the default value of the dummy variable set. A strong asymmetry effect would indicate that the fluctuations are biased toward growth or dropping of links over time. At present, it is not possible to state what aspects of the three industries' existence were responsible for these effects, but they are present nonetheless.

SUMMARY

This chapter considered the growth of social networks beginning with dyadic relationships. If the attractiveness of the two individuals to each other is relatively symmetrical, the progress of the relationship is one of increasing social exchange until a saddle point is reached. At the saddle point, the relationship may dissipate or proceed further toward asymptotic stability. The dynamics become more complex, however, if the attractiveness between the parties becomes asymmetrical. Virtual communities grow in the same pattern of increase (in numbers), saddle, and progress toward asymptotic stability. The growth of such communities can also be understood as a bandwagon cooperative game and as a May–Oster population growth function.

Several pieces of information have now been learned about organizational networks, and probably network behavior more generally. (a) Measures of centrality and network growth share an interest in number of links as a critical criterion of network system behavior. (b) The growth in network density is at first highly unpredictable with the models that have been tried thus far, but then it becomes chaotic once it has self-organized to a limited extent. (c) The dynamics of network growth were best represented by the cusp catastrophes, of the three models that were tested. The cusp contains a bifurcation manifold, which effectively sorts organizations into those that will continue to be plugged into the network and those that are "out of the loop." (d) Control variables in the cusp process appear to be related to events that differ across industries. The industry-specific events have not yet been identified explicitly, but they are probably linked to the nature and quantity of interactions among members of organizations within an industry.

8

Work Group Coordination

In Chapter 6 we identified a few reasons why groups might not always be more effective than the most competent individuals. The task needs to be defined as a group task rather than a task that is presented to a collection of individuals; there must be some interdependence among the group members' activities. The rewards associated with the task also need to be defined for the group. In the particular case of brainstorming groups, we found that blocking effects and critical mass effects could make the difference between ineffective and effective group efforts.

There are just as many occasions, however, when a group is more effective than an individual. To explain why that might be the case, Laughlin (1988, 1996) and coworkers (Laughlin, Chandler, Shupe, Magley, & Hulbert, 1995; Laughlin & Futoran, 1985; Laughlin & McGlynn, 1986; Laughlin & Shippy, 1983; Laughlin, VanderStoep, & Hollingshead, 1991) have developed a theory of collective induction. In this context, groups would be more effective than individuals because they can examine information more thoroughly. Groups also have the potential to retrieve errors more reliability, rely on skills and knowledge bases from a greater number of people, and make a true solution to a problem (usually of the convergent, optimizing variety) apparent to each other. The process of making an optimal decision apparent to other members, or the "truth wins" process, is only possible in cases where there is a verifiable solution to the problem. When the group members disagree, they resort to techniques such as randomly selecting an alternative from the available proposals, voting, taking turns among the proposals, actually demonstrating the superiority of an alternative, and generating new emergent alternatives. This chapter covers some additional group performance phenomena, which involve coordination. The United States military appears to have recognized the special need for coordination through its regular scheduling of military exercises that involve large quantities of personnel. One may glibly dismiss these adventures as simply examples of learning and training, but to do so does not explain the psychology of what the operations personnel were learning. During World War II, the military introduced three acronyms to describe possible maneuver outcomes. The acronyms have become part of common language: the *snafu* (situation normal, all fouled up, used as a noun or adverb), the *fubar* (fouled up beyond all recognition, used as an adverb or noun), and the less well-known noun, the *janfu* (joint army–navy foul up).

At present it does not appear that psychological theories of group behavior have adequately addressed the fu-family of group behaviors, which are all about coordination. Recently, there have been some good starts, however, and the major push forward comes from an integration of game theory and NDS. The first section of this chapter unpacks the distinctions between coordination and phenomena that look similar on first blush. The second and subsequent sections describe the contributions of game theory, implicit learning and NDS. Following are the results of some recent experiments that illustrate the core phenomenon, the particular role of verbal, as opposed to nonverbal, communication, and what happens when personnel are replaced in a coordination task. The chapter concludes with some thoughts about the coordination among social institutions.

THE SOCIAL PROCESS

Group *coordination* occurs when two or more people take the same action, or compatible actions at the same time (Friedman, 1994). Coordination is vital to group effectiveness in situations where a successful outcome for the entire group is the end result of numerous contributions or efforts by all group members and where successful contributions by one participant are contingent on a correct and timely contribution by another participant.

Coordination is a phenomenon distinct from group *cohesion*, which the extent to which group members "stick together" as a group of people (Zander, 1994). The two are probably related, but that relationship is left to future research. Both are related to the quality or amount of work performance of groups. Group coordination is not social loafing. *Loafing* is a situation in which members of a group are supposed to share the work and share the rewards, but some people end up doing far more work than others (Latané, Williams, & Harkins, 1979). Coordination and loafing are actually connected by way of game theory, but they represent different phenomena.

Coordination among team members has been recognized as an important correlate of team performance (Bowers, Bakers, & Salas, 1994; Brannick, Prince, Prince, & Salas, 1995; Brannick, Roach, & Salas, 1993; Cannon-Bowers & Salas, 1998; Cannon-Bowers, Tannenbaum, Salas, & Volpe, 1995; Coovert, Campbell, Cannon-Bowers, & Salas, 1995; Dailey, 1980; Leedom & Simon, 1995; Stout, Salas, & Carson, 1994). Coordination has been operationalized in some cases by an observer's ratings of the team members' communication patterns (Brannick et al., 1993; Dailey, 1980). In other cases, coordination was negatively defined by the amount of time one team member spent waiting for another member before engaging in a joint effort (Coovert et al., 1995).

In the simulations that have been conducted so far, these measures of coordination have not been consistently linked to group performance. On the other hand, it is not clear how important coordination is in every team work situation, or whether it takes more possible forms. Bowers et al. (1995) suggested, however, that job analysis ratings could be used to determine the extent to which coordination is required in different work situations.

Walker and Dooley (1999) developed a simulation to analyze situations that require coordination. They worked from the vantage point of information flows, which in turn induce patterns of self-organization within a system. At the most general level, situations can be distinguished with regard to their levels of centralization or decentralization of task executions. Centralization or lack of it is in turn the result of four other system properties: *Throughput* or *fluency* is the "tendency to pass signals through with one input held constant." *Memory* is the "sensitivity of the present behavior to [its] previous self-state." *Homogeneity* is the "overall similarity in output state" (p. 16). As we will see later on in this chapter, coordination involves rules that organize the activity. In a heterogenous system, there would be different possible rules in place. *Autonomy* is the extent to which a rule is actually guiding the system outcomes.

The complexity of the system states becomes greater as the number of players increases, according to Walker and Dooley (1999). Furthermore it is important whether all members can interact with equal probability, or whether there is a management function that controls their relationships. Another feature of coordination is the length of time that a system can run without interruption; this is the system's cycle length. Cycle lengths are longer if the system has a means to prevent errors from creeping in. Systems are more stable if their cycle lengths are longer. System outputs can become unstable, however, if members have unequal likelihood of making errors.

Several other authors have noted the importance of good communication in different ways (Brannick et al., 1993, 1995; Cannon-Bowers & Salas, 1998; Dailey, 1980). Xiao, Patey, and Mackenzie (1995) found that breakdowns in coordination within hospital emergency rooms could be traced to two groups of faults. One group of faults consisted of interruptions of task flow. The interruptions arose from conflicting plans, inadequate delegation, diffusion of responsibility, or inadequate support. The other group of explanations consisted of verbal communication faults.

Group cohesion, on the other hand, is the sum of forces acting on group members that maintain their participation in the group, such as cooperation and help giving, mutual psychological support, interpersonal attraction, commitment to the task, and group pride (Mullen & Copper, 1994; Zander, 1994). There is a consistent trend in the empirical research showing that cohesion is an important contributor to effective group performance (Evans & Dion, 1991; Mullen & Copper, 1994). The reviewers found no support, however, for the moderator hypothesis that greater degrees of interaction would promote effective performance by improving coordination and smooth operation of a group's activities (Mullen & Copper, 1994, p. 213; also Leedom & Simon, 1995). This latter finding is not surprising in light of the number of ways that communication patterns might be organized, according to Walker and Dooley (1999).

GAME THEORY AND IMPLICIT LEARNING

Game theory is a formal mathematical approach to economic behavior for two or more economic agents and the cognitive aspects of social interaction (von Neumann & Morgenstern, 1953; Zagare, 1984). Gaming experiments commonly manipulate the motivational and payoff structures available to players for their selection of options within a game. Coordination occurs when two or more players select the same option. Coordination takes on different forms depending on whether a cooperation–competition game, such as Prisoners' Dilemma, is used, or whether the game is strictly cooperative (Friedman, 1994). Two important strictly cooperative games, Stag Hunt and Intersection, are described next.

Stag Hunt and Social Loafing

In a strictly cooperative coordination game, the outcome for the group is dependent on the efforts of all members. If one member makes too little effort, or too many mistakes, the outcome for the group is reduced to that of the least effective person (Crawford, 1991; McCain, 1992; Rankin, Van Huyck, & Battalio, 2000). In Stag Hunt, all players are working toward a common goal and share a common reward if the goal is attained. Players assume the role of a hunter in a group that is trying to surround a stag. If enough hunters do not respond adequately, the stag has an opening through which to slip to evade the hunter group, and no one obtains a reward. In a 2×2 game, each hunter has the option of joining the stag hunt or hunting rabbits individually.

The social loafing phenomenon is essentially a game of Stag Hunt. Social loafing occurs when a group is supposed to be working for a common outcome; the rewards are shared by all the participants, but some people work much harder than others (Albanese & Van Fleet, 1985; Latané et al., 1979). "The social loafer, like the free rider, profits from the work of other group members without working up to his or her level of potential" (Comer, 1995, p. 649). When inequities are experienced the best workers become dissatisfied and remove themselves from such a situation if possible, particularly if the group is perceived to be functioning poorly overall (Comer, 1995).

Social loafing is likely to occur when the group is large, and when each group member does not have a personal definable role to play in the group. Under those conditions, the contribution of a single person is seen as small, and unimportant. "Why bother? What difference does it make?" One recommended antidote for loafing is to segment the group into relatively small units. Larger groups exhibit lower cohesion, and are less well coordinated by people in coordinating roles. Alternatively, one may introduce more coordinator roles, or define tasks in a way that permits individual roles, responsibilities, and contributions to overall group performance objectives at the same time. Increased individual accountability might ensure a more equal distribution of group labor (Albanese & Van Fleet, 1985).

Not all examples of differential participation from group members are examples of loafing, however. For instance, suboptimal group effectiveness may arise from inappropriate task and reward structures (Shepperd, 1993), or personality characteristics that are antithetical to working in groups on a continuing basis (Earley, 1989, 1993; Guastello, 1995a). More to the point, inferior group performance with unequal input by individuals can arise from poorly synchronized efforts of the group as a whole. Thus, the coordination phenomenon is a group-level dynamic that is not adequately characterized as a simple sum of individual inputs.

On the other hand, if the group members are not equally competent, it becomes rational for some group members to do more than other members in the long run. The point was illustrated in Stag Hunt and in other games where defection strategies pay off if one player is fully aware of the other's strategy choices (Colman & Stirk, 1998).

INTERSECTION

Intersection games resemble the behavior of automobile drivers when they approach a four-way stop situation. If the drivers perceive the correct turn-taking system adopted by the preceding drivers and follow the sequence, then all cars pass through the intersection in a minimum amount of time with the lowest odds of a collision. In a real-life intersection, the drivers could adopt any of several possible rule systems. Each driver approaching the intersection needs to observe the strategy that is actually in effect (Crawford, 1991), then makes the correct action. If the correct action is not made, an accident could occur, or at the very least, other players would need to revert to ad lib actions to untangle the confusion at the intersection.

The Intersection form of coordination is predicated on individuals learning the rules of successful sequential interaction. Learning requires effort, as in the case of Stag Hunt, but the input of effort is not sufficient in this case. The coordination of players is not localized into a separate coordinator role. Rather, the responsibility of coordination is distributed among all players. Players learn not only the task, but also the awareness of how other players' input affects their next actions.

Coordination in the sense of Intersection games would appear to explain group performance phenomena such as the improvisational flurries of a jazz band or theater group. Here the script, chart, or task is sufficiently structured so that players know what piece they are performing and where they are in the unfolding of the piece. At the same time, there are spontaneous elements that emerge whereby each performer makes a simultaneous or subsequent contribution that enhances, develops, or supports the contributions of particular soloists.

Knowing the rules of baseball, football, soccer, basketball, lacrosse, or other team sports is only the beginning of what it takes for a team to be effective. Excellence in elementary skills such as running, passing, catching, shooting baskets or goals, or subverting the actions of opposition players is also necessary but insufficient. Coordination among players constitutes a good deal of what remains.

Intersection-type coordination also appears to aptly describe the health care services provided by hospitals to inpatients. Physicians, nurses, and technicians of different specialties need to provide the right actions in the right sequence for a regular flow of patients who have individual requirements. There are additional interactions between physicians, nurses, housekeeping, and dietary staff, and whoever is responsible for scheduling people, events, and physical facilities. Successful care delivery is related to timeliness and synchrony as well as it is to individuals' skills.

As mentioned in Chapter 5, a game can be formalized as a matrix of utilities, showing the options available to each player on each axis of the matrix. Table 8.1 lists the options and utilities for the Intersection game actually played in the experiments that are reported here. The utilities of a particular pair of options are listed in each cell of the matrix for each player, separated by a comma. The

TABLE 8.1
Matrix of Utilities for the Coordination Game

		Group of Three Players		
		All Coordinated	*Partially Coordinated*	*Not Coordinated*
Target Player No. 4	Coordinated	4,4	1,1	0,0
	Not	1,1	0,0	0,0

game was composed of four players, and the options in the table are listed for one player compared to the collective action of the remaining three. Partial coordination occurred when three out of four players illustrated that they had figured out the game rule. The utilities for the individual and the group were the same, and a fully coordinated action was preferable to all players. These utilities were translated into the performance scoring and feedback system used in the ensuing experiment.

Implicit Learning

Implicit learning is essentially an unconscious thinking process that is typically coupled to an explicit learning set. Several types of unconscious learning sets that have been captured include artificial grammars and production management in a simulation of a sugar factory (Berry & Broadbent, 1988; Reber et al., 1980; Seger, 1994). Subjects would be trained in the explicit learning objectives, then tested later on the implicit objectives. Knowledge of the implicit objectives was substantially greater than chance.

Implicit learning occurs to a greater or lesser extent compared to explicit learning depending on the salience of the information to be learned and the selectivity of the learner. In many natural conditions, an implicit rule will not be any less salient than explicit information; in those cases learning is less selective. In the case of salient targets, explicit instructions to learn an implicit rule (to experimental treatment subjects) results in greater learning than that observed for control subjects. In the case of a nonsalient target, there is less learning with the explicit instruction than that observed for control subjects (Berry & Broadbent, 1988). It also appears that implicit learning sets are learned in parallel with explicit learning sets. At some point in the process, the implicit learning set becomes salient to the learner, and thus might become explicit at that time (Willingham & Goedert-Eschmann, 1999).

Coordination learning (Intersection type) has both explicit and implicit components. The explicit goal is to learn the rule by which a sequence of events should take place. The implicit goal is for team members to anticipate moves by their coworkers, read their timing signals, and execute a move at the right time and place. Therefore, it should be possible for a group to learn a coordination rule in one experimental set then learn a second rule faster, assuming an equal level of rule difficulty, in a second experimental set. This type of transfer was examined explicitly in the ensuing experiment.

Not all coordination learning involves repeated interactions among the same players. In an actual four-way stop intersection, each driver has few repeated interactions with specific other drivers. Much of the explicit learning is derived from watching others. The implicit learning is the sum of experience with other drivers and intersections, coupled perhaps with some level of expectation that the other drivers will act reciprocally. Another part of the implicit learning is knowing what patterns a driver should look for when trying to figure out what rule is in motion. For instance, three common rules are: two cars heading east–west alternating with two cars heading north–south, counter-clockwise rotation, the car that arrived first passes through first, and the car on the right goes first (standard driver's manual rule). There are other conventions that drivers adopt when trying to make left turns; left turns through congested intersections are often made by two cars making a left turn approaching from opposite directions.

Although implicit learning explains coordination learning, coordination learning is not ordinary implicit learning because learners interact with other learners. In common learning experiments, individuals learn something from stimuli presented by the experimenter who controls the presentation of stimuli. In coordinated groups or teams, each participant provides stimuli and some sort of feedback for the others in addition to the feedback associated with the explicit task. All learners in a coordination situation must be successful to some extent if any are to claim the group reward (Guastello & Guastello, 1998, p. 424–425).

In a complex job environment, coordination acquisition learning should be remembered as an element of learning that occurs in the middle of other forms of learning. First, there is the content domain. Group members should be matched for equivalence on shared mental models and job knowledge. Social skills for getting along with coworkers, leaders, or subordinates are also part of the process (Cannon-Bowers & Salas, 1998).

NONLINEAR DYNAMICS AND COORDINATION

It was mentioned in Chapter 5 that a connection exists between iterated games, evolutionary processes, asymptotic stability, and Nash equilibria. The section below explores self-organization phenomena for humans and animals, and the specific dynamics of learning. As mentioned earlier, systems in a state of chaos, or in far-from-equilibrium conditions, self-organize by building feedback loops among their subsystems. Systems thereby shape their own structures. These feedback loops serve to control and stabilize the system in a state of lower entropy. Patterns of stimuli and responses can be interchangeably understood as communication flow patterns (Bak, 1996; Guastello, 1999a; Kauffman, 1993, 1995; Haken, 1988, 1999; Prigogine & Stengers, 1984)

Local Rules in Organizations

In organizations, explicit policies and implicit cultural norms evolve to permit or require certain actions, facilitate (or catalyze) others, and inhibit yet others. Positive feedback loops facilitate growth, development, or radical change in the extreme. Negative feedback loops have the net impact of inhibiting organizational change. At times, the policies of an organization, or the cognitive processes of a human individual, will contain illogical components that make no sense to an impartial outside observer. Upon closer inspection, however, they serve the purposes of inhibiting change or challenges to the internal relationships within the organization or logical system (Goertzel, 1994; Goldstein, 1994).

Haslett et al., (2000) have proposed *local rules* theory to explain how local interactions between people and their work give rise to global patterns in work behavior. They presented an example from the Australian Postal Service wherein the post office staff observe their work load on a given day and set their work pace for the day in light of particular incentives given to them by the administration. The administration allowed them to collect a full day's pay if the whole day's work was completed before the end of the day. If they whole day's work was not completed in time, perhaps because of seasonal volume, the postal workers were allowed overtime pay plus a meal allowance.

The postal workers exhibited a bistable work pace collectively. If the mail load for a day was light, they sped up the process so that they could go home early. If the mail load was heavy, they dragged the job out until they qualified for a meal allowance, then finished. They tried to avoid days where there was exactly one day's work done in one day's time. Haslett et al. (2000) showed that the global changes in the lengths of work days followed a nonlinear dynamical process, specifically a fold catastrophe model. The stable state was the short day. The unstable state was the long one. The control parameter was the daily work volume.

The same model was replicated over five mail centers; R^2 coefficients for the nonlinear model ranged from .61 to .90. Those values compared favorably to their strongest linear counterparts, which ranged from .40 to .76.

The coordination of postal workers with respect to work pace undoubtedly involved a mixture of verbal exchanges and nonverbal observations of each other's work pace. There is reason to suspect, however, that a separation of the verbal and nonverbal aspects of the process could bring to light important new findings about coordination behavior in work groups.

Animal Model

Reynolds (1987) developed an application of self-organization that explains the flocking behavior of birds, which is a nonhuman coordination phenomenon. The formation and travel paths of flocks can be explained by a set of only three rules. (a) Avoid crowding or colliding with flockmates. (b) Steer toward the average heading of the flockmates. (c) Stay close to the average location of the flockmates.

Bird flocks function without leaders or verbal mediation. Geese, although they fly in a characteristic V-formation, do not have an actual leader. They take turns at the vertex and other positions. The role rotations represent another instance of coordination.

Similar dynamics have been ascertained for schools of fish, and animal herds. In a school of fish, the pattern of individual swimming is for fish that start on the outskirts of the school to swim inward. The fish that start toward the center, meanwhile, veer outward. This intermingling of contraction and expansion routines is characteristic of the trajectories inside a chaotic attractor. Leaderless herds follow the same regimen.

The chaotic motion has adaptive value to the school or herd: The critters on the outskirts are those most likely to be picked off by a predator. Critters that are ill cannot easily keep up the speed of the group and fall behind consistently. They are thus the ones most likely to be targeted by the predator. Those on the interior have a better chance of survival; the members of the flock or herd share the protected status.

The key finding from the animal models that is of relevance to human group coordination is that leadership or hierarchical structures are neither necessary nor sufficient for coordination. Intersection-type coordination is also closely analogous to the type of biophysical coordination that exists among human muscle groups. They too function by means of communication links and without hierarchy and (obviously) without verbal mediation (Saltzman, 1995; Turvey, 1990). This pattern was speculated as an explanation for coordination among human social agents on at least one previous occasion (Baron, Amazeen, & Beek, 1994).

Learning Dynamics

Group coordination is a form of implicit learning. In implicit learning, individuals often learn information and procedures are that incidental to some other learning objective. Implicit learning is thought to occur when group members adapt to each other's behaviors in order to accomplish some task. The ability of a team member to make an adaptive response to a suboptimal move by another team member could make the difference between a successful or an unsuccessful coordination outcome (Egidi & Ricottilli, 1998).

A new element that is introduced here, however, is that all group members are entraining on each other; thus the coordination phenomenon is a type of collective learning. As a form of collective learning, it can be considered a form of self-organization as well. Each member of the group provides feedback to all other members, which is in turn instrumental toward stabilizing a behavioral process. As the following experiments will illustrate, coordination can be learned in one situation and observed to transfer to another. Because coordination is believed to be a learned function, a group's coordination over time would increase toward a fixed-point attractor. Difficult coordination tasks would promote the behavioral signs of chaos before self-organization and the attraction to the fixed point of asymptotic stability sets in.

ORIGINS OF COORDINATION EXPERIMENT

The first hypothesis was that coordination dynamics in the sense of a group process actually exist, and that coordination is learned by the experimental subjects in a novel situation in a manner that is not mediated by leadership functions or verbal communication. The second hypothesis was that groups learn to coordinate themselves in a self-organizing manner. There would be a transfer of coordination from one rule situation to the next. Thus, when experimental groups are moved from one task to a similar task with a different but equally difficult rule structure, the learning curve for the second coordination challenge would be sharper, and the overall learning greater, than in the first learning curve.

A synopsis of the experimental data, analysis, and results appear next. Details of each aspect appear in the original publication (Guastello & Guastello, 1998).

Method and Analysis

A card game experiment for studying coordination in teams or work groups was developed from the theoretical properties of the Intersection game. Twelve groups of four undergraduates earned points by learning both the correct sequence of plays and the rule specifying the correct sequence. Game iterations were divided into blocks representing learning transfer to a tasks of equal or greater difficulty. Results of the split plot ANOVA showed, given the experimental controls that were in effect, that coordination is learned phenomenon, and distinct from other group dynamics such as cooperation, competition, social loafing, and not mediated by leadership actions or verbal exchanges. Transfer of coordination was positive to a task of equal difficulty, but less readily so to a more difficult task (Fig. 8.1).

The graph of the results shows increased performance over time as the groups learned the rules for scoring points. The learning curves are a bit battered, though, and the next step, therefore, was to look for nonlinear dynamical evidence of learning. In principle, there should be a fixed point attractor indicated where learning was stabilized. A chaotic process might be observed if the groups did not fully self-organize into a coordination regime.

The nonlinear properties of the game evolution were analyzed using the structured equation technique that was detailed in Chapter 3. In the simplest model tested, the essential tool for analyzing the dynamics of the data was the Lyapunov dimension (D_L):

$$z_2 = \theta_1 \exp[\theta_2 z_1] + \theta_3 \qquad (3.18)$$

where,

$$D_L = \exp[\theta_2], \qquad (3.19)$$

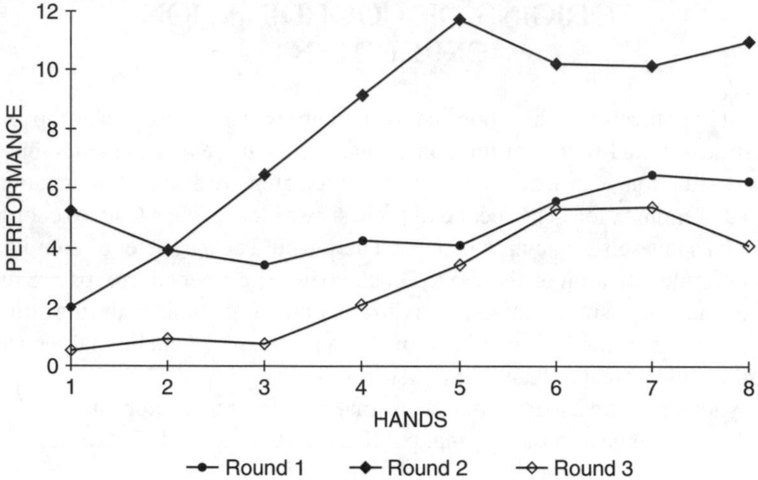

FIG. 8.1. Coordination acquisition trends for all 12 groups over eight hands of play. From Guastello & Guastello (1998, p. 430); reprinted with permission of the American Psychological Association.

where θ_2 was the critical exponent, θ_1 and θ_2 were constants (of little consequence), and z_2 and z_1 were consecutive values of our dependent measure, y, in a time series that was in turn corrected for location and scale. In this experiment, y was the performance of the group during the card game; values of y were taken at the conclusion of each *hand* of cards. There were eight hands to a *round*. There were three rounds, which were the starting task, a shift to a task of equal difficulty, and a shift to a more difficult task. In Equation 3.19, all time lapses were equal intervals, t, were thus set to the trivial value of 1.

The second model in the series is the case where there is an unknown bifurcation variable. This test for the structure was made by estimating the bifurcation variable, θ_1, as a regression parameter:

$$z_2 = \theta_1 z_1 \exp[\theta_2 z_1] + \theta_3. \quad (3.20)$$

In this case, dimension was calculated as

$$D_L = \exp[\theta_2] + 1. \quad (3.21)$$

The +1 is for the control parameter that produces the bifurcation effect. If there was a variable that could be tested as hypothetical bifurcation variable, it would be entered into Equation 3.21 between θ_1 and z_1. Again, R^2 coefficients would be compared against those obtained with linear models, or with a simple nonlinear regression model.

Resulting Dynamics

The better models contained the unknown bifurcation effect (Equation 3.21) and were adopted for further examination. Rounds 1 and 2 exhibited the negative Lyapunov exponents and the fixed point when they were iterated from different initial conditions; R^2 coefficients were .50 for the starting task and .29 for the shift in Round 2. Those values compared favorable against the benchmark linear effect of .12. D_L for the two conditions were 1.78 and 1.75, respectively.

Round 3 was the transfer to the more difficult game rule. The prediction level for Round 3 was initially low, so a search was made for the possibility of a second function lurking in the residual. The search for the second function, which has not been the usual practice in these nonlinear regression analyses for dynamics, was guided by an element of the coordination theory itself. Coordination acquisition is a form of self-organization, and self-organization is thought to underlie other forms of learning as well (Vetter, Stadler, & Haynes, 1997). If learning is incomplete, there may be a nontrivial amount of chaotic behavior in the data instead of the fixed-point dynamic that is associated with learning curves. Because the two dynamics involve exponents with opposite signs, the larger of the two functions would show up first, and must be removed before the second one can be identified and extracted.

Indeed, there was a second function with a positive Lyapunov in Round 3. The two functions together raised R^2 from .14 for just the convergent function alone to .44 when the second function was added in. Codimensionality increased to 3.11. There were no second functions in Rounds 1 or 2.

The combined function that was obtained from Round 3 was iterated for various initial conditions. When the two functions were given natural unequal weights, learning displayed an extinction curve with an asymptote at zero. When the two functions were given equal weights, however, learning declined to an asymptotic nonzero level.

A simulation was conducted to answer the last question: What would be the impact on learning if the game utilities were somehow doubled? Very different simulation outcomes were obtained for 150% inflation and 200%. At 150%, the coordination level still went into extinction. At 200%, however, a sudden positive spike in learning (or performance) was observed. Figure 8.2 illustrates the search for the critical multiplier, which turned out to lie between 194% and 195%. These results show that increasing the motivation value of the game can work wonders for expected performance.

Discussion

The foregoing experiment was devised so that the human subjects did not talk, had no prior work experience together, and did not work under any leadership influences. The experiment isolated the core features of coordination that are

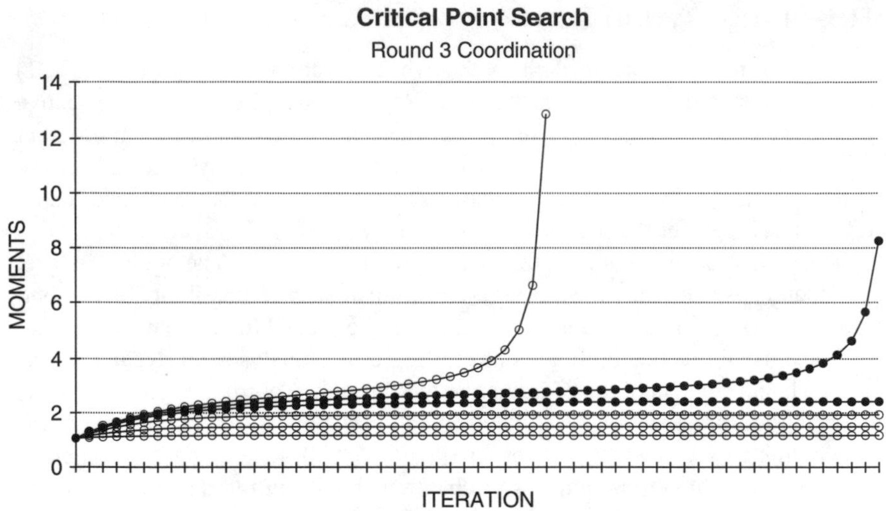

FIG. 8.2. Search for the critical multiplier effect located between 194 and 195% inflation of utilities obtained for Round 3. Trajectories closest to the critical point are designated by closed circles. From Guastello and Guastello (1998, p. 434); reprinted with permission of the American Psychological Association.

independent of leadership, verbosity, prior group history, and are thus generalizable to all coordination situations in that form. Also important was that coordination learning generalized to a task of equal difficulty. The task of great difficulty exhibited both a chaotic and self-organization component, which is what would be expected if learning was only incomplete or inconsistent across the twelve groups.

VERBALIZATION AND REPLACEMENT OF PERSONNEL

The next experiment (from Guastello, Bock, & Caldwell, 1999) used the same card game task as the one used in the previous experiment. This time, however, two new variables were manipulated. The first variable was whether the groups were allowed to talk to each other or not. The second was that some personnel were replaced after two rounds of play. The personnel exchange manipulation tested how much prior shared coordination was sufficient to maintain coordination of the group. This manipulation concomitantly captured one important aspect of a group's prior history of working together.

Data and Analysis

The card game was played once again with groups of four players. This time 12 groups were allowed to talk to each other, and 12 groups were not allowed to talk as in the previous experiment. The card game was played in rounds of eight hands again. There were four rounds this time, however. Round 1 was the same starting task as in the previous experiment. Round was the same difficult task that was played in Round 3 of the previous experiment. Round 3 here was a return to the starting task, but this time new players replaced one, two, or three out of four original players. Round 4 was a return to the difficult task with no further replacements introduced.

Equal numbers of verbal and nonverbal groups were assigned to one of three replacement conditions. In the three conditions, one, two, or three of the four players were replaced. The replacement players did not observe the first two rounds of play. Data were first analyzed using a split plot ANOVA. Fixed effects were the verbal and nonverbal conditions. Repeated effects were the four rounds and the eight hands of the game. Interactions among the four effects allow for additional hypotheses regarding interaction hypotheses: Did the ability to verbalize produce a sharper learning curve? Did the ability to verbalize compensate for the replacement of personnel? Did the number of replaced personnel compromise the transfer of coordination learning across rounds?

The ANOVA analysis showed that verbalizing groups outperformed nonverbal groups overall. Furthermore, the interaction between hand of the round and verbalizing conditions indicated that verbalizing groups displayed sharper learning curves than nonverbal groups. Verbalization did not compensate for the number of replacements, however.

Figure 8.3 shows the total coordination score for groups that replaced one, two, or three players; total scores are shown separately for each round. It turned out that a positive transfer occurred from Round 1 to Round 3, and from Round 2 to Round 4 only if one or two people had been replaced. If three out of four players had been replaced, no transfer occurred. On the basis of this experiment, 50% replacement appears to be close to the upper tolerance limit.

Nonlinear Dynamics

The same analytic strategy was used here as in the previous experiment. Verbalizing and nonverbal groups were analyzed separately here, however. For the nonverbal groups, the bifurcation model (Equation 3.20) was optimal for Rounds 1 (starting) and 4 (difficult with replacements and transfer). The R^2 coefficients were .47 and .68 respectively, and D_L were 1.68 and 1.93, respectively. The Lyapunov exponents were negative, indicating convergence to a fixed point. Note that one dimension out of 1.68 or 1.93 was associated with the bifurcation parameter, and less than one dimension was associated with the immediate dynamics of the fixed point.

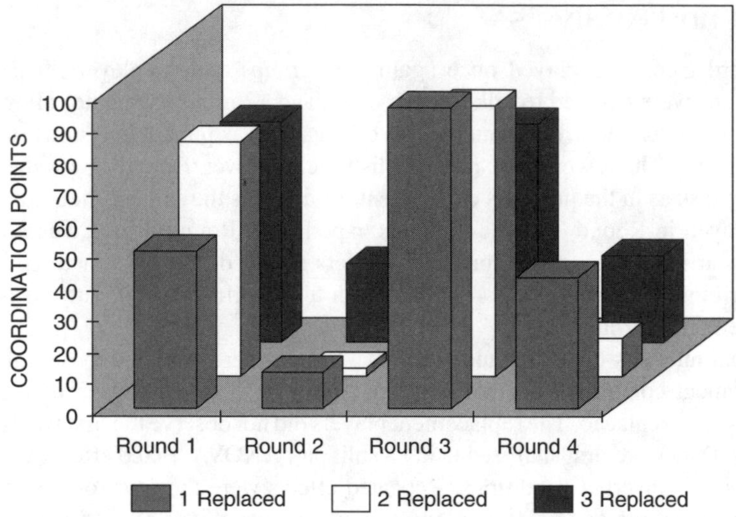

FIG. 8.3. Total level of coordination obtained over four rounds of the game for groups with one, two, or three members replaced at the beginning of Round 3.

For nonverbal groups in Round 3, however, the optimal model was a simple chaotic effect (Equation 3.20). R^2 was .37; D_L was 1.44. The foregoing values compared favorably with the linear benchmark value of .16. Neither structural model could explain behavior in Round 2; we are left to surmise that nothing was learned or even partially self-organized there.

For verbalizing groups, the bifurcation model (Equation 3.20) was optimal for Rounds 1 (starting), 3 (starting task with replacements) and 4 (difficult with replacements and transfer). The R^2 coefficients were .32, .68, and .73, respectively, and D_L were 1.53, 1.72, and 1.67, respectively. The Lyapunov exponents were negative, indicating convergence to a fixed point.

For verbalizing groups in Round 3, however, the optimal model was again a simple chaotic effect (Equation 3.20). R^2 was .27; D_L was 1.39. The foregoing values, once again, compared favorably with the linear benchmark value of .16. The ensemble of trajectories for the chaotic process in Round 3 is shown in Fig. 8.4 for both verbalizing and nonverbal groups.

Discussion

The second experiment showed that verbalization did improve coordination over and above what occurs naturally from nonverbal processes. Some generalizations are now warranted, as follows. Verbalization improves the overall result and the sharpness of the learning curve. It does not compensate for the replacement of

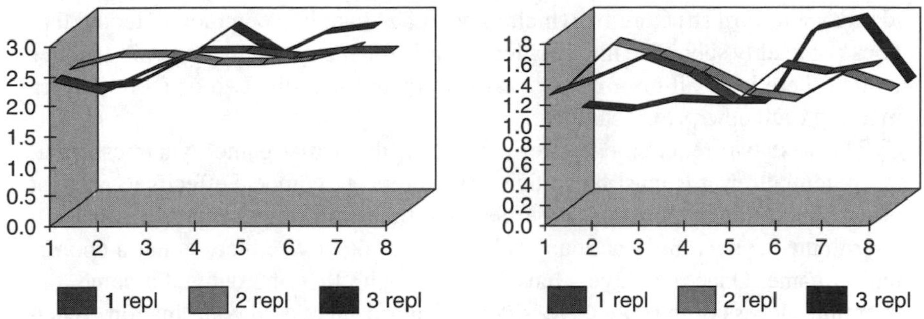

FIG. 8.4. Predicted values of coordination for verbal groups (left) and nonverbal groups (right) based on the chaotic function obtained in Round 3. Separate series are given for one, two or three replaced group members.

personnel, however. Replacement of personnel does not produce a critical disruption in coordination transfer when 25% or 50% of personnel are changed. If more than 50% are changed, however, the disruption undermines the transfer of coordination from previous task experiences.

Under conditions where learning has been relatively successful, the group performance indicator proceeds over time to its usual asymptotic maximum. There we find a negative Lyapunov exponent. In conditions where learning has been seriously challenged, a positive Lyapunov exponent is observed, which denotes that there is a deterministic chaotic process underway. In the most difficult conditions, however, the group performance is close to zero from start to finish; we observe only noise, with no dynamical structure.

SOCIAL INSTITUTIONS AND VIRTUAL COMMUNITIES

It would appear that coordination gaming would explain the real onset of a social institution, which could be a regular business organization or a nonprofit organization. The range of possible social institutions includes social service organizations that rely on a large component of volunteerism to do their work, or that rely on other agencies to provide financial grants to support the work and employ people.

The prior conditions for the onset of a social institution, in this application of game theory, would first require that two or more groups locate each other and determine that they have common interests and objectives. That is, they would experience utilities that would enhance the chances of a cooperative and coordinated activity as opposed to mutual disinterest. The second prior condition is that they identify a reward structure by which they could share in a common outcome that does not readily subdivide into smaller rewards for each participating unit. In other words, there is an all-or-none outcome associated with the two or more players meeting each other's expectations.

The next two requirements are intrinsic to the actual game dynamics. First, the potential rewards must be sufficiently large as to compete effectively against other uses of the participants' time. Second, the result must be obtained through coordinated synchronous actions of the players, otherwise there is not a coordination game. Once the players have located each other and defined a game, the eventual success of the collective is dependent on successful coordination. When these hypothetical groups engage in repeated (iterated) games, they become for all intents and purposes an institution. Literal mergers among the groups into a single organization may be forthcoming as a further means of enhancing coordination on future tasks.

There may be more than one explanation for the onset of all social institutions. For instance, governments may develop agencies or granting programs for the purposes of catalyzing coordinated efforts among groups. Even here, however, a coordinated effort as described above is still required on the part of some groups of people to administer the grant program. More coordinated effort is required from additional groups of people to do the work once the grant has been awarded. Conferences may serve the function of facilitating groups meeting groups. Here the reward structure is often intangible or intrinsic in nature. The publication of a proceedings volume may be a more tangible reward, however.

The bandwagon game has substantial implications as well. In a bandwagon situation, the utilities to each newcomer to a social aggregate increases to the extent that there is a greater number of members already participating. Similarly, the cost to each new participant decreases as the social aggregate increases. This is the utility structure that was thought to underlie the development the virtual community on the Internet that was mentioned in the previous chapter (from Guastello & Philippe, 1997).

SUMMARY

The chapter began with a summary of some known reasons why individuals can sometimes outperform groups or why the opposite could be true. The social process of coordination was then described along with patterns of information flow that could facilitate or disrupt it. Coordination was also contrasted with the phenomenon of group cohesion.

Two strictly cooperative games were described. The Stag Hunt game is a close analogy to the social loafing phenomenon, where some people in a group work harder than other people. Not all examples of differential effort are the result of social loafing, however.

The Intersection game represents a class of work activities where group members must figure out a rule that allows them to make a series of correction actions. In spite of the premium placed on communication and information flow by coordination theorists, basic coordination can occur without verbal communication, leadership, or other hierarchical structures. Very difficult coordination tasks may be facilitated by sharply increasing the utility payoff to the players.

When verbal communication is introduced, however, we do see an increase in coordinated behavior and more rapid coordination learning. Verbal communication does not compensate for coordination that is lost by personnel changes, however. It appears that a group that has already learned coordination can withstand personnel changes up to 50% of its membership. Beyond that point there is a noticeable decline in coordination.

The nonlinear dynamics of coordination comprise a transition between chaos and self-organization. When coordination is learned, it displays the dynamics of a fixed point with a bifurcation function. When coordination learning is in its early stages, the behavior pattern is chaotic.

Finally, the coordination dynamics that apply to groups can also be applied to large social institutions. However, the growth of institutions might be better explained by bandwagon dynamics.

9

The Emergence of Leadership

Management and leadership are not the same thing. Ideally, an organization's administrators would exhibit both qualities, but there is often a subtle division of labor among people who can manage well and those that inspire or harass others to greater heights. Outside the organizational context, we observe different forms of leadership in political situations and leadership in creative works or technological settings. Some of the contrasts between the different forms of leadership are unfolded in this chapter.

Several years ago, my colleagues and students perused Clark and Clark's (1990) book, *Measures of Leadership* to see how the contributors handled the distinction between leadership and management. The short answer is "not particularly well," but the results of our investigation were instructive nonetheless. Most measures of leadership reported by Clark and Clark's contributors were the results of factor analyses of performance measurements in use in various organizations. We went through the sets of factors that were given as empirical results, and we wrote a brief description of each on index cards. There were 36 cards including the duplicates. The organizational behavior students then sorted the cards into as many categories as they needed, but no more categories than what they needed.

After trimming a couple loose ends we came up with five categories of leader–manager behavior: *Ability to motivate*—This is the extent to which the incumbent motivated and developed subordinates and built a cohesive work team. *Problem solving and resourcefulness*—This is the extent to which the incumbent demonstrated competency in solving difficult problems and generating new ideas and strategies. *Communication*—This is the extent to which the incumbent kept co-workers and upper management properly informed about important matters, and the quality and clarity of communication. *Commitment to the organization*—This is the extent to which the incumbent is committed to organizational goals and policies as demonstrated by actions. We noted that any lack of commitment should not be confused with thoughtful, reasonable, or professional disagreement or differences of opinion. *Planning and control*—This is the extent to which the incumbent maintains control over his or her responsibilities and makes work plans to carry out objectives (Guastello & Rieke, 1993, p. 4).

After all that card sorting, we were still not very close to what seems to be the philosopher's stone of leadership—What is charisma? According to French & Raven (1959) charisma is closely linked to the use of two forms of power in organizations: expertise and referent power. Expertise is subject matter knowledge. Referent power is the extent to which the constituency identifies with the values and behavior patterns of the leader. Forty more years of leadership research suggested that there was still more to be learned about charisma.

There are four general ways of studying the characteristics of successful leadership. First, one can study biographies of famous leaders. Of course, the available biographical information is biased toward leaders who have been interesting enough to generate books. Second, there is the method of correlating traits with behavioral measures of leadership behavior and leadership success; for a recent compendium that includes a wide range of theoretical perspectives, see Clark, Clark, and Campbell (1992). Third, there is the training method. In the training method, people are placed in a training program that is designed around the premises of a theory, and the participants are measured on relevant behaviors before and after training. Ideally, their differences in behavior should be compared against those of a control group. All the usual discussion points regarding what constitutes a reasonable control group should be remembered here.

Fourth, there is the method of studying leadership emergence. In this scenario, a mixture of people is placed into a leaderless group situation where they are given a common task. Then magic happens, and someone is designated the leader at the end of the work period. The data analysis then determines who emerged as the leader and why. Leadership emergence scenarios are also frequently used as devices to assess the leadership potential of individuals who are candidates for promotion in large organizations.

The biographic method lends itself to some great stories, dramatic examples, and basic material from which to build theories. The latter three methods lend themselves more readily to empirical work. The studies of self-organization and leadership in this chapter were conducted within the emergent leadership modality. (Is this a surprise?) The emergent leadership medium of study can be used with almost any theory of leadership; thus it is a flexible tool for NDS studies of leadership emergence as well.

The following section of this chapter recounts some of the landmarks in leadership theory. Special attention is given to those links in the conceptual chain that have led to current thinking about leadership as a self-organizing, emergent process. Next, the theory of emergent leadership is recounted along with the results of empirical studies of nonlinear structures.

CONVENTIONAL THEORIES OF LEADERSHIP

Leadership Traits

Are leaders born or made? Leadership seems to involve a bit of both—a true example of the nature—nurture balance that developmental psychology thinks so much about, and which biographies of famous people seem to suggest. Some observers would say that there is a bit of luck involved. For instance, what if the car the hit Winston Churchill while he was crossing a street in New York had killed him instead (Schlesinger, 1988)? Other observers might point out that there is a skill to being in the right place at the right time. Comics might observe, on the other hand, that being a *perennial annoyance* is different from being a *leader*, but some people can't tell the difference.

Luck and environment notwithstanding, traits play an important role. A *trait*, strictly speaking, is a long-term enduring individual characteristic. The reality is, however, that many traits can be shaped, or the behaviors associated with the traits can be learned. Thus, we can imagine situations where some people gravitate to leadership experiences naturally, while others have to work harder to overcome their natural inclinations.

Intelligence is a relevant trait. People who fit the 16PF personality profile of leaders tend to be, on the average, one standard deviation above the population norm on mental ability, in the sense of general IQ (Cattell et al., 1970; Guastello & Rieke, 1993). In other words, leaders are smarter than 85% of the herd, *on the average*, and more intelligent than the group that they are leading. Intelligence is not synonymous with having a particular knowledge base, which may be relevant to a specific leadership situation. The catch appears to be, however, that the emerging leader only needs to be one standard deviation above the average to qualify in the minds of the constituents. Any increments of intelligence greater than one standard deviation tend to go unrecognized. On the other hand, if the constituency has an opportunity to compare people who have performed the leadership job, then differences in performance might be predicted based on comparisons with leaders of the past.

There are some consistent, or at least traditional, personality traits of leaders, as we discussed in Chapter 6. Successful leaders tend to be warm and participative, friendly and outgoing, assertive and socially bold, rule-bound and attentive to details, practical rather than imaginative, traditional as opposed to experimental, group-dependent as opposed to self-sufficient, and self-restraining rather than impulsive. Creative personalities share the assertive and social bold characteristics, but they lean toward the imaginative, experimental, independent, and impulsive poles of the other variables. Oddly, the latest wave of leadership theories is placing greater emphasis on creative input and how creativity might be enhanced in a work force (Rieke, Guastello, & Conn, 1994).

Leadership Styles

The first work on leadership styles was done in the late 1930s by Lewin, Lippett, & White (1939) who identified three distinct styles: the autocratic leader, the democratic or facilitative leader, and the laissez-faire types. The *autocratic leader* rules by persuasion and control, and typically does not solicit participation; this type of leadership is consistent with the Likert's (1961) System 1and 2 leadership, and may possibly, but not necessarily be predicated on Theory X beliefs (per McGregor, 1960). This type of leadership draws heavily on position power to move and control events. Another curiosity of this style is that the autocratic leader often interrupts workers from their tasks in projects to put them on other tasks. This technique has the effect of dissociating the worker from the task, and necessarily lowers involvement.

The group members in emergency situations often prefer autocratic style, however. If an incumbent leader is not responding effectively to an emergency situation, the group is likely to install a "stronger" (i.e., autocratic) leader. When the emergency is over, the group will be likely to expect the leader to revert to a democratic style (Hamblin, 1958).

The *democratic leader* rules by participation. The prime directive here is to use the leadership position as a means to help the group attain its collectively set goals. This type of leader pays less attention to position power and typically tries to produce an egalitarian atmosphere. Democratic or facilitative leadership is particularly appropriate when the leader does not have much position power, such as when a team of people from around the organization is brought together for a special project. Any hierarchies that could exist in the project team are very temporary at best, and may not reflect the members' "regular" organizational status.

Democratic or facilitative style is generally regarded as more effective than autocratic leadership. Objective indicators are the amount of the work accomplished, and the level of conversation about work among the group members, and general atmosphere of conviviality while work is taking place.

Laissez-faire, or permissive leadership, lets people do what they want to do. There is little direction, although the leader probably performs administrative duties adequately. The 16PF trait profile for this type of leader is inversely correlated with the general leadership profile, meaning that the laissez-faire leader is essentially not a leader at all (Sweney, 1970).

Although the permissive leadership style is generally ineffective, there are cases when it is indeed appropriate. In those situations, the work group has been together for a long time, and has ironed out its internal coordination problems long ago. They all know how to do their jobs, and not much change in taking place, either with the work or the group membership. Additional input from a leader is superfluous. One might be inclined to think that anarchy is the best policy under these conditions.

The notion of leadership style denotes a pattern of leader–follower interactions. The three styles that Lewin et al. (1939) identified do not constitute the only way of looking at leadership style. Indeed there is a long history of research on the nature and relative effectiveness of leadership styles (Zander, 1994). The transformational leader, which is considered later on, is another style concept that is gaining particular attention today. Other researchers are trying to identify other style concepts as well. According to path-goal theory (House & Mitchell, 1975), however, a successful leader is one who can invoke any of a variety of styles depending of the demands of the situation. In doing so, the leader identifies a viable path toward the group's goals and utilizes a combination of directiveness (or task structure), supportiveness (or consideration), participativeness, and achievement motivation.

Studies of communication patterns uncovered a similar theme. Fisher (1986) observed that the communication behaviors of emerging leaders are not really different from those emanating from conventional group members; leaders just tend to exhibit more of them at the right times. Similarly, Guastello (1995a, 1995b) reported that leaders of creative problem solving groups, as perceived by the peers, exhibited greater amounts of several types of contributions to a conversation—asking questions, providing information, tension reduction, clarification, gatekeeping, initiating new lines of conversation, and following others' lines of thinking. The emergent leaders simply contributed a wider repertoire of behavior than other group members did.

Structure, Consideration, and Development

The Ohio State Studies of leadership (Fleishman & Harris, 1962) began as an extensive military leadership project, although civilians were involved. The research procedure began by asking people to describe favorable and unfavorable aspects of their supervisors' or managers' performance. The free-form descriptions were boiled down to about 1,800 succinct statements about a manager. Statements were redeveloped into a questionnaire in which the respondent indicated how accurately a statement described his or her immediate supervisor. A factor analysis of the results yielded two factors: *structure and consideration.*

Structure is the extent to which the leader defines tasks for workers, gives directions, and organizes projects and affairs. *Consideration* refers to the leader's attentiveness to individuals' needs, social relationships among group members, and willingness to be flexible with rules to accommodate individual needs. Criterion-related research eventually showed that both structure and consideration were important components of work group performance, and that the two factors did not compensate for each other. Too much structure without consideration resulted in increased levels of turnover and grievances. Too much consideration without task orientation didn't get the work done.

Two questionnaires based on this research survive today, and are regularly used in leadership research along with more contemporary measurements. They are the Leader Behavior Description Questionnaire (LBDQ) and the Leadership Opinion Questionnaire (LOQ). Workers complete the former as they describe their bosses. A supervisor completes the LOQ, often as part of a management development program or as a personnel selection instrument. Blake and Mouton (1964) capitalized on these findings to produce a very popular management concept known as the Managerial Grid^{R}. Management trainees complete the Managerial Grid questionnaire, which gives them scores on two factors: *concern for the task* and *concern for people*, each on a 1–9 scale. A version of the Grid is displayed in Figure 9.1 with a third dimension that reflects a current-day embellishment, which is considered in turn below. With the two scores of concern for people (consideration) and concern for the task (structure), a manager can be placed on a two-dimensional grid as follows:

9,1: The slave driver, shows concern for task accomplishment with little attention to building relations with the work force, or for establishing a good social climate. *1,9: The country club manager*, shows great concern for social relationships. The leader hosts a great party but little is accomplished. *1,1: The do-nothing manager.* Self-explanatory! *5,5: Conventional management* usually does a little

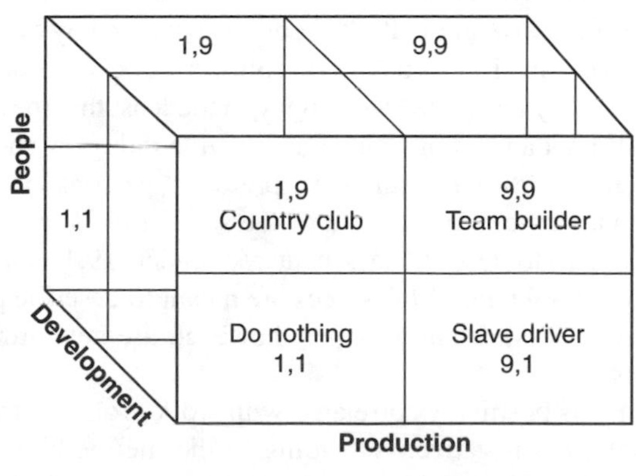

FIG. 9.1. A three-dimensional taxonomy of leadership styles showing concern for production, people, and development of personnel.

good in both areas, but generally not enough. *9,9: The team-builder*, according to the model. This is the training goal.

Lindell and Rosenqvist (1992) observed that leadership theories have focused too often on the immediate concerns for people and the task and not enough on the development of employees. The deficit is particularly acute where the team is regularly involved in the production of creative products. Thus, a developmental axis is shown in Fig. 9.1 to depict the actions of leaders that enhance the capabilities of group members to do more creative, or otherwise better, work. Further thought is given to the situational demands of leadership next.

Contingency Model

Characteristics of leaders interact with properties of the job situation to produce high or low levels of performance. Fiedler's (1964; Fiedler & Chemers, 1984) contingency theory seeks to explain why those interactions occur by utilizing the following concepts. *Leader—member relations*: Do the subordinates like the leader? *Task Structure*: Is there a clearly mapped-out way to carry out the work, or are the workers solving problems with many unique features? In the Fleishman and Harris (1962) and Blake and Mouton (1964) theories, task structure is not grossly different from concern for the task. Slave driving types tend to overstructure things and minimize the need to accommodate the needs and individual differences among the workers. *Decision verifiability*: How do we know when we've done it right? *Goal clarity*: How clear were the goals in the first place? (5) *Path-goal multiplicity*: Are there several different ways in which the problem can be solved? *Solution specificity* is the degree to which there is more than one correct solution to the problems. The *position power of the leader* is also relevant; some leadership positions do carry broad sweeping powers, while other contain all responsibility and little power to mandate events.

Finally, *Leadership style* in Fiedler's theory is measured by the Least Preferred Coworker (LPC) measure. LPC is defined as follows: Supervisors are asked to think about the coworker they have liked working with the least that they can remember. The supervisors fill out a form in which they provide ratings of the least preferred person's characteristics. Some of the least preferred persons are rated very low, some still high, and some in the middle of the scale; this is the LPC score. Low LPC scores are meant to describe task-centered leaders (9,1 more or less on the Managerial Grid^{R}), while high LPC scores are meant to describe people-centered leaders (1,9 more or less). Many scholars, however, are not sure about what the LPC score means.

Sometimes LPC is positively correlated with work group performance. Sometimes the correlation is negative. According to the theory, high performance is a combination of the four variables. High LPC leaders are desired in situations where the LPC-performance correlation is positive, and low LPC leaders are desired in situations where the LPC-performance correlation is negative. The trick is to match the leader's style with the right situation.

Although the LPC concept seems to have dissipated, other lines of research on the connection between situational variables and optimum form of leadership continue. Neuman and Wright (1999) found that in a conjunctive office work task, group performance was the result of the group's level of cognitive ability in three areas and two personality traits: agreeableness and conscientiousness. In a *conjunctive* task, the group's performance is limited by the ability of the least competent member. Agreeableness was related to the individuals' ability to resolve conflicts. Conscientiousness was related to the individuals' ability to organize, plan, and attend to the details of the work. Although the study did not address leadership phenomena, organizing and planning the work and resolving conflicts are well-known facets of leadership behavior (e.g., Fleishman & Harris, 1962).

Neuman and Wright (1999) also noted that other types of tasks and task structures would probably require different composites of traits for the group to be successful. Other task structures might be additive, "where the contributions of each member are combined into a single group product," or disjunctive, "where the group's output is determined by the performance of its best member" (Neuman & Wright, 1999, p. 377; Steiner, 1972). Similarly, other types of tasks might require different levels of trait homogeneity. The general preference for group heterogeneity in creative problem-solving groups is well known although the opposite is the case when the group task involves repetitive production (Zander, 1994).

Tasks might also differ in their motivational structure when they are presented to groups, and leaders might have the opportunity to frame the motivational properties of a situation to elicit the best results. There are at least three motivational structures evident in game theory when strictly cooperative outcomes are involved; the Stag Hunt, Intersection, and Bandwagon were described in earlier chapters. The Bandwagon is a situation where increased production facilitates further production levels. The dominant leadership behaviors can be regarded as just one part of an organization's adaptive strategy, which evolves along with its product, distribution of power, need to acquire and use information, risk-taking stance, and competitive elements in its external environment (Kagano, Nonaka, Sakabara, & Okumura, 1985).

Transactional, Transformational, and Visionary Leadership

According to Bennis (1988), academic leadership theories hitherto known to humankind are pretty worthless in that they do not describe the realities under which the big time leaders must work. His *Why Leaders Can't Lead* began with a saga of a university president driving his car off a cliff. (That got *my* attention!) Bennis then explored what happened to the poor fellow. Bennis described an unconscious conspiracy taking place, which prevents leaders from actually doing any leading or changing anything meaningful about the system. Uninspired administrators who value the status quo and resist change surround the leader. They, in concert with other forces that they can muster, involve the leader in lackluster administrative trivia, which they might accomplish by behaving incompetently when the leader tries to delegate those functions back to the administrators. As a result, the leader has little time for thinking up new ideas, developing them, or moving them through the system.

Enter the visionary leader. The visionary is one who imagines a course of action for the organization, if not an entire way of life for the organization including products, processes, and social climate within the company (Sashkin, 1984; Sashkin & Burke, 1990). The vision implies goals, methods for their implementation, and values often enough. Such a leader, if successful, is not only able to concoct such visions, but can also impart those visions to other organizational members. A third broad and critical feature of visionary leadership is that the leader delegates enough discretionary power to other organizational members. By doing so, the others can internalize the vision, explore what it means to them and their span of control, and operationalize that vision the way they see it.

A key problem with visionary leaders often lies at the third step. A would-be visionary may fall into the trap of trying to "own" the vision, and accept no alternative view of it than what he/she saw originally. Subordinates' attempts to internalize the vision thus become thwarted by feedback that says, "That's not the way I see it, so it can't be correct." A visionary who is more likely to succeed is one who is willing to let the subordinates think the vision was their own idea rather than the leader's.

According to Bass (1985; Bass & Avolio, 1994), the prevailing theories of leadership all shared a common focus on *transactional* leadership, which is how leaders go about their daily chores of getting tasks accomplished, building teams, choosing the right style for the occasion and so forth. *Transformational* leaders, however, can induce people to think in new ways and to imagine new goals and desired states. Transformational leadership requires: attractiveness as a role model, ability to motivate the group to envision desirable new states and goal pathways, stimulating intellectual products from the leader, an environment that supports a positive climate for innovation, and positive one-on-one relations between the leader and the group members. The latter element is indicative of leader–member exchange theory, which is considered in the next main section of this chapter. The requirements for intellectual stimulation and a positive climate for innovation are particularly germane to creative problem-solving situations. According to one report, (Guastello, 1995b) leaders of creative problem-solving groups, as perceived by their peers, were also the group members who exhibited greater amounts of original creative input and who helped other people generate their own ideas.

Here we have the distinction between transactional and transformational leadership. The transactional leader is the managerial functionary who, consistent with the academic leadership theories of the past, succeeds in mobilizing the work force to accomplish tasks that are already laid out. The transactional leader can also resolve any interpersonal difficulties among work group members that might arise.

The transformational leader, by contrast, is capable of conceptualizing new viewpoints and convincing others of the new viewpoints and engaging them in pursuit of new goals. Transformational leadership by this definition is not substantially different from the visionary described above. The transformational leader is characterized by the *four i's*:

1. *Idealized influence.* Transformational leaders behave in ways that result in their being role models for their followers (Bass & Avolio, 1994, p. 3). This is essentially the use of referent power in the French and Raven (1959) power scheme.

2. *Inspirational motivation.* Here the leader finds ways of getting the group to envision desirable states, make them foam at the mouth, and so forth. The so-called "motivational speaker" comes to mind here, although some of those characters on late-night paid-program TV tend to be more glitz than substance. Most will, however, explain to their audiences the value of visioning their desired goals.

3. *Intellectual stimulation.* Here innovation and creativity on the part of the leader are essential means for inspiring others to do the same. The leader supports a positive climate for innovation, as discussed earlier in conjunction with creativity and the management of innovation and innovative work units.

4. *Individualized consideration.* Here the leader builds one-on-one relationships with team members by listening and paying attention to individual needs and achievements. Here the delegation of tasks and decisions is carried out in such a way as to develop the subordinates, which may mean not treating them all exactly alike in every instance.

Charisma Continues

So far we have landed on the latest version of charisma—the transformational leader who convinces people to think differently about situations—and presented it in its more desirable form. At some point, however, charisma ends and demagoguery begins.

In common parlance, a mission statement and a vision statement can be closely similar. A mission statement will state the purpose of the organization and its general plans of operation. A vision statement will state what the organization is going to do next concerning its active and future business activities. Mission statements lean toward static views of a situation. Visions have some potential for dynamical interpretations of events. Depending on who is in charge, there can be a fuzzy boundary between the two. According to Conger and Kanungo (1998), the ordinary leader will confine the vision message to pragmatic statements such as "Expand our North American sales." The charismatic leader will expand on the deep importance of the North American sales territory. The verbiage would place the specific sales objective in the context of the greater whole of the organization's operations.

Charismatic leaders are as creative with the use of language as they are with the substance of their messages. They create meaning and motivation with their word choices. In Chapter 4 we visited Weick's (1996) ideas on organizational culture and the manufacturing of meaning. Here we can see how the charismatic leader might take an active hand in shaping the meaning. A slogan or two at the right time can facilitate this objective. Conger and Kanungo (1998) give the example of Mary Kay Ash, of Mary Kay cosmetics, who coined the slogan, "God first, family second, and careers third!" This particular slogan was an appeal to the value system of the vast majority of organizational members who were women, religious, and part-time. F. D. Roosevelt's slogan, "There's nothing to fear except fear itself" was a winner in a very different place and circumstance.

Baum, Locke, and Kirkpatrick (1998) isolated seven different characteristics of effective vision statements: brevity, clarity, abstractness, challenge, future orientation, stability, and desirability. They studied vision statements, and lack of them, generated by CEOs of 183 organizations (with statistical controls for prior growth, organizations' age and size, CEO tenure, and so forth). Of the 183 organizations, 127 had vision statements available. Some vision statements were communicated in writing, others by spoken language, and others by both means of communication. Ratings of the seven vision attributes were then correlated with publicly available information about the organizations' growth. Additionally, the content of the vision statements was examined for growth-related imagery. The researchers found significant correlations between organizational growth with high scores on the seven vision attributes (in the form of a single scale, $r = .37$) and growth-related imagery ($r = .30$). The take-home message here is that some vision statements are better than others.

The vision and the poetry can mask a few personality problems, however. According to Conger and Kanungo (1998) there is a shadow side of charisma, and they found several contrasts with the good guys: The Shadow Guy's motivation becomes increasingly self-serving and fixated on his personal vision. In doing so, the leader's direction becomes further removed from the concerns of the rest of the constituency within the organization and from what the public wants to buy. Resources are severely miscalculated. The Shadow Guy is oblivious to changes in the environment or market demand. Some faults show up in communication content. The Shadow Guy exaggerates his own expertise and the claims of the vision itself. Negative information is censored while supportive information is distributed widely.

Some visionary leaders in technology circles began their career with legitimate claims to fame—great inventions that became immensely popular. Success propelled some technology leaders to continue doing what they did right. Other technology leaders, however, became caught up in their inventions for the sake of the inventions and became oblivious to their horrendous R&D budgets and gross miscalculation of the market demand for their products. Although every leadership saga has a few examples of exemplary people, I will forego the temptation to expand on particular lives. Instead it is left to the reader as an exercise to consider the messages conveyed by any luminaries in politics, business, science, or other quadrants of the galaxy and ask: Was there a clear vision? Was it compelling? Did the leader do anything about it besides talk? Were actions consistent with the message? What happened when people disagreed?

DYNAMICS OF LEADERSHIP EMERGENCE

The psychological background to the leadership emergence phenomenon dates back to Cattell & Stice (1954), according to whom, leadership is more widely distributed in the population than appearances might indicate. A large and complex social structure creates important roles for less prominent, or more specialized group members. Group members thus define their roles and express leadership tendencies in more specific ways such as: technical experts on different topics, purveyors of rare commodities, public relations specialists who communicate with other groups, and those who specialize in resolving conflicts among group members.

Different profiles of personality traits may be associated with the different role types. In their landmark experiment, Cattell and Stice (1954) organized a sample of military personnel into groups of 10 people. Each group was given a problem to solve. Part way through the deliberations, the group was given an opportunity to elect a leader. Later, the group was given an opportunity to choose a new leader if the one they had selected earlier was not effective. Those leaders who were both selected at first and retained later on became the reference sample for the personality trait profile.

How does one emerge as a leader in problem-solving situations? There is a default theory of leadership that says that the leader is person who just talks the most. Bottger (1984) was able to explicitly demonstrate, however, that expert content is more related to endorsements of leadership than simple "air time." The social quality of the interactions also counts for a lot. Leader–member exchange theory (Graen & Uhl-Bein, 1995) explains that the building block of leadership is the dyadic relationship between the leader and each of the other people in the group. High-quality dyadic interactions display four characteristics: loyalty, respect, contribution, and positive affect. High-quality interactions are in turn responsible for better work group performance, commitment, and satisfaction. Leaders emerge through the interaction process when some people accumulate greater frequencies of high-quality interactions with greater numbers of people. As group members change, tasks change, and the interactions among people that are generated by those tasks change, different leaders can be expected to emerge. The notion of leader–member exchange quality denotes a concept of interaction style, or leadership style as discussed earlier.

Self-organization and the Swallowtail Catastrophe Model

Self-organization is the tendency for systems that are in a highly unstable, or "far-from-equilibrium" state to create new and stable structures. New structures are built with feedback loops, or information flow patterns, among the subsystems. In leadership emergence situations, the information flows occur in the communications and other interactions among group members. Asymmetries in the interaction patterns eventually occur whereby some group members interact with others to a greater extent, and in more diverse ways.

It is the intricacy of the information flows among the subsystems that puts the "complexity" into "complexity theory." The flows are also responsible for the low impact of change initiatives that might be introduced by outside agents. Change in one localized aspect of the system tends to induce local adaptations from adjacent parts of the system, with the net result that nothing important will happen to the system. In order to induce meaningful change, it is necessary to identify the *dynamical key* to the system. The dynamical key, like a cornerstone of a classic (architectural) Roman arch, is linked to the rest of the system in such a way that if it is removed, the rest of the system will unravel or topple. At that time there is an opportunity to induce self-organization toward a different pattern of information flow (Hubler, 1992). The available research to date on leadership emergence has not gone so far as to unravel a group structure once it has been formed. The creative problem-solving task that the participants in the experiments perform, however, does involve finding a dynamical key in a complex set of problems they are trying to solve.

The rugged landscape model of self-organization is particularly germane to the emergence of leaders and other social structures in an undifferentiated group. The swallowtail catastrophe model (Fig. 3.4) and its probability distribution (lower portion of Fig. 3.1) is adopted here as a mathematical model for the discontinuous changes that occur in rugged landscape scenarios generally, and in leadership emergence specifically. Puu (2000b) noted some important similarities between Darwinian biological evolution and the form of evolution that occurs in the development of inventions. Both forms of evolution involve small mutations. Some mutations favor survival, some antagonize survival, and some are trivial. When an important evolutionary step does occur, however, it involves a bifurcation that separates the new idea or organism from the previous variety. Inventions, like organisms, can be regarded as sets of traits. The airplane, for instance, was "invented" many times, but it was not until the proper combination of wing design, fuselage strength, and engine power was discovered that a viable transportation device resulted. Similar arguments can be made for economic or social institutions. The common denominator is that a confluence of traits will support survival by one means or another; when the means switches, a bifurcation, by definition has taken place. Only the large switch, which is denoted by the catastrophe models, actually matters; the slow mutations are subcritical.

The swallowtail response surface is four-dimensional and describes two stable states of behavior and one unstable state. It is the set of points in which

$$\delta f(y)/\delta y = y^4 - cy^2 - by - a = 0, \tag{3.25}$$

where y is the dependent variable, or order parameter, and a, b, and c are control parameters.

Change between the behavior states in a swallowtail model is a function of three controls, *asymmetry* (a), *bifurcation* (b), and *bias* (c). The response surface requires sectioning for cases where $a = 0.0$ and cases where $a > 0.0$. For the cases where $a = 0$, behavior can take on two forms, one stable and one unstable. For the more interesting case where $a > 0.0$, the behavior can change between two adjacent stable states, or fall through a twist and gap in the surface and leave the surface entirely.

When the point leaves the surface it passes through a region when very few points fall. That vacant region contains the a *swallowtail point*. The swallowtail point is known for its role as the most unstable point on the surface.

On the other side of the vacant region is a region of high, but unstable, point density (as when $a = 0$). The vacant region thus separates the unstable area from the two stable states. The two stable states are separated by a small vacant area that is represented by the twists in the surface, as shown in Figure 3.4. As the bifurcation parameter b becomes large, there is increasing differentiation of the two stable behavior states from the unstable area that exists when $a = 0$. Parameter c, the *bias* parameter, governs the degree of separation between the two stable states.

It is important to remember that leadership and creativity are both exponentially distributed throughout a population, rather than normally distributed (Guastello, 1995a, 1995b; Simonton, 1988; West & Deering, 1995). Exponential distributions are hallmarks of a nonlinear dynamical process.

The rugged landscape model of self-organization applies to leadership emergence as follows: The group is, at first, undifferentiated with respect to social roles. It is then presented with a sufficiently challenging task, which is analogous to the environmental assault to the species on the mountaintop. The group is bounded because membership in the group is definite, and there are no other boundary-role personnel. This assumption was deliberately introduced into recent experiments on creative problem-solving groups; real-world situations might not always have firm boundaries. Next, the group members communicate in the natural course of their creative problem-solving efforts. Self-organization then results from information flows such that the group members structure themselves into a leader, secondary roles, and general others. Thus, leader–member exchanges all begin a member–member exchanges.

The NDS studies of leadership emergence in creative problem-solving groups were carried out using a simulation called "Island Commission" (Gillan, 1979; Guastello, 1995a, 1995b, 1998b; Guastello, Hyde et al., 1998; Zaror & Guastello, 2000). Island Commission is usually played by groups of eight people; the game is described in Appendix B. At the end of the game, which typically lasts one hour, the participants rated all members of their groups as to who exhibited the characteristics of the leader to the greatest extent, and who exhibited the characteristics of the leader to the second-greatest extent. Participants were not given any limiting definitions regarding what characteristics should be germane to leadership. Instead they had to rely on their own best judgment, which is what happens in the real world.

A frequency distribution of the ratings of leadership behavior by each player for each fellow player was plotted and analyzed for its degree-of-fit to the swallowtail catastrophe distribution (Guastello, 1998b), which is depicted in Figure 9.2. The analysis revealed that clear primary and secondary leaders did emerge, as evidenced by the presence of statistical modes and antimodes and a strong degree of fit overall ($R^2 = .99$). The computational strategy utilized the method of nonlinear regression for a catastrophe probability density function given in Chapter 3. The data in Figure 9.2 were based on 140 participants who worked in groups of 7 to 9 people. The important point is that a form of self-organization did occur within the group, and that the structural model for discontinuous change should be pursued further.

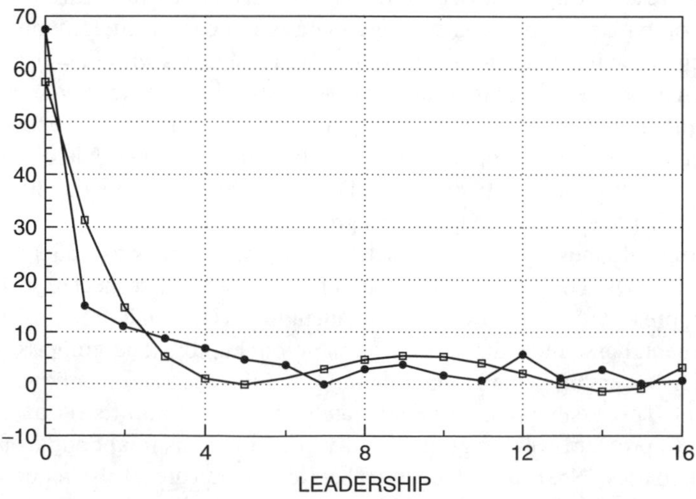

FIG. 9.2. Comparison of actual frequencies for leadership ratings with values expected from the quartic polynomial fit; groups contained an average of eight people. From Guastello (1998b, p. 312); reprinted with permission of Human Sciences Press and Kluwer Academic Publishers.

The foregoing results were replicated on a sample of undergraduates at a Chilean university (Zaror & Guastello, 2000). The language and cultural differences between the North and South American samples made no impact on the dynamics of the leadership emergence process.

Control Variables for Creative Problem-solving Groups

The next study in the series of NDS experiments with creative problem-solving groups (Guastello et al., 2001) pursued the identification of control parameters in the leadership emergence process. Island Commission was the experimental medium in that study also. As mentioned earlier, leaders in the Island Commission studies were group members who exhibited a wide repertoire of social and conversational behaviors. Thus, we expected to find a substantial number of conversational contributions on parameter *a*. The conversational contributions would correspond to Kauffman's (1993) *K* for adaptation-relevant traits in the rugged landscape model of self-organization. In the extreme case, no leaders would emerge if no conversation took place. As the repertoire of contributions to a conversation increases, the individuals with the widest repertoires would be the most likely candidates for primary or secondary leadership.

Parameter *b* describes the strength with which a bifurcation takes places. Bifurcations occur when the entropy of the system increases to the point where the system becomes more efficient by making a separation of its behavioral regimes. Creative input to the conversation would induce the necessary entropy, according to previous studies on the relationship between creativity and chaos (Guastello, 1995a, 1998b). Bifurcation would then be observed as the extent to which the leaders are separated from the rest of the group in terms of the leadership endorsements they receive. Because it also appears to be the case that leadership, creativity input, and the facilitation of the creativity of others are closely related, parameter *b* would be expected to contain elements of both creative input and facilitative style.

Parameter *c* governs the degree of separation between the primary and secondary leaders. According to the psychological part of the theory, secondary leaders have specific relevant abilities, but not as wide a range of them as the primary leaders. It is unclear how primary and secondary leaders might be distinguished, but the answer probably lies in the composition of the group somehow. For purposes of these experiments, a factor analysis of relevant traits may produce a candidate variable that is worth testing as parameter *c*.

This particular experiment used eight groups with an average size of 16 people, for a total of 114 participants in the study. The intention was to see if the swallowtail shape would appear with a larger group. It turned out that it did. After the groups played the game, they completed a questionnaire in which they rated all the group members on leadership and other variables. The other variables included those defined in Table 6.1: requesting information, giving information, tension

TABLE 9.1
Additional Group Process Ratings for the Creative Problem-Solving Group Experiment

Creative Ideas. Which person in the group offered the most creative ideas for solving the Island's problems?
Facilitating. Which members of the group did the most to help the other members of the group develop their ideas?
Controlling. Which members of the group did the most to control the direction of discussion?
Task-orientation. Which members of the group showed the greatest concern for successful completion of the budget allocation task?
Competition. Which members of the group competed most strongly for their own (role's) interests in the budget allocation outcome?
Consideration. Which members of the group showed the greatest concern for other players' interests in the budget allocation outcome?
Development Orientation. Which members of the group showed the greatest concern for the development of the Island's infrastructure?

reduction, clarifying responses and ideas, gatekeeping, initiating, following, and harmonizing. There were seven other items also which are defined in Table 9.1.

The ratings, with the exception of Leadership, were factor analyzed using the maximum likelihood method of factor extraction and oblique rotation. (Oblique rotation allows for the possibility of correlated factors.) Three factors were extracted. The first and largest factor was named "Control of the Conversation." It was composed of ten survey items. Five of the items were conversational elements. The other five were facilitating, controlling the conversation, task orientation, consideration of other players' interests, and concern for Island's infrastructure development. It now appeared that a substantial range of conversational elements and leadership style elements were related to the players' perception of who controlled the conversation.

The second factor was named "Creative Role Play." It was composed of four survey items: giving ideas, creative nature of the contributions, competitive behavior, and concern for Island's infrastructure development. The competitive behavior question was framed in terms of the extent to which the players argued for the interests of their game roles. Thus, the connection between competition and creativity represented fanciful nature of the role-play.

The third factor was named "Tension Reduction." It was composed of two items: tension reduction and creativity again. This factor appears to indicate that the funniest jokes emanated from the more creative people.

The three resulting variables were tested as control variables in the swallowtail model. The results turned out as shown in Fig. 9.3. Control of the Conversation contributed to parameter a, and thus accounted for the major separation between the large unstable mode and the region of the surface where local stability, and thus, self-organized behavior, was located. In other words, without this large repertoire of behavior, no movement of individuals to a local leadership mode would have

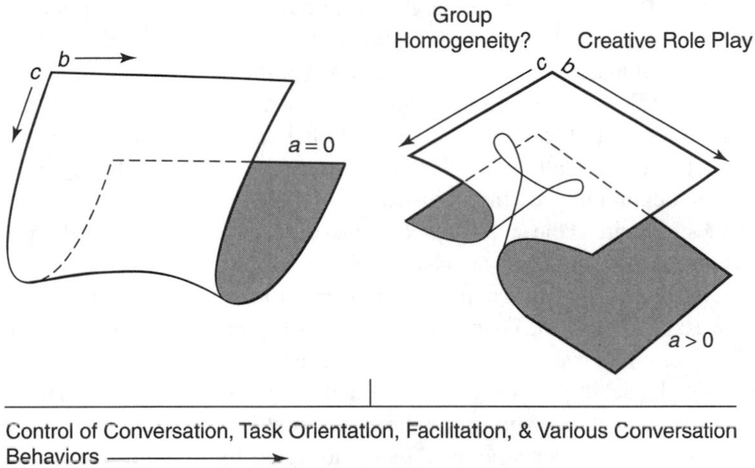

FIG. 9.3. Swallowtail catastrophe model for leadership emergence obtained for creative problem-solving groups.

been possible. Creative Role-Play contributed to the bifurcation parameter (b), and thus accounted for the extent to which an individual reached either of the two locally stable modes. Tension reduction did not contribute to any of the three control parameters.

At the end of the analysis we remained in the lurch as to what might explain parameter c. It was probable that c was the result of a variable that we did not manipulate in the experiment. One plausible concept was group homogeneity. The groups were drawn from the same population base, and they all shared the same objectives during the game time. Had there been some players with goals that clearly contradicted those of other players, different results might have been obtained. Heterogeneous groups may be more likely to promote greater asymmetry in social interactions sooner than homogenous groups; time will tell.

It should be mentioned that the Island Commission game does allow for the possibility of competitive behavior. In my experience, however, only about one group in 30 will exhibit seriously competitive behavior while trying to maximize some objectives from the Island Commission's task of budget allocation.

Finding the Dynamical Key

One "Environmental Bulletin" that is presented to the Island Commission participants pertains to the Friendly Power Navy Base, from which 10% of the Island's income is derived. The bulletin begins by stating that two facilities that must expand are competing for the same space. The bulletin continues, "The Friendly Power Navy has recently learned and has proof that a large part of the economy of

Independent Island has depended on the illicit cultivation of opium poppies. The Navy has stated that if the traffic in opium is not eliminated, it will pull out of its installation" (Gillan, 1979, p. 104). The removal of the navy base was a dynamical key to the Island's socioeconomic system. It was a potentially risky act to remove it, because of the hypothetical loss of 10% of the Island's income. Removal of the navy base, however, would allow for different uses of land, buildings, resources, and accommodation of growing industries.

The questionnaire at the end of the game just described also contained a question that was not part of the factor analysis: Did you support the removal of the navy base? Inevitably the question comes up in discussion as to whether the navy base should be asked to leave the island. Seldom does the group advocate its removal. In this experiment, however, we deliberately correlated the answer to the navy base question with leadership ratings. It turned out that people who advocated removing the navy base, i.e., those who found the dynamical key, tended *not* to receive as strong leadership endorsements as those who opted for keeping the navy base. This result leads to some questions we can ponder in our spare time regarding leadership and actual correct solutions. Perhaps the correct solution was too risky for the average leaders' preference.

Leadership Emergence in Production Groups

In the last completed work in the series, we (Guastello et al., 2001) investigated how leaders would emerge from a situation where the group task was production centered. There is some precedent in psychological theories of leadership to support the notion that production-centered groups have leadership requirements that are different from those of creative problem-solving groups. According to the contingency theory of leadership (Fiedler, 1964; Fiedler Chemers, 1984), the optimal choice of leadership style is predicated on the quality of leader–member relationships and the inherent structure of the task. A task low in structure is one that is often encountered by creative problem-solving groups: there is more than one possible solution, more than one possible solution could be satisfactory, and there are multiple ways of arriving at any of the possible solutions. Repetitive production tasks, on the other hand, typically have their goals and procedures figured out in advance of production. Thus, many of the interactions peculiar to creative problem-solving would occur in a production task to a much smaller degree.

The experimental groups began their tasks as leaderless groups. The total of 30 groups ranged in size from 4 to 8 people for a total of 197 participants. The hypothetical scenario explained to them was that they were in the business of producing coloring book covers for a publisher. There were provided with a stack of uncolored drawings and three boxes of 16 crayons. Their first task (of three) was to generate a color scheme and produce five exact copies of the product. This phase of the work required approximately 20 minutes.

The second task began when the first was completed: Each experimental group was handed an "order form" from the "customer" for two dozen (65 participants), three dozen (65 participants), or four dozen (67 participants) covers. The work order specified that they (their hypothetical work organizations, as they were not paid in cash) would earn \$3.00 per dozen if the order was completed within the next 20 minutes. If it was not completed on time, they would earn only \$2.50 per dozen for the work completed. Pay was \$0.20 per copy if a full dozen was not completed. Thus, there was, in principle, a motivational element encouraging faster work built into the production scenario.

The third task took place after the "work" was "delivered." Participants were given name tags showing designations of Player A, Player B, and so on. They were then given a questionnaire in which they reported which members of the group behaved more like leaders, exhibited various leadership styles, and contributed other social influences. The questionnaire contained the questions already used in previous leadership emergence studies: ratings of leadership, the items in Table 6.1, and the items in Table 9.1. The items already given in the tables were reworded to reflect "the production task" rather than anything to do with "The Island."

Three factors were extracted. The first and largest factor was composed of three survey items. One item, initiating a line of conversation, was a conversational element. The other two were giving creative ideas and controlling the conversation. It now appeared that a substantial range of conversational elements and leadership style elements were wound up with the players' perception of who controlled the conversation. This factor was named "Creative Control."

The second factor was composed of five survey items. Three items were conversational elements: clarifying, gatekeeping, and following. The other two were controlling the conversation and tension reduction. This factor was named, "Production Control."

The third factor was composed of three conversational items: giving information, tension reduction, and harmonizing. The combination of tension reduction and harmonizing suggested that this factor captured efforts to reduce conflicts among players and keep morale up. This factor, therefore, was named "Tension Reduction."

There was one other important variable in the study, which was Goal Realism. Goal Realism was a variable introduced from the experimental manipulation of groups, who were given goals of two, three, or four dozen book covers to complete. The groups that were assigned two or three dozen covers produced more covers than those that were assigned four dozen covers, but there was no difference in production between the two-dozen and three-dozen groups. The result was interpreted as an example of Goal Realism: people will work toward their goals if the goals are reasonable, and ignore the goals if the goals are off-the-wall. For the swallowtail analysis, Goal realism was coded dichotomously, where 1 = realistic (groups assigned to the two-dozen or three-dozen conditions), and 0 = unrealistic (four-dozen condition).

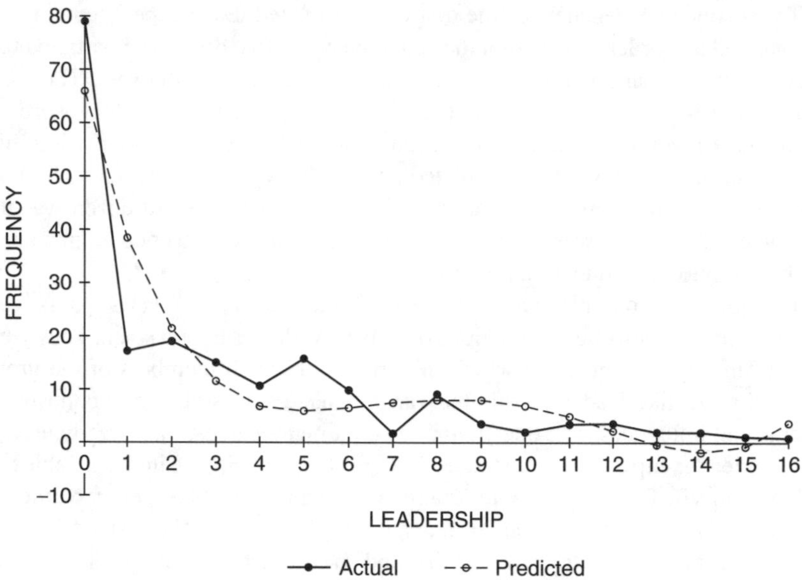

FIG. 9.4. Comparison of actual frequencies for leadership ratings with values expected from the quartic polynomial fit; groups contained an average of 16 people.

The swallowtail catastrophe analysis once again produced a distribution of leadership scores that was similar to the ones found previously, although the first locally stable mode of behavior was less distinguished from the unstable area; see Fig. 9.4. The R^2 for goodness of fit to the swallowtail structure was beyond .99, however.

The analyses involving the control variables showed that parameter *a* consisted of two variables: the Tension Reduction factor and Goal Realism. Note that leaders were less likely to emerge at all in the unrealistic condition. Both Creative Control and Production (or Task) Control contributed to parameter *b*. There was a greater distinction, and stabilization, of leadership if a group member exhibited greater control in both areas. Parameter *c* was as elusive as ever. The other variables were tested in the *c* position, just in case they might do something, but nothing new was uncovered by that exercise. Once again, the group homogeneity, or goal homogeneity explanations, are the top speculations for what parameter *c* might represent. The final model is shown in Fig. 9.5.

I should remark before concluding this section that the R^2 values for the swallowtail models actually dropped somewhat when the control variables were introduced. The final R^2 value for the swallowtail model with control variables for the creative problem-solving task was .74, and the final value for the production task was .62. In each model, however, statistical significance ($p < .05$) was obtained for all elements containing control parameters.

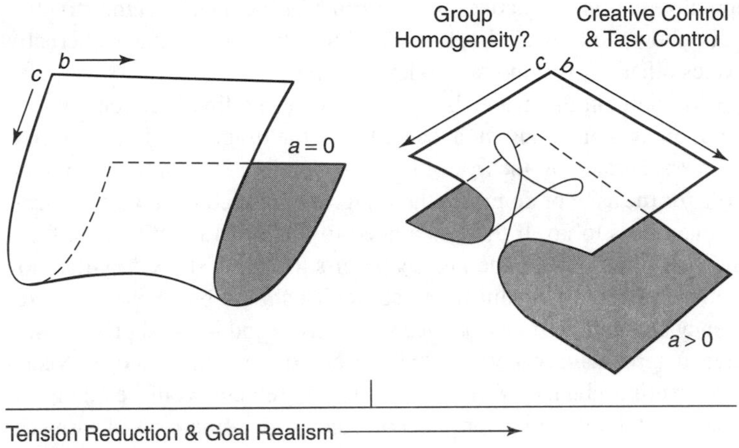

FIG. 9.5. Swallowtail catastrophe model for leadership emergence obtained for a production-intensive task.

Leadership Emergence in Coordination-Intensive Tasks

The latest experiment in this series is still in progress. The group task is the coordination task described in Chapter 8. Some groups will be able to verbalize and others will be required to work speechless. It is possible that verbal communication may contribute to parameter *c* in this instance, but we have been fooled before. Watch this space for new developments.

Chaos and Vision

"Chaologists" have expressed some important differences of opinion on the role of vision. Wheatley (1992) regarded vision as an important component of a cultural change initiative. Once the organization has reached its bifurcation point, management needs to define attractors and make them strong enough to draw unstable "points" into their basins. Clear visions of the desired of the desired culture and goals are needed to define attractive objectives. As for introducing the change itself, it is preferable to *let* it happen, rather than to *make* it happen. Goldstein (1994) emphasized this latter point also.

Stacey (1992) differed on the matter of vision, as discussed earlier. Visionary leaders often invent immutable visions that no one is allowed to seriously alter or contradict. Visions can be barriers to creative thinking, particularly when the organization needs to develop strategies in an environment that is fundamentally unstable. Thus, mission statements or vision statement can prevent more change than they can induce. A better management strategy, according to Stacey, is to conceptualize action alternatives in the form of a fractal branching structure, such as the one shown in Fig. 4.7. Each new action activates some new alternatives and deactivates others. It is important to know which is which.

My own view on the matter is that there is a fine line between a vision and a hallucination. It is one thing for a leader to see the rugged landscape clearly and to report back accurately to the rest of the organization. It is another to manufacture attractors for the sake of doing so; the imaginary attractors could represent places that no one needs to go. If there is a need to manufacture attractors, that should be done "out there" where the landscape of survival is shaped by the movement of organizations. Internal adjustment strategies should be devised to increase the consistency and compatibility between objectives and internal processes.

I have to agree with Stacey's (1992) observation about mission or vision statements preventing change. A useful mission statement would explain what just happened after the organization has adjusted from some type of turmoil. It is a way of locking in a set of behaviors and turning them into a zone of local stability, as indicated by the general organizational development model in Fig. 4.2. I did have the dubious pleasure of participating on a committee some years ago in which our assignment was to concoct some future objectives on paper for the future of our functional unit. What would have been a noble cause was instantly tainted by one further instruction: Pay close attention to the organization's mission statement and write a consistent mission statement for the unit. The individual who was appointed chairman of our little threesome took the mission instruction very seriously, to my dismay. We spent three-quarters of our available work time twiddling with the fine points of mission verbiage, and had to scramble terribly fast to throw the substance portion of our work together. Meanwhile, when last I checked, there was an organizational committee dedicated to the tweaking of the organizational mission statement. After 5 years of monthly meetings they produced a 250-word document which, as far as I could tell, said nothing about the future of the organization. Oh well. . .

In any case there is no substitution for being able to see the dynamics of present and future events clearly and to communicate the story effectively. I will return to this point in Chapter 12. Perhaps the most strategic stance with regard to vision is to combine a loose vision with both flexibility and preparedness for adaptive change (Zimmerman et al., 1998).

SUMMARY

The chapter began with a tour of leadership theory as it existed before the NDS applications. The literature has addressed the importance of personality traits, styles, situational influences, and cross-cultural effects. The distinction between transactional and transformational styles is the one most closely associated with nonlinear organizational dynamics because of its emphasis on creativity, intellectual stimulation, and organizational change. The dynamical impact of vision statements was contrasted with that of the mission statement.

Psychological theories of leadership emergence have emphasized the importance of individuals' trait clusters for determining social roles and the quality of interactions among members. Asymmetries form after repeated interaction, which result in self-organized role structures.

The rugged landscape model of self-organization bears a close similarity to the leadership emergence phenomenon. Psychological traits, or behaviors related to them, correspond to Kauffman's *K* for adaptation-relevant traits. Other behavioral constellations correspond to the separation (bifurcation) of primary and secondary leaders from the rest of the group members. Catastrophe models generally explain the phase shift in a system before and after a self-organization phenomenon and the branching that occurs in an evolutionary process. The swallowtail catastrophe model was identified as the catastrophe model most similar to the dynamics of leadership emergence. The swallowtail model consists of two stable states, an unstable state, and three control parameters.

Empirical studies of leadership emergence dynamics showed that different, but related, models were required for groups that were primarily involved in creative problem-solving and those that were primarily involved in a production process. Swallowtail parameter *a* corresponded to *K* adaptation-relevant traits; different combinations of traits appeared in the two group situations. The mode for creative problem-solving groups included several variables related to assertiveness and control of the conversation. The model for production groups included tension reduction and goal realism as contributing variables.

Swallowtail parameter *b* included creative role-play ability in both task situations. In the production task, however, the control of the group task shifted from parameter *a* to parameter *b*. The content of swallowtail parameter *c* is unknown at the present time, but it is believed that group homogeneity or heterogeneity may be relevant here. Heterogeneous groups are hypothesized to promote greater asymmetry in social interactions sooner than homogenous groups as studies on leadership emergence continue.

The emergence of leaders from a leaderless group is the first step in the formation of an organizational hierarchy. The next chapter considers the dynamics of workflow within hierarchies of two and three levels along with the interesting case of what happens when the hierarchy contracts instead of expands.

10

Work Flows in Hierarchies

In the previous chapter we saw how leaders emerge from situations that had been initially leaderless. That was the first step in the emergence of a hierarchical structure in an organization. A quick look across the business landscape suggests that the growth of hierarchies is inevitable. A quick tour of the mechanisms of self-organization (e.g., as we did in Chapter 2) indicates that even nonliving systems can generate hierarchical structures.

At the same time, however, there are two emerging ironies that we must address. First, in spite of the ubiquity of hierarchies in work organizations, there has been a negligible amount research since the beginning of Industrial Psychology (circa 1910) on the subject of work flows up and down hierarchies. What have been studied often are the relationships between some attributes of the managers or organizational culture and the performance of work groups. A downward flow of *something* is consistently assumed. In the time of the Participation Renaissance there was a new value placed on *upward* communication. There again, however, was a downward flow of something that should disinhibit, if not also encourage, upward communication.

In contrast, the NDS perspective on organizations makes note of two important points. First, self-organization occurs from the bottom up. As a result, there is greater instability at the top than appearances would indicate. Second, the number of links in the communication chain grows in a hierarchical formation, which would only serve to slow and to distort communication up or down the hierarchy. Hierarchical pathways would also produce balkanized chains of information flow such that some people would get some part of the story but no one would get all the parts. Many times, what management calls the "need-to-know basis" really means, "We'll tell you if you ask, but the task of telling everyone everything would be overwhelming." At other times "need-to-know" means, "We plan on telling as few people as possible."

The next section of this chapter addresses the conventional approach to the study of phenomena related to hierarchies. Here we encounter nonhierarchical organizations and autonomous work groups (once again), "reengineering the firm," and the incredible saga of downsizing. Afterwards we will see that a closer look at relevant NDS theories make conflicting predictions about what does, or should, occur in a hierarchical work flow situation. Then come the (real-time) experiments where hierarchical workflows were studied from an NDS perspective. In the case of the downsizing experiment, we see the organization's performance as naturally occurring chaos in a production situation, the hierarchical and codependent relationships among organizational subunits, self-organization, and the control of the system.

CONVENTIONAL APPROACH TO HIERARCHIES

The first review of the studies of organizational structure variables (Porter & Lawler, 1965) indicated that there was no relationship between the number of levels of hierarchy in an organization and attitude or performance phenomena inside. By the early 1980s, however, large hierarchies such as the steel manufacturers in the United States saw the need to do something differently in order to compete effectively with steel manufacturers from Japan. Besides technological innovations, they reduced their hierarchies by as many as six levels in some instances. The hierarchy reduction was based on the Japanese preference (Ouchi, 1980) to push decisions downward so that the lowest-level person who could possibly make the decisions makes them. Thus, we see in the steel mills how decision control crept up the hierarchy and probably propelled hierarchical growth. Some hierarchical levels became unnecessary once the decisions were pushed downward.

The Rationale for Downsizing

Many industries in the United States and Europe underwent radical reductions in workforce in attempts to improve their efficiency and profitability. A great deal of downsizing activity took place in the 1987–1997 era, which occurred in the wake of a rabid flurry of mergers and acquisitions. Arguably, these broad trends are another example of self-organization at work. The results of the downsizing efforts were often disappointing, and the rationale behind some of them may have been misguided. The main motivations for downsizing efforts are considered next, followed by a summary of the results.

One rationale is based on the nature of maturing industries. As industrie mature, they are compelled to compete with each other on the basis of lower cost (Tucci & Sweo, 1996). A significant amount of variability in downsizing effectiveness depends on the economic sector involved (Baily, Bartelsman, & Haltiwanger, 1996), because within a particular industry, such as oil and energy, there may be little relationship between an organization's efficiency of operation and its profitability (Thompson, 1993).

A counterargument for the maturing industry rationale can be found in the economic theory developed by Sraffa (1960), who viewed an economy as an interlocked matrix of inputs and outputs that includes trade among industries. Sraffian economics made two points germane to the downsizing issue. First, industries that are experiencing zero growth will attempt to increase their profitability by hammering their wage base. Options available today fo reducing wages include a one-for-one substitution of highly paid workers by lower paid workers, technology substitutions and deskilling, and blatant workforce reductions. If many low-skill workers could be replaced by a smaller number of higher-skill workers, then the change would occur in the opposite skill direction.

The second pertinent point from Sraffa (1960) was that organizations that seek to enhance their profits by reducing their productive labor complement would experience a deficit. In more contemporary times, Filardo (1995) reported that the combined use of computers, plant investment and downsizing have not increased profits economy-wide. Revenge effects from computerization have been noted, such that innovations that are meant to reduce time and work actually create work or merely shift work from one form to another (Tenner, 1996).

Dates count for something in this discussion. Filardo's (1995) research was conducted at the dawn of what was to become one of the longest-running epochs of economic growth in the United States. By mid-afternoon, the U.S. government permitted greater commercialization of the Internet, which triggered a rapid growth in the number of e-commerce firms. Profitability for many of them soared. More traditional organizations found new ways to use the World Wide Web to enhance their operations and sales. Unemployment and inflation both reached 30-year lows, and stock market gains reached record highs. Curiously, however, average wages and salaries did not keep up the growth or inflation. Thus, disposable income decreased. The boom was pronounced "over" by November 2000. E-commerce and technology stocks were hit the hardest by the economic contraction. The most resilient sectors were the energy stocks and traditional organizations that had adapted well to their new technological option. Sraffa would probably have said, "I could have told you so."

A "red queen" effect appears to be operating here with regard to wage hammering and technology absorption. If all constituents of a zero-growth economic sector reduce staff, or take any other common action to compete with each other on the basis of cost, then all participating organizations end up in the same place relative to each other. The only way out of the dilemma is to "run faster," which would mean either adapting much faster than the competition or expanding into new growth areas of commerce.

Another rationalization for downsizing was to reduce redundancies in work operations created by leveraged buyouts and mergers (Wiersema & Liebeskind, 1995). The high costs of the buyouts themselves could counteract the advantages of redundancy reduction. On the other hand, it is valuable to consider the effects of reducing redundancy in the absence of leveraged buyout costs. It is well known in human factors engineering that redundancy improves the reliability of a system, but with the added cost of slowing the system down. Contemporary computer technology is only becoming faster, however, and a substitution of one human for an *expert system* of some sort, while retaining one or more other humans, is not a bad idea. In fact, it was the initial intention behind expert systems that they should provide a "coworker in a can;" the silicon employee would automatically generate design ideas and troubleshoot technical specifications. Optimal use of expert systems is based on another well-known dilemma in human factors engineering: What is the best way to allocate functions between the human and the machine? There are some classic answers regarding what functions each can do best. The realization of specific solutions depends on the specific situation.

Reengineering the Firm

In any case, the reduction of redundancy was a touchstone addressed by Hammer and Champy (1993, 1996) in their concept of reengineering the firm. Unwanted redundancies creep into an organization, or they become obsolesced by new technology. The search for redundancies would promote microlevel decisions about which people or functions to downsize out of the organization. It should also be obvious by now that videoconferencing, or even simple e-mail, can reduce the need for staff meetings and interplanetary business travel.

The information-handling activity of middle management was frequently the target of downsizing in the 1987–1997 era. Perhaps there was a lot of redundancy in those work systems that could be replaced by efficient computer programs. On the other hand, the economics literature indicates that the stage was set for middle management downsizing several decades beforehand. During the 1948–1957 epoch, labor costs in manufacturing increased 17% for wage earners, but 63% for salaried personnel. Roughly the opposite was true in the 1939–1948 epoch in which wages increased 93%, but salaries only 53% (Schultze, 1959, p. 25). "Similarly, in manufacturing almost the entire reduction in employment takes place among production workers—nonproduction worker employment [referring to management and salaried personnel] declines very slightly" (p. 56).

There's another important part of the reengineering concept. Hammer and Champy (1996) advised managers to think of new things that they can do with new technologies rather than simply replace one process with another process. They give several examples in which they convert an "old rule" to a "new rule" that takes form with the use of a "disruptive technology." For example, "*Old rule*: Field personnel need offices where they can receive, store, retrieve, and transmit information. *Disruptive technology*: Wireless data communication and portable computers. *New rule*: Field personnel can send and receive information wherever they are" (p. 614). In this case, the obvious substitution is the physical office with the virtual office; travel time can be reduced and the employee can be reached more quickly.

Some of their suggested substitutions were of dubious value. As another example, Hammer and Champy contended that with expert systems, an expert job can be done by "a generalist" (1996, p. 612). On the one hand, if the need for expertise is confined to the simpler tasks that a true expert might have to offer, I can see the point. There is probably a lot of true expertise going to waste every day on elementary tasks. On the other hand, if a great deal of investment is to be made in a product produced by a untrained middle manager with a point-and-click interface, and with no back-up from a human expert, the potential for costly errors increases sharply. In the long run, if society does not support true expertise, who will be left to revise the computer programs? (Another middle manager with a better computer program, of course . . . okay, I feel better now.)

As a last word on the topic, French and Bell (1999) observed that reengineering is not an example of OD in the usual sense. The reengineering process is driven top-down, and there is no explicit provision for upward participation. French and Bell (1999, p. 231) did find a few hand waves to "human resources," "organizational infrastructure," and "values and beliefs," but that appears to be as far as the participative element goes. French and Bell also noted that reengineering often resulted in substantial layoffs. One can anticipate an internal human relations watershed.

Research on Downsizing

Empirical studies on the effectiveness of downsizing showed no systematic profitability advantage from the workforce reductions (Baily et al., 1996; Brush & Karnani, 1996; Cascio, 1993; Filardo, 1995; Ganster & Dwyer, 1995; Hitt, Keats, Harback, & Nixon, 1994; Mentzer, 1996; Mick & Wise, 1996; Thompson, 1993). Some specifically negative outcomes were reported, many of which involved the human component of the organization. These included decreased trust,commitment, and loyalty (Buch & Aldridge, 1991; Richey, 1992) decreased innovation level (Dougherty & Bowman, 1995), "paralysis" and decreased productivity within the organization (DeMeuse, Vanderheiden, & Bergmann, 1994; Krau, 1995; Lind & Sulek, 1994), and drops in liquidity ratios (Mick & Wise, 1996). Some of the foregoing problems may have been tied to the leveraged buyouts, which triggered downsizing efforts (Link & Sulek, 1994).

The possible explanations for why downsizing efforts failed include the neglect of appropriate attitudes during and after the downsizing activity (King, 1996), and poor strategies for protecting training investments, technical and leadership expertise (DeWitt, 1993; Hitt et al., 1994; Labib & Appelbaum, 1993). A good many downsizing efforts were initiated by an archaic command, control, and compartmentalization approach to management (Cascio, 1993), which went uncorrected during and after the downsizing event (Weller, 1995). Downsizing often involved the break-up of information networks and workflows that had actually been effective in getting anything accomplished (Dougherty & Bowman, 1995; Lind & Sulek, 1994). As a result, many organizations resorted to rehiring their terminated employees back as consultants, often at triple the cost of the individuals' previous salaries (Mitroff, 1993).

Organizations that experienced no positive effect, or productivity losses, from downsizing sometimes resorted to second and additional downsizing episodes with no improvement (Vandaveer, 1995). If downsizing was so often ineffective, why did it persist as a strategic option? Aside from superstitious behavior, poor management, or bad manners, two other explanations have surfaced. First, the stock market during the downsizing era responded favorably to corporations who announced significant staff reductions well before there was any chance to observe the effects of those reductions. In the case of General Dynamics Inc., the return rate to the stockholders from market appreciation of their holdings reached 553% (Dial & Murphy, 1995), and bonuses were paid to the top executives. Decreased company loyalty was noted in a survey of survivors in one division of that organization (Richey, 1992).

The second explanation for the continued use of downsizing strategies was rooted in the power relationships between top and middle management. According to Krau (1995), the work reconfigurations generated by downsizing resulted in a disempowerment of the middle managers which in turn served to enhance the power objectives of top managers.

The same work is often shared by a smaller number of people. These group-defined tasks have led industrial–organizational psychologists to ponder the "death of the job," at least in its traditional sense (Pearlman, 1995). With growing frequency, employees do not have individually-defined jobs; rather, baskets of tasks are assigned to groups of people who will be expected to get them all accomplished "somehow." The changed nature of the jobs themselves produces some well-known stress conditions—role ambiguity and role conflict, and job insecurity. The effects of stress on work performance are also well known, and Shaw and Barrett-Power (1994) have argued that the effects of downsizing should be managed from the point of view of stress management. Organizational development techniques, especially team development, also have been recommended as solutions to the work reconfiguration problem (Buch & Aldridge, 1991).

NONLINEAR DYNAMICS, PRODUCTIVITY, AND HIERARCHIES

Lind and Sulek (1994) studied the entropy resulting from downsizing in one organization from a Newtonian point of view. In that situation, "entropy" was defined as the human energy that is wasted on maladaptive responses to strong stimuli. The example of a "strong stimulus" was a downsizing event, which occurred on the heels of a leveraged buyout. In their example, management responded to the downsizing requirements with rigidity, restricted information flow and processing, and a reversion to mechanistic command and control behavior. The negative impact on productivity and profitability began to reverse itself as a return to predownsizing behaviors within the organization ensued. Lind and Sulek made a brief acknowledgment of the experience of "chaos" in that organization during the downsizing transition.

As noted earlier in other ways, the break-up and reconfiguration of work networks signal a problem in synergetics and self-organization. The next stage of this exposition turns to nonhierarchical organizations. That is followed by perspectives game theory, synergetics, and related work on coupled processes. There are three objectives for theory-building here. The first is to examine coordinated work behavior in a hierarchical structure where strict cooperation rules (i.e., noncompetitive) would apply. The second is to examine the links between individual work dynamics and long-run outcomes at the upper levels of the system hierarchy. The third objective is to assess the specific effects of downsizing disruptions.

Nonhierarchical Structures

The wheel-shaped network that appears in Fig. 7.1 is essentially hierarchical because of the asymmetry in the communication flows among group members. Group members in a wheel only talk to the member in the middle. Real people might try to behave in an egalitarian fashion, and probably should do so in many cases. A nonhierarchical version of the same group of people would emphasize communication links among all people in the group.

O'Neill (1984) showed that the wheel-turned-pentagram example is only the first of many possible nonhierarchical arrangements. He developed a set of nonhierarchical organizational structures by using an extension of the same graph theory that produced much of the formal work on social networks. His resulting structures contained some important properties: homogenous information flow

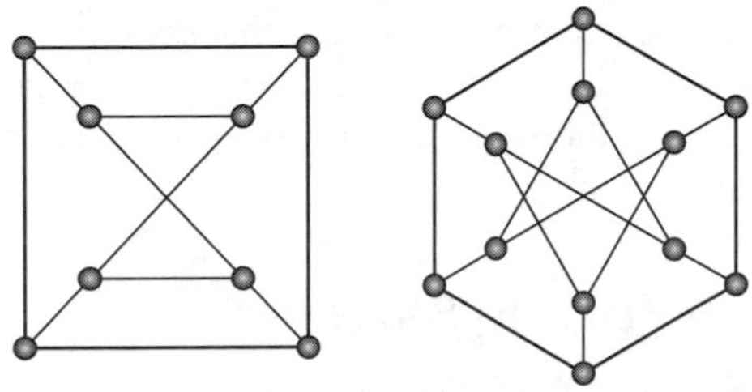

FIG. 10.1. Two examples of nonhierarchical organizational forms: an 8-person organization (left) and a 12-person organization (right).

throughout the organization, and a minimum number of meetings to convey the information, with a minimum number of people in each meeting. As we know, large numbers of people in a meeting can present a coordination problem. Figure 10.1 shows two examples from his set of [*n*, 3, 2] organizations. In [*n*, 3, 2], an information packet flows across the organization consisting of *n* people with a minimum of three meetings per person, each of which contains two people. This series can accommodate 4 to 20 people and allow for incremental growth. If more people are added to the groups, another configuration in the series is formed.

There is also a series of nonhierarchical models that require meetings of three people (not shown). The set of [n, m, 3] organizations can accommodate 7 to 30 people.The number of meetings varies for different organizational members, but each meeting consists of three people. The structures are modular, meaning that two or more structures can be combined to form another nonhierarchical organization. For instance, two [5, 2, 2] organizations become a [10, 3, 2] organization. Eventually, there is an end to these neat structures. Nonetheless, the series of structures is flexible with regard to the number of people involved, preferred meeting size, and modular organization. Hierarchical structures can be minimized at least.

Game Theory

Game theory offers one possible prediction for behavior in hierarchies, which is that, in the long run, the dominant behavior strategies for a hierarchical system are equivalent to the evolutionarily stable states (ESS) for individual players. This prediction, which is also known as "the folk theorem," requires the assumption of subgame perfection. This assumption is generally untenable (Friedman & Samuelson, 1994), but it runs as follows: Imagine that a game is a set of strategy combinations, each with a utility associated with it. If the game is allowed to branch into different utility structures as iteration progresses, then a *subgame* is the strategy–utility combination associated with one of the branches. In a *proper subgame,* the sets of strategies and utilities available to each player are all included in the set of strategies and utilities that comprise the general game. A game is *subgame perfect* if the utilities associated with subgame strategy combinations produce the same equilibrium strategies as the general game. In the absence of subgame perfection, anything can happen.

Synergetic Drivers and Slaves

A second type of prediction for behavior in hierarchies emanates from the theory of synergetics (Haken, 1984). With enough entropy, individual-level agents self-organize to create a hierarchical structure. This hierarchical structure acts as a driver of individual level behavior; the latter would be regarded as a "slave." "Entropy" in this sort of a system would take the form of a large amount of unprocessed information coming into, or generated by, the organization at a sufficiently fast rate. Hierarchical driver–slave structures are thought to explain a wide range of self-organization structures from the point of view of information flows. For the downsizing problem, synergetics theory would probably argue that the work flows, productivity, and profits are driven by top management actions. This proposition is apparently supported by studies that cited poor management and strategy formation as explanations for the negative consequences of downsizing, and would further suggest that top-level adaptation responses are primarily responsible for an effective reorganization after downsizing. Synergetic dynamics would also suggest that conventional command-and-control management strategies would, in the long run, remain supremely effective, which we know is not accurate for work organizations.

The third perspective runs contrary to the top-down orientation of synergetics theory. There is another level of reasoning that suggests that self-organizational processes are bidirectional, if not multidirectional. Rosser et al. (1994) observed that shocks (sudden bursts of energy) can emanate from the worker level and have the potential to disrupt the management hierarchy. In other words, there could be a "revolt of the slaved variables." Such shocks are more likely in some systems than in others, but they could in theory disrupt the driver–slave relationships. The implication here is that the real roots of self-organization begin at the work group level; this premise is consistent with that of organizational development, generally that the work group is the building block of the organization.

CHAOS EXERCISE EXPERIMENTS

The Chaos Exercise (Michaels, 1992) is a group dynamics simulation that provides its participants with an experience of chaotic change in the continuity of workflow. The players are organized into production groups and management groups. The "organization" is thus a complex system that exists within an environment that is generating spontaneous events that threaten the continuity or stability of production efforts.

There are several teams working simultaneously in the game. Members of each team toss a ball in a circle. The goal for each group is to have all members handle the ball at least once before returning to the team leader. When a ball has completed its cycle, the group tosses a separate "report ball" to the management group, and a group member who is equipped with a pencil and clip board records the completed toss cycle as a unit of work. The index of productivity is the number of completed toss cycles that transpire in 20-section periods for that group. Management then collects one "report ball" from each group and completes a set of reports. When a set has been assembled, management yells "sale" and marks down the time at which the sale was registered and returns the report balls to the production groups for continued work. Meanwhile, the game facilitator interrupts the process with "power outages," "strikes," and "tornadoes," and reassignments of group members from one group to another.

Two-level Hierarchies

The first study with the Chaos Exercise involved 14 participants, who were a combination of graduate students and management consultants. They were organized into three work groups and one management team. The configuration of the game hierarchy is shown in Fig. 10.2. Chaos was hypothesized to exist at both the work group level and the management level because the "organization's" work output was the result of three coupled oscillators. The three oscillators in this situation were the three work groups, which produced "report balls" almost periodically. There was no requirement placed on the "workers," however, their output was to be constrained to regular limit cycles.

The results showed that the production trends for the work groups were chaotic over time as signified by a positive Lyapunov exponent and dimension which was calculated on the production data series. Lyapunov dimensionality was calculated through the nonlinear regression method (Chapter 3), and resulted in 90% of variance accounted for by the simplest model of the series. A phase portrait of one work group's performance appears in Fig. 10.3.

It was not possible, however, to analyze the management production records because management was in such a state of confusion they could not record the data.

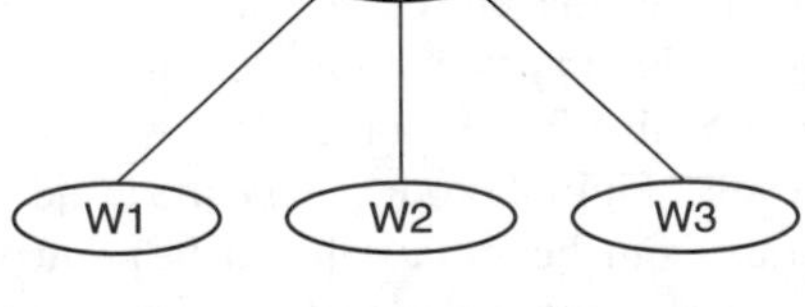

FIG. 10.2. Two-level hierarchy configuration for the Chaos Exercise.

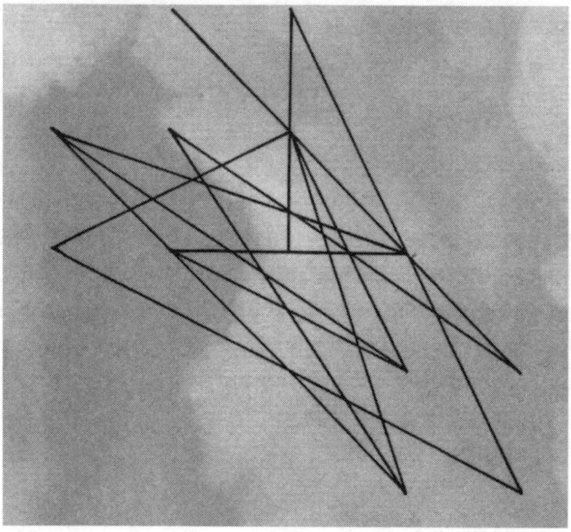

FIG. 10.3. Phase portrait of a group of workers' performance in a two-level hierarchy. From the case first published in Guastello (1995a, p. 353).

Interestingly, two management consultants, who were selected at whim, formed the (incompetent) management team. The study made an important point, nonetheless, that the erratic production behavior that is often described as the subjective *experience* of chaos is indeed symptomatic of mathematical chaos. Furthermore, the chaos function accounted for the majority of the production variance; there was comparably little noise by social science standards.

The second study of a two-level hierarchical production system (Guastello, 1999a) generated some different results. The two-level hierarchy was configured with three work groups, one management team, and a total of 14 participants (same as the previous configuration). The participants this time were graduate students in human relations. Most of them held regular jobs.

There was a bifurcation effect observed for the work groups, however, and R^2 was lower than before (.51), which meant that noise (variance unaccounted for) was higher. The function was

$$\Delta z = -0.374 z_1 e^{(0.292 z_1)} + 1.09. \tag{10.1}$$

The bifurcation effect indicated that entropy in the system varied over time and that there was a pattern of instability in production over time that could lead to a state of chaos if it became large enough. When Equation 10.1 was extrapolated over time for groups with different levels of initial productivity, the projections showed that performance made a sharp arc from the initial value to the point of asymptotic stability. The conditions that could have contributed to the bifurcation effect were not known.

The management team in the two-level organization was able to manage the workflow and produce readable data, in contrast to the previous experience. Their work production function was chaotic with 91% of variance accounted for by the nonlinear model. There was no bifurcation effect present. I explained to the group the difference between their performance and the performance of the previous group. One of the management players responded that he had spent 20 years in the military and "We had to manage chaos all the time."

The contrast in results for the two 2-level cases suggested that in the more recent case, management was successful in self-organizing its function, which had the effect of controlling chaos at the worker level. This interpretation is based on the combination of events where (a) the deterministic function for management was strong with low noise, and (b) the strength of the workers' deterministic function was reduced leaving greater levels of noise. These dynamics were consistent with expectations from synergetics theory insofar as the system displayed stronger and simpler dynamics at the management level. The inconsistent aspect, however, was that the work groups did not display the same functions in both experiments. On the other hand it could be argued that bottom-up transient patterns were stifled by the strong management function.

Three-level Hierarchy

The first example of the Chaos Exercise with a three-level experimental organization (Guastello, 1999a), produced some colorful results. The hierarchy consisted of six work groups, two middle management groups, one top management group, and a total of 85 participants, who were all undergraduate students in psychology courses. The configuration of this game is shown in Fig. 10.4.

A variety of effects emerged. First, the work groups' behavior was chaotic, with the net result of a steady increase in production efficiency over time. There was no apparent fixed stable point when their nonlinear function was projected in time. Middle management showed a chaotic function for their production of subassemblies for sequential units of time, which eventually stabilized. Their

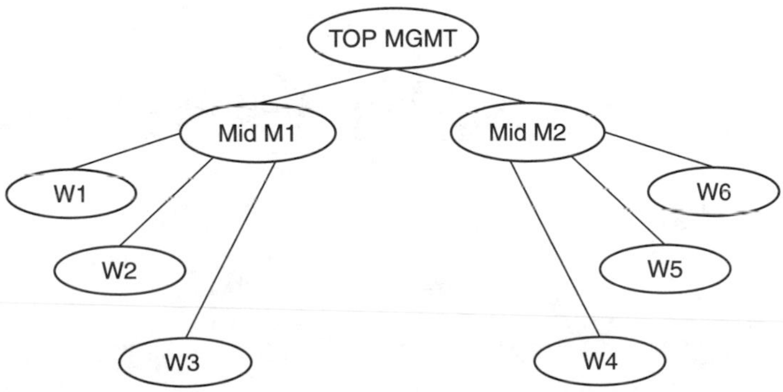

FIG. 10.4. Three-level hierarchy configuration for the Chaos Exercise.

efficiency levels, which were negatively defined as the time elapsed between two subassemblies, showed a dampening oscillation in one case, and an accelerating oscillation in another. Top management showed chaotic and oscillatory behavior for both its final assemblies completed per unit of time and efficiency. The oscillations accelerated in the case of completed assemblies, and dampened in the case of efficiency.

The functions that were obtained for top management were iterated in simulated time using different initial conditions. Those results are shown in Fig. 10.5. The number of sales in a time period would oscillate more widely for management groups that were initially low performers. High performers would oscillate also, but not as much. The efficiency of work displayed the dampening function that is shown in the lower portion of Fig. 10.5. Oscillation did not disappear entirely over time.

The results of the hierarchical production study offered some evidence that there was an element of truth inherent in the main theoretical relationships drawn from game theory, synergetics, and Rosser et al. (1994). First, the two-level system

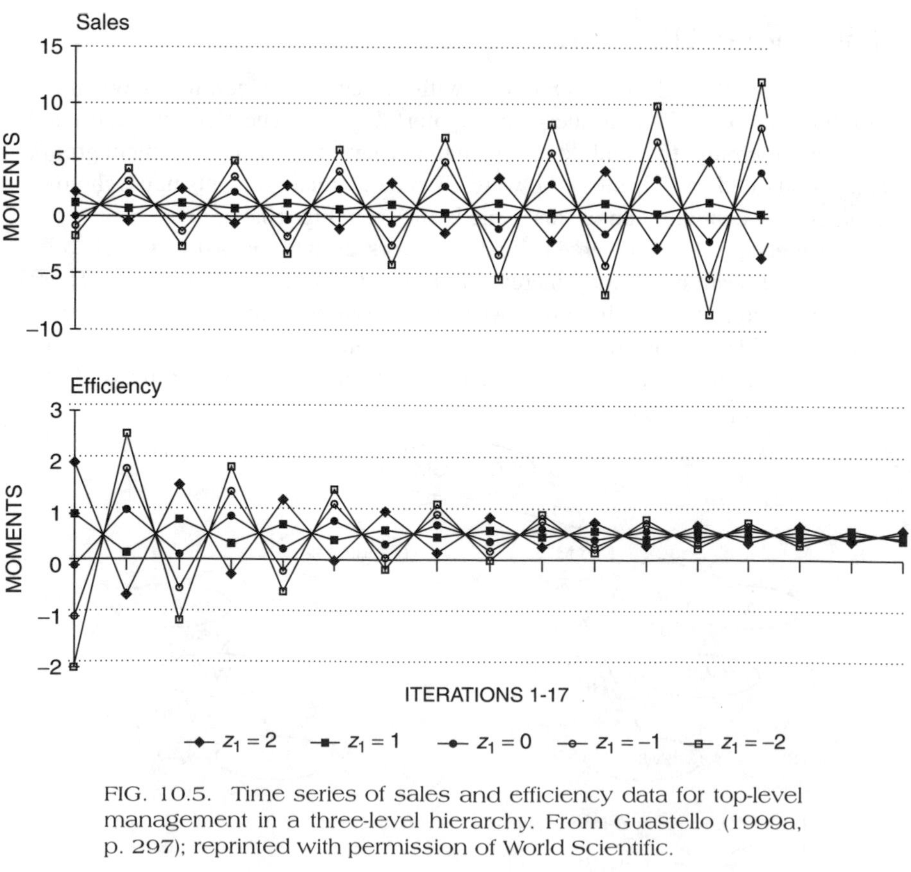

FIG. 10.5. Time series of sales and efficiency data for top-level management in a three-level hierarchy. From Guastello (1999a, p. 297); reprinted with permission of World Scientific.

displayed results that were possibly consistent with a subgame perfect assumption, although the results, and hence the assumption, did not generalize to the three-level case. Specifically, the stable and chaotic work performance that was observed in the first experiment (Guastello, 1995a) was evident at the management level in the second (Guastello, 1999a), where the two games involved the same configurations of participants and the same rules. The consistency with the subgame perfect assumption was not complete, however, because the same dynamics were not identified at both levels of the organization within the same game.

Third, a bifurcation effect was present in the management data in the three-level hierarchy, which denoted a pattern of instability. Instability at the management levels would be consistent with the "revolt of the slaved variables" dynamics, wherein sufficient entropy from the lower levels of the organization could disrupt the management. The overall pattern of results suggests that a cognitive process could be explaining all the results, which is the managerial control of chaos. We return to this theme in Chapter 12. Meanwhile, the management teams encountered so far showed a full range of responses ranging from total disarray to close control.

In further analyses, we (Guastello & Bock, 2001) used Abarbanel's (1996) principal components procedure to determine if the phase portrait of the top management time series for sales should be embedded in more than the standard two dimensions. In doing so, we analyzed the first half (49 observations) of the time series and compared those results to results based on the entire time series. The objective of the comparison was to determine whether the time series itself was stationary; in other words, we were interested in finding out if the same dynamics occurred through the series or whether different dynamics were occurring at different times.

It turned out that the sales data unfolded in two dimensions, or components, for the short series, and five dimensions in the full data series. The exponential functions that we extracted were a bit simpler than the original version, but there were more of them. The upshot was that the sales data were not chaotic. Rather, management maintained a reasonable amount of control in the early part of the game. As things happened, management control weakened, but control was regained toward the end. The phase portrait shown in Fig. 10.6 is a three-dimensional projection of the two largest components. Tight and loose winding of the trajectory can be see therein, along with a transient trajectory out of the dominant plane.

A phase portrait for a system of five components would require a set of six 3-dimensional projections, which appear in the original article. The deep mystical importance of the added dimensions was not entirely apparent.

Downsizing Experiment

The experiment that follows (for full details, see Guastello & Johnson, 1999) was another Chaos Exercise situation. Three organizations with three-level configuration were studied in which different amounts of downsizing were induced during

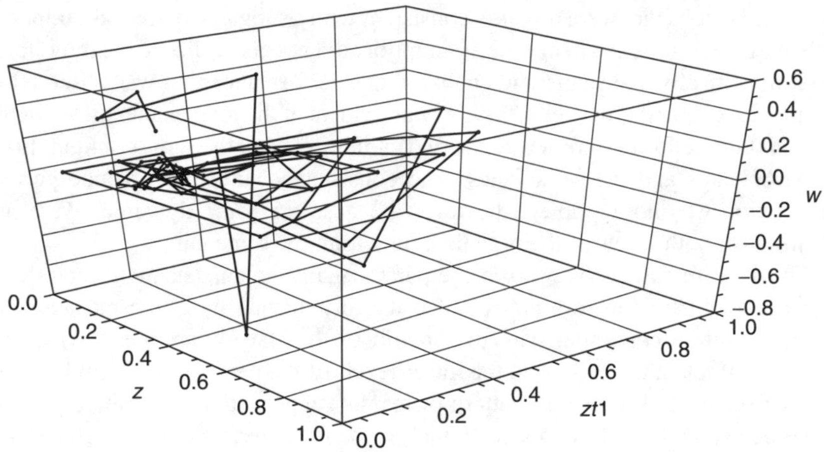

FIG. 10.6. Three-dimensional phase portrait of sales data for top-level management in a three-level hierarchy. From Guastello & Bock (2001); reprinted with permission of Human Sciences Press and Kluwer Academic Publishers.

the game. Indicators such as the complexity of the structural equation governing the work output, Lyapunov dimensionality, and bifurcation structure were examined as indicators of the effects of downsizing. The downsizing intervention itself was hypothesized to contribute a bifurcating effect on the system.

The focus of attention was the effect of downsizing on the management of the workflow. Thus, as a matter of experimental control, the downsizing manipulation used in this study affected management teams only; work groups were not downsized. This manipulation was predicated on conditions where the existing work groups were absolutely necessary for completion of the work, and circumvented the complications that arise in real situations where workers react to being downsized themselves.

A total of 80 undergraduates who were enrolled in psychology courses participated in the study. They all played the Chaos Exercise in one of three experimental conditions using the three-level hierarchy shown in Fig. 10.4. The downsizing manipulation was enacted after ten minutes of play. Downsizing affected top and middle management groups, but not worker groups. For Condition A (28 players), management groups were reduced from three to two players each. For Condition B (19 players), management groups were reduced from two to one player each. For Condition C, (33 players) management groups were reduced from three to one players per management group. Timekeepers were never removed during the downsizing so that data collection would be consistent. The game continued for another 5 minutes after downsizing with additional power outages and tornadoes at approximately 2-minute intervals. Although every attempt was made to allot equal numbers of participants to each experimental condition, irregularities developed because some scheduled participants did not show up at the appointed time of the study.

The dependent measures again consisted of the number of completed ball tosses in each 20-second interval. For middle and top management, the recording was such that it was possible to indicate the production efficiency associated with each "sale" or subassembly; in principle, a shorter amount of time indicated greater efficiency. The time records were later converted to the number of subassemblies or sales for 20-second periods; this measurement allowed some further comparability with the work output from worker groups.

The same nonlinear model structures were tested as in the previous cases. In this experiment, however, there was one more variable to include. G was a dichotomous variable that was scored 1 before the downsizing manipulation and 2 afterwards. After dividing through by its scale parameter, it was tested as a bifurcation variable:

$$z_2 = \theta_1 \, G z_1 \, e^{\theta_2 z_1} + \theta_3. \tag{10.2}$$

Once again, θ_1 and θ_3 are garbage constants. Occasionally, a dynamical process is more closely related to the change in z (Δz), rather than z itself. In those situations, Δz replaces z_2 in Equations 3.19, 3.20, and 10.2. In those cases, dimensionality is still defined for the Δz function per Equations 3.18 or 3.21; the integral of $e^x dx$ is e^u, which is convenient. Models were, therefore, also tested with Δz in place of z_2 in Equations 3.19, 3.20, and 10.2. The linear comparison model for this experiment was

$$z_2 = b_0 \; b_1 z_1 + b_2 G. \tag{10.3}$$

The complete statistics for the study are reported in the original article. I will simply summary the main trends here. It was possible to extract a significant linear model, and a slightly better nonlinear model, for work groups in all three experimental conditions. The nonlinear dynamics for the experimental conditions A and C were similar to each other, but different from Condition B. Conditions A and C produced two-parameter simple exponential models, chaos, and 52–56% noise. Condition B required a three-parameter bifurcation model, and produced 91% noise; R^2 increased from .09 to .36 when the criterion was changed from z_2 and Δz.

A bifurcation effect for the downsizing intervention was tested on all three conditions, as shown in Equation 10.2. Three significant weights were obtained for Condition B only ($R^2 = .09$). The Lyapunov exponent for Condition B was once again negative.

Figures 10.7 and 10.8 show plots of the functions that were obtained for the middle management groups in subassemblies completed per 20 seconds, and for efficiency. In all cases, the nonlinear models were more accurate than the linear models. The two middle management groups within each experimental condition

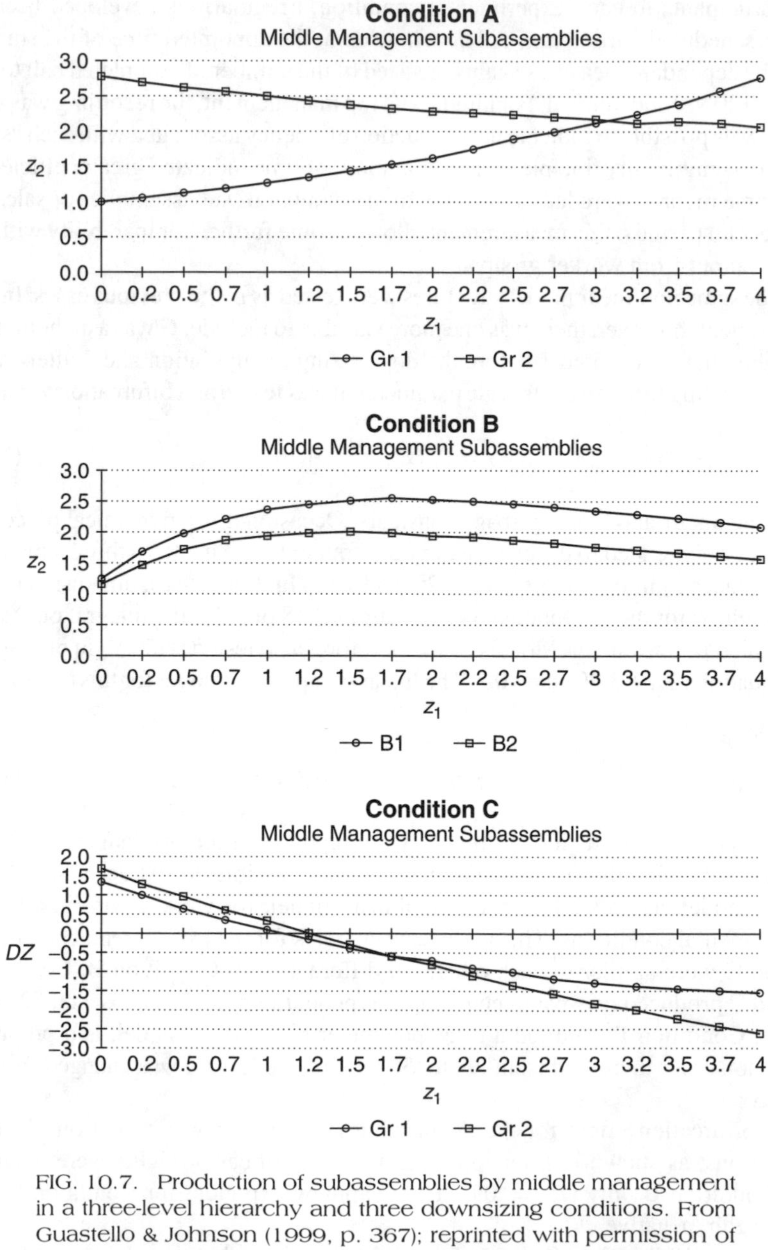

FIG. 10.7. Production of subassemblies by middle management in a three-level hierarchy and three downsizing conditions. From Guastello & Johnson (1999, p. 367); reprinted with permission of Human Sciences Press and Kluwer Academic Publishers.

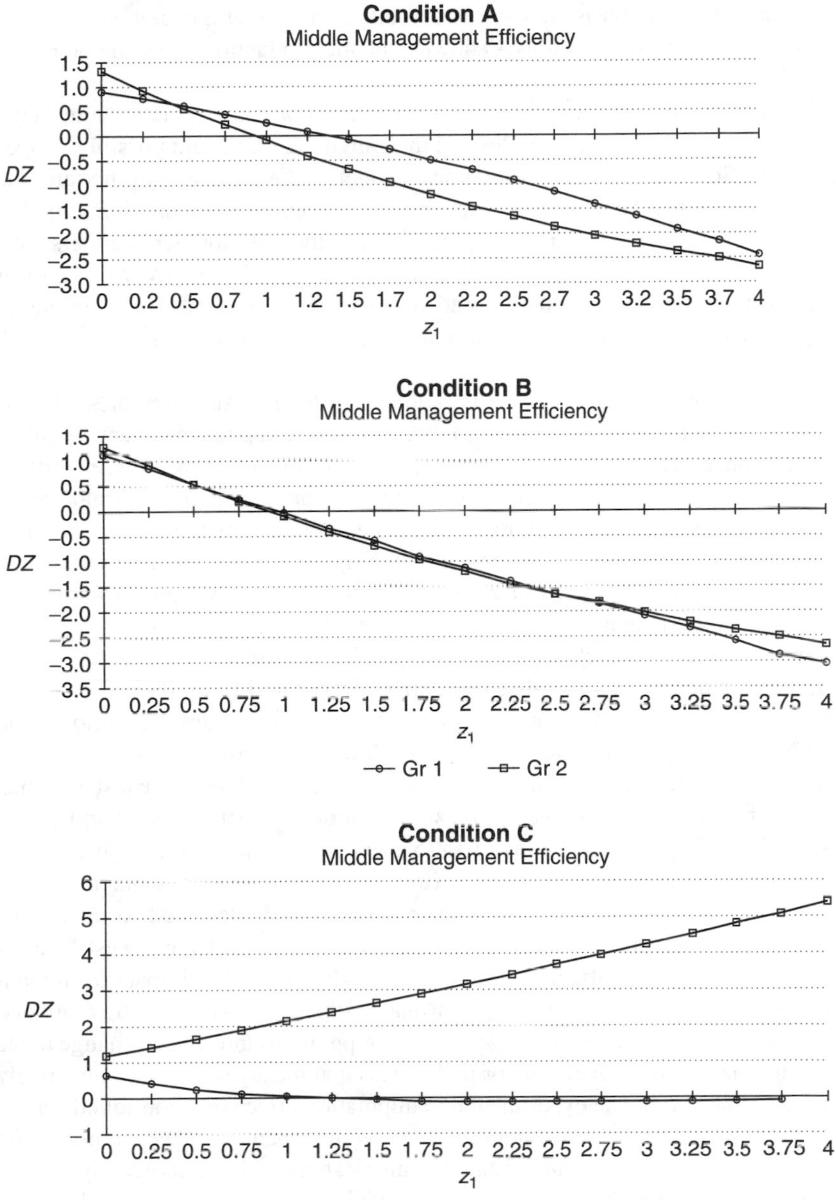

FIG. 10.8. Efficiency data for middle management in a three-level hierarchy and three downsizing conditions. From Guastello & Johnson (1999, p. 368); reprinted with permission of Human Sciences Press and Kluwer Academic Publishers.

sometimes showed consistency with each other and sometimes not. One middle management team in Condition A showed chaotic production while the other five teams did not.

The results for top management showed that nonlinear models were better than linear models in all cases. Beyond that, anything that could possibly happen happened. Some of the optimal nonlinear models were bifurcation functions, but others were represented better by the simple exponential function. Some models were best characterized with Δz in place of z_2 as the criterion, while others were best characterized with z_2 as the criterion. For sales, the Lyapunov exponent was negative for Conditions A and C, and positive for Condition B. For efficiency (which is an indication of a profit rate), the Lyapunov exponent was positive in all three cases.

Of the various data displays, the iteration of the top management sales function (Fig. 10.9) was the most meaningful. For Condition A, top management would, in the long run, stabilize its rate of sales; the function was not especially sensitive to initial sales performance levels. For Condition B, top management would appear to perform in a stable fashion for a while, but explosive growth in sales over time would occur. This function was sensitive to initial conditions insofar as organizations that were the better performers would explode sooner than others would. For Condition C, top management would display gradual steady growth.

The variable G, which represented a possible bifurcation effect that would have taken place before and after downsizing, registered a significant impact on the worker function in Condition B only. In the other workers' conditions, and all middle and top management conditions, downsizing produced only "chaos as usual." Even there, the dynamics were not always chaotic. They were just unstable. The downsizing interventions can thus be regarded as just another form of the externally applied shocks that organizations experience, such as the experimental introduction of strikes, power outages, riots, and personnel reassignments.

The experimental manipulations in this study were designed to assess the impact of downsizing on management behavior. Workers at the lowest level of the hierarchy were not affected directly. Although a watershed impact from management was possible, their work performance functions did not portray any disturbance. For the management players, the manipulations induced no change in the number of levels of management or in the tasks that management was collectively required to perform. The experimental manipulation effectively controlled for social forces that exist in real situations such as management power motives, job insecurity, organizational climate and communication, and stockholder dynamics.

The foregoing results offered several provisional conclusions about downsizing. (a) When the production dynamics are considered in isolation from other organizational factors, management downsizing to the minimum number of managers to cover the jobs *can possibly* produce either increased production units or improved efficiency per unit. These effects cannot be generalized to subminimal staffing, however, on the basis of this study, and do not extend to downsizing

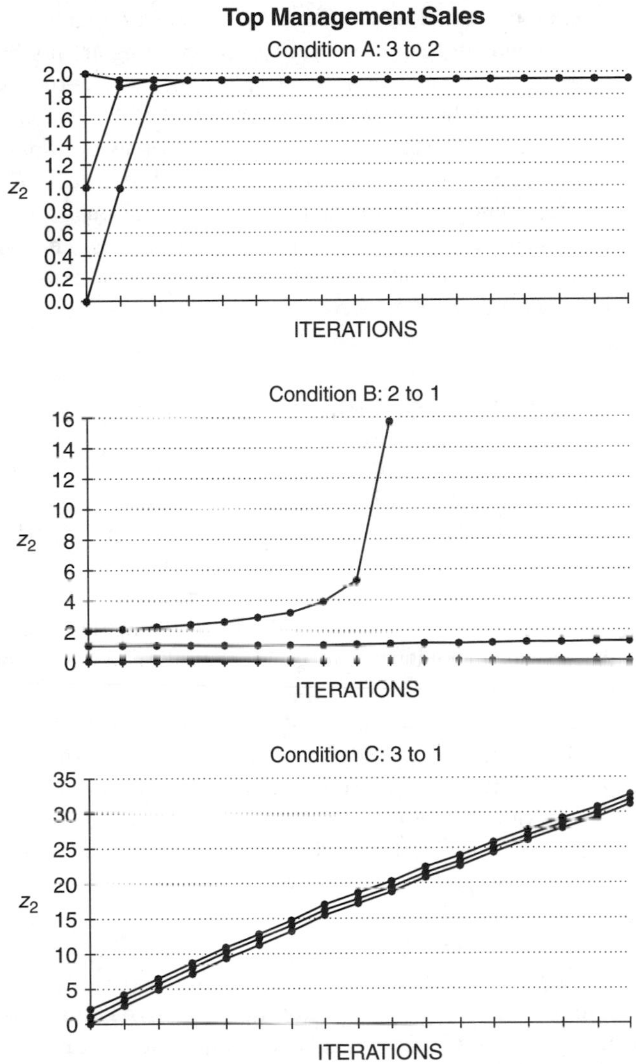

FIG. 10.9. Top management sales data in a three-level hierarchy and three downsizing conditions. From Guastello & Johnson (1999, p. 372); reprinted with permission of Human Sciences Press and Kluwer Academic Publishers.

of production personnel. (b) A trade-off between production units and efficiency per unit is often encountered. (c) The effects of downsizing are not homogenous at different levels of the organization. (d) A variety of production responses are possible at the top and middle management level, not all of which appear adaptive.

The average R^2 across the three experimental conditions for workers was .31 for the linear models and .34 for the nonlinear models. The average R^2 across the three experimental conditions for top and middle management groups combined was .04 for the linear models and .35 for the nonlinear models. The modest levels of prediction are possibly indicative of transient behavior patterns that were not captured by the models that were tested.

Implications for Hierarchical Dynamical Systems

Some interpretations are warranted. First, the assumption of subgame perfection, which is required for the game theory prediction that consistent productivity patterns are generated at different levels of the hierarchy, is not to be assumed when trying to forecast the outcomes of a downsizing intervention. In this experiment, worker utilities remained the same across the three manipulations; all changes occurred in the management levels. Subgame perfection was thus deliberately disrupted.

Little in the way of a downward watershed effect from downsizing was observed, where the dynamics of the worker groups could be traced to the dynamics of top and middle management. The dynamical spillover might have been suggested from the top-down driver–slave principles of synergetics. Similarly, there was no upward revolt of the slaved variables implicit in the downsizing exercises between the two lower levels. Rather, any destabilization among management players was confined within the two management levels.

A common theme appears to be emerging with regard to the cognitive aspect of the management activity. It appears that management responses to the production dynamics and the disruptions, involve a form of cognitive control. That control seems to require a trade-off between production quantity and efficiency levels. Potential conflicts between those two organizational objectives have not been systematically addressed in the organizational literature, other than the "economies of scale" arguments in economics. It now appears that efficiency can drop with increased production, and if so, the drop has more to do with the efficiency of the management than with the principle of the economy of scale.

The generalizability of the results of the hierarchical workflow studies to the full range of real conditions is still somewhat limited at the present time. New studies should systematically introduce a reduction of management levels, redefinition of the management tasks, and the staffing of the worker groups themselves. Conditions should be sought that would induce the organizational "paralysis" noted by some researchers. Additionally, other forms of organizational behavior should be investigated where production levels could potentially conflict with profit margins.

SUMMARY

The growth and contraction of organizational hierarchies is a form of organizational change, although some would hesitate to call it OD in the true sense. Several reasons for the downsizing efforts that transpired over the last 15 years were discussed. Some reasons for downsizing appeared more rational than others. It is also true that multiple forms of utility were involved in the downsizing decisions.

Both the patterns of workflow within a hierarchy and downsizing decisions, in principle, defy the formalisms of game theory because the assumption of subgame perfection could not be met. For some management strategists, the short-term utilities of pay, hiring, and downsizing decisions were very different from long-term utilities. Sraffian economics, which is actually based on a concept of complex systems and predates complexity theory, would have predicted the poor results the organizations derived from downsizing.

Studies of work flow within an organizational hierarchy did not exist before the NDS studies reported in this chapter. Possible dynamical theories offered different suggestions as to how they would take place. Perhaps the control of work flow *should* be top-down, as suggested by the synergetics school of thought, but in actuality it was not. Rather, the studies occasionally showed Rosser et al.'s (1994) "revolt of the slaved variables." Instabilities in the lower levels of the organization destabilized management control, particularly when three levels of hierarchy were involved. Downsizing manipulations turned out to be just another form of destabilizing disruption.

It was also possible to discern differences in managers' ability to control chaotic flows. The two examples of two-level hierarchies were played with professional managers in the management roles. One team lost control completely, while the other rode the tidal wave well. The analysis of the three-level game (Guastello & Bock, 2001) showed an effort by the student mangers to gain control after control got away from them. Games with the downsizing of management showed a variety of possible responses, some of which were adaptive while other responses were not. These observations strongly suggest that there are individual differences in the ability to navigate dynamics and control chaos that should be studied by psychologists. Indeed that is the topic of Chapter 12. But before we go there, it is important to gain a grip on the sources of instability from outside the organization that could trigger an adaptive response from inside.

11

Nonlinear Economics for Organizations

It is not uncommon for organizational theories to speak of "the environment" as if it were a formless fountain of stimuli. Most academic approaches to organizational behavior tend to dismiss economics as somebody else's topic and problem. In contrast, an NDS theory of organizational behavior recognizes that some of the dynamical events that take place in "the environment" fall into both the domains of economic theory and the enlightened understanding of organizational behavior. True, it is impossible to condense all nonlinear economics into one chapter. Rather, it is necessary to focus on a few topics that are proximally related to organizational life, and save the rest for other authors such as Leydesdorff and van den Besselaar (1994), Puu (1993, 2000b), Rosser (1991, 1999, 2000a), and Zhang (1996).

The chapter begins with the concept of the simple price equilibrium and the classical economic system that goes with it. The limitations of classical economics, such as the assumption of perfect competition, are well-known today, although classical and neoclassical thinking persists. The chapter then continues with some nonlinear economic themes that are, on the one hand, important to organizational life, and on the other hand, nonclassical in their content. They are the nonlinear market theory, theories of unemployment and inflation, information economics, and natural resource economics.

CLASSICAL CONCEPTS

Some of what follows in this section is familiar to many readers. The objective here is to connect some dots between classical thinking and current thinking about self-organization and nonlinear economic dynamics.

Law of Supply and Demand

As the demand for a commodity becomes greater, people are willing to pay more for it if there is excess demand beyond the present supply. As the commodity becomes more available, the price goes down after the supply exceeds the demand. The relationships between supply and price and demand in price are commonly represented by two nominally nonlinear curves, as shown in Fig. 11.1. (In other words, there is no need to assume linearity or even a specific nonlinear function at this point.) The point at which the two curves cross is the (Walrasian) equilibrium point, where supply and demand levels stabilize.

In the NDS lexicon, the Walrasian equilibrium is a fixed point (Dore, 1998). If we were to introduce some temporal dynamics of demand, such as lumber to build houses in the spring, or the longer-term trends in demands for industrial chemicals, the fixed point becomes a limit cycle. It is not difficult to imagine a more complex economy with multiple goods traded in limit cycles and dependencies among some of those markets. We would quickly attain the minimum conditions required to produce chaos in commodity prices in some sectors of the economy, although not all combinations of three limit cycles produce chaos (Puu, 1993).

Next we can introduce some variability among suppliers and competition among them. For purposes of this exercise, assume that the utility of a good is the same from all suppliers, and the same to all consumers. The supplier who can produce the same goods at lower prices gets more business. The economy of scale principle kicks in here: Sellers who sell in greater volumes can withstand smaller profits per

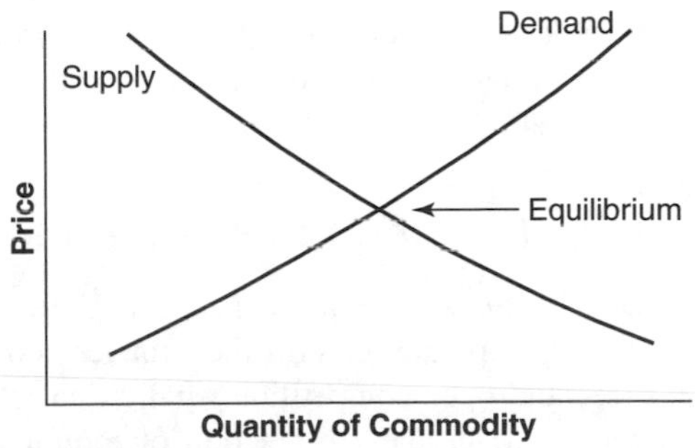

FIG. 11.1. The classical equilibrium between supply, demand, and price.

trade if the volume of trading is large enough to make a living. Other some sellers have an advantage in that they can produce goods less expensively because of a more favorable market experience for raw materials or a more efficient value-added process; their profits also increase with greater volume.

Marginal Utility, Traders, Money

The foregoing tale of supply and demand assumed the existence of money. Bartering markets persisted after the invention of money to the extent that they were more convenient and satisfactory to potential traders. The next question is why a trade ever takes place.

A market forms when there are at least two traders with at least one commodity to trade. Each has an oversupply of something and a demand for something else. It is also important that each trader have a different *marginal utility* associated with each of the commodities. A marginal utility is the willingness one trader (customer) to pay more for a commodity than another trader (supplier) would do. In other words, all traders would rather have something other than what they are holding at the moment.

We need some catalyzing events in order to find someone who is willing to swap some corn for our melons. One possibility is a middleman who collects commodities and then resells them to potential buyers. Another is the formation of a common location for traders such a bazaar or grain exchange. The third is the development of money, which allows trades to be made on the basis of a common index of value. The three elements often work in combination. Economists thus speak of the free market as an "unbiased auctioneer" who referees the sales of all goods to any highest bidder.

The history of money itself is long story, but the common theme has always revolved around widely accepted norms of value, such as precious metals. Monetary exchange then evolved by substitution of paper money for metal, then electronic impulses for paper. Currencies issued by different nations today sustain their value through—guess what—another market. The accounting system for monetary trades is paid for by a combination of agreements between the buyers and sellers, and these costs of doing business are passed on to the buyers and sellers. Thus, money itself has a cost.

The Invisible Hand of Resource Allocation

Adam Smith introduced the Invisible Hand concept in 1776 to summarize how individual market events extrapolate to form the broader economy (Baumol & Blinder, 1979). With free and open competition, egalitarian relationships among traders, and an absence of government protection of monopolies, an economy gropes toward efficiency. Here "efficiency" means that the suppliers who supply the best goods for the best prices to the largest markets survive, and the dubious characters find another job. The "natural" balance of supply and demand shapes the number of participants in any particular market.

The societal division of labor progresses as markets expand. As organizations become larger, labor becomes more specialized. Sociotechnical systems theory holds that the best process for dividing labor is to allow people to find their own best means of organizing and executing the work. The method that people eventually choose will be the one that maximizes human capabilities. Capabilities are physical, mental, and social. Any solution to the division of labor involves asymmetries in interaction. Thus, the formation of networks of suppliers and consumers, or of specialized markets, is inevitable. The process is one of self-organization—or so it appears.

Classical Assumptions

There are several assumptions of classical economic theories for phenomena. If the assumptions are met, perfect equilibria, rather than instability, will occur in markets. Furthermore, the behavior of the macro-economic system can be explained by no more than a few market-oriented rules. They do not hold well in practice, however. On the other hand, the demise of classical assumptions, together with several major nonclassical economic systems, has promoted the development of NDS explanations for economic phenomena. The division of labor was an example discussed in Chapter 4, and by Chapter 11 we saw a reversal of labor division within organizations.

The assumption of *perfect competition* means that every economic agent has an equal opportunity of interacting with every other agent. All agents are working to maximize their own outcomes in self-interested fashion. If there were perfect competition, then there would be no collusion among buyers, or among sellers, to force prices up or down. All agents would have equal access to markets and information about markets.

It would appear that, if a market equilibrates on a price for a commodity, all new entrants to the market who trade at market prices will reinforce the status quo. Thus, in essence, the collusion is built in. On the other hand, such equilibration does not, in principle, favors buyers more than sellers. Certain combinations of agents, meanwhile, would prefer to do business with each other, rather than with other agents, because of good mutual outcomes in the past. Thus, some relationships are going to repeat themselves at the exclusion of other possible relationships.

In the case of labor, Daly and Goodland (1994) noted that the current age of global economics and electronic money is bringing a new challenge to perfect competition. The challenge concerns the mobility of labor and capital. Money can move quickly around the world and to different enterprises. Labor, on the other hand, is (more commonly than not) geographically entrenched and not able to switch skills and technologies at whim. This asymmetry in mobility is detrimental to the interests of labor, and favors the interest of capital.

The assumption of *perfect rationality* is that agents have an unlimited capacity to utilize information about commodities, prices, markets, and their futures and to make optimal decisions. Although the agents may be indeed working in their own self-interest, their rationality is *bounded* nonetheless. The notion of bounded rationality itself gave rise to several areas of productive psychological research concerning biases in decision making, the limits of human cognitive abilities, computer programs that emulate the thinking of "experts," and so on. According to classical thinking, if there is perfect rationality, speculative bubbles are not possible (Rosser, 1997). This point is expanded later in this chapter in the section on stock market behavior.

The notion of perfect rationality carries with it the idea of *market efficiency*, which is based on the instant *flow of information*. On the one hand, all necessary information about products is equally distributed among agents at lightning speed. On the other hand, all information about a commodity, such as the future value of a share of a corporation, is immediately encoded into the market price for that commodity. Information flows are, of course, a favorite focus for theories of self-organized behavior. A subsequent section of this chapter considers what happens when information itself is the subject of market trading.

Classical economics assumes that agents are trading only *one commodity per agent*. If this assumption holds, then all market trades are independent of all other trades. Anyone who has ever been to a department store knows this assumption is not always true.

The assumption of the *unbiased auctioneer* is that the market arbitrators are treating all players equally. A good deal of human energy goes into making local laws and international trade agreements to ensure this assumption. The formation and enforcement of monopolies is, of course, the opposite state of affairs. Both happen.

The last assumption on my list for now is the assumption of *equal utility of money*. In other words, classical economics assumes that $100 to one agent is valued at the same amount by every other agent. According to Dore (1998), it is possible that the only universal law in economics is the opposite state of affairs, due to Engels: The marginal utility of money is much less for the rich than it is for the poor. Thus, markets pander to the needs of the richest sectors of society before working their way down the food chain.

Multiple Basins

The concept of multiple basins in economics dates back to Robinson (1933; Puu, 2000b). Products, such as automobiles or kitchen appliances, come in many variations with different features and different prices attached. The variation in qualities and prices are meant to appeal to people who wish to make their purchases within certain price boundaries. How many times have we been asked by the salesperson, "How much do you wish to spend?" We have probably also noticed that occasionally a manufacturer will redesign a product with the result that the price increases or drops by a psychologically significant amount. The redesign of products and prices often occurs after new technological advances are introduced.

The concept of multiple basins is nonclassical, or at best neoclassical, because it involves a deviation from the assumption of perfect competition. In classical thinking, there should only be one equilibrium for a product's market. Balasko (1978a, 1978b, 1979a, 1979b), on the other hand, discovered a paradox between some dynamics within differential topology and single-equilibrium reasoning. He proved that a set of stable and minimally contiguous basins would give rise to a stable global equilibrium for the system of basins. Furthermore, it was possible to predict properties of the global equilibrium from knowledge of the local stability, and vice versa. The requirement of "minimally contiguous basins" meant that the basins needed to be connected at only a very small window of points.

RATIONALITY IN THE STOCK EXCHANGE

If perfect rationality was a legitimate assumption, all traders on the stock exchange would make their purchases and sales using the *fundamentalist strategy* of earnings per share, price–equity ratios, asset values per share, debt levels, dividend rates, and so forth. There would be no speculative bubbles, boom and bust cycles, or foolish purchases of any kind. And Mona Lisa would have worn a mustache.

The interesting question is, rather, how do speculative bubbles form, and which nonlinear processes are involved? That question is followed closely by another one: What do traders do to create one or another dynamical event? According to Rosser (1997), several taxonomies of investor strategies have been proposed over the years. The types that seem to have the most robust relationship to dynamics are the fundamentalist, the chartist, the beauty contest judge, and the noise trader.

The fundamentalist strategy, as mentioned a moment ago, is based on the economic behavior of the organization (or entity) whose stock is being traded. It is also influenced by global economic factors that, in principle, predict future earnings, such as inflation, unemployment, and international events that affect currency trade or natural resource availability. An opportunity for irrationality occurs here. Most of us, since the day we first dropped out of the tree, have regarded unemployment as "bad," and employment as "good." Some economic theories have rested in part on the assumption that full employment is a desirable goal. On the other hand, the last decade of New York Stock Exchange activity has reacted with widespread price increases when a quarterly increase in unemployment was announced. The common reasoning is that there is an inverse relationship between unemployment and inflation, and if employment increases, then the ugly specter of inflation must be just around the corner. Also common is the reasoning that if there is an oversupply of labor, labor costs go down, and thus corporate profits go up. The specific dynamics of unemployment and inflation are addressed later on in this chapter.

The expectations of corporate profits resulting from an announcement of downsizing were addressed in the previous chapter.

The *chartist* strategy is to predict the future price of a stock based on trends in the prices. Chartists will probably prefer to make purchases that show both good fundamentals and charts, but when in the absence of fundamentals, they work the charts. Sharp price movements often signal that a speculation is in play. Some speculations are well reasoned. They can be triggered by the introduction of a new product that promises to revolutionize something or other. When a bubble forms, the best profits go to those who get in and out quickly. The next round of speculators sees that others have already made a good profit on a stock that "is going up." The hot potato is then passed on to the third wave of still-less-informed buyers. Eventually, the bubble bursts and someone is holding it.

Somewhere in the collection of chartists is the *beauty contest judge*. According to Keynes (1936–1965), the real winner of the beauty contest is the judge who can determine which contestant will be preferred by the other judges. The personal judgment of the attractiveness of the contestant is not quite so relevant. People who trade in antiquities develop a well-honed sense of beauty contest judgment.

The fourth noteworthy trading entity is the *noise trader*. Prices fluctuate, as we know. When fundamentals are adequately represented in a price, there are upward and downward blips nonetheless. A noise trader will work those shifts and realize some profit by doing so. A blip in a price that is greater than average can potentially give a false signal to investors that a real movement is afoot. A bubble can thus self-organize around such a blip of noise.

Cusp Catastrophe Model

The cusp catastrophe model of stock market behavior evolved in a series of papers by Zeeman (1974, 1977), Weintraub (1983), Guastello (1994, 1995a), and Rosser (1997). The model is shown in Fig. 11.2. The asymmetry control parameter that affects price shifts consists of the fundamentals. The bifurcation parameter consists of variables that reflect the raw volume of price movement in either the up or down direction. Bubble formation occurs at the high-bifurcation side of the surface, while trading that is dominated by fundamentalist trading occurs on the low-bifurcation side.

According to my analysis of the New York Stock Exchange trading in the 1983–1989 period (Guastello, 1995a), the most active asymmetry variables were the dividend rate and reliability, interest rate sensitivity, and brokers' ratings. The ratings reflected price–equity ratios, alternative evaluations for organizations that suffered a loss in the prior year, interpretations of the organizations' levels of indebtedness, and other fundamental events that were specific to a stock. The most active bifurcation variables were the prime interest rate (an indication of inflation or inflation expectation on the part of the Federal Reserve Bank), the moving standard deviation of the stock in the prior two years, and the total market volume

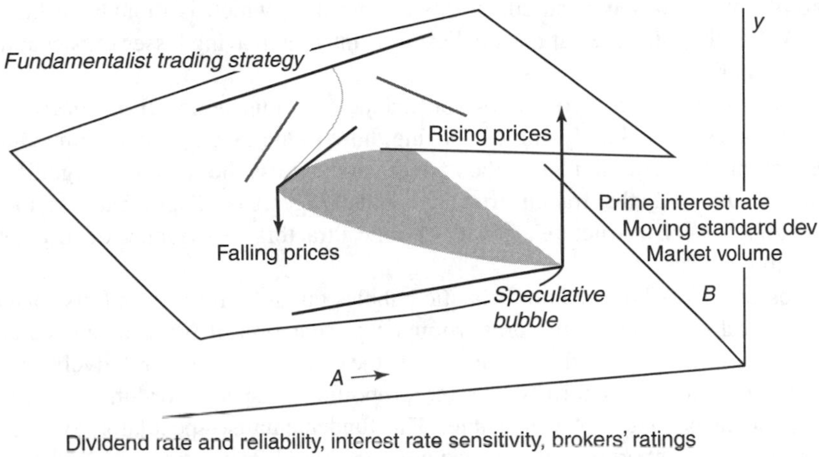

FIG. 11.2. Cusp catastrophe model for New York Stock Exchange prices.

in millions of shares traded. Of additional interest, the control variables affecting the market were not always the same in each quarter-year in which differences were taken. Phenomena such as the January Effect (a depression in prices that occurs in the second week of January after a high volume of end-of-year trades), and 2-year trading trends also emerged at during that epoch. Overall, the gap in accuracy between the nonlinear model and the linear comparison was greatest for quarter-years in which "greater uncertainty" was expressed by market observers.

Chaos in Capital Markets

Is it noise, or is it chaos? There seems to be some consistent support for the chaos interpretation, which is contrasted against the "random walk" interpretation. The formal empirical question actually goes back to some of Mandelbrot's (1966) early work on fractal structures in stock market prices. What appears to be noise actually contains deterministic processes. Peters (1991) considered the process to be chaotic, and brought into evidence fractal dimensions in time series of stock prices. The now-obvious problem, however is that the presence of a fractal does not automatically signify chaos. In his later episode, Peters (1994) retrenched his arguments into fractal structures and what they could do for prediction, and was less concerned whether chaos itself was present. He expanded the fractal concept into what became the fractal market hypothesis.

Peters (1994) observed the relationship between the time series of market trades at hourly, daily, and longer intervals, noting similarity in structure, and posited the fractal relationship between market basins, where trading lags represent different forecasting horizons and securities markets. Fractal theory further holds that the stability of markets is ensured by this relationship, which is thought to buffer shock. Shock is absorbed at the smallest time interval, leaving lesser impact at the broader horizons.

The fractal market theory does not include any contribution from macroeconomic forces to market dynamics, leaving those to the assumption of immediate absorption of information. The theory does not address the matter of ergodicity, which would imply that fractal structure could change markedly. In that case, there might not be such a structure after all. Chaotic attractors are evidence of structural stability.

Rosser (1997) explored how chaotic bubbles might be formed and dissipated. The critical ingredient is the proportional representation of fundamentalists and "trend-chasing sheep." If the balance favors the fundamentalists, a relatively stable fixed-point attractor is formed. As the proportion of speculators increases, the center point becomes very unstable. The fundamentalist–speculator dynamics occur in the neighborhood of the cusp point in Fig. 11.2.

The following is an original analysis of the Dow Jones Index (DJI) that was taken from 1995–1997. There was a total of 3,902 data points representing approximately 2 years of hourly trading. The time series was analyzed for dimensionality using the simple exponential function (Equation 3.19). The goal was to determine compare Lyapunov exponents for hourly, daily, weekly, and longer-term trades. If the fractal market theory held up, it would be possible to obtain the same dimension value, D_L for all time windows. The model was

$$z_2 = \theta_1 e^{(\theta_2 z_1)} + \theta_3, \tag{3.19}$$

where z is the DJI taken at two points in time.

The results of the analysis showed that θ_1 was extraneous; thus it was dropped from the analysis. The model was calculated at lags of 1, 5, 10, 20, and 40 hours, which would correspond to periods of one hour, approximately a half-day, approximately a day, a half-week, or a week. Table 11.1 below shows the results for parameter estimates, D_L, and R^2 at those five lag lengths. The usual corrections for location and scale were applied.

The results showed very little change as a function of lag length. R^2 varied by only .008, and D_L by only .01. Most of these changes occurred between lag

TABLE 11.1
Summary of Regression Results, Unbleached Data

Lag	R_2	θ_2 *(exponent)*	θ_3 *(constant)*	D_L
1	.965	.406	−.448	1.501
5	.964	.406	−.448	1.501
10	.965	.407	−.445	1.502
20	.963	.408	−.440	1.504
40	.957	.410	−.428	1.510

lengths of 20 and 40. The regression parameters in Table 11.1 were all statistically significant. Thus, one may conclude that the exponent was nonzero, and thus the function was nonlinear.

A linear comparison function was also tested whereby the DJI was regressed against the hourly time interval. Here the linear relationship was very strong, such that $R^2 = .938$. The incremental advantage of the nonlinear function amounted to 1.9% to 2.7% of variance accounted for by a model.

UNEMPLOYMENT AND INFLATION

Unemployment Dynamics and Policy

Phillips (1954) identified a nonlinear relationship between unemployment and inflation. The Phillips curve was derived from Keynes' (1936 1965) examination of the two quantities in his *General Theory*. By the late 1960s, however, the curve was found not to hold up against data that had been accumulated (Phelps, 1967), and it was replaced by the concept of the natural rate of unemployment (Friedman, 1968). This so-called natural rate was conceptualized as a Walrasian equilibrium (fixed-point attractor). Economic policy in the United States in the 1990s, nonetheless, continued to regard unemployment as a voluntary market function, and to define the natural rate of unemployment as whatever the current rate happened to be (Freedman & Kriesler, 1994; Seccareccia, 1991).

Lerner (1951), on the other hand, suggested that the actual level of full employment should be targeted relative to the inflation rate. If inflation is already low, then higher full employment is possible without triggering high rates of inflation. Income policy was thought to be the key variable for controlling both inflation and unemployment. To Sraffa (1960), however, income levels were far less connected to market forces than they were to power relationships between employer and employee. In a no-growth economy (different from a Keynesian expanding economy), an employer would seek to increase profits by pressuring wages, which could be done by lowering wages directly, or indirectly by forcing higher turnover and bidding down the next wave of job applicants.

A natural rate of unemployment, should it exist, is a convenient assumption for national-level policy makers who adjust central bank interest rates on the basis of money supply, inflation rates, unemployment, and international currency exchange trends. Yet observers of U.S. federal monetary policy have expressed concern that the central bank has engaged no consistent policy in its adjustments in interest rates during the 1985–1995 decade (Galbraith, 1994; Papadimitriou & Wray, 1994). From one vantagepoint, the focus of policy may have shifted from monitoring price stability to managing employment levels (Davidson, 1995). In other words, there seemed to be enough residual belief in the Phillips curve for policy makers to increase interest rates in order to generate more unemployment deliberately.

Inflation

The relationship between inflation and unemployment is somewhat related to the relationship between money and interest. Other explanations involve market dynamics for the goods being exchanged, the supply and demand for money. The market dynamics for products and money then affects movements in wages, which in turn have different possible effects on future prices of goods.

According to Keynes, "In a static society or in a society in which for any other reason no one feels any uncertainty about the future rates of interest, the . . . propensity to hoard . . . will always be zero in equilibrium" (1965, pp. 208–209). Today we might examine the true dynamical structure of "equilibrium" inasmuch as several structural possibilities (different types of attractors or bifurcations) could exist, and each type of structure could have different implications. Keynes also noted that even if lending institutions chose to generate zero profit, they would still require nonzero interest rates to cover their operations costs. Thus, the very existence of a banking system contributes a small amount to rising prices, which begins with the cost of money.

In classical economics, the supply of money was the sole and simple explanation for inflation and deflation. Keynes (1965) noted, however, that the monetarist theory was flawed in that it did not separate the impact of the money supply from changes in the wage unit. Classical monetarist and Keynesian explanations for inflation coexist only in the untenable conditions of full employment and no tendencies to save or to hoard cash.

There are two perverse consequence of the money–interest dynamics (Keynes, 1965). One is runaway inflation, in which expectations of the lower future value of money are countered with high interest rates and high prices. The second is rigid deflation, which characterized the U.S. depression of the 1930s, whereby cash was hoarded by both individual economic agents who avoided any spending, and by lending institutions who were averse to making loans, presumably because of a high perceived risk of default. Both extremes suggest the presence of self-organized economic policies that reinforce these self-fulfilling prophecies.

The consequences of runaway inflation and rigid deflation represent anything but stability. In the case of runaway inflation, economic agents (individual and institutions) are constantly responding to dramatic price and interest shifts. In the case of rampant unemployment and deflation, the individuals are prone to resort to political mechanisms for social change, or to balkanized economies that are somewhat insulated from the macroeconomic conditions. Script-based bartering economies started to emerge in the United States in the early 1990s, then appeared to have dissipated once the economic boom took form.

As mentioned earlier, inflation policy in the 1985–1995 decade attempted to hold inflation to a near-zero level by increasing interest rates whenever the unemployment rate dropped. Schultze (1959) identified two dynamics, however, that suggest alternative causal relationships between employment and inflation.

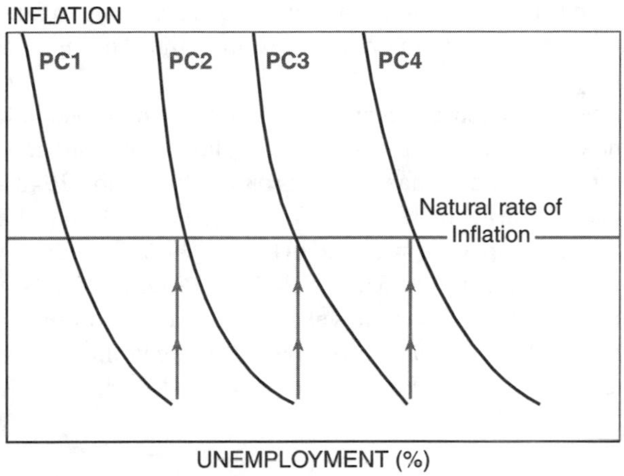

FIG. 11.3. The horizontal Phillips curve, adapted from Freedman and Kriesler (1994, p. 16).

According to the demand-pull explanation, the demand for a product induces the supplier to raise prices. In the wage push explanation, the demand for wages induces prices to rise. A wage push could reflect labor's demand to participate to a greater extent in the profits already flowing to a prosperous enterprise. A wage push would also occur if labor's spending power had shrunk too far.

Freedman and Kreisler (1994) proposed an improved model that appears to account for the inflation–unemployment dynamics that actually occur. According to their "horizontal Phillips curve," increases in unemployment pull inflation down below a critical point that is a natural rate of inflation. Once inflation declines low enough, it springs back to the critical point, but at a higher-adjusted level of unemployment. The downward pull between unemployment and inflation is now shifted to another curve that is parallel to the first. This mechanism is depicted in Fig. 11.3.

The product of one economic sector may be a resource or supply for another. The interrelationships among producers, business consumers, individual consumers, and labor costs form a complex network that includes the entire economy if it is conceptualized broadly enough (Sraffa, 1960). Some NDS theorists have drawn attention to the self-organization of supply chains (Borges & Guastello, 1996; Kauffman, 1995). Thus, the sequence of excess demand, increased prices, high profits, and upward wage push may operate in one sector, but a sequence of increased supply cost, flat demand, decreased profit margin, and downward wage push could exist in another sector. Thus, the sequence of excess demand, increased prices, high profits, and upward wage push may operate in one sector, but a sequence of increased supply cost, flat demand, decreased profit margin, and downward wage push could exist in another sector. According to Schultze (1959), excess demand is not expected to drive prices up in times of high unemployment or excess capacity.

There are other asymmetries regarding how labor within one industrial sector shares the same experience with wage trends. The major distinction is between the trends for production and managerial groups. During the 1948–1957 epoch, labor costs in manufacturing increased 17% for wage earners, but 63% for salaried personnel. Roughly the opposite was true in the 1939–1948 epoch in which wages increased 93%, but salaries only 53% (Schultze, 1959, p. 25), as mentioned in Chapter 10. Nonlinear dynamics studies also report that the flow of money between the real economy and investment economy and between financial institutions is enough to generate globally destabilizing effects (Andresen, 1999; Keen, 1997).

NDS Hypotheses and Results for Unemployment and Inflation

In response to the building controversies, I tested several NDS hypotheses concerning unemployment and inflation using the structural equations technique. The first three concerned unemployment (Guastello, 1999b, 2000b): (a) The natural rate explanation suggests that unemployment rates have a fixed-point attractor. (b) As an alternative to (a), the policies based on a natural rate assumption or a loose Keynesian mechanism suggest that instabilities over time are the norm, although some instabilities are greater than others. (c) The complex system of economic forces that affect unemployment rates can produce both upward and downward effects. This pushing and pulling suggests chaotic dynamics.

The second three hypotheses concerned inflation (Guastello, 1995c, 2000b): (a) Policies that target zero inflation assume that zero inflation is an optimal equilibrium value. According to Keynesian theory, however, the optimal equilibrium is nonzero. According to the Horizontal Phillips model, a nonzero equilibrium must exist. (b) Instabilities in inflation rates are known to have occurred historically worldwide. (c) The complex system of economic forces that affect inflation rates can produce both upward and downward effects. This pushing and pulling suggest chaotic dynamics.

The last hypothesis concerned point estimation: What are the critical values of employment and inflation stability and instability if they exist?

Data for the analysis were seasonally adjusted monthly unemployment rates for the period January 1948 to December 1994. Seasonally adjusted data conveniently control for an effect with which we are familiar already. If the seasonal correction adjustment is off by a smidgen, however, the difference between predicted and actual seasonal effects will be retained as one more form of random shock. On the other hand, if errors in seasonal adjustment were somehow *dependent* on an underlying nonlinear dynamical process, then those deviations would further contribute to the R^2 for the dynamical model. Data were analyzed at quarterly intervals (lag lengths of 3 months) as suggested by pilot analyses. There were 563 observations available at two time frames.

Similarly, monthly annualized inflation rates for the Producer Price Index (PPI) and the Consumer Price Index (CPI). The former is an indicator of inflation at the wholesale level. The latter is an indicator of inflation at the retail level. The essential findings were as follows:

Unemployment rates do not have a fixed-point attractor, and therefore are not "natural rates" in the sense of fixed-point attractors. The best characterization of unemployment rates identified a bifurcation effect, which denotes instabilities over time. Rates in this model were inclining through 6.6% but were not expected to stabilize. The second-best characterization of the unemployment data indicated a chaotic attractor, which had an epicenter at 3.4%. The chaotic structure may be interpreted as the closest alternative to a fixed-point natural rate.

If the economic system is given a strong shock, then allowed to recover, unemployment will equilibrate at a level greater than the preshock level. This same postshock level will occur with or without government intervention, although an intervention could speed up the equilibration process. The effects of shock were determined through a simulation based on the bifurcation effect that was extracted from the real-world data. Figure 11.4 illustrates the variety of possible outcomes with and without government intervention, and for two different levels initial unemployment severity. The hypothetical shock was measured at 10 times the current entropy level of the actual economy in the 1948–1994 epoch. The shock was set to

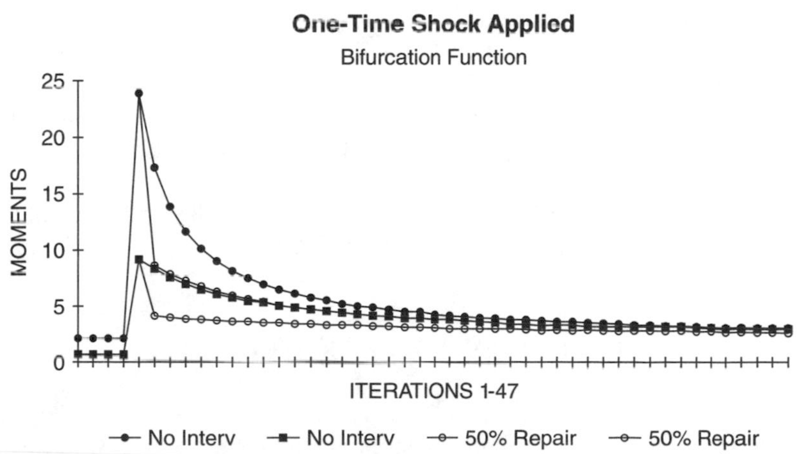

FIG. 11.4. Iterations of the bifurcation model with one-time excessive shock, with and without a governmental intervention (from Guastello, 1999b, p. 41). Both the 1994 average and epicenter of the chaotic attractor were used as initial conditions.

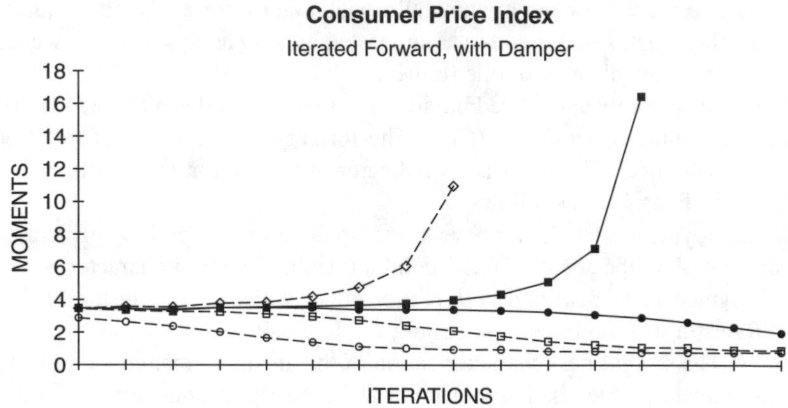

FIG. 11.5. Iterations of the chaotic attractor function for the Consumer Price Index. From Guastello (1995c, Fig. 7); reprinted with permission of *Chaos Network*, People Technologies.

occur once, and produced a sudden unemployment rate equal to that of the Great Depression in the United States (1929–1940).

A nonzero equilibrium in price inflation exists; the structure is chaotic and may be interpreted as the closest alternative to a fixed-point natural rate. The epicenter of the PPI attractor is located at −0.26%, signifying a slight downward pressure on prices. If the PPI rate is iterated forward in time, it stabilizes at a rate of 1.93%. The forward iteration of the function, which contains a negatively valued constant, appears to represent a boundary condition. Goods producers and federal economic policy probably hold the boundary in place by a combination of cost-cutting initiatives.

The epicenter of the CPI attractor is located at −0.76%, again signifying a slight downward pressure on prices. If the CPI rate function, which also contains a negatively valued constant, is iterated forward in time, it stabilizes at a rate of 2.78%. If the CPI reaches a critical point between 11.75 and 11.78%, runaway inflation will occur. The iteration chart for the runaway CPI function appears in Fig. 11.5.

INFORMATION ECONOMICS

The media have chattered for several years about the "information society" and the "information economy." Management professionals exclaimed, with a dab of drool on their lower lips, that the information economy is providing us with an ever-renewing natural resource. Those of us in the information biz should not be so impressed: In the more traditional economic viewpoints, a natural resource has no value except in terms of the cost of its extraction or the rents one must pay to others to use their resources. This valuable versus valueless tension thus propels us to take a look at contemporary thinking about information economics.

Boisot (1995) observed that value is a function of rarity and utility in common market dynamics (the limitations of classical theory were noted above). Information functions as an important resource insofar as it enlightens market players on the rarity and utility of commodities and products. In an economy where information itself is a commodity, knowledge of utility, if distributed too far, affects the rarity of the information, thus decreasing its value. Hence, traditional market concepts do not readily apply to information as a commodity.

Boisot (1995) then developed the concept of *information space*, or the *I-Space*. A unit of information is characterized by three parameters: its level of abstraction, codification, and diffusion. *Abstraction* is the degree to which the information is concrete and specific versus generalizable. *Codification* is the extent to which the information is actually written down in forms readable by others. *Diffusion* is the extent to which the information is circulated throughout a society. The rationalization for the I-Space was drawn from voluminous works in philosophy of science and psychology pertaining to knowledge structure, abstraction, encoding, and learning style.

Social learning dynamics can be modeled as trajectories through the I-Space as shown in Fig. 11.6. Someone who "learns by doing," for instance, makes a transition from high diffusion and codification, with moderate abstraction, to low diffusion and codification at the same level of abstraction. Society, meanwhile, engages in a learning cycle in which knowledge continually refreshes itself in a curvilinear path around the I-Space. Barriers to abstraction, codification, or diffusion are sometimes encountered in the process of societal learning.

The backdrop of social learning dynamics triggers an interesting question about the role of creativity in the new information economics. Boisot's (1995) answer was not an obvious one: "The source of variation that expands the range of choices for the exercise of evolutionary selection may not be individual inventiveness at all, as it is commonly supposed, but possibly the idiosyncratic conservatism of certain individuals who cannot help seeing the world in the way they do. They become cognitively committed to a vision that sets them apart from their fellow humans" (p. 220).

Institutions of different types utilize information differently. Boisot (1995) identified four relevant institutional forms: fiefs, clans, bureaucracies, and markets. The locations of those institutional forms in the I-space are shown in Fig. 11.7. Fiefs form around information that is generally concrete, uncodified, and undiffused. Clans form around information that is more diffused, a bit more abstract, and more often codified. Bureaucracies form around abstractions that are usually written down, but their content is typically undiffused. Information may go in freely, but it does not flow outward particularly well.

Markets involve information that is typically well diffused, abstract, and codified. A high level of abstraction means that the information is generalizable. High

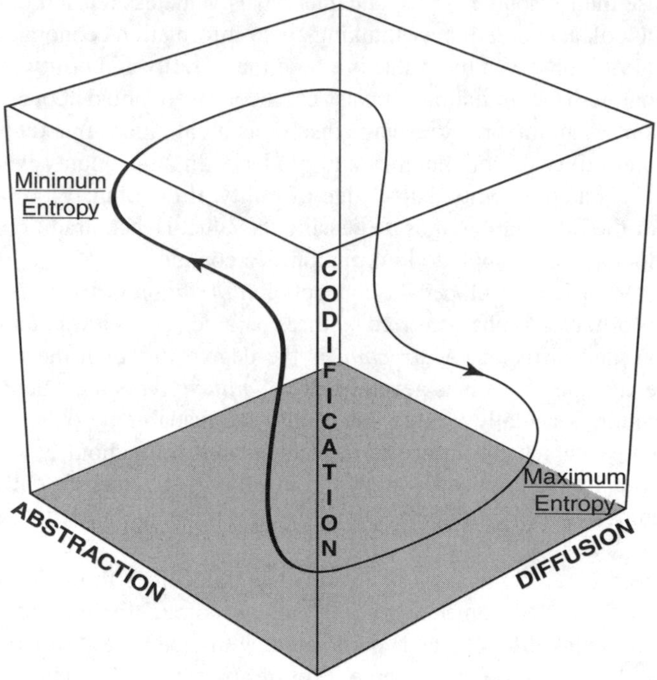

FIG. 11.6. Information space and social learning. From Boisot (1995, p. 188); reprinted by permission of Routledge.

codification indicates that publishers sell what is written, printed, or otherwise committed to a salable concrete form. The place of markets in the broader scheme of the information business is not especially large. Ideal market forms, according to Boisot (1995), are a matter of degree and are short-lived.

In his conclusion, Boisot (1995) devoted some attention to information as a natural resource. He addressed the tension that exists between environmentalists and orthodox neoclassical economists with regard to the implications of economic growth. The imposition of limits to economic growth would transform all further economic activity to a zero-sum game among economic players. Accelerated schisms and conflicts between social classes might result. Information markets and distribution could break many of those economic deadlocks, however.

I should remark here that in the United States there is a different fear of economic growth, which takes the form of a fear of inflation; the fear occasionally circulates within the stock and bond markets and the Federal Reserve Bank policy. A restriction on economic growth could produce a supply shortage of information by at least two mechanisms. In one scenario, information would more often become the property of a bureaucracy or a fief, and thus would not diffuse, in

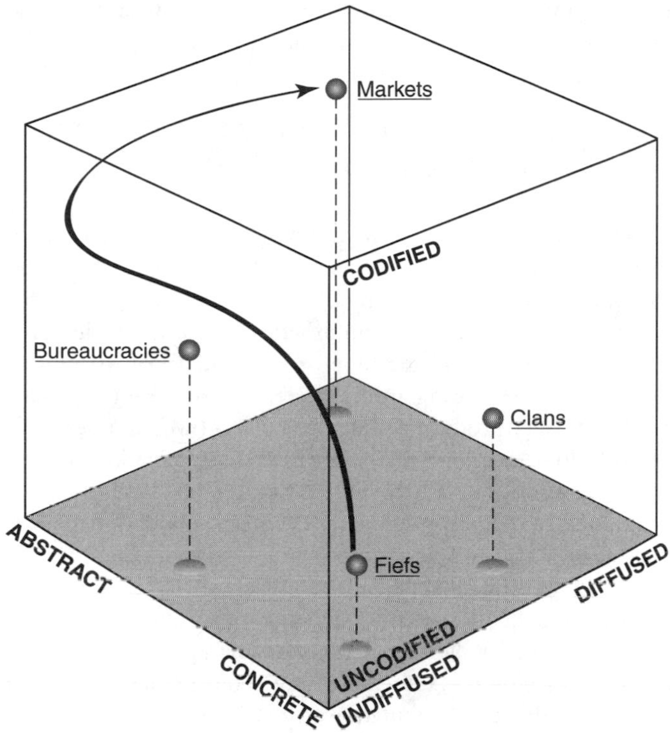

FIG. 11.7. Information space and institutional forms. From Boisot (1995, p. 317); reprinted by permission of Routledge.

order to maintain certain competitive advantages. There would be a proliferation of "trade secrets" where free flow of information would have been the norm. In another scenario, institutions would avoid paying the information worker to produce information that is too likely to be useful to the general public. Institutions would support instead information that had limited arcane value.

Finally, one might relate I-Space concepts to cultural evolution principles that characterize information as an evolutionary driving force (Banathy, 1996; Csányi, 1989). The role of information can be viewed from the biological to the societal level of analysis. To Csányi, information plays a catalytic role in the self-organization of institutions. The role of the information worker in the economic food chain of the near future is not well defined at the present time, but it is loaded with possibilities. Sraffian principles of input-output analysis (Sraffa, 1960) could offer further insights to the role of information in the next wave of economics activity. I will leave it to the reader as an exercise to list all the ways in which information is involved in bringing a new product to market. How would social structures change if certain kinds of information were available? Unlike some natural resources, information has the potential to reproduce quickly if external restraints, such as copyright protection, are not applied.

POTENTIAL COLLAPSE OF OCEANIC FISH HARVESTS

Open-sea fishing harvests have been declining worldwide since their peak in 1989 (Weber, 1994). The purpose of this project was to determine whether nonlinear dynamics could capture these trends, and whether it was possible to obtain a prediction for the recovery of the main fisheries. The work behind this fish story was completed in 1996 around the time of the collapse of the cod fisheries in Northeastern Canada, and during a time of serious trouble for Louisiana shrimp. Hard times for a fishery produce a watershed effect (no pun intended) on entire communities that do business with people who do business with the sea. The story is important because of the NDS principles that are involved in ecological economics and because of the implications for the management of fisheries, if not for the management of natural resources more generally.

Several lines of reasoning suggest that nonlinear dynamics could be involved, although the available theory does not point to a consistent picture. The first point of departure is the Lotka–Volterra functions for prey–predator relationships. The system is defined as a closed system consisting of one predator and one prey, e.g., foxes and rabbits. As the rabbit population grows, the food supply for the foxes also increases and does the fox population. Once the collective appetites of the foxes become too great for the rabbit population, however, the rabbit population contracts. The fox population contracts shortly thereafter, allowing the rabbit population to increase again. The time series for such a function would be quasi-cyclic showing increases and decreases in the populations of foxes or rabbits. More specifically, the quasi-cycles are thought to be cusp-catastrophic hysteresis functions (Thompson, 1982). On the other hand, analyses of actual time series for Canadian lynx showed quasi-cyclically as expected, but, ultimately, chaotic trends (Stewart, 1989; Tong, 1990).

The open-sea fishing environment is not a closed system. Rather, the predators are human-operated, corporation-owned, factory fishing trawlers. These compete with local, less industrialized fishers and with each other. By current estimates, the world's fishing fleets are already operating at 50% overcapacity relative to the fish that they actually catch (Weber, 1994). Under strictly ecological conditions, these fleets would have contracted substantially, but often continue to operate with the help of financial backing of their governments. Additionally, the human population can leverage itself with other food supplies, and the fleets can switch to new food species, drag the ocean more deeply, and switch to different oceanic basins when the harvest from one location falls short (Rosser, 1991). Part of the problem in the management reasoning is the use of heavy *discount factors*, by which the value of having a supply tomorrow is far less valuable than a profit today (Rosser, 2000b).

Another operating principle concerns the size of fish in each successive harvest, which follows a simple exponential decay function over time (Brown & Parman, 1993; Kirkpatrick, 1993). The biomass available to be caught decreases with each successive harvest because the fish are not allowed to grow to their full and mature size. Eventually, if the target species did not become ecologically extinct, they would become commercially extinct. Repeated harvesting also plays havoc with fish reproductive cycles, which are highly variable, as are their mutation rates. Thus current fishing practices are thought to have a strong evolutionary impact on fish (Policansky, 1993).

Although it is common for fisheries managers to consider the case of each species individually, a certain amount of collective or aggregated analysis is required to understand some of the emerging properties of the oceanic ecosystems (Sugihara et al., 1994). For instance, the sharp decline in the Peruvian anchovy was met with a sudden increase in the sardine; the anchovy population did make a sharp recovery eventually. The cod in the Newfoundland fishery, however, might not have a high chance of returning as the ecosystem vacated by the cod has been filled by migrations of dogfish (Weber, 1994).

Method

The analytic approach of the present study was, therefore, focused on the harvested biomass of the 16 major oceanic basins without regard to the specific species involved. Data were the peak catch levels of each basin (expressed in millions of tons), the catch level for 1992, and the number of years that elapsed between the peak and 1992. Data were reported in Weber (1994). (Note: Although the world peak was 1989, the separate basins varied in their peak catch years.)

The data were analyzed using the method of structural nonlinear regression equations. Because there were unequal time intervals in the original data, the variants of the structural models with time as a variable were used. Three models were tested. The first was the simple chaotic process:

$$z_2 = e^{(\theta_1 z_1 t)} + \theta_2, \qquad (11.1)$$

where z was the harvest level corrected for location and scale. The second model tested for the presence of a bifurcation effect where the bifurcation variable itself was not known:

$$z_2 = \theta_1 z_1 e^{(\theta_2 z_1 t)} + \theta_3. \qquad (11.2)$$

The third model tested for time itself as a bifurcation variable:

$$z_2 = \theta_1 z_1 e^{(\theta_2 z_1 t)} + \theta_3. \qquad (11.3)$$

A comparison linear test was automatically built into these analyses with the test on the exponential regression weights.

Results

Parameter estimates, R^2 coefficients, and dimensionality calculations are shown in Table 11.2. All regression weights, except θ_2 for Equation 11.2, were significant.

Because of its low degree of fit, Equation 11.1, the simple chaotic model, was ruled out as an explanation of the data. Equation 11.2 showed that there was a simple linear decline in fishing harvests from the peak to 1992. Because its regression weight in the exponent was zero, its dimensionality was 1.00. It had the highest degree of fit of the three models tested. Figure 11.8 shows an iteration plot of Equation 11.2 for different initial conditions. The outcome was beguilingly linear; each successive annual catch is expected to be only 92% of the catch for the previous year. Eventually an asymptotic minimum would be reached.

Equation 11.3 also showed a high degree of fit, although it was not the best of the three. It was interpreted nonetheless because it illustrated the initial theoretical premises. The dimensionality was close to 3.00, and thus signified a cusp-catastrophic process characteristic of the ideal Lotka–Volterra function. The Lyapunov exponent was also positive, and thus denoted that the stable states of the system were chaotic rather than fixed points. Figure 11.9 is an iterative plot of the resulting function with various initial conditions. Fishing harvests were projected to crash suddenly by 1995 (consistent with the Canadian cod and Louisiana shrimp events), then remain grim for nearly 36 years. After that, a catastrophic recovery is expected.

Discussion

The results of the analysis showed that it was possible to extract more than one viable and theoretically expected relationship from the data. The model with the better fit illustrated the simple harvest–decay function. It essentially meant that the international fishers would fish the oceans to exhaustion, all things being equal, and the prognosis would be that the exhaustion was permanent. This model tells

TABLE 11.2
Regression Estimates, R^2 and Lyapunov Dimensionality for Oceanic Fishing Models

Eq.	θ_1	θ_2	θ_3	R^2	D_L
11.1	0.033	−0.532	NA	.27	1.04
11.2	0.924	−0.003	0.00	.99	1.00
11.3	0.011	0.734	0.370	.80	3.08

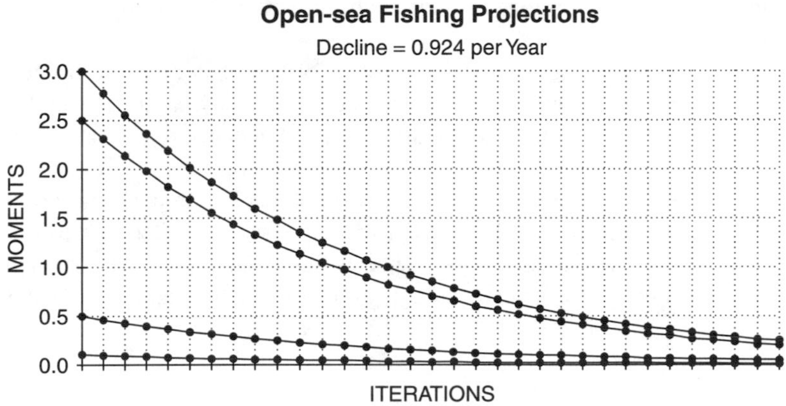

FIG. 11.8. Open-sea fishing harvest projections, based on Equation 11.2.

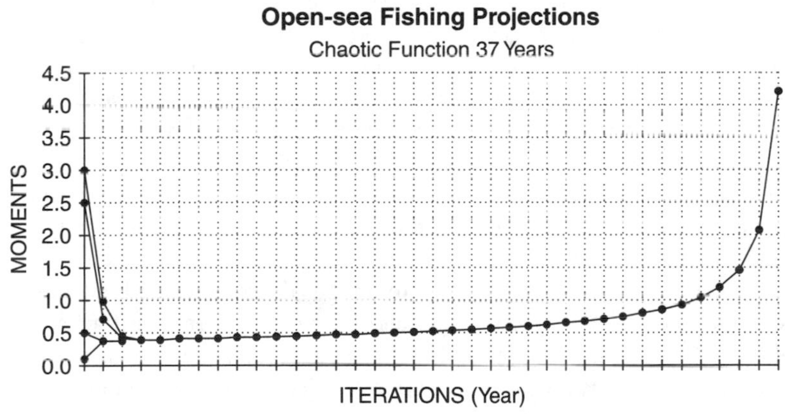

FIG. 11.9. Open-sea fishing harvest projections, based on Equation 11.3.

the story from the point of view of the fishers, what they would capture, and how long the harvests could be maintained.

The model with time as the bifurcation term, however, illustrated both the Lotka–Volterra function at the expected level of dimensionality. It also showed the chaosticity that contemporary researchers also identified through different numerical means and with other data sets. Its projections, however, were from the point of view of the fish; their population dynamics do not anticipate further adaptive responses from the fishers. Rather, if the fish populations were allowed to restore themselves, they would be back in full force. Of course, their populations would not explode as the end of Fig. 11.9 suggests; there would be a limit to the carrying capacities of their environments that was not built into the model.

On the other hand, Fig. 11.9 shows results for total fish quantity. It does not presume that the same species that disappeared will be the ones to recover. For all we know, the recovery would take the form of an abundance of carp and dogfish, rather than orange roughy and cod.

Finally, Fig. 11.9 suggests that the catastrophic decline in harvests should be occurring right about now. Again, adaptive responses by fishers are to dredge deeper than before and to identify new species that were once considered junk. It is probable that these maneuvers would just forestall the inevitable, as depicted in Fig. 11.8.

SUMMARY

This chapter began with a brief summary of the nature of markets and how they self-organize. The assumptions of classical economics, which were once thought to explain most economic phenomena, were considered next. Markets become unstable to the extent that the classical assumptions are not met, and they are often not met. Four types of economic activity were then considered—stock markets, unemployment and inflation, information flows, and natural resource harvesting. The dynamics of each are better explained by nonclassical theories in conjunction with nonlinear dynamics. In each case, individuals and institutions exert strategies for their economic gain, which require at least an intuitive understanding of the nonlinear dynamics that are involved.

Stock market activity is the result of four types of strategy: the fundamentalist, the chartist, the beauty contest judge, and the noise trader. The four strategies involve second-guessing the instabilities generated by other economic actors to some extent. The overall dynamics of price activity was modeled empirically as a cusp catastrophe in earlier research, and the essential points were recounted here. Another dynamical theme is whether the time series for price activities exhibit fractal structure. A new analysis of DJI prices using the method of structural equations supported the fractal market hypothesis.

Unemployment and inflation levels are related according to nonclassical theorists. NDS studies indicate that unemployment does not have a natural rate in the form of a fixed-point attractor (or "equilibrium") as some classicists would maintain. NDS analysis of unemployment dynamics in the United States uncovered two possible trends instead. One trend showed an instability that could have led to a gradual and steady increase in unemployment to approximately 6.6%, which is where the unemployment rate was heading at the time the data series ended in 1995. The other trend indicated the presence of a chaotic attractor with an epicenter of 3.4%; the national unemployment rate in the United States for the year 2000 was 4.0%. The latter might be regarded as the nearest alternative to a natural rate interpretation. A simulation based on the bifurcation function that was extracted from the unemployment data showed that if a large shock were delivered to the economic system, the system could recover, but its new asymptotic low would be higher than its starting level.

NDS analysis of inflation in the United States for the same time period indicated the presence of a chaotic attractor in both the PPI and CPI. Both functions indicated downward pressures on prices at their epicenters. Forward iterations of both functions indicated the presence of boundary effects and an eventual stabilization at 1.9% and 2.8% price growth, respectively.

Information plays an important role in the design and marketing of products as well as in regulating the efficiency of ordinary markets. The distribution and flow of information does not always conform to ordinary market rules, however. Instead, flow is determined to a great extent by the form of the information, as depicted in Boisot's I-Space concept, and the type of institution that generates it. Theorists have considered the catalyzing self-organizing effect of information on social structures in various ways.

Global fishing harvests that had once reached all time highs have begun to decline, and important fisheries have failed. NDS analyses indicate that the prey–predator relationships, such as humans catching fish, show a cusp catastrophe dynamic overall with chaotic dynamics in the regions of population levels immediately proximal to the attractors. NDS analysis of fishing harvests worldwide indicated two possible trends. One trend indicated an exponential decay that would eventually become terminal. The other trend indicated a sharp drop in fish populations that would continue for approximately 37 years before rebounding. Rebounding would require a serious decline in predator activity, which surrounding economics conditions did not appear to support.

12

Management and Control of Dynamical Systems

Chapter 10 introduced the thought that there are individual differences in managers' ability to predict and control chaos and other dynamical events that occur within an organization. Chapter 11 introduced several situations in which decisions must be made concerning dynamical events in the external economic environment. Collective decisions by individuals and institutional policy makers contribute to economic dynamics as much as they respond to the dynamics. It is believed that many of the same forecasting skills are at work in both the internal and external arenas.

This chapter describes some methods for predicting the future and explores some of the psychology that is allegedly involved. The first methods date back centuries before the scientific era. Conventional psychology has made some notable contributions also, most of which are better known for other reasons. NDS concepts play progressively larger roles as we move toward present-day approaches to futurism. Subsequent sections of the chapter highlight various means of predicting and controlling chaos, catastrophes, and self-organization explicitly. This chapter perhaps contains the greatest amount of speculative material, but a good deal of it is empirically grounded. On the other hand, it is not possible to ride off into the sunset without a sunset.

Decision theories and computer programs for decision-support techniques are designed to assist decision-makers to maximize their outcomes and minimize decision errors. Decision support programs may be ineffective when the management decisions involve information that is incomplete, inaccurate, and changing over time. Decision-makers are likely to pay for certainty by selecting options that involve less risk, or by accessing the missing information sources that would serve to reduce uncertainty.

Uncertainty in decision making takes several forms: (a) The decision maker knows what the possible outcomes would be and knows the probabilities associated with each outcome, but is compelled to guess which of the outcomes will actually take place. (b) The decision-maker knows what the possible outcomes would be, but does not know the probabilities associated with each outcome. (c) The decision-maker has an incomplete knowledge of the possible outcomes, and hence, the probabilities associated with any of the known options are speculative. (d) The decision-maker has incorrectly identified the problem, and as a result identified all the wrong options.

Decision aids may take the form of single simple equations, such as a multiple linear regression equation, or a complex computer program such as an "expert systems." The connection between complexity theory and the control of uncertainty dates back to the late 1940s. The landmark contributions are chronicled here in four epochs: artificial life and artificial intelligence, control of chaos from the mathematical point of view, controlling catastrophes, and control of dynamical events from the point of view of social processes. Attention is given to both the general procedures and the specific variables that have surfaced in psychological or economics research.

At the broadest level of analysis, the control of dynamics systems requires a perspective that allows change and fluctuation as normal, rather than a perspective that insists on fixed-point equilibrium control. Sensitivity to initial conditions and synchronization play important roles in system control; system control may focus on the mathematical control of engineering systems, or the social expression of control in organizations (Ditto & Munakata, 1995; Kaas, 1998; Stacey, 1992, 1993).

PREDICTIONS OF THE FUTURE

People often see advantages in knowing something about the future. Questions might pertain to the fate of a single business transaction or a global trend, such as energy consumption patterns, population and environment shifts, health care utilization, economic flow and distribution of wealth, and relationships among institutions (e.g., businesses, universities, and other educational environments; governments; scientific enterprises; labor representatives; etc.). This section of the chapter describes some landmarks in the technology of forecasting, some current ideas and issues, and the type of thinking that takes place.

Later sections of this chapter expand on several points concerning the cognitive processes that are involved specifically in the prediction of chaos and other unstable events: artificial intelligence and artificial life programs, cognitive processes in the prediction of chaotic number series, use of chaotic controllers in a system, manipulation of control parameters that are known to a situation, and techniques that facilitate the self-organization of a system. The foregoing techniques assume a certain level of knowledge of the system, the nonlinear dynamics that are involved, and the control parameters that are included.

Several other cognitive processes relevant to futurism were identified in Chapters 5 and 6: There is expectancy theory whereby the rat guesses where the cheese will be, based on prior experience. There is game theory, whereby individuals choose strategies based on utilities to themselves and others; each player in a game tries to second-guess the other players' responses. There is divergent thinking of the type inherent in the Consequences test, which compels people to think of a complex system and its possible outcomes. More generally there is divergent thinking and cognitive style.

A certain amount of skill, however, needs to be developed whereby the vizier can form a clear picture of the current state of a system, capture its underlying complexity, and envision possible future scenarios of what might happen if certain other events are introduced. Note here the distinction between the monolithic visions of the visionary leader and the multiplicity of vision that occurs in futurism. Of interest, there are research institutes all over the world dedicated to futuristic thinking and producing meaningful results.

Oracles

Two thousand years ago, the local oracle was the management consultant of choice for a person who needed to know something important about the future. The querent would pose the question to the oracle staff consisting of a priest and a couple of writhing 14-year-old girls (Jaynes, 1976; oracle staff would undoubtedly vary from place to place.) The priest then interpreted the girls' words and motions for the querent. The logic of the oracle was superstitious and magical; there were no cause–effect relationships between the oracles' performance and the course of any real-world events. On the other hand, the experience may have been dramatic, poetic, and creative enough to spark some innovative or useful ideas in the mind of the querent.

The performance of oracles brings us to the set of thought processes called *hermeneutics*, which is the art or technique of interpretation. Hermeneutics do not have a direct counterpart in psychological theory. Psychologists seem to prefer to study particular kinds of interpretation, such as conclusions about statistical data, diagnoses drawn from a set of psychological tests, or the tasks of expert systems. In the case of oracles, however, the interpreters might have been engaging in a round of creative thinking inspired by the performance of the writhing individuals. The dynamics of chance, chaos, and creativity were probably part of a satisfying oracle experience.

Divining Devices

This group of innovations consists of astrology, tarot cards, *I Ching*, and related methods of divining the future. As a rule, this group of techniques was more systematic than the oracle. Tarot cards represent a systematic pattern of cosmic concepts, which are organized in a 4×14 grid pattern plus a set of 22 major arcana (or trump) cards. The card reader may use any of several patterns for laying out cards. Frequently, the cards in different positions in the layout correspond to past influences, present influences, future influences, and a final outcome. The content of each card is a complex grouping of metaphors, and has a positive and negative meaning (Kaplan, 1978). Tarot cards first emerged in Europe in the late 14th century, although their contributing concepts date back to the Egyptian civilization. Many of the contributing concepts surfaced in Jung's writings on the archetypes of the unconscious (see Chapter 4).

The Fool (Fig. 12.1) is one of the more enchanting tarot concepts. The court jester in medieval times was as much an advisor to the king as he was an entertainer. In his finer moments, the entertainer skillfully captured alternative and contradictory points of view on an important matter. The Fool typifies a situation that can have many possible outcomes. Some of the outcomes are products of wisdom, while others are the result of folly. The difference between wisdom and folly could be the result of differing points of view.

The next card in the series, The Magician, manipulates the rational and irrational in the form of creative illusions. He characterizes luck, chance, and coincidences that are not really chance occurrences. Combs and Holland (1996) observed that synchronicities or coincidences have captivated people's imaginations since time immemorial. The Greeks ascribed the occurrences of these events to the works of the god Hermes, or the One Who Brings Luck.

I Ching, or *The Book of Changes*, dates back to China, 1200 BCE (Confucius, trans. Legge, 1969). Its concepts are organized in a binary grid of 64 patterns of short and long lines, which are in turn the result of tossing six copper coins heads or tails. The resulting combination of heads and tails describes patterns of change at an abstract level. The patterns of change are the results of two opposite cosmic forces, yin and yang.

Figure 12.2 depicts one of the hexagrams, *Kun* (also *Chun*). Kun depicts the struggle of a plant to rise out of the earth, then flourish. The struggle is, furthermore, a metaphor of the formation of a political state from confusion and disorder after a great revolution. The political future of the state is enhanced by the appointment of suitable feudal lords, but even then the future is not guaranteed. There is success in small goals over a period of 10 years. Large undertakings (e.g., imperial expansion) can have dire consequences, however. Other variations of the Kun scenario describe the folly of a hunter chasing a deer through the woods without the assistance of capable forester. In some possible interpretations, Kun depicts the edge-of-chaos phenomenon.

FIG. 12.1. The Fool, from the 1JJSwiss Tarot Deck; reprinted by permission of AGM AGMüller, CH-8212 Neuhausen/Switzerland, © 1974.

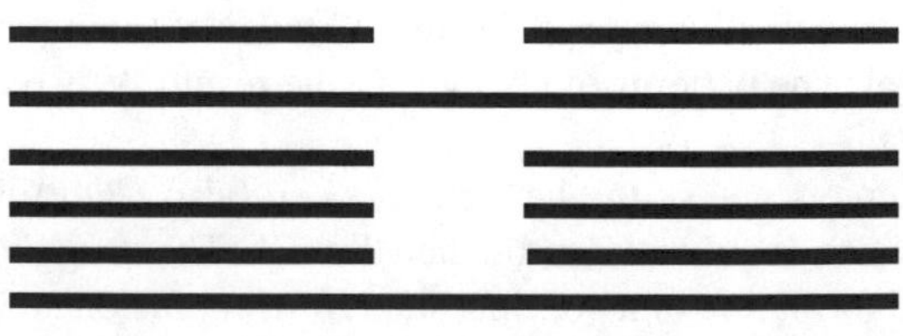

FIG. 12.2. The Kun (Chun) hexagram from *I Ching*.

In the case of astrology charts, the course of human events was somehow parallel to the complex course of the planets, sun, moon, and stars as it unfolded between the moment a person was born to the present time or to the time of the future event in question. The future that is told by astrologers is determined by the positions of the celestial bodies. Because there are myriad possible futures that could arise from within the logic of the system, less fatalistic interpreters would describe an astrological future that would transpire unless the querent did something to influence the situation. The same could be said about tarot cards with regard to the types of futures it might tell. The *I Ching* reports are phrased in a way that suggests a course of action for the querent; thus the individual's participation in the future is always implied.

Statistics

The advent of statistics brought a modicum of scientific procedure and objectivity into the process of futuring. Several basic concepts of statistics are especially germane. First, randomness is natural, not supernatural. "*Random*" initially meant "the motions of a horse that its rider does not control" (Mandelbrot, 1983). Second is the notion of *probability*: We can determine the *odds* of a set of events taking place even if don't know for sure which event will occur on a given occasion.

Third, the odds of events can be determined by counting *samples* of events. Sampling allows us to collect a small portion of the information available from a population or pool of information and draw inferences about the events in the entire sample based on what is observed in the sample. The results of the sampling activity are generalizable to the extent that principles of random sampling have been observed. In a *random sample*, every member of the population has, in theory, an equal chance of appearing in the sample.

Fourth, relationships may exist between two or more variables that could be cause-and-effect relationships or not, depending on how the data were collected, nature of the phenomenon, and so on. In either case we can apply an *inferential statistic* to determine the odds of a particular relationship occurring by chance.

Fifth, a correlation coefficient (or its latter day relatives) and its accompanying regression equation allow numeric predictions of one variable from the knowledge of another. Although a good amount of social science is predicated on the X and Y measured at the same point in time, another good amount attempts to predict Y tomorrow based on Y and X today, as we have seen throughout this book. Regression equations can also be used to model human decision processes. As every statistics student learns, however, correlation is not causation, but if X really does cause Y, we should be able to see a correlation between X and Y; and, oh yes, the relationship between X and Y is linear.

Sixth, the correlation coefficient (and some of its relatives) also denotes the size of the effect that is present in the data. That is, we can know the relative contributions of a deterministic, and thus predictive, effect and the amount of random variation in the events that we observe.

Finally for this list, the left-over random variation is usually placed into a garbage can of unknowns such as "measurement error," "modeling error," Type I and Type 2 errors, and random shocks. In classical measurement theory (Lord &

Novick, 1968), all errors are assumed to be independent of all other errors and measurements. NDS theory, however, now shows that the independence of errors is a dubious assumption when nonlinear forms of determinism are involved.

Models and Simulations

A model is an abstraction of a real system. A model is a metaphor in the sense that some real-world properties are included while other properties that are thought to be nonessential are ignored, held constant, or randomized. This exercise in reductionism, however, prepares a logical trap for the model-maker, however. The simplification of a real process into a convenient model implies throwing away information that could be critical. Wishing away intractable variables or subprocesses does not make them any less relevant.

A good model, nonetheless, has much in common with a good experiment. A good experiment allows us to vary some variables, hold others constant, and observe outcomes. A more complex experiment can allow the simultaneous manipulation of several variables. A good experiment requires internal logic and external validity. Ultimately we ask, "Does the model capture the real world phenomenon with an adequate degree of fidelity?"

The external validity question has plagued the development of expert systems over the years, but methods for determining the validity of a variety of expert system structures have been forthcoming (Guastello & Rieke, 1994). Deficits in simulation strategies have been traced to a lack of external validity. In one of the more dramatic examples, the ecological catastrophes that were predicted in *Limits to Growth* (Meadows, Meadows, Randers, & Behrens, 1972) never came to pass. On the one hand, it is the planet's good luck that the predictions did not come true at the scheduled time. On the other hand, the predictive deficiency supported the interests of anti-ecological profit-seekers. On the third hand (first foot?), the *Limits to Growth* debate generated an awareness of problems, such as overpopulation, that needed to be addressed (Rosser, 1991).

Artificial Life and Artificial Intelligence

Although John von Neumann is perhaps best known for the theory and development of electronic computers, he also created a vision for software that became known as "artificial life." The central premise was that all life could be expressed as (reduced to) the processing of information. Artificial life unfolded in a series of important and complex steps over the subsequent 50 years (Levy, 1992). Decision software evolved in three epochs, which were dominated by game theory, expert systems, and evolutionary programming. Expert systems involve some interesting connection between human decision making and computer programs, but most of the story falls outside of NDS theory. Interested readers should see Guastello and Rieke (1994) and Liu, Dooley, and Anderson (1995) for overviews of expert system architecture and validations strategies.

Artificial life models involve different classes of applications and rule structures compared to expert systems, but the underlying issues are relatively the same. Artificial life computations, by some opinions, could produce more realistic models than did expert systems because the behavioral systems that are being modeled involve a comparably small number of rules. Three principal types of complex computations have evolved nonetheless. Although they have some relevance as tools for forecasting and policy development for complex system, their potential remains to be mined more completely.

A neural network is a computation that is designed to emulate the behavior of neural structures. Neural networks originated as structures for robotics where the motion of limbs required modeling along with some semblance of learning and binary decision-making capability. There have been some reported attempts to use neural networks as black box computational devices that would search for nonlinear patterns of events, create a model for those events internally, and proceed to use that model to predict the outcome of new cases. Neural networks have some attractiveness because they allow decision-makers to engage the computation without a theory, hypothesis, or clue regarding what nonlinear structure could underlie the process. It remains to be shown whether, and under what conditions, neural networks describe nonneurological events with greater accuracy than other state-of-the-science statistical practices.

Genetic algorithms are computational strategies designed to track possible mutations of genes, or entire species, as a result of different mutation rates, breeding conditions, and environmental assaults. They are particularly attractive for their ability, in principle, to identify emerging life forms. There exists a counterpoint, however, between the theoretically grounded biological processes that comprise the rule structure of a true genetic algorithm, and the locally modified deviation from theory, known as evolutionary computation. The theoretically pure varieties tend to be less accurate than the situationally modified varieties, although the latter sacrifice generalizability for adaptiveness to constrained problems. It also remains to be shown whether, and under what conditions, genetic algorithms and evolutionary computations can describe nongenetic events with any greater accuracy than other state-of-the-science statistical practices.

Cellular automata are computations that have been useful for illustrating how local interactions between elementary system members can produce global structures and patterns. Although "cell" in this case is analogous to the cell of an organism, it need only be a patch of space in any topography, or the cell of a grid or sheet of graph paper. Each cell can take on two or more discrete states. A cell's state is determined by rules that are based upon what the cell's eight surrounding neighbors are doing. There is no restriction on the nature or complexity of the underlying rules; rules should be chosen on the basis of the constraints and properties of the system under study. Cellular automata have been used to describe the diffusion of attitudes (Latané, Nowak, & Liu, 1994), patchiness of aquatic ecological systems (Medvinsky et al., 2000), and the irregularities of land use across Belgium and Senegal (Allen & Sanglier, 1981; Englen, 1988; Englen, White, & Uljee, 1997; White & Englen, 1997; White, Englen, & Uljee, 1997).

Nonlinear Dynamical Futures

NDS offered a number of new concepts for modeling events that change over time, and hence for forecasting. One of its more enchanting insights is that many phenomena that appear to be random are actually predictable by simple deterministic equations. The trick is to find the correct equations. The more prominent equations are those that describe chaos or fractals, although it is well understood that chaos and fractals are only two species of nonlinear dynamics in the "topological zoo." The creatures that are most friendly to organizational phenomena were described in Chapter 2, and the group includes self-organization and sensitive dependence.

Several other NDS concepts are relevant to futuring. Processes are *controlled* rather than caused. Events of different levels of complexity exhibit different signatures, or identifiable patterns, as they unfold over time. The unfolding processes are, by and large, *autonomous*. They can be of an evolutionary or revolutionary nature. Many NDS processes are irreversible. Systems may be ergodic or dissipative, although most human systems fit the latter category. As the later parts of this chapter indicate, chaos can be controlled by some peculiar means.

For a brief period of time, NDS theorists suggested that NDS might replace statistical reasoning altogether, but contemporary analytic techniques use statistical procedures, such as nonlinear regression, to separate chaos from noise. In so doing, it is possible to obtain greater accuracy of prediction for nonlinear phenomena using NDS models compared to what would be the case for common linear alternatives. For the more volatile NDS processes, short-term predictions may be satisfactory, but the prediction decays as the prediction window increases.

Now that it is possible to separate chaos from noise conceptually, physicists are now discovering, however, that the complete range of statistical processes, as observed in statistical mechanics, is not captured by chaos or other nonlinear dynamics (Zaslavsky, 1999). There still remains the problem of transient dynamics. Transients often display a recognizable NDS trajectory for a brief time, but then disappear or change as suddenly as they appear. The behavior of transients is linked in part to the assumption of ergodicity and to two properties of the system that are implied by the ergodicity assumption. The limiting conditions are that the boundary of the system is rigid and the volume of the system remains constant. If those two conditions are met, trajectories within the system are less unstable than if the conditions are not met.

PSYCHOLOGY OF PREDICTION

The understanding of the psychology of predicting chaos is an outgrowth in the understanding of the psychology of predicting anything else, according to Loye (1978, 1995, 2000). There is an undercurrent in cognitive psychology on the topic of planning, and how people use it to make future events both predictable and desirable to the greatest possible extent. Most noteworthy is the motivational theme of *achievement* (McClelland, 1961) whereby people set goals, plan moderate risks, and formulate plans. In most cases, we are trying to generalize from what we know to what we do not know. Historical epochs of economic advancement in the United States, and local experiments in India and Mexico, have been coupled with widespread achievement motivation in those societies.

In the particular case of NDS prediction, Loye (1995) observed three scenarios where prediction is desirable. One case is the prediction of the behavior of points within a chaotic attractor. Another is the prediction of chaos from systems that can be described by the logistic map, wherein "new patterns, new order, [and] new predictabilities emerge" (1995, p. 347). The third is the prediction of the emergence of new structures that occur through processes of self-organization. These points are expanded later on in this chapter.

Loye observed that, although numerical prediction of chaotic events is short-term at best, the human ability to envision outcomes is more robust. He labeled the special capabilities of humans as an "arrow through chaos" (1995, 2000). He likened this special ability to the work of a logger who can walk on logs while they are running downriver, and hop from one log to another at unpredictable intervals of space (between logs) and time. Vaill (1989) also used an aquatic metaphor by comparing the art of management to rafting on whitewater. Both versions of the metaphor target the well-known chaotic flows of fluids and gasses.

Loye (1995) also gave some thought to individual differences in the ability to predict future events, drawing upon several empirical studies. He found that people who were able to predict future political events were those who were more open-minded, creative, imaginative, tolerant of ambiguity, displayed incomplete brain hemisphere dominance (i.e., the left- and right-brain capabilities work equally well), and exhibited systems sensitivity. In other words, successful predictions were more likely among people with a complete creativity syndrome, with emphasis on the *Consequences* type of divergent thinking.

Skilled politicians, furthermore, were able to forecast future events because of an ability to extract information about political intentions through "ideological dialectic." Although attitudes are notoriously poor predictors of future behavior (except where a narrowly defined behavior and a high degree of commitment are involved), ideologies represent consistent patterns of political preferences.

The psychology of prediction could legitimately extend to the study of psi capabilities (e.g., precognition, telepathy), but the support for the existence of these capabilities is equivocal and not generally accepted. Hardy (1998), on the other hand, suggested that a phenomenon that *resembles* psi could occur in a community that has widely shared semantic lattice contents. In principle, if enough lattice content is shared, a person could predict someone else's behavior, or a group behavior, by examining their own knowledge structures.

Finally, a good future vision requires a good sense of timing. Koehler (1999) introduced the concept of *time ecologies* to refer to the time scale on which events occur. Knowing *what* is going to happen is important, but knowing *when* could be at least half the problem. Elected policy makers, for instance, may be working within 2-, 4-, or 6-year cycles that are specified by their election terms, even though the events they wish to affect may involve time horizons that extend 10 or 20 years. When they face problems that they know affect future generations, a 30-year horizon may seem good enough (depending on the density of voters by age group), although lifetimes may be affected in reality. An economist would mention discount factors in decision processes (e.g., Rosser, 1991): How does a benefit today weigh against a cost that will not occur until tomorrow?

Ecological decisions are notable examples of conflicting time horizons (Pherigo, Lee, Nehman, & Eve, 1999). Problems start out subcritically and suddenly blossom in a nonlinear pattern over time. Because of the relationships among the components of the biosphere, activity in one component eventually affects others. Well-intentioned policies, however, often do not respond to the temporal dynamics of the situation. Policies are formulated based on the way things look at a particular point in time, legislation is passed, and the management moves on to the next topic. An improvement would be to build in contingencies for reevaluating the specifics of the policy and responding to temporal dynamics.

CONTROL OF CHAOS

This section describes four techniques for controlling dynamical processes, especially those that involve chaos: tracking nonlinear processes, adding chaos to control chaos, using system control parameters, and the method of forced periodicity. Some of those ideas, but not all of them, have received some attention in psychological experiments. The interest in controlling chaos applies to both directions of control: Sometimes the goal is to minimize the unpredictability associated with chaotic processes by regularizing the business stimuli in some fashion. At other times, the decision goal is to identify future business states and options that will become available, and compute the odds of success for various adaptive responses.

Tracking Nonlinear Dynamics in Systems

There are three groups of studies that address some aspect of human ability to track complex dynamic processes. In one series of experiments (Metzger, 1994;

Neuringer & Voss, 1993; Smithson, 1997; Ward & West, 1994, 1998), human participants were presented with numeric series that were generated from the Verhulst (or logistic map) equation:

$$X_2 = CX_1(1 - X_1). \tag{2.5}$$

The participants' task was to predict the next value in the series. Correlations between actual and predicted values ranged from .55 to .85 in the study from this series by Ward and West (1998; Fig. 12.3). Decision-makers were found to have engaged in two heuristics that assisted their forecasts. In one heuristic, the respondents ignored the tiny differences in numerical values that were associated with extreme decimal places; thus the gross swings in actual values were more important to their forecasts than the fine details. The second heuristic was based on the forecasts of sequential pairs of actual values. Thus, the intuition of a sequential point in the series depends on the direction and size of the previous movement in the actual values.

In an important variation on the same theme, Heath (2000a) prepared a series of chaotic (Henon attractor) "outdoor temprature readings" and asked subjects to forecast the temperature over the next 4 days. A control group was given a set of temperature readings that was prepared from a surrogate data set that contained the same autocorrelation and variability levels, but was not a chaotic sequence. The human subjects predicted the chaotic series more accurately than they did the surrogate series.

In another series of studies (Mosekilde, Larssen, & Sterman, 1991; Sterman, 1988) respondents played a computer simulation of a beer distributorship. Their task was to place orders and receive deliveries from breweries and make deliveries to restaurants, bars, and stores without overflowing their warehouse capacity or running out of stock. Meanwhile, the beer production and deliveries were interrupted by "strikes," "transportation problems," and "demand shifts." Respondents' beer inventories were found to be chaotic over time. It is noteworthy that only 11% of players were capable of maintaining a beer inventory between the two limits for the duration of the game.

The third series of studies pertained to the management of workflow in a hierarchical organization. In the experiments, which were described in Chapter 10, contrived work consisted of three to six work groups plus one or two levels of management. The organization's work routine was aperiodically interrupted by "blackouts," "strikes," and "personnel changes," and other interventions. The empirical results showed that the output of work groups was chaotic over time, but the relative amounts of determinism versus noise seemed to vary across experimental situations. Management's ability to manage the collective performance varied widely across situations also.

First-level work groups gradually produced more work per unit of time as a general rule. Some management teams, however, improved performance gradually

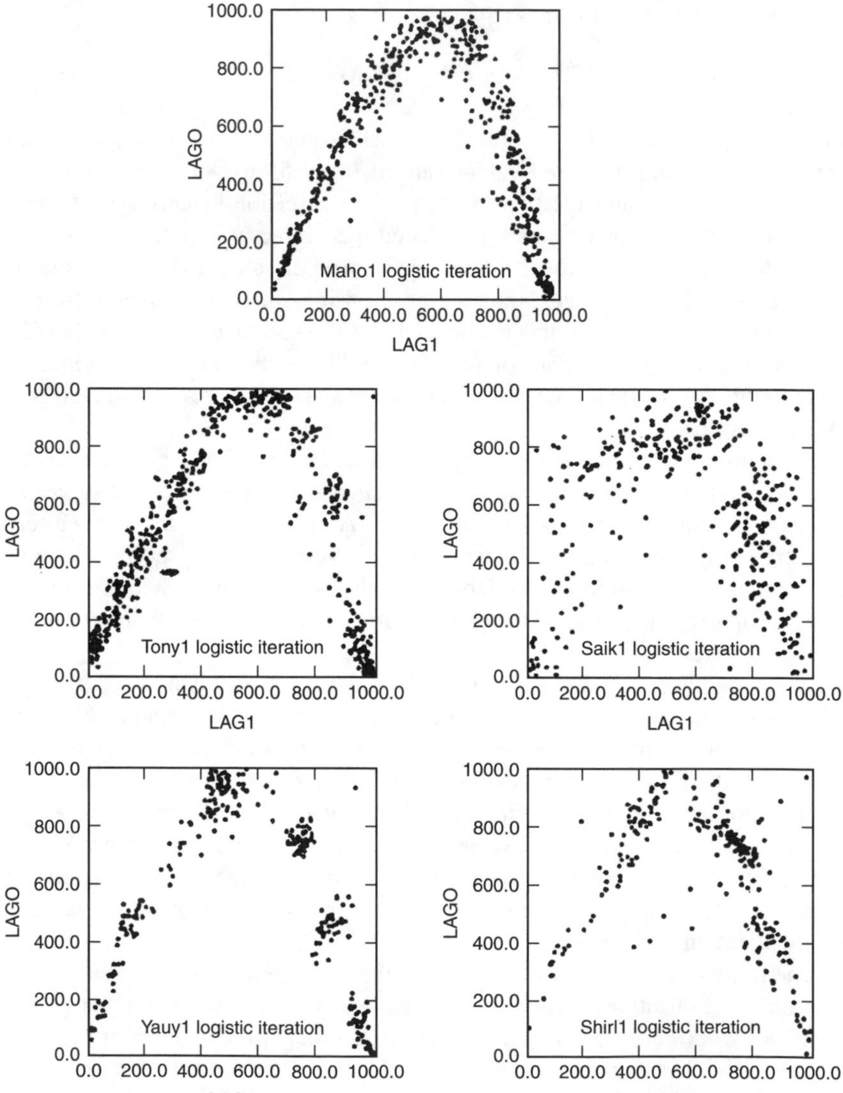

FIG. 12.3. Comparisons of actual chaotic function and predicted values given by human participants in Ward and West's experiment (1998, p. 268). Reprinted with permission of Human Sciences Press and Kluwer Academic Publishers.

while others declined. Most management teams exhibited instability in performance with transient dynamics. The collective result of this group of studies showed that the cognitive control of work performance in hierarchies is unstable at best. Thus, the type of top-down driver–slave relationship that is observed in physical systems with emerging hierarchies does not necessary occur in human work systems. Rather, it would appear that a dynamical forcing function from lower to upper management would occur more often than the other way around.

The ability to intuit nonlinear dynamics is valuable even when dynamics simpler than chaos are involved. Consider the following real event: A university president, who had just taken over the job, noticed an increase in enrollments over the most recent few years. The increase in enrollments was coupled with new concerted efforts on the part of the admissions and recruitment staff to increase enrollments. The president extrapolated the trends in a straight line, and proceeded to spend large sums of money based on those expectations of future revenue. The president missed a population trend, however, that was already reported in other universities whereby a local decline in enrollments should have been expected.

Controlling Chaos with Chaos

The concept of a *chaotic controller* was developed in the early 1990s (Breeden, Dinkelacker, & Hubler, 1990; Jackson, 1991a, 1991b), but very little was heard about it in the social sciences, especially since the time I mentioned it last (Guastello, 1995a). Chaotic controllers are based on Ashby's Law of Requisite Variety, which states that the controller of a system must be at least as complex as the system itself (Stacey, 1992). Chaotic control works counterintuitively by first adding a small amount of low-dimensional noise into the system. The reasoning is that the amount of sensitivity to initial conditions is not uniform throughout the attractor space. Sensitivity is less in the outer edge of the basin of the attractor and least in the center, compared to the middle regions of the attractor space. The level of sensitive dependence may be affected by the attractor's proximity to another attractor. Adding noise to the system allows the attractor to expand to its fullest range.

The controller can then respond in one of two ways. One is to apply a filter that allows a special range of values to pass through. The second option is to mimic the chaotic motion of a point, predict where it is going, and respond in a strategic manner.

The chaotic controller concept has not received more than a few minutes of speculation in management or social science applications. Conceivably, however, an organization might want to increase its entropy to propel an organizational change, to enhance its repertoire of adaptive responses to the economic and social environment, or to initiate original business ideas. It may be desirable, therefore, to couple a chaotic process to another behavior. For instance, creative thinking resources appear to have potentially chaotic output. An adaptive organization would thus develop a culture that is conducive to creative thinking with respect to both original initiatives and adaptive responses.

Occasionally a manager will declare the need to "shake things up" without really having much of a plan regarding what is to be shaken, or what the shaking is supposed to mean when it happens. Directionless efforts might indeed help a member of the work group to make a new observation or solve a problem. Pointlessness is not the same as chaos, however.

Periodic Entrainment

The Ott, Grebogi, and Yorke (OGY, 1990; Ott et al., 1994) method for controlling chaos is based on the relationship between oscillators and chaos: Three coupled oscillations are minimally sufficient to produce chaotic time series. Many economic and biological events exhibit periodic behavior, or are the result of coupled periodic oscillators. Although not all possible combinations of oscillations do produce chaos, it is still a viable analytic strategy, nonetheless, to decompose chaos into its contributing oscillating functions.

The OGY method for controlling chaos involves targeting unstable periodic functions, and strengthening the attractiveness of one periodic function so that it becomes dominant. As a particular oscillation increases in strength, points from nearby trajectories become entrained on the stable manifold of the dominant orbit. The complexity of temporal motion then simplifies to a simple periodic orbit.

In one simulated economic example of the OGY method (Ahmed & Hassan, 2000), two competing firms experienced a chaotic fluctuation in their respective market shares. Eventually they became entrained with respect to their production and sales cycles. A first-strike advantage was also discovered whereby the firm that locks into its own orbit first dominates the other firm.

The OGY method has some limitations in situations where its computations are to be taken literally to model behaviors of real, rather than simulated, systems. The principle problem is its susceptibility to disruption from noise. An external shock will be carried through subsequent iterations of a chaotic system. The disruptions become magnified and the tracking of the stable manifold becomes impaired. For this reason, the literal application of the OGY method may give way to targeting methods in practical or policy-making settings.

Control Parameter Manipulation

The logistic map equation received a great deal of attention in complexity studies because of its one control parameter that governs changes in system behavior from fixed to periodic, aperiodic, and chaotic states. Although there is no guarantee that a real system can be controlled through all those states by just one parameter, it is intriguing, nonetheless, that a wide range of behavior patterns could be controlled by a very few well-chosen parameters.

One application of chaotic control is found in the tatonnement process, whereby buyers and sellers haggle prices for goods (Bala, Majumdar, & Mitra, 1998). The final prices are Walrasian equilibria. The process begins by the two parties each setting a target price at which they want to buy or sell the commodity. The bargaining partners state their targets to each other, and in the usual case, sellers set higher target prices than buyers. The bargaining partners then give each other adjusted price targets, the difference between the price targets narrows, and the process continues until a mutually acceptable price is reached. The typical fluctuations in price targets are thought to follow the logistic map pattern while the control parameter decreased in value over time. At the present time, the control parameter has not yet been defined, but its existence is implied by the logistic map, or dampened oscillator process that is taking place.

The targeting method has also been shown to be an efficient remedy for organizations that are producing and selling goods at chaotic levels of profit (Hoylst, Tagel, Haag, & Weidlich, 1996; Kopel, 1997). Sale prices are related to supply and demand levels. Supply levels, in turn, fluctuate in concert with changing production volumes and interest rates. Under these circumstances, organizations are likely to adjust their prices and production chaotically. Mean sales and profitability can be improved by targeting a production policy that is dynamically an unstable fixed point. This form of targeting, once again, involves some systematic trial and error.

Table 12.1 contains a summary of the chaotic organizational behavior models that have been identified thus far. The table shows links between the phenomena and the control processes that are thought to be responsible. For the most part, chaotic behavior was determined empirically. Items 1 though 11 appear in the foregoing chapters. Item 12 is elaborated in this chapter under the topic of cognitive strategies for complex systems. Items 13 through 15 appeared in my earlier exposition (Guastello, 1995a) and did not resurface previously in this book. The suggested control variables have varying levels of support, some of which is only theoretical. By lining the models up in this fashion, however, it is possible to rethink what types of new studies should be attempted, and what types of control variables might be plausible in new situations.

A few qualifications to the list are in order nonetheless. Strategic cooperation, Item 2, involves game matrices. Gaming strategies can become chaotic if the matrix is 4 by 4 or of greater proportion. Chaotic behavior can occur in smaller games if the evolution is long and players induce chaotic response choices.

For Item 3, motivational flow, time spent working was determined by empirical analysis. The role of structure in personal schedules was inferred by the nature of the clusters of people who participated in the study.

In Item 4, some of the suggested control variables were borrowed from the mushroom catastrophe study in which chaos and catastrophe were both present. A similar liberty was taken with the control variables listed for NYSE prices in Item 8.

TABLE 12.1
Nonlinear Dynamical Phenomena in Organizations and Their Known Control Parameters: Chaotic Processes

Phenomenon	*Factors Affecting Entropy or Behavioral Complexity*
1. Organizational change and development	Sociotechnical embeddedness, levels of hierarchy, vested interests of incumbents, information, supplies of materials, differences of opinion regarding organizational strategies
2. Strategic cooperation or competition	Set by problem situation, subgame perfect structure, defection and cooperation rates among players, use of oligarchic control strategies
3. Motivational flow	Individual lives, interests, time spent working, structure in personal schedule
4. Creative problem-solving groups	Complexity of problems and the ease of finding their dynamical keys, use of chaotic or linear cognitive styles, people–topic combinations, number of discussion threads, creative ability, knowledge domain, risk-taking attitude, intrinsic motivation for creativity
5. Population dynamics in virtual communities	Rate of diffusion or joining the community, crowdedness factor
6. Coordination of work groups	Number of possible behavior spectra that the group intends to control, number of options available, level of practice for group members, personnel replacements within communication trained groups, verbal versus nonverbal communication only
7. Work performance in hierarchies	Configuration of work groups and levels of hierarchy
8. NYSE stock prices	Interest rates, moving average, proportion of speculators
9. Economic inflation	Interest rates, money supply, national debt policy [unemployment]
10. Unemployment	Money flow between real and investment economy [inflation]
11. Fish Harvesting	Ecological niche colonization, fish mutation rates, demand for fish
12. Complex group performance under turbulence	Openness to experience and toleration of ambiguity, self-reference, boundary reparation, coaction
13. Population dynamics in the construction trades	Hiring rate, termination rate
14. International polarization	Not known
15. Magnitude of war	International polarization

The control variables that are listed for Item 5 were drawn from the theory concerning diffusion limited aggregation and the May–Oster population dynamics. A similar inference can be drawn from the construction trade study, reported elsewhere (Guastello, 1992b, 1995a), where the May–Oster dynamics were in evidence.

Little is known about the control variables that affect chaotic production in hierarchies. At the present time, the most plausible explanations are tied to the number and configuration of work groups and levels of management.

The control variables listed for inflation (Item 9) and unemployment (Item 10) are based on the apparent conclusion that the Phillips curve does not actually work. If the relationship that Keynes originally identified is rigorous, however, we have to add that unemployment and inflation are control variables with respect to each other. Kaas (1998) observed that unemployment and inflation can be controlled more effectively, compared to standard policy approaches by using a combination of OGY entrainment and targeted values of equilibria. The common limitation of targeting approaches has been the inability to locate (what we know today as) the attractor centers for the targets. An example solution to that procedural problem appeared in Chapter 11.

The listing for fish harvests (Item 11) requires a bit of explanation. As a prey–predator relationship, the supply of prey controls the population of predators, and vice versa. On the other hand, the supply of fish is also subject to fish mutation rates and niche colonization rates as stated earlier. Allen and McGlade (1987) observed that there are two cognitive strategies among the humans for finding fish, which they characterize as the *determinists* and the *stochasts*. The stochasts put significant effort into exploring for new sources of fish. They do not expend the entire supply before searching for a new area. The determinists, on the other hand, hang around waiting to see where other boats, which are probably operated by stochasts, are finding fish. Once they lock onto an area, they mine the area until the supply of fish is exhausted.

The stochasts obtain a competitive advantage from their ability to hunt for new locations. In so doing they are able to stay a few jumps ahead of their competitors. They bear a cost in the form of exploration energy. The determinists obtain a competitive advantage by free-riding on the exploration energy of the stochasts. They run a risk, however, of arriving at the fishing hole too late and coming up empty after only a short while.

Finally, for this group of models, control variables for Item 14 is not known. Polarization was, in earlier times, thought to be a predictor of the magnitude of international war, but the process affecting polarization itself is not well understood.

CONTROL OF CATASTROPHIC PROCESSES

Catastrophe models have a convenient feature in that the control variables usually have to be known before the model is finished. Table 12.2 summarizes the known catastrophe models in organizations that have been developed to date. Items 1 through 8 were developed in the foregoing chapters. Items 9 through 20 were appeared in my earlier exposition (1995a) and did not resurface here. Again, the latter group is summarized here for possible further suggestions regarding how some organizational processes might be modeled and controlled.

TABLE 12.2
Nonlinear Dynamical Phenomena in Organizations and Their Known Control Parameters: Catastrophic Processes

Phenomenon	*Asymmetry Parameter*	*Bifurcation & Other Parameters*
1. Length of work day, Australian Post Office	Amount of work received	
2. Organizational development	Pressure to change	Resistance to change
3. New product adoption by consumer (or business consumer) public	Awareness of products & opinions about it	Variety of accessories available; prior adoptions by other consumers
4. Work motivation, performance, absenteeism, turnover, creative input	Abilities, aptitudes	Extrinsic motivation, intrinsic motivation, management enhancement of motivational factors
5. Personnel selection, performance and turnover	Abilities, aptitudes, prior pay grade. Relevant control variables change during the course of one term of enlistment in the Air Force	Pay raises, career interest, intrinsic motivation, management enhancement of intrinsic motivation. Relevant control variables change during the course of one term of enlistment in the Air Force
6. Creative problem solving, individual outcomes	Personality characteristics: warmth and participativeness, unpretentiousness, social boldness, assertiveness; creative ability, content domain knowledge	External shocks from the problem environment, enriched environment for ideas supply, idea flow from other problem solvers, risk taking attitude, intrinsic motivation for creativity
7. Stability in a social network		Establish linkages with other network incumbents
8. Leadership emergence, creative problem-solving situations	Broad repertoire of contributions to a conversation	Creative role-play and creative facilitation
9. Leadership emergence, production-centered situations	Tension reduction, goal realism	Control of task and conversation
10. NYSE Stock prices and speculative bubbles	Dividend rate, reliability, interest rate sensitivity, p–e ratios, other fundamentals	Inflation level, moving variance, market volume, proportion of speculators and noise traders in market
11. Prison riots	Tension	Alienation
12. Diathesis-stress, work performance	Leadership–management support	Cognitive functions that are stress-prone

(Continued)

TABLE 12.2
(Continued)

Phenomenon	*Asymmetry Parameter*	*Bifurcation & Other Parameters*
13. Sports performance	Physiological arousal	Cognitive anxiety, self-confidence
14. Buckling stress and work performance	Work load	Elasticity versus rigidity, physical height, body balance
15. Fatigue and work performance	Compensatory strength source	Lean body mass, total work accomplished, exercise habits, labor experience
16. Occupational accidents	Environmental hazard level	Safety program quality, perceived control, anxiety, stressors, work pressure, shift work, group size
17. Stress-related illness	Environmental hostility	Organ integrity, immune system activity, stress avoidance
18. Organizational security	Crime exposure	Gatekeeping, pro-social attitude among employees, humanistic–fascistic management style
19. Competition–cooperation in groups	Group size	Group diversity
20. Urban pattern formation	Attractiveness of city to newcomers and current residents	Population growth, rigidity of the suburban ring
21. National security	Environmental hostility	Competence of military and police, norms for civil liberty, mechanisms of internal control
22. Elitist versus democratic government juntas	Inequality of income	Legitimacy of present government, span of control over individual lives, use of coercion for controlling people

Because the cusp is the most common catastrophe model, it was convenient to separate control variables into the two main groups of asymmetry and bifurcation. In the case of the more complex catastrophe models, bifurcation and higher-order control variables are grouped together in Table 12.2. The interested readers should consult the original text if the models have not been indelibly emblazoned in long-term memory already.

A few qualifications are in order, nonetheless, regarding the catastrophe models. Item 1, the length of the workday at the Australian Post Offices, was a fold catastrophe model, and thus did not have a bifurcation parameter. Items 4, 13, 18, 21, and 22 were butterfly catastrophe models. Item 6 was a mushroom catastrophe model. Item 7 was a cusp, but the asymmetry parameter has not been identified yet. Items 8 and 9 were swallowtail catastrophe models; the swallowtail (third) control parameter has not been identified yet in either case. Item 20 was actually an annihilation bifurcation, and not a member of Thom's elementary catastrophe series.

The catastrophe control parameters have specific functions in the models. The asymmetry parameter brings the system into the active region of the bifurcation manifold. The parameters on the bifurcation manifold determine the size and extent of the discontinuous change. The combination of asymmetry and bifurcation parameters creates gradients that pitch the direction of change toward one basin of local stability or another.

COGNITIVE STRATEGIES FOR COMPLEXITY

The psychological methods for adapting to nonlinear dynamical processes, discussed so far, include several abilities and cognitive strategies. There appears to be an ability to discern fixed point, periodic, and chaotic patterns over time. Individuals also differ in their abilities to track chaotic behaviors where sensitive dependence is critical. They differ in their abilities to manage and produce stable work outflows from complex systems that typically have parallel processes. All of these strategies may be considered as "computations" made by living systems. Although it is possible to use literal computer simulations for decision making, simulations are not common practice. Heuristic substitutes in the form of targeting are useful also.

Five Strategies Based on NDS

Eoyang (1997) suggested five more cognitive strategies for organizational management. These candidates are based on the dynamics of boundaries, fractals, feedback loops, self-organization, and coupling. All five have been offered as descriptions of internal behaviors of the organization. Four out of the five represent aspects of self-organization; the exception would be the fractals. The substantiation for any claims of fractal structure in organizations have, to date, rested upon plausible analogies rather than literal data analysis.

The fractal concept implies that it is often instructive for organizations, when attempting to plot new strategies and solve problems, to examine how basic themes of organizational life repeat themselves throughout the organization. One might then look for themes that represent computational "seeds," then search for evolutionary variety. One might also examine the extent to which there are "scaling effects" whereby a theme that is found at a micro-level of the system reappears at a broader organizational level. In some further thinking on the possible applications of fractals, Eoyang and Dooley (1996) suggested that fractals might show up in complex boundaries between the organization, its vendors, suppliers, and so on. The need for actually assuming a fractal structure was not clear, except that it might be a convenient assumption in a forecasting program of some sort.

The dynamics of self-organization are described in other chapters in this volume. For present purposes, however, Eoyang (1997) emphasized that self-organization is the tendency for systems to create cohesive structures when they are subjected to prolonged states of chaos or entropy. Structure forms through the development of feedback loops among subsystems. As a result of the feedback structure, subsystems may become tightly or loosely coupled. Strategists might want to examine the conditions under which structures have formed, and the nature and placement of the feedback loops.

It was mentioned in earlier chapters that a successful diagnosis of conditions and strategy formation is predicated on finding a dynamical key to the system. A dynamical key represents the central connections among feedback loops within a system. The failure to break up the key connections typically results in a reformation of the earlier structures; sometimes with small mutations that counteract an ineffectual intervention.

Boundary conditions, finally, are known to affect the self-organization of systems. Their shape, placement, and permeability affect the flow of information across the system's boundary and the formation of structures within. Although it is convenient to think of boundaries in concrete terms, boundaries are also well known in creative problem-solving where they take the form of situational constraints and assumptions. A strategist then considers the extent to which the constraint is really necessary or overrepresented.

Predisposition for Self-organized Behavior

According to Smith and Comer (1994), groups that are working under conditions of turbulence will perform better to the extent that the groups are better prepared for self-organizing behavior. The actual groups were 10 teams of students who carried out assignments in courses on group development or innovation management. Group members completed questionnaires that measured five variables: Openness or Symmetry Breaking, Experimenting Behavior, Self-reference, Boundary Reparation, and Coaction.

Openness and Experimenting Behavior are similar in meaning to the personality traits of the same name found in the 16PF taxonomy (mentioned in previous chapters) and other personality trait taxonomies. One of Smith and Comer's (1994) measures pertains to communication openness and the willingness to express negative feelings and negative expectations. The other pertains to playfulness and taking small interpersonal risks. Self-reference refers to members' level of commitment to the task, task vision, and expectations for their own creativity. Boundary Reparation referred to the interpersonal boundaries among individual members. The desirable circumstance is one in which members seek each other's help, do not behave passively toward each other, and show some interpersonal concern. Coaction refers to the members' expectations of their ability to work together as a group.

The experimenters found that groups that scored higher averages on the self-organization variables performed better at the end of their courses. Smith and Comer (1994) did note, however, that only 10 groups were involved and rank-order correlations were used. Experimental designs with a greater numbers of groups would be needed in future studies. I would add that a variety of task situations would need to be involved also.

DYNAMICS OF EMERGENCY MANAGEMENT

Emergency responses to earthquakes, floods, and similar disasters, require coordination among many public and private organizations, central government, and individual citizens. Although most major cities have a disaster response plan of some sort, the received wisdom is that, what then time comes, the best-laid plans of mice and management become suddenly rearranged. Goals and effective choices of action change rapidly. The pace of activities often outruns the prediction horizon; emergency medical facilities experience serious bottlenecks in the early phases of the disaster response. Traditional approaches to planning try to be general enough to fit any situation, but the specific nature of collective activities and architecture often pose limitations to the general plan (Samurcay & Rogalski, 1993). NDS concepts of sensitivity to initial conditions, fractal organization, and self-organization have been useful for interpreting what actually occurs (Comfort, 1996, 1999; Koehler, 1995, 1996a).

Sensitivity to Initial Conditions

Where did the earthquake strike, and at what time of day? If the earthquake strikes outside the city with damage extending to the interior, the projection is that casualties in the city will receive medical and other attention faster than casualties in the outlying districts (Koehler, 1995). On the other hand, if the epicenter of the quake falls closer to the urban center, another set of problems arises. The state of California determined that 8 out of 26 major medical facilities in the San Francisco area were built before the last round of seismic engineering standards went into effect. As much as a third of the best medical resources could, therefore, be wiped out in the quake, and greater stress would be placed on the remaining facilities along with the transportation resources to use them (Koehler, 1996b).

If the earthquake disrupts a major highway system in the city during the middle of the night, we have one set of problems. If the earthquake disrupts the same highway at rush hour, we have another set. In both cases, there will be a drain on major highways running in and out of the affected area. People will leave the disaster area by any means possible, especially if they have somewhere they can go. Emergency vehicles will need to get around during full-tilt commotion. Emergency supplies will need to get inside the affected area.

Time of day would also affect the response of telephone and electrical utilities. For the most part, the utility companies have already evolved their own inner logic as to how much power they can commit to certain locations at different times of day. They will inevitably have a more difficult time shutting down operations and diverting resources during the day than in the middle of the night.

Fractal Organization

Two points concerning fractals have been proposed, and both are based on the diffusion-limited aggregation principle. According to Koehler (1995), the organization of an emergency response is similar to the organization of a fractal structure. Before the onset of the disaster, the individual emergency capabilities, such as fire, police, private organizations, and hospitals, work in a disjointed fashion as they go about their ordinary business. There are small amounts of connection among them, but no overall pattern. Once the disaster strikes, however, the networks solidify. Some agencies become located at the central control node, others become located close to it, and others become located progressively further away.

As the network "percolates," more work teams are added to the peripheral nodes. Private organizations that are not usually involved in disaster-relevant business often emerge in active roles in locating survivors, supplying care, or reconstruction of facilities. Organizations that do not usually work together now interact very often.

The second diffusion-limited aggregation phenomenon is tied to the geography of the disaster region. There will be an epicenter and an area immediately surrounding it, which will have the greatest toll in casualties and property losses. There will be trajectories of disaster emanating from the epicenter and following the fault line itself in case of an earthquake. The main disaster arteries will have branches of progressively less severity. At the most distant regions, the casualties are reduced to a little broken glass and few frightened moments.

Self-organizing Behavior

While the usual disaster response units are gathering their forces, a good deal of emergency action is already taking place where the disaster has struck. According to Comfort (1996) and sources in the state of California, about 75% of able-bodied survivors are engaged in some aspect of the relief effort within hours after the onset of the disaster. When "official" personnel arrive in the trouble locations, they must usually integrate their efforts with those already in progress. The emergency response itself unfolds in three phases: extraction and stabilization of critically injured people; the restoration of homes, jobs, civic functioning, communication and transportation; and the "reassurance" squads of clergy, social workers, and psychologists (Comfort, 1999).

Comfort (1996) observed that the distribution of severity of injury resembles an N|K distribution. The rugged landscape analogy would be an attractive mental model of situations such as earthquakes. Philippe (2000) would probably classify the injury distribution as an inverse power law, which appears to characterize many epidemic outcomes. Hospitalization lengths would be an operable indicator of severity. In either case, the nonlinear dynamical signposts are clearly visible.

The self-organization process itself is facilitated by good communication networks and relatively new information technology tools (Comfort, 1999). Simple actions are sometimes the most valuable, however. As soon as people living outside the disaster region get wind of the disaster, they telephone into the region obviously to check or friends or family. Unfortunately, these calls jam the telephone system's carrying capacity and interfere with communications that are essential to the actual work of disaster response. Thus, the first policy move is to block as many nonessential communications as possible until the internal situation is more or less under control.

Timing is critical and problematic. For instance, one decision-maker can ascertain that a hospital emergency room has a certain amount of carrying capacity at a particular moment, and then dispatch some victims to that hospital. By the time the batch of victims arrives, other decision-makers had the same idea and dispatched victims to the same location, thus producing a bottleneck. Other critical events are connected to the discovery of new victims or the prevention of concomitant disasters, such as fires in the wake of an earthquake, or the change in the path of a forest fire caused by a sudden shift of the winds change rapidly. Human communication and the physical movement of people and equipment are not always fast enough to compensate.

Koehler (1996b) also observed that the psychological representation of time by disaster respondents and victims is strongly constricted to the needs of the present moment. The ability to see the future, even in the short horizon of a disaster response, is greatly impaired. The problem persists in a different way in the later phases of the disaster and reconstruction where many people have difficulty getting on with their lives, or making long-term adaptive plans. He cited the habit of people to move back onto a flood plain after a flood as a probable example of that mentality.

Information technologies can speed things along, but there is no guarantee that there will be enough time to boot up the little desktop computer and run simulations. There is no guarantee that the needed data link-ups are still operable. In short, the disaster scenario is loaded with destabilizing events, and there is great potential for management to exacerbate a situation that is already chaotic. In spite of these challenges, however, postepisode analysis of emergency responses to major California disasters showed that the symphonies of management and action have had stabilizing, rather than destabilizing, effects (Priesmeyer & Cole, 1996).

Some disasters are managed better than others, and much depends on whether there are collisions between predisaster planning and the actual requirements for a successful self-organization process. Comfort (1996) compared the collective responses to two earthquakes that occurred in Marathwada, India in 1993, and Kobe, Japan in 1995. The Marathwada earthquake registered 6.4 on the Richter scale. The Kobe earthquake registered 7.2.

About 80% of Marathwada's 12,264 regional citizens were employed in agriculture, and the overall adult literacy level of the area was about 45%. There was no prior awareness of seismic risks in the population or in the government geological reports (they know better now). There was a strong social cohesion in the population, however, that kicked into high gear when the disaster started. Communication with the regional capital was greatly facilitated by the presence of a satellite system that had been installed by the Indian government. The problem was detected quickly, and the response was prompt. The greatest response came from the local village councils, which addressed the needs for medical attention, shelter, food, and water. The transportation routes were sparce and underdeveloped; fortunately, they were not terminally disrupted. What was missing in central planning, knowledge, and municipal preparedness was compensated by flexibility in grass-roots responses.

Kobe, on the other hand, is a city with a population of about 1.4 million and an adult literacy level in excess of 95%. Seismic risks were well-known, but at the same time, the population held little concern because their last earthquake in 1916 was not as bad as the later one in Tokyo in 1926. Nonetheless, there had been considerable investment in seismic architecture and seismic monitoring technology. Although private organizations had made substantial investments in information technologies to meet their own needs, there was little connection with municipal agencies. Thus, it took the privately owned gas company 6 hours to turn off the gas in the areas of the city that were on fire. There were 60 fires burning simultaneously just after the eruption, and 85 burned simultaneously in the next 3 hours. The total response capability, however, consisted of 11 fire stations, 176 engines, and 663 personnel (Comfort, 1996, pp. 130–131).

The industrialized society of Kobe did not have the social connectivity that facilitated reclamation in Marathwada, which Comfort (1996) described as an "internal model or schema for voluntary action" (p. 135). To make matters worse, however, well-intentioned rules and regulations actually stifled a number of aid efforts in Kobe. For instance, there was a law in place preventing police and fire from giving emergency medical care without the presence of a physician; as a result there was an added layer of communication, waiting, and personnel shortage. In another example, a law restricted the use of dogs from hunting for humans. One emergency response team would have brought in dogs to search for survivors, but was prevented from doing so. The dogs were only allowed to search for dead bodies.

The death rate in Marathwada was counted at 10%, or 1,220 persons. The death rate for Kobe was estimated at 0.5%, or upwards of 6,000 people. Other relevant indicators are the number of injured persons, survival rates for people rescued, homes destroyed, and the gross financial impact of the disaster. The value of time is sobering in any case; Fig. 12.4 illustrates the numbers of people

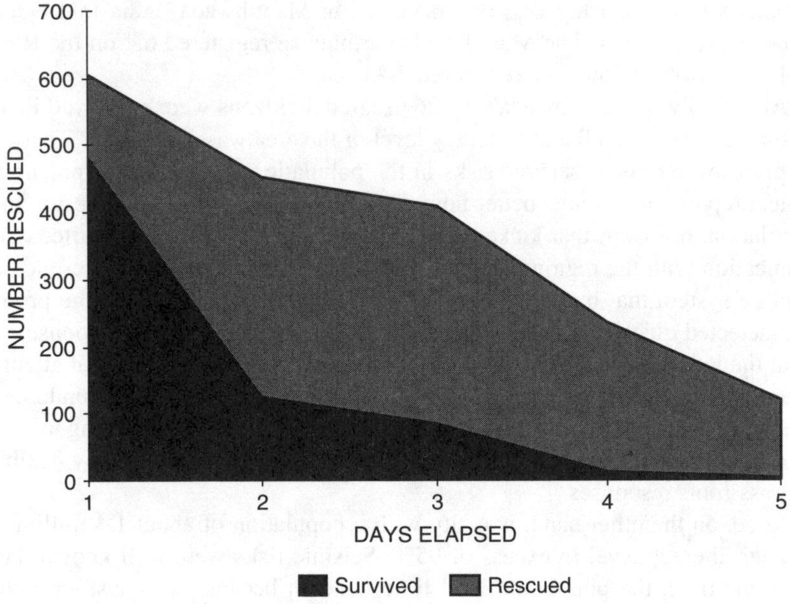

FIG. 12.4. Number of people rescued during the Kobe earthquake as the number of days since the quake increased. Based on tabular data from Comfort (1996).

rescued in Kobe and the number of rescued people who survived for day of the disaster. The likelihood of survival after rescue declines rapidly with each day of the disaster.

It is not fair to make blanket judgments as to which community "did better" or which final outcome "was worse." There were major differences in the initial population levels, infrastructure density, and chance events. The lesson that should be extracted, however, concerns what could be done effectively, and how the initial conditions affected the self-organization of the global response system.

SUMMARY

This chapter examined what is known about the psychological processes that involved in predicting the future and the decision tools that have evolved over the eons. All techniques have evolved to minimize different types of uncertainties. Ancient devining methods include oracles, astrology, tarot cards, and *I Ching*. Contemporary tools involve the use of statistics, models and simulations, expert systems, and nonlinear-based techniques. Nonlinear analytical techniques include NDS principles generally as a frame of mental reference, the types of analyses used throughout this book, plus artificial life techniques such as genetic algorithms, neural networks, and cellular automata.

The psychology of prediction and prediction ability was considered next. It appears that some prediction of the future is well-known in motivation theory and almost taken for granted. People who have shown the strongest abilities to predict the future also show many of the characteristics of creative people. They also have an ability to predict the future of chaotic events even though numerical prediction would be generally poor.

Several types of control for chaos were introduced. Some were first identified as phenomena of physical systems then transported into human decision schemata. They were the ability to track chaos, controlling chaos with chaos, the OGY method of periodic entrainment, and control parameter manipulation. A table listed the known chaotic human systems (within the scope of this book) and the control parameters that regulate them. The principle of control parameter manipulation was also expanded to include the control of catastrophic systems. A table listed many of the known catastrophic human systems (within the scope of this book) and the control parameters that regulate them.

Several additional control strategies for complex systems were introduced that pertained to boundaries, fractals, feedback loops, self-organization, and coupling.

The final section of the chapter explored the dynamics of emergency management. Several NDS principles were involved that pertained to sensitivity to initial conditions, diffusion-limited aggregation and fractal percolation, and self-organizing behavior. The challenges of coordination and mental representations of time horizons were considered also. Earthquake response outcomes were used as examples.

Epilogue

Whatever Happened to Everything?

The continuing developments on NDS applications to organizational behavior have resulted in new knowledge about many related phenomena. This concluding section of the book summarizes what we have learned and the relative salience of some things we already knew. The summary addresses the predictive and quantitative advantages of the NDS approach, the qualitative understanding of phenomena that was shaped by nonlinear dynamics research, and the special role of specific nonlinear dynamics in each of those situations.

THE UTILITY

A theory that explains everything explains nothing at all. A better theory will explain some phenomena well, and it will explain many phenomena with a minimum number of propositions or assumptions. One might argue that simple linear models and concepts are somehow better than NDS ideas because of the inherent simplicity of linear models. Ian Stewart (1989) has pointed out in no uncertain terms, however, that a science that is dominated by linear models is a precisely an example of using one model to explain everything. He characterized the linear thought pattern as not much different from insisting that every animal in a zoo is an elephant.

Alternatively one might argue, as I have (e.g., Guastello, 1981), that a well-formulated nonlinear model can subsume many elementary concepts and thus represent more efficient explanations. Hopefully, the heuristic advantage of NDS concepts for explaining specific phenomena has been apparent in the foregoing pages. Hopefully also, it has catalyzed a critical reorganization of our shared ideas concerning what an organization is, and what happens inside it.

It is a fair question to ask how well the NDS concepts actually describe the *data*. In *Chaos, Catastrophe, and Human Affairs*, I concluded that, in the cases where the NDS model was actually adopted as the preferred explanation for a phenomenon, the NDS model accounted for more variance in the data compared to its best linear alternative by a ratio of 2.1:1. Table 13.1 makes the same comparison. This time, the studies contributing to the average are those that were cited in this book, and for which the data were published after *Chaos, Catastrophe, and Human Affairs*. In other words, let's just look at the new material and see if the same advantages can be observed.

Indeed they can. The averages at the bottom of Table 13.1 indicate that, in situations where a nonlinear model was adopted, the predictive accuracy of the nonlinear model was 1.8:1 based on the R^2 coefficients. Those averages did not include three studies listed in the table where a linear comparison R^2 was not available. It may be justifiable to say, however, in the case of the symbolic dynamics studies where the linear model was undefined, that the inability of linear thinking to formulate a competing hypothesis is tantamount to saying that linear models accounted for 0% of variance in those instances. If we head in that direction, then the average R^2 for the nonlinear models still rounds to .67, and the average R^2 for the linear models decreases to .34. The resulting average then increases to 2.00 : 1.

It is noteworthy, however, that my colleagues and I have encountered a couple situations in leadership emergence, where the nonlinear model was well formed, but the linear model showed somewhat greater accuracy. In those cases, we tentatively adopted the nonlinear models with the expectation that they would improve eventually once the missing control parameters were found. The excellent fit between the distribution of leadership ratings and the swallowtail catastrophe distributions suggested that we could be on the right track.

THE PHENOMENA

Our NDS adventures began with the saga of the San Francisco earthquake of 1906. Events such as the earthquake correspond to colloquial notions of "chaos." More importantly, the earthquake story contains several dynamical events that fit the formal definitions; the most important dynamics were (probably) self-organization from the bottom of the system upward, and hierarchical driving downward.

TABLE 13.1
Comparison of Linear and Nonlinear Models

Phenomenon	*Authors*	*Linear Model R^2*	*Nonlinear Model R^2*	*Preferred Nonlinear Model*
Local work rules	Haslett et al., 2000	.59	.77	Fold catastrophe[a]
Product adoption	Lange et al., 2000	.95	.996	Cusp catastrophe
Personnel selection, turnover, Air Force	Chapter 5	.21	.30	Cusp catastrophe
Motivational flow	Guastello, Johnson, & Rieke, 1999	.05	.25	Simple exponential, chaotic[b]
CPS group output	Guastello, 1998a	.56	.57	Chaotic with periodic driver[c]
CPS number of active threads	Guastello, 1998a	.75	.75	Periodic[c]
CPS conversation response type; real-time discussion	Guastello et al., 1998	UNDEF	.63	Symbolic pattern,[d] string length = 4
CPS conversation response type; list-server discussion	Guastello, 2000a	UNDEF	.51	Symbolic pattern,[d] string length = 2, social interaction protocol
CPS conversation response type; list-server discussion	Guastello, 2000a	UNDEF	.95	Symbolic pattern,[d] string length = 3, problem completion protocol
Inclusion in a network of organizations	Chapter 7	.04	.70	Cusp catastrophe
Formation of a CPS virtual community	Guastello & Philippe, 1997	.88	.99	Exponential, May–Oster population dynamics
Coordination group performance task	Guastello & Guastello, 1998	.12	.40	Fixed point attractor function with bifurcation[e]
Difficult coordination task	Guastello & Guastello, 1998	.12	.44	Chaotic attractor *plus* fixed point attractor function with bifurcation.
Coordination task verbal groups only	Chapter 8; Guastello, Bock, & Caldwell, 1999	.16	.50	Exponential chaotic in one case, bifurcation unknown in three additional cases[f]
Coordination task nonverbal groups	Chapter 8; Guastello, Bock, & Caldwell, 1999	.16	.36	Exponential chaotic in one case, bifurcation unknown in three additional cases[f]
Leadership emergence, CPS	Guastello, 1998b	.33	.999	Swallowtail catastrophe response surface
Leadership emergence, CPS	Zaror & Guastello, 2000	.33	.998	Swallowtail catastrophe response surface
Leadership emergence, CPS, larger group	Chapter 9; Guastello et al., 2001	.40	.995	Swallowtail catastrophe response surface
Leadership emergence, CPS, larger group	Chapter 9; Guastello et al., 2001	.80	.74	Swallowtail catastrophe with control variables introduced[c]
Leadership emergence, production task	Chapter 9; Guastello et al., 2001	.44	.999	Swallowtail catastrophe response surface
Leadership emergence, production task	Chapter 9; Guastello et al., 2001	.75	.62	Swallowtail catastrophe with control variables introduced

(Continued)

TABLE 13.1
(Continued)

Phenomenon	*Authors*	*Linear Model R^2*	*Nonlinear Model R^2*	*Preferred Nonlinear Model*
2-level production hierarchy, workers	Guastello, 1999a	.04	.51	Exponential with bifurcation unknown[g]
2-level production hierarchy, managers	Guastello, 1999a	.02	.91	Exponential chaotic function
3-level production hierarchy, workers	Guastello, 1999a	.23	.24	Exponential chaotic function
3-level production hierarchy, all 3 management groups	Guastello, 1999a	.03	.51	Exponential with bifurcation unknown[g]
3-level hierarchy, workers, managers downsized	Guastello & Johnson, 1999	.31	.34	Exponential chaotic in 2 conditions; bifurcation unknown in 1 condition[h]
3-level hierarchy, all management groups, managers downsized	Guastello & Johnson, 1999	.04	.35	Variously chaotic, bifurcation unknown, with ordinary and differenced criteria; 18 models total[h]
Dow-Jones stock prices	Chapter 11	.94	.96	Chaotic, with fractal structure at 5 different lag lengths
Unemployment	Guastello, 1999b, 2000b	.32	.88	Chaotic attractor; also an instability with bifurcation unknown[i]
Producer price index	Guastello, 1995c, 2000b	.02	.75	Exponential chaotic
Consumer price index	Guastello, 1995c, 2000b	.40	.85	Exponential chaotic
Oceanic fishing harvests	Chapter 11; Guastello, 1997	.99	.80	Chaotic Lotka-Volterra with time as a bifurcation variable[j]
Average without UNDEF entries		.378	.671	Ratio = 1.78: 1
Average with UNDEF entries		.343	.673	Ratio = 1.96: 1

Abbreviations: NG = Not given in the handout. UNDEF = Linear models were not defined for these situations.

[a] R^2 entries are the means of values taken from 5 samples.

[b] R^2 entries are the means of values taken from 24 individuals' time series.

[c] Linear models actually capitalized on nonlinear trends inherent in the data.

[d] ϕ^2 was used to approximate R^2.

[e] R^2 entries are the means of values taken from 2 similar experimental conditions.

[f] R^2 entries are the means of values taken from 4 experimental conditions.

[g] Criterion was a difference score (Δz).

[h] R^2 entries are the means of values taken from 3 experimental conditions.

[i] The R^2 entry for the nonlinear models is the average value for the two interpretations.

[j] The linear model was actually produced from an exponential structure, which showed asymptotic stability over time.

The upward self-organization dynamic took the form of local interactions between people and their environment. There were many reports of near-instantaneous adaptive responses by local groups and individuals as well as maladaptive responses by other parties. Coordinated rescue teams formed as a result.

The downward hierarchical driving took the form of management of the civic organizations, such as police, firefighters, and health care. Individual citizens joined those formal organizational units on demand. Many of the important decisions were not observed directly, but the manifestations that people remembered involved interactions between police and people, police and military, and every organization with the life-threatening environment.

The rebuilding of a city involved a very different set of dynamics. It involved building an attractor structure that combined a geographical location that was already regarded as desirable, job offers, and a chance for individual and collective creative expression. In spite of the 1906 disaster and others like it since that time, San Francisco is a thriving city today. Its architecture reflects the latest available developments in seismic control. Its population shares a special knowledge of how to respond to an earthquake during the tremors and afterwards that might not be so widely shared outside the state of California.

Ironically, the San Francisco earthquake occurred before the concept of bureaucracy was formally introduced to sociology, organizational behavior, or management. Today, the story typifies a major transition in the thinking about what is an organization. The dominant paradigm over the last century has evolved from an organization that is bureaucratic, mechanical, impersonal, and wholly rational to an organization that is a complex adaptive system. The complex adaptive system exhibits structure and fluidity; rational, emotional, and intuitive, thinking; and individual and collective rationality. It took the better part of a century to explore these attributes among individual humans, and there is no sign that the job has been completed. It is not a surprise, therefore, that it has taken at least a century to interpret an organization.

Organizations, like other life forms, change. The old paradigm of opposing forces has given way to catastrophe dynamics where pressure to change and resistance to change have more complicated roles in change phenomena. Pressure and resistance have now acquired new levels of meaning as well. The general model suggests many possible specific manifestations. So far, just a few examples of catastrophe dynamics have been recorded for phenomena that were defined at the organizational level of analysis. Group-level examples are much more prevalent at the present time.

We can also shift focus from the broad and obvious aspects of organizational change to the microdynamics of change. Here we can now see logical connections within an organization that take the form of work flows, communication pathways, and sociotechnical structures. Organizational change, or *organizational development* in the more deliberate case, involves a process of building entropy, trust, and the consolidation of new structures. That is done with *ideas*.

Ideas are elements of information. Like molecules, some ideas are more complex than others. Their contributing elements, like atoms, vary in complexity as well. The important point here is that two types of thought drive organizational dynamics: Creative or *divergent thought* generates options and possible actions and *convergent thought* selects the most profitable options.

The motivation chapter unpacked the convergent thinking aspect into several important parts. There is *utility seeking* as expressed by game theory, expectancy theory, and the strategy that underlies personnel selection. Utilities take two heuristic forms–the *extrinsic and intrinsic*. Exterior agents deliver extrinsic rewards. Intrinsic rewards are generated by the task itself. In both cases, the optimization of rewards requires a sense of what will happen in the future; hence we have the notions of *expectancy* and *instrumentality*.

Creative thinking requires a combination of intellectual skills, a personality that is comfortable with the experiences that stem from change, a flow of ideas, organization of new ideas, and resulting changes in one's view of the world. It thrives under conditions of intrinsic motivation and environment that is rich in idea resources. The results of creative thinking are most successful if the thinker, or collection of thinkers, has a wide repertoire of *cognitive schemata* (styles) for utilizing intellectual abilities.

Both types of thinking lend themselves to group problem-solving processes. There are several channels of communication operating. There is nonverbal expression and verbal expression. The *nonverbal communication* in a coordination task bears a strong similarity to the behaviors of bird flocks, fish schools, and herds. Verbal expression promotes a *shared problem* and the *sociable interaction* that keeps a problem-solving group together for its own sake. The discussions that are directly related to the problem are organized in two tracks: *general information flow* or (participation) and *especially creative information transactions*. Some groups generate higher volumes of information flow than others.

Individuals have long been known to have both conscious and unconscious mental processes. A *collective unconscious* was suspected to exist within a society. Today, there is recognition of *collective intelligence* and collective unconscious thought, especially within organizations or work units where the members have entrained to each other's thought processes to some extent. The shared storehouses of ideas, or semantic lattices, extend to shared lattices in the broader society.

There is a blurred distinction between a group and a *social network*. A group begins with a collection of individuals who have a common purpose and who share information and make other exchanges that can be represented as information. A group has a *boundary* that is shared by its members, although groups differ in the extent to which their boundaries are rigid or permeable. Networks, on the other hand, are defined by information flows. Networks generally do not have boundaries and may be composed of groups that have partially overlapping memberships. Similarly organizations may form networks by virtue of their frequent and complex patterns of bilateral exchanges. A variety of influences from technology, information content, and the particular people involved combine to form the basis of a social network. Social networks have their own patterns of interaction. Many of the vicissitudes of the interaction patterns have yet to be explored.

The interactions among group members become asymmetrical as the volume of interaction increases. The social quality and expertise content of the interactions is at least as important as the raw volume. At first, some members can be observed as being more centrally located in the group interaction patterns than other members. Eventually, a group that started as a leaderless group self-organizes into role structures, wherein *primary and secondary leaders* can be observed. The group members who are most likely to be recognized as leaders are those who display a wide repertoire of *social interaction patterns*. The different interaction behaviors in the conversation have different effects on the role structures and leadership emergence, depending on whether the group objective is creative problem-solving, production of a quantity of work, or some other objective.

Leaders and creative people are known to have some similar personality traits and other traits that are polar opposites. Theorists have begun to recognize the role of creativity in leadership and the leadership impact of creative thinking. In both cases, the ability to *envision the future* is an important part of leadership influence. The historically important visionaries have varied widely with regard to the content of their visions, methods of implementation and influencing other people, and the long-term positive regard that they received. Although a leader's expertise contributes to the widespread popularity of the leader, there is no reason to believe that the reverse is true; popularity does not necessarily foreshadow optimal decisions.

A considerable amount of research from the last half century addressed the general question of how leadership styles and behaviors affect the performance and adjustment of constituent work groups. Autonomous work groups, which involve no *hierarchical management*, have been strikingly effective. The studies of hierarchical work organizations represent the first attempts to study the reverse problem of how the temporal dynamics of groups' work flows affect management's ability to maintain a stable and efficient work flow of its own. The downsizing manipulations, which affected only the management groups in the experiments, did not have a consistent effect in either the stable or unstable direction. It is probable that the hierarchical structure studies generated more questions than they answered. If so, one scientific objective has been served.

Organizational psychology has paid a fair amount of lip service over the years to "economic factors" that "affect decisions." Chapter 11 was explicitly concerned with four types of economic decisions. Some involved *ordinary markets*. Some involved *hierarchical structures* in the economy such as inflation and unemployment. Some involved *markets for information* which do not follow common market dynamics; the flow of information is dependent on institutional structures. Some involved the utilization and marketing of *natural resources*, which again do not conform to common market dynamics. There are other decision forms, of course; the *game theory* applications from earlier chapters comprise another diverse class of economic decisions.

The conventional leadership theories that address the topic of *vision* portray leaders' visions as if they are static concepts. Some theories recognize that visions transmute when other people get a hold of them. The ability to *predict future events*, however, is a specialized type of vision. NDS research has uncovered a variety of cognitive strategies for interpreting, predicting, and controlling future events and event scenarios. We have only begun to learn about many of them.

THE DYNAMICS

We can now reintroduce mathematical structures that underlie organizational events and observe some patterns. Organizational change dynamics can be described by the logistic map, which could denote several classes of events—stability, entropy, critical points, oscillation, additional bifurcations of the oscillations, and chaos. Systems in a state of chaos reorganize into new stable structures. The process of self-organization into a new stable structure is essentially the formation of an attractor. A cusp catastrophe model represents the change in the system from the old structure to the new one. The bifurcation manifold of a cusp governs whether the change process is gradual, evolutionary, and stable; or whether it is discontinuous, revolutionary, and locally stable. This understanding is bolstered by some more general relationships between catastrophe dynamics, the differentiation of a rugged landscape, and the jump that an organization (for instance) might make between fitness peaks.

Work motivation requires a butterfly catastrophe model to explain the full range of work performance types, attractor levels, bifurcations, and control parameters. We saw in earlier investigations (Guastello, 1995a) how learning and motivation are parts of a common dynamical process. The complexity of the behaviors of the system, together with the learning–motivation connection, allows us to rationalize models that are cusp subsets of the butterfly model. The subsets for training or program evaluation and personnel selection may prove to be the most useful. In the particular case of personnel selection, there is a substantial heuristic advantage to considering individual performance and turnover as part of a common behavioral spectrum.

Intrinsic motivation is commonly imagined as a steady state of mind or semi-permanent set of attributes of the work environment. A closer look, however, showed that individuals' intrinsic motivation levels fluctuate in a low-dimensional chaotic manner in the course of a week. Furthermore, three different patterns of motivational flow were uncovered. One pattern reflected little in the way of flow itself and may be indicative of an anhedonic disposition. A second pattern reflected a relatively high volatility over time. A third pattern reflected long, comparatively stable, periods of flow experience. There may be other patterns that have not yet been identified.

Creative behavior has lent itself to a variety of NDS analyses. The default theory suggested that creative mental events were chance occurrences, and that all one had to do was to plug into idea-rich environments. Of course, if that were true, there would be no individual differences in divergent thinking skill or cognitive style. Nonetheless, the environment does play an important role in the NDS theory of creativity; if anything, the contribution of the environment is augmented by the recognition of social dynamics within the environment. The distributions of creative events display deterministic structures. The particular structures depend on what aspect of the creative process the researcher wishes to view. In any case, fractal inverse power laws, sand pile self-organization, moderately high-dimensional chaos, mushroom catastrophes, logistic map bifurcations, and coupled dynamics have all been observed in one context or another.

Creative thinking involves, among other things, divergent thinking, which in turn involves cutting new paths across one's semantic lattice structures. Semantic lattices are shared to some extent among a group of problem solvers; hence we have the notion of *shared mental models*. Semantic lattices appear to be a critical deep structure in the creative process, and the lattice structures evolve with frequent interactions with the environment. Psychologists recognize the evolution of lattices as consisting of two processes: *assimilation* and *accommodation*. I have speculated, but have not yet been able to prove, that the evolution of a lattice is similar to the percolation of a fractal.

The indicators of network density and network membership can be represented by some familiar dynamics. Inclusion in, or deletion from, a network can be represented as a cusp catastrophe. As such, the model bears a strong similarity to the dynamics of personnel selection.

When a network grows sufficiently large, by virtue of its perceived value to new potential members, it may be regarded as a *community*. Some communities are *virtual*, while others are the more terrestrial variety. In the virtual case, the community acts as an *attractor* to new members. The strictly cooperative *bandwagon* game explains the utilities of community membership. The size of the community is a May–Oster population growth dynamic as it changes over time.

There are critical points in the development of relationships between two people and in the population growth of a virtual community. The two phenomena share the same dynamical pattern: Increasing levels of exchange maintains attractiveness. A saddle point is reached, whereby the relationship could continue to grow or dissipate. If it continues to grow, it gravitates to a fixed-point attractor.

Work group coordination is the result of a convergence of several psychological and NDS phenomena. Psychological phenomena include optimizing decisions made by groups, implicit learning, and a particular form of cooperative behavior that overlaps with game theory. Furthermore coordination is based in part on the dynamical connections between learning and motivation. When coordination is not successfully attained, the behavior of the group is chaotic. When coordination is successfully attained, the early chaotic behavior self-organizes into the coordinated behavior, which is in turn observed as evolutionarily stable state or a fixed-point attractor. Bifurcations are observed that govern the rapidity of the coordination acquisition over time.

High-quality interactions among work group members generate entropy. With sufficient entropy, the group self-organizes into role structures whereby leaders emerge. The pattern of self-organization strongly resembles the scenario of a species of organism that differentiates as it explores and colonizes different ecological niches in a rugged landscape. The distribution of leadership characteristics is best represented as a swallowtail catastrophe model. The control parameters of the swallowtail model differ depending on the type of task that is involved. In some cases, the nature of the control parameters is not fully understood at the present time.

Once can reasonably argue that the emergence of a leader is an example of a synergetic process in which a hierarchical structure is formed; the upper level of the hierarchy then acts as a driver that dominates the dynamics of the lower level of the hierarchy. Hierarchies in work organizations only partially resemble that description, however. In two-level hierarchies it has been possible to observe work groups that act as strong chaotic drivers, which in turn render management completely out of control. In another case, the work group generates a mixture of chaos and noise, to which management responds in a chaotic and stable manner.

In three-level hierarchies, management can be seen as oscillating in its performance and dampening the oscillation. In other instances, management's oscillation behavior expands as if a bifurcation manifold or positive feedback loop were in place. The top management may display periods of relative stability and instability. Finally, it is possible to observe the same dynamics from different roles within the same experimental organization. The inevitable conclusion is that there are individual differences in managers' ability to navigate volatile temporal dynamics.

The economic environment that surrounds an organization can act as a driver; the dynamics of the driver can take on many forms. Market behaviors may exhibit fractal properties if viewed from one perspective. Markets may exhibit speculative bubbles, which take the form of cusp catastrophes.

In the particular case of labor and money, markets self-organize by virtue of the interrelationships among market sectors, thereby forming a Sraffian complex system. Asymmetries in power develop which, in essence, create hierarchical relationships among economic agents. Power asymmetries are mediated to some extent by another level of hierarchy, which we observe in the form of governmental economic policy. The possible presence of natural rates of inflation or unemployment could only be assessed as NDS problems. Fixed-point attractors, which would have denoted classically defined natural rates, were not observed. Instead, there was a stability of inflation that was characterized by a chaotic attractor, as well as a scenario whereby a bifurcation effect would trigger runaway inflation if a critical point were reached. Unemployment trends could be interpreted as unstable, growing, and susceptible to an underlying bifurcation dynamic. Alternatively, the same data could be interpreted as the behavior of a chaotic attractor. It was possible to identify critical points in both unemployment and inflation data.

Global trends in fishing harvests reflect predator–prey dynamics. Different theorists have characterized predator–prey dynamics as cusp catastrophes or chaotic phenomena. The data analysis indicates that both interpretations are true. The harvest levels were chaotic, and they were of sufficient complexity to support an underlying cubic potential. There was an important alternative model, however, that indicated an asymptotic decline in fishing harvests over time if the trends that were captured in the data were allowed to continue.

The tasks of management in organizations occur at the interface between complex dynamics within the organization, and complex dynamics from environmental sources. It is no surprise that individuals differ in their ability to surf the tides. The final chapter explored various means by which complex dynamics are understood and how adaptive responses might be formulated. We found individual differences in the ability to track temporal dynamics. We found some possible uses of dynamical systems to induce other dynamical events. We also posited that knowledge of specific dynamical models for specific situations can provide, and should provide, a lexicon of control parameters that available to a would-be manager.

Another special skill is the ability to conceptually analyze a complex system and identify its dynamical key. The key is the critical thread in a ball of yarn, which, if we find it and pull it, unravels the entire problem. That is more easily said than done, of course. If we are really good at what we do, however, we should be able to navigate some of the most challenging disasters that an organization could face. There are unpredictable initial conditions of time and place, a fast-moving evolution of events, the self-organization of resources, and a strong need to anticipate near-term events and the potential for collateral disasters. Not all challenges portend disaster; some simply represent the opportunity to do great things as compared to doing nothing at all.

Decisions that we make at one moment affect our available options at the next moment. With that in mind, I'll end the book. Now where did I put that sunset?

Appendix A

Data Analysis with Structural Equations

The method of structural equations that is described in Chapter 3 can be executed on standard statistical packages such as the *Statistical Package for the Social Sciences* (SPSS). The original analyses that are presented in this book and all others that were based on structural equations methods were accomplished in that fashion. A brief instructional guide appears below. Instructions are specified in terms of statements that can be used in a mainframe SPSS program. The same commands can be used in the PC versions with only minor modifications; the mainframe syntax is easier to explain, however.

CATASTROPHE MODELS WITH POLYNOMIAL REGRESSION

The data set for catastrophe models needs to be organized so that each observation contains the dependent measure (the variable that is hypothesized to show catastrophic behavior) at two points in time, and the values of the control value at Time 1. The user then needs to specify some COMPUTE statements before specifying the actual regression subprogram. COMPUTE statements are needed to transform dependent measures and other control variables with respect to location and scale.

```
COMPUTE z2 = (y2 - L) / S                                    (A1)
```

In statement A1, $y2$ is the dependent measure at Time 2, L is the value of location, and S is the value of scale. Actual numbers would replace L and S. The same syntax would be used for control variables and for changing $y_1 \rightarrow z_1$. Compute statements are also needed to define power terms such as z^3 (statement A2), a similar quadratic term, bifurcation interactive terms (A3), and the difference score (A4) that is used as the dependent measure in the catastrophe models.

```
COMPUTE zpow3 = z1**3                                        (A2)
COMPUTE bz = b*z1                                            (A3)
COMPUTE deltaz = z2 - z1                                     (A4)
```

The variable b listed in statement A3 is a variable that is hypothesized to function as a bifurcation term in a cusp. A particular application can have several variables called b. The variable called a in statement A5 is a variable that is hypothesized to function as an asymmetry variable.

Proceed to the main program statements after completing the COMPUTE statements. Use the regression subprogram.

```
Regression descriptives/ missing=pairwise                    (A5)
      /variables = dz zpow3 zpow2 bz a
      /dependent = dz/ enter zpow3 zpow2 bz a
```

Next inspect the significance tests for each of the terms in the model. If the regression weight for zpow3 is not significant, drop zpow2 and try it again. In the event that there are several variables being tested as a and b variables, drop any variable for which the p-value on the regression weight is greater than .10. Then try the reverse hypothesis, that the variables first thought to behave as b are really a's and vice versa. To do so define some more compute statements for the new bifurcation terms (A6) and run the regression as a two-step process (A7).

```
COMPUTE az = a*z1                                            (A6)
REGRESSION descriptives/ missing=pairwise                    (A7)
      /variables = dz zpow3 zpow2 bz a b az
      /dependent = dz /enter zpow3 zpow2 a /enter az b
```

Statement A7 assumes that the variable that was first thought to behave as b was not significant, and that both zpow3 and zpow2 were acceptable:

Finally, the two linear alternative models would be defined as A8 and A9:

```
REGRESSION descriptives/ missing=pairwise                    (A8)
      /variables = dz b a
      /dependent = dz /enter a b
REGRESSION descriptives/ missing=pairwise                    (A9)
      /variables = z2 z1 b a
      /dependent = z2 /enter z1 b a
```

EXPONENTIAL SERIES WITH NONLINEAR REGRESSION

Nonlinear regression offers much greater flexibility in the definition of models compared to polynomial regression and its variations on the GLM. Because of its flexibility in defining a model, the nonlinear regression subprogram of SPSS requires a more specific statement of the intended models, and there is little automatic processing with regard to putting variables in or out of the model.

The data set up requires that the observations be ordered in time series, where each subsequent string of data represents observations at successive points in time. The control program again requires COMPUTE statements, but not generally as many. The definitions of $y \rightarrow z$ go in first along with the conversions for any control variables. Define the z as z_2 (statement A10) then use the LAG syntax to define z_1 at a lag of 1 time period (A11).

```
COMPUTE z2 = (y - L) / S                                     (A10)
COMPUTE z1 = lag(z2, 1)                                      (A11)
```

Next we define the three program statements for nonlinear regression. All three begin in the left-most space of the line; there is no indentation on the second or third command. The first line specifies the variables that will appear in the model as nonlinear regression weights. Nonlinear regression is an iterative calculation process whereby the user specifies some initialized values of the regression weights (a, b, and c in this example). The program then fits the initial values with the model function to the data, makes an adjustment, then fits the result to the derivative of the function, makes an adjustment, then refits the principal model to the data again, and so forth, until the resulting corrections become trivial.

```
MODEL PROGRAM a = 0.5, b = 0.5, c = 0.5                      (A12)
```

It is usually good to specify initial values of the regression weights that are close to the final values, if the final values are known. I usually use 0.5 for initial values of all parameters in these studies. I have experimented (or rather fiddled) with possible strategies for using different initial values, but I have not yet found any strategy better than the equal estimates where nonlinear dynamics are concerned.

The second specifies the nonlinear model,

```
COMPUTE PRED = a*exp(b*z1) + c                                    (A13)
```

The third specifies the dependent measure and executes the program,

```
NLR z2 with z1                                                    (A14)
```

Nonlinear regression programs should offer options such as constrained nonlinear regression or different methods of specifying error terms. Constrained nonlinear regression keeps the parameter estimates within certain boundary values, which are typically chosen based on previous studies of similar functions with similar data. In the absence of any good reason to constrain values one way or another, I recommend using the unconstrained nonlinear regression, which is specified in statement A14 by the command NLR.

Another option that is sometimes available involves the selection of the principle of maximum likelihood for calculating the error component of the regression model instead of the principle of least squares. I have used the least squares method for all nonlinear regression analyses reported in this book.

The nonlinear regression analysis concludes with an ANOVA table and a value of R^2 for the model overall. Tests on the specific regression weights are listed by SPSS as estimated values and their confidence intervals at the 95% level. If the upper and lower boundaries of the confidence interval are both positive or both negative for a particular regression weight, then the confidence does not include .00, and the results can be interpreted as significant at $p < .05$.

The weight on the exponent is the critical element of the analysis. If statistical significance is not obtained for that weight, then delete the less essential components from the models, namely, the constants. Statements A12 and A13 change to A15 and A16, respectively, while A14 remains the same:

```
MODEL PROGRAM b = 0.5                                             (A15)
COMPUTE PRED = exp(b*z1)                                          (A16)
NLR z2 with z1                                                    (A14)
```

To test the bifurcation model, Statements A12 and A14 remain the same, and A13 becomes A15:

```
COMPUTE PRED = a*z1*exp(b*z1) + c                                 (A15)
```

Finally, there are times in which a nonlinear regression model fits so poorly that a negative R^2 is produced. Those values should be interpreted as equivalent in meaning as .00, meaning that the model fit was extremely poor.

CATASTROPHE PDFS WITH NONLINEAR REGRESSION

The test for the catastrophe pdfs is not substantially different from the exponential regression models just considered. There are two additional steps in data preparation, however. The first step requires a frequency distribution on the raw scores of the dependent measure *y*, that will produce the cumulative probability (or percentile) of *y*. Second, use a RECODE command to substitute the cumulative probabilities of *y* for *y* and give the result a new variable name, PCTY (A16):

```
RECODE Y (0 = .500) (1 = .617) (2 = .683) (3 = .725)          (A16)
      (4 = .750) (5 = .775) (6 = .800) (7 = .825)
      (8 = .842) (9 = .842) (10 = .883) (11 = .933)
      (12 = .950) (13 = .967) (14 = .999) (15 = .999)
      (16 = .999) into PCTY
```

The decimal values shown in A16 were those that were actually used in the leadership emergence study by Zaror and Guastello (2000) in which we were looking for a swallowtail catastrophe pdf. We still need to convert *y* to *z*. SPSS sometimes encounters an computational overflow when running nonlinear regression if, on one of the iterations, the numerical argument to the exponent exceeds 88. The problem is solved by multiplying *S* by 100 as shown in A17.

```
COMPUTE z = (Y - L)/(S * 100)                                  (A17)
```

We can now proceed to the three statements for the nonlinear regression model:

```
MODEL PROGRAM x= 0.5, a= 0.5 b=0.5 c=0.5 d=0.5 e=0.5           (A18)
COMPUTE PRED = x*exp(a*(z**5)+b*(z**4)+c*(z**3)+d*(z**2)+e*z)
                                                               (A19)
NLR PCTY with z                                                (A20)
```

In the event that statistical significance is not obtained for each of the regression weights, the least essential element in the model can be dropped. In this case, we would drop "b=0.5" from A18, and "+b*(z**4)" from A19; A20 would not change.

The next analysis that goes with the catastrophe pdf is one that determines the location of critical points. The critical points are the local modes and antimodes of the statistical distribution. A regression program can do the job much more easily than solving a differential equation by hand. To begin, create a data set that contains two columns: *Y* and the Frequency of *Y*, based on the frequency distribution was the previously obtained.

The analysis is a polynomial regression of Frequency of y as a function of y. The PSI-PLOT program from Poly Software International can perform the analysis instantly with a point-and-click to polynomial regression. The job can be done through SPSS, nonetheless. In either case, the conversion of y to z is not necessary for this type of problem. First compute polynomials of y^2, y^3, and y^4 using the syntax given in Statement A2. Then define the regression program to enter the polynomials from lowest to highest:

```
REGRESSION descriptives /missing = pairwise                    (A21)
     /variables = FREQY, y, ypow2, ypow3, ypow4
     /dependent = FREQY
     /enter y /enter ypow2 /enter ypow3 /enter ypow4
```

For data such as the leadership emergence data, there were only 17 values of y, so it was no surprise that all power polynomials showed statistical significance. The regression results, nonetheless, give regression weights that can be used to compute a predicted frequency of y. A plot of the predicted frequency of y gives the underlying modes and antimodes for the frequency distribution.

ANALYTIC ALTERNATIVES

The method of structural equations is perhaps the oldest approach for testing NDS models with real data, although some aspects of the technique described here and in Chapter 3 are older than others. The conventional wisdom for any form of data analysis is to choose the right tool for the right job, and three approaches to structural equations modeling have been needed so far. The polynomial regression method for the catastrophe models is straightforward and does not require the estimation of an exponent; it can be executed with a standard statistical package as we have already seen. It does require that: (a) the dependent measure be measured at two points in time at least, from which the difference score criterion is computed; (b) the Time-1 score for the dependent measure (order parameter) has some variability; and (c) the researcher has a fairly well-developed theory regarding which experimental variables contribute to the latent control parameters.

The polynomial regression method for catastrophe models does not do well for static distributions or for examples such as leadership emergence where the Time-1 score for leadership was zero for all cases. In that type of situation, the nonlinear regression method for catastrophe distributions would be recommended.

In the event the researcher has many possible variables that could act as control variables, and no strong theory regarding what goes where, the GEMCAT method developed by Lange et al. (2001; the improved version, of course) might be a good method to try. Otherwise the researcher should develop a more explicit theoretical model.

The nonlinear regression method for the exponential series of models is well-suited to the analytic requirement of estimating an exponent. The models themselves define a limited set of possible equations that will reflect the presence or absence of chaos, bifurcation effects, and other structures. Their predictive accuracy has been very good in addition to their descriptive value for phenomena to which they have been applied.

In the event that the researcher is confronted with some nonlinear-looking data and the exponential model series does not produce any results, it may be useful to try Abarbanel's (1996) procedure for decomposing the order parameter with principal component analysis. Other statistical methods for nonlinear time series analysis have been proposed, and intrepid researchers are encouraged to see what nuances can be extracted from their data using techniques developed by Heath (2000b), Kanz and Schreiber (1997), or Tong (1990).

Finally, the symbolic dynamics method, called orbital decomposition, is not yet available in a smooth-operating program. All the necessary steps for calculation, however, are mapped out in Guastello (2000a). The entire procedure can be executed with a common spreadsheet and frequency distributions and hand calculations.

SCTPLS DATA LIBRARY PROJECT

There are, of course, other ways of analyzing dynamics and new programs have become available in the past few years. At the time of this writing, The Society for Chaos Theory in Psychology & Life Sciences had just announced its new Data Library and Analysis Project. The goal of the project is to facilitate the testing of new software, algorithms, and computational procedures for nonlinear dynamical phenomena. The full description of the project is currently housed on the Society's web site www.societyforchaostheory.org. The file on the web site, "How to Contribute a Data Set" gives a preview of the data set descriptions that the Society wishes to acquire. The data sets themselves will be housed either on the Society's web site or on the contributor's site, depending on which method represents the cybernetic path of least resistance. Downloading instructions are given at the point of access. The Society will not provide analytic software or licenses for software, although it will provide as complete information as possible about available software on the node of the web site designated "Other Resources/Software."

The analytic strategy that a researcher might choose to pursue depends, of course, on the type of data being considered, and the programs that could be applicable to such data. Please refer to the web file, "Suggestions to Include in a Data Analysis," for a further discussion of possible options, "Formatting Your Research Report for this Web Site," for preparation of final reports.

After a collection of reports has started to grow, some of the reports will be selected for publication in *Nonlinear Dynamics, Psychology, and Life Sciences*, which is the Society's research journal. The choice of papers will be based on the reviews of the journal editors. The usual considerations of depth, clarity, originality, and topic coverage will apply. The authors whose work has been selected in this fashion will be contacted sufficiently in advance of publication to ascertain their interest in such publication.

Appendix B

The Island Commission Game

The Island Commission Game is credited to P. Gillan (1979). The game is usually played with eight participants. They are seated at a conference table. If a conference table is not available, they move their seats into an arrangement that is approximately circular. They are each given a name tag on a random basis that identifies the player as one of eight roles: Director of City Planning, Director of the Chamber of Commerce, Organizational Development Consultant, Council Member Dentist, Director of Community Action, General Manager of the Food Company, Council Member Farmer, and Council Member Lawyer.

In one variation of the game I have used 16 players and made up additional name tags such as Director of Transportation, General Manager of the Hospital, and so forth. It was important not to define roles that implied hierarchical relationships among the players' roles. For games of 16, the name tags were placed around the conference table. As players entered the room they were invited to take a seat anywhere they felt comfortable. The objective of that procedure was to induce a possible form of self-organization between the players and the roles they selected.

Players are then given an information sheet consisting of two pages. One page contains the Island Commission Major City Information Sheet along with the map. The second page contains the Island Commission Task Agenda Sheet. The moderator reads the two pages aloud while the players read for themselves. Players are then asked to start any time. Furthermore, they are instructed that if a piece of information about the Island or their role is not explicitly stated in the materials, they may make up any missing information as they please.

The game is played in four rounds of 15 minutes each. At the end of the first, second, and third round, they are given an Island Commission Environmental Bulletin. The three bulletins are printed on separate strips of paper. They are asked to complete their budget allocations by the end of the last round. Some groups manage to finish, but others do not. One person in the group usually accepts the task of writing down the group's decisions. When the game is played as part of an experiment, a questionnaire is handed out at the end of the fourth round. Questionnaire items and their research purposes were described in Chapters 6 and 9.

ISLAND COMMISSION MAJOR CITY INFORMATION SHEET

Major City is located on the coast of Independent Island (250 square miles), 200 miles from the mainland of Friendly Power. The population of 200,000 has grown rapidly in recent years because of immigration. (See Fig. B.1 for map.)

These are 40 square miles of city and suburbs. The surrounding area is good agricultural land. Little unused land remains in the urban area.

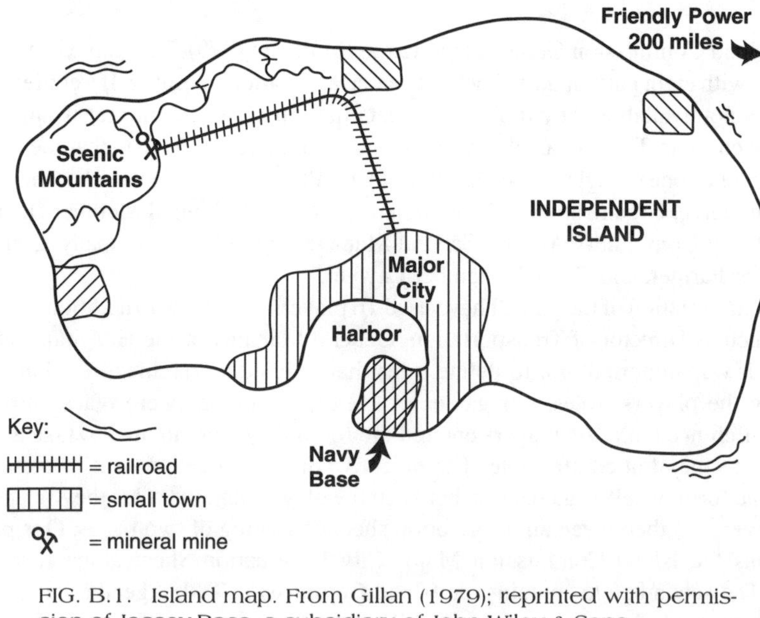

FIG. B.1. Island map. From Gillan (1979); reprinted with permission of Jossey-Bass, a subsidiary of John Wiley & Sons.

All power for domestic and industrial use depends on fuel imported from Friendly Power. The present power plant is being operated at 98% of capacity. The sewer and water plants are now operating beyond design capacity.

Major City's economy depends on the processing and export of the agricultural production of the island (35%), minerals mined on the island (15%), tourism (25%), the Friendly Power naval base (10%), and miscellaneous income (15%). Although the general economy is good, there is some unemployment and a sizable population of poor people.

Half of Major City's food is grown on the island. In addition to the beaches and climate, the major attractions are the island's unspoiled rural scene and the fresh fruits and vegetables, available all year, that are the basis of the famous native cuisine.

The airport, located on the navy base, is used jointly for military and commercial planes. The harbor has been famous for centuries. Although picturesque, it is a very busy port, suitable for modern ships.

ISLAND COMMISSION TASK AGENDA SHEET

Background

You have been recruited by the mayor of Major City to be a member of a special commission. You accepted enthusiastically, because you want to have an impact on the important long-range recommendations that the commission will develop. You are widely respected on the island and are known to be an expert in your specialty. The mayor has indicated that your frame of reference will be important to the commission's functioning.

The Job of the Commission

The commission was formed as one of the requirements for getting a large grant for Major City. A total of 20 million dollars has been earmarked for the city—four million a year for 5 years. The mayor has formed the commission to: (a) Formulate a plan for consideration of the important factors affecting the city's future; and (b) Make specific recommendations to the Major City Governmental Council for the use of the funds.

The funds will begin arriving in 18 months, and the mayor has given the commission 12 months to complete its work. The mayor has explained that he formed this blue-ribbon commission so that the recommendations would have the greatest possible weight and that he will work for the adoption of all the commission's recommendations.

One important background factor is that no more than 50% of the funds may go into capital development; i.e., human service programs must comprise at least one-half of the commission's recommendations.

The Meeting Schedule

The next hour represents the four major quarterly meetings of the commission. Each meeting will last about 15 minutes in "real time."

1. At the first meeting, the assignment is to create a "chart of work" for the commission's next three meetings.
2. The second and third meetings are for carrying out the chart of work.
3. A product of the last meeting will be an actual set of recommendations for the use of the 20 million dollars over the next 5 years. (You also will be asked to hand in this list on a sheet of newsprint.)

Note: Take a minute to get into the feeling of your role. Imagine what a person in your role would think. What viewpoints would you hold? What would be important to you as you act out your role? Having thought about these things, behave from this frame of reference as you participate in the commission meetings.

ISLAND COMMISSION ENVIRONMENTAL BULLETIN 1

The schools of Major City have become badly overcrowded, and a study just released to the news media states statistical proof that the quality of education is slipping.

The supply of transportation fuel has, without warning, been cut by 50%. Reports indicate that this is not a temporary shortage.

The heavy tourist influx from Friendly Power is just beginning, and the car rental people are expecting a big season.

ISLAND COMMISSION ENVIRONMENTAL BULLETIN 2

Growth in Major City has resulted in the need to expand the hospital facilities. The food-processing industry on which the city depends heavily also needs to expand in order to survive. The hospital and the industry are competing for the same space; no other space is available within the city limits.

The Friendly Power Navy has recently learned and has proof that a large part of the economy of Independent Island has depended on the illicit cultivation of opium poppies. The Navy has stated that if the traffic in opium is not eliminated, it will pull out of its installation.

ISLAND COMMISSION ENVIRONMENTAL BULLETIN 3

The Aviation Administration has stated that the airport cannot handle the large transport and passenger jets now in almost exclusive use by all major airlines serving the island.

Organized low-income residents demand that no expenditures be made until housing for the poor is provided. The older, established residents are demanding two-acre zoning for all new housing starts, in order to preserve the character of the city and the island.

References

Abarbanel, H. D. I. (1996). *Analysis of chaotic data*. New York: Springer-Verlag.

Abdullaev, Y. G., & Posner, M. I. (1997). Time course of activating brain areas in generating verbal associations. *Psychological Science, 8*, 56–59.

Abraham, F. D. (1995). Dynamics, bifurcation, self-organization, chaos, mind, conflict, insensitivity to initial conditions, time, unification, diversity, free will, and social responsibility. In R. Robertson, & A. Combs (Eds.), *Chaos theory in psychology and life sciences* (pp. 155–173). Mahwah, NJ: Lawrence Erlbaum Associates.

Abraham, F. D. (1996). The dynamics of creativity and the courage to be. In W. Sulis & A. Combs (Eds.), *Nonlinear dynamics in human behavior* (pp. 364–400). River Edge, NJ: World Scientific.

Abraham, F. D. (1997). Nonlinear coherence in multivariate research: Invariants and the reconstruction of attractors. *Nonlinear Dynamics, Psychology, and Life Sciences, 1*, 7–34.

Abraham, F. D., Abraham, R. H., & Shaw, C. D. (1990). *A visual introduction to dynamical systems theory for psychology*. Santa Cruz: Aerial Press.

Abraham, R. H., & Shaw, C. D. (1992). *Dynamics, the geometry of behavior* (2nd ed.). Reading, MA: Addison-Wesley.

Adams, J. S. (1965). Inequity in social exchange. In L. Berkowitz (Ed.), *Advances in experimental social psychology* (Vol. 2, pp. 265–299). San Diego: Academic Press.

Agu, M. (1983). A method for identification of linear or nonlinear systems with the use of externally applied random force. *Journal of Applied Physics, 54*, 1193–1197.

Ahmed, E., & Hassan, S. Z. (2000). On controlling chaos in Cournot-games with two and three competitors. *Nonlinear Dynamics, Psychology, and Life Sciences, 4*, 189–194.

Albanese, R., & Van Fleet, D. D. (1985). Rational behavior in groups: The free-riding tendency. *Academy of Management Review, 10*, 244–255.

Albritton, D. W. (1995). When metaphors function as schemas: Some cognitive effects of conceptual metaphors. *Metaphor and Symbolic Activity, 10*, 33–46.

Allen, P. M., & McGlade, J. M. (1987). Modeling complex human systems. *European Journal of Operational Research, 30*, 147–167.

Allen, P. M., & Sanglier, M. (1981). Urban evolution, self-organization, and decision making. *Environmental Planning, A, 13*, 167–183.

Amabile, T. M. (1983). *The social psychology of creativity*. New York: Springer-Verlag.

Anderson, P. (1999). Complexity theory and organization science. *Organization Science, 10*, 216–232.

Andresen, T. (1999). The dynamics of long-range financial accumulation and crisis. *Nonlinear Dynamics, Psychology, and Life Sciences, 3*, 161–196.

Argyris, C., & Schon, D. (1978). *Organizational learning: A theory of action perspective*. Reading, MA: Addison-Wesley.

Arnold, V. I. (1974). Normal forms of functions in the neighborhood of degenerate critical points. *Russian Mathematical Surveys, 29*, 10–50.

Arthur, W. B. (1989). The economy and complexity. In D. L. Stein (Ed.), *Lectures in the sciences of complexity* (pp. 713–740). Redwood City, CA: Addison-Wesley.

Atkinson, M. W. (1964). *An introduction to motivation.* Princeton, NJ: Van Nostrand.

Axelrod, R. (1984). *The evolution of cooperation*. New York: Basic Books.

Axelrod, R., & Hamilton, W. D. (1981). The evolution of cooperation. *Science, 211*, 1390–1396.

Baba, M. L., & Ziegler, B. P. (1985). Evolution and innovation in sociocultural systems: A punctuated equilibria model. In J. R. Nesselroade & A. van Eye (Eds.), *Individual development and social change: Explanatory analysis* (pp. 1–30). Orlando, FL: Academic Press.

Baer, J. (1993). *Creative ability and divergent thinking: A task specific approach.* Hillsdale, NJ: Lawrence Erlbaum Associates.

Bailey, K. D. (1994). Talcott Parsons, social entropy theory, and living systems theory. *Behavioral Science, 39*, 25–45.

Bailey, K. D. (1997). The autopoiesis of social systems: Assessing Lyhmann's theory of self-reference. *Systems Research and Behavioral Science, 14*, 83–100.

Baily, M. N., Bartelsman, E. J., & Haltiwanger, J. (1996). Downsizing and productivity growth. *Small Business Economics, 8*, 259–278.

Bak, P. (1996). *How nature works*. New York: Springer-Verlag.

Bak, P., & Sneppen, K. (1993). Punctuated equilibrium and criticality in a simple model of evolution. *Physics Review Letters, 24*, 4083.

Bala, V., Majumdar, M., & Mitra, T. (1998). A note on controlling chaotic tatonnement. *Journal of Economic Behavior of Organizations, 33*, 411–420.

Balasko, Y. (1978a). Equilibrium analysis and envelope theory. *Journal of Mathematical Economics, 5*, 153–172.

Balasko, Y. (1978b). Economic equilibrium and catastrophe theory. *Econometrica, 46*, 557–569.

Balasko, Y. (1979a). Economies with finite but large number of equilibria. *Journal of Mathematical Economics, 6*, 145–147.

Balasko, Y. (1979b). Number and definiteness of economic systems. *Journal of Economic Theory, 40*, 168–195.

Bales, R. F., & Cohen, S. P. (1979). *SYMLOG: A system for the multiple level observation of groups*. New York: Free Press.

Banathy, B. A. (1996). Information-based design of social systems. *Behavioral Science, 41*, 104–123.

Banks, D. L., & Carley, K. M. (1997). Models for network evolution. In P. Doreian & F. B. Stokman (Eds.), *Evolution of social networks* (pp. 209–232). Amsterdam: Gordon & Breach.

Barnett, W., & Freeman, J. (1999, November). *Too much of a good thing? Product proliferation and organizational failure*. Paper presented to INFORMS '99, Philadelphia, PA.

Baron, R. M., Amazeen, P. G., & Beek, P. J. (1994). Local and global dynamics of social relations. In R. R. Vallacher & A. Nowak, A. (Eds.). *Dynamical systems in social psychology* (pp. 111–138). San Diego: Academic Press.

Bass, B. M. (1985). *Leadership and performance beyond expectations*. New York: Free Press.

Bass, B. M., & Avolio, B. J. (Eds.). (1994). *Improving organizational effectiveness through transformational leadership*. Newbury Park, CA: Sage.

Baum, J. R., Locke, E. A., & Kirkpatrick, S. A. (1998). A longitudinal study of the relation of vision and vision communication in extrepreneurial firms. *Journal of Applied Psychology, 3*, 43–54.

Baumol, W. J., & Blinder, A. S. (1979). *Economics: Principles and policies*. New York: Harcourt, Brace, Jovanovich.

Benne, K. D., & Sheats, P. (1948). Functional roles of group members, *Journal of Social Issues, 4–5*, 41–49.

Bennis, W. (1988). *Why leaders can't lead: The unconscious conspiracy continues*. San Francisco: Jossey-Bass.

Berry, D. C., & Broadbent, D. E. (1988). Interactive tasks and the implicit-explicit distinction. *British Journal of Psychology, 79*, 251–272.

Bevales, A. (1948). A mathematical model for group structures. *Human Organization, 7*, 16–30.

Bigelow, J. (1982). A catastrophe model of organizational change: *Behavioral Science, 27*, 26–42.

Billings, S., Guastello, S. J., & Rieke, M. L. (1993). A comparison of the construct validity of three measures of authoritarianism. *Journal of Research in Personality, 27*, 328–348.

Birkhoff, G. D. (1932). Sur quelques fermées remarquables. *Bulletin du Société Mathématique de France, 60*, 1–26.

Blake, R., & Mouton, J. S. (1964). *The managerial grid: Key orientation for achieving production through people*. Houston, TX: Gulf.

Blau, P. M. (1967). *Exchange and power in social life*. New York: Wiley.

Boisot, M. H. (1995). *Information space*. New York: Routledge.

Boisot, M. H., & Child, J. (1999). Organizations as adaptive systems in complex environment: The case of China. *Organization Science, 10*, 237–252.

Boland, R. J. Jr., & Tenkasi, R. V. (1995). Perspective making and perspective taking in communities of knowledge. *Organization Science, 6*, 350–372.

Booth, M. (1996, March 17). Is loyalty dead? *Denver Post*, p. 16A–17A.

Borges, L. A. J. (1997, August). *Dynamics of policy shifts involving three-way trade-offs among process, product, and human resources.* Paper presented to the 7th Annual International Conference of the Society for Chaos Theory in Psychology & Life Sciences, Milwaukee, WI.

Borges, L. A. J., & Guastello, S. J. (1996). Integration and strategy: A chaos theory approach. In C. A. Voss (Ed.), *Operations in a global context* (pp. 97–102). London, UK: London Business School.

Borges, L. A. J., & Guastello, S. J. (1998). Chaos theory applied to TQM: A survey. In W. L. Baker (Ed.), *Proceedings of the 52nd Annual Quality Congress* (pp. 578–585). Philadelphia, ASQC.

Bottger, P. C. (1984). Expertise and air time of actual and perceived influence in problem-solving groups. *Journal of Applied Psychology, 69*, 214–221.

Bowers, C. A., Bakers, D. P., & Salas, E. (1994). Measuring the importance of teamwork: The reliability and validity of job/task analysis indices for team-training. *Military Psychology, 6*, 205–214.

Brannick, M. T., Prince, A., Prince, C., & Salas, E. (1995). The measurement of team process. *Human Factors, 37*, 641–651.

Brannick, M. T., Roach, R. M., & Salas, E. (1993). Understanding team performance: A multimethod study. *Human Performance, 6*, 287–308.

Breeden, J. L., Dinkelacker, F., & Hubler, A. (1990). Noise in the modeling and control of dynamical systems. *Physics Review A, 42*, 5827–5836.

Brock, W. A., Hseih, D. A., & LeBaron, B. (1991). *Nonlinear dynamics, chaos, and instability: Statistical theory and economic evidence*. Cambridge, MA: MIT Press.

Brouwer, S. (1998). *Sharing the pie: A citizen's guide to wealth and power in America*. New York: Holt.

Brown, J. S. (1948). Gradients approach to avoidance responses and their relation to motivation. *Journal of Comparative and Physiological Psychology, 41*, 450–465.

Brown, J. S., & Parman, A. O. (1993). Consequences of size-selective harvesting as an evolutionary game. In T. K. Stokes, J. M. McGlade, & R. Law (Eds.), *The exploitation of evolving resources* (pp. 248–261). Berlin: Springer-Verlag.

Brush, T., & Karnani, A. (1996). Impact of plant size and focus on productivity: An empirical study. *Management Science, 42*, 1065–1081.

Buch, K., & Aldridge, J. (1991). OD under conditions of organizational decline. *Organizational Development Journal, 9*, 1–5.

Bunde, A., & Havlin, S. (1996). Percolation I. In A. Bunde & S. Havlin (Eds.), *Fractals and disordered systems* (2nd ed., pp. 59–113). New York: Springer-Verlag.

Byrd, R. (1986). *The C & RT index*. San Diego: University Associates.

Byrne, D. G., Mazanov, J., & Gregson, R. A. M. (2001). A cusp catastrophe analysis of changes to adolescent smoking behavior in response to smoking prevention programs. *Nonlinear Dynamics, Psychology, and Life Sciences, 5*, 115–138.

Callahan J. (1980). Bifurcation geometry of E_6. *Mathematical Modeling, 1*, 283–309.

Callahan J. (1982). A geometric model of anorexia and its treatment. *Behavioral Science, 27*, 140–154.

Campbell, D. T. (1960). Blind variation and selective retention in creative thought and other knowledge processes. *Psychological Review, 67*, 380–400.

Cannon-Bowers, J. A., & Salas, E. (1998). Team performance and training in complex environments: Recent findings from applied research. *Current Directions in Psychological Science, 7*, 83–87.

Cannon-Bowers, J. A., Tannenbaum, S. I., Salas, E., & Volpe, C. E. (1995). Defining competencies and establishing team training requirements. In R. A. Guzzo & E. Salas (Eds.), *Team effectiveness and decision making in organizations* (pp. 333–380). San Francisco: Jossey-Bass.

Carroll, L. (1988). *Alice in Wonderland*. Newmarket, England: Brimax. (Originally, 1865).

Cartwright, D., & Zander, A. (1960). *Group dynamics*. Evanston, IL: Row, Peterson.

Cascio, W. F. (1993). Downsizing: What do we know? What have we learned? *Academy of Management Executive, 7*, 95–104.

Casti, J. L. (1989). *Alternate realities: Mathematical models of nature and man*. New York: Wiley.

Casti, J. L. (1995). Cooperation: The ghost in the machinery of evolution. In J. Casti & A. Karlqvist (Eds.), *Cooperation and conflict in general evolutionary processes* (pp. 63–88). New York: Wiley.

Cattell, R. B. (1966). The scree test for the number of factors. *Multivariate Behavioral Research, 1*, 245–276.

Cattell, R. B., Cattell, H. E. P., & Cattell, A. K. S. (1994). The *Sixteen Personality Factor Questionnaire* (5th ed.). Champaign, IL: Institute for Personality and Ability Testing.

Cattell, R. B., & Drevdahl, J. E. (1955). A comparison of the personality profile (16PF) of eminent researchers with that of eminent teachers and administrators, and the general population. *British Journal of Psychology, 46*, 248–261.

Cattell, R. B., Eber, H. W., & Tatsuoka, M. M. (1970). *Handbook for the Sixteen Personality Factor Questionnaire*. Champaign, IL: Institute for Personality and Ability Testing.

Cattell, R. B., & Stice, G. F. (1954). Four formulae for selecting leaders on the basis of personality. *Human Relations, 7*, 493–507.

Christensen, P. R., Merrifield, P. R., & Guilford, J. P. (1958). *Consequences*. Palo Alto: Human Sciences Press.

Clair, S. (1998). A cusp catastrophe model for adolescent alcohol use: An empirical test. *Nonlinear Dynamics, Psychology, and Life Sciences, 2*, 217–241.

Clark, K. E., & Clark, M. B. (Eds.). (1990). *The measurement of leadership*. West Orange, NJ: Leadership Library of America.

Clark, K. E., Clark, M. B., & Campbell, D. P. (Eds.). (1992). *The impact of leadership*. Greensboro, NC: Center for Creative Leadership.

Clayton, K., & Frey, B. F. (1996). Inter- and intra-trial dynamics in memory and choice. In W. Sulis & A. Combs (Eds.), *Nonlinear dynamics in human behavior* (pp. 90–106). Singapore: World Scientific.

Clayton, K., & Frey, B. F. (1997). Studies in mental "noise". *Nonlinear Dynamics, Psychology, and Life Sciences, 1*, 174–180.

Cobb, L. (1981). Multimodal exponential families of statistical catastrophe theory. In C. Taillie, G. P. Patel, & B. Baldessari (Eds.), *Statistical distributions in scientific work* (Vol. 6, pp. 67–90). Hingam, MA: Reidel.

Cobb, L., Koppstein, P., & Chen, N. H. (1983). Estimation and moment recursion relationships for multimodal distributions of the exponential family. *Journal of the American Statistical Association, 78*, 124–130.

Cohen, S. G., Ledford, G. E. Jr., & Spreitzer, G. M. (1996). A predictive model of self-managing work team effectiveness. *Human Relations, 49*, 643–676.

Colman, A. M., & Stirk, J. A. (1998). Stackelberg reasoning in mixed-motive games: An experimental investigation. *Journal of Economic Psychology, 19*, 279–293.

Combs, A., & Holland, M. (1996). *Synchronicity: Science, myth, and the trickster*. New York: Marlowe.

Comer, D. R. (1995). A model of social loafing in real work groups. *Human Relations, 48*, 647–667.

Comfort, L. (1996). Self-organization in disaster response: Global strategies to support local action. In G. Koehler (Ed.), *What disaster response management can learn from chaos theory* (pp. 94–112). Sacramento, CA: California Research Bureau, California State Library.

Comfort, L. (1999). Nonlinear dynamics in disaster response: The Northridge, California earthquake, January 17, 1994. In L. D. Kiel & E. Elliott, E. (Eds.), *Nonlinear dynamics, complexity, and public policy* (pp. 139–152). Commack, NY: Nova Science.

Confucius (1969). *I Ching: The book of changes*. Translation J. Legge. New York: Bantam.

Conger, J. A., & Kanungo, R. N. (1998). *Charismatic leadership in organizations*. Thousand Oaks, CA: Sage

Constant, D., Sproull, L., & Kiesler, S. (1997). The kindness of strangers: On the usefulness of electronic weak ties for technical advice. In S. Kiesler (Ed.), *Culture of the Internet* (pp. 303–322). Mahwah, NJ: Erlbaum.

Contractor, N. S., & Siebold, D. R. (1993). Theoretical framework for the study of structuring processes in group decision support systems. *Human Communication Research, 23*, 528–563.

Coovert, M. D., Campbell, G. E., Cannon-Bowers, J. A., & Salas, E. (1995, May). *A methodology for a team performance measurement system*. Paper presented to the Tenth Annual Conference of the Society for Industrial and Organizational Psychology, Orlando, FL.

Cordery, J. L., Mueller, W. S., & Smith, L. M. (1991). Attitudinal and behavioral effects of autonomous group working: A longitudinal field study. *Academy of Management Journal, 34*, 464–476.

Crawford, V. P. (1991). An "evolutionary interpretation of Van Huyck, Battalio, and Beil's experimental results on coordination. *Games and Economic Behavior, 3*, 25–59.

Crutchfield, J. P., & van Nimwegen, E. (1999). The evolutionary unfolding of complexity. In L. F. Landweber, W. Winfree, R. Lipton, & S. Freeland (Eds.), *Proceedings of the DIMACS Workshop*. New York: Springer-Verlag.

Csányi, V. (1989). *Evolutionary systems and society: A general theory of life, mind, and culture*. Durham, NC: Duke University Press.

Csikszentmihalyi, M. (1988). The flow experience and its significant for human psychology. In M. Csikszentmihalyi & I. Csikszentmihalyi (Eds.), *Optimal experience: Psychological studies of flow in consciousness* (pp. 15–35). Cambridge: Cambridge University Press.

Csikszentmihalyi, M. (1990). *Flow: The psychology of optimal experience*. New York: Harper-Collins.

Csikszentmihalyi, M. (1993). *The evolving self: A psychology for the third millennium*. New York: Harper-Collins.

Csikszentmihalyi, M. (1996). *Creativity: Flow and the psychology of discovery and invention*. New York: Harper-Collins.

Csikszentmihalyi, M., & Getzels, J. W. (1973). The personality of young artists: An empirical and theoretical exploration: *British Journal of Psychology, 64*, 91–104.

Csikszentmihalyi, M., & LeFevre, J. (1989). Optimal experience in work and leisure. *Journal of Personality and Social Psychology, 56*, 815–822.

Cunningham, B. (1995). *Soaring profits–but workers don't share* (Report No. 82). Washington, DC: AFL-CIO Economic Research Department.

Dailey, R. C. (1980). A path analysis of R&D team coordination and performance. *Decision Sciences, 11*, 357–369.

Daly, H., & Goodland, R. (1994). An ecological economic assessment of deregulation of international commerce under GATT. *Ecological Economics, 9*, 72–92.

Davids, K., Button, C., & Bennett, S. (1999). Modeling human motor systems in nonlinear dynamics: Intentionality and discrete movement behaviors. *Nonlinear Dynamics, Psychology, and Life Sciences, 3*, 3–30.

Davidson, P. (1995). Letter to the Editor, *New York Times*. Electronically retrievable document by File Transfer Protocol: PKT Archives, 25 January, 1995, csf.colorado.edu.

Dawkins, R. L. (1976). *The selfish gene*. New York: Oxford.

DeBono, E. (1985). *Six thinking hats*. Boston: Little Brown.

Deci, E. L. (1972). *Intrinsic motivation*. New York: Plenum.

DeGreene, K. B. (1978). Force fields and emergent phenomena in sociotechnical macrosystems: Theories and models. *Behavioral Science, 23*, 1–14.

DeGreene, K. B. (1991). Emergent complexity and person-machine systems. *International Journal of Man-Machine Studies, 35*, 219–234.

DeMeuse, K. P., Vanderheiden, P. A., & Bergmann, T. J. (1994). Announced layoffs: Their effect on corporate financial performance. *Human Resource Management, 33*, 509–530.

Deming, W. E. (1986). *Out of the crisis*. Cambridge, MA: MIT Press.

Dennis, A. R., & Valacich, J. S. (1993). Computer brainstorms: More heads are better than one. *Journal of Applied Psychology, 78*, 531–537.

DeWitt, R.-L. (1993). The structural consequences of downsizing. *Organization Science, 4*, 30–40.

Dial, J., & Murphy, K. J. (1995). Incentives, downsizing, and value creation at General Dynamics. *Journal of Financial Economics, 37*, 261–314.

Ditto, W., & Munaka, T. (1995). Principles and applications of chaotic systems. *Communications of the ACM, 38*, 96–102.

Dooley, K. J. (1997). A complex adaptive systems model of organization change. *Nonlinear Dynamics, Psychology, and Life Sciences, 1*, 69–97.

Dooley, K. J., & Van de Ven, A. H. (1999). Explaining complex organizational dynamics. *Organization Science, 10*, 358–372.

Dore, M. H. I. (1998). Walrasian general equilibrium and nonlinear dynamics. *Nonlinear Dynamics, Psychology, and Life Sciences, 2*, 59–72.

Dougherty, D., & Bowman, E. H. (1995). The effects of organizational downsizing on product innovation. *California Management Review, 37*, 28–44.

Drexler, J. A. (1977). Organizational climate: Its homogeneity within organizations. *Journal of Applied Psychology, 62*, 38–42.

Duysters, G. (1996). *The dynamics of technological innovation: The evolution and development of information technology*. Cheltenham, UK: Edward Elgar.

Earley, P. C. (1989). Social loafing and collectivism: A comparison of the United States and the People's Republic of China. *Administrative Science Quarterly, 34*, 565–581.

Earley, P. C. (1993). East meets West meets Mideast: Further explorations of collectivist and individualistic work groups. *Academy of Management Journal, 36*, 318–348.

Egidi, M., & Ricotilli, M. (1998). Co-ordination and specialization. In F. M. Guindani & G. Salvadori (Eds.), *Chaos, fractals, models* (pp. 120–134). Pavia, Italy: Italian University Press.

Eisenberger, R. (1992). Learned industriousness. *Psychological Review, 99*, 248–267.

Englen, G. (1988). The theory of self-organization and modeling complex urban systems. *European Journal of Operations Research, 37*, 42–57.

Engelen, G., White, R., & Uljee, I. (1997). Integrating constrained cellular automata models, GIS, and support tools for urban planning and policy making. In. H. Timmermans (Ed.), *Decision support systems in urban planning* (pp. 125–155). London: Chapman & Hall.

Enzle, M. E., & Ross, J. M. (1978). Increasing and decreasing intrinsic interest with contingent rewards: A test of cognitive evaluation theory. *Journal of Experimental Social Psychology, 14*, 588–597.

Eoyang, G. H. (1997). *Coping with chaos: Seven simple tools*. Cheyenne, WY: Laguno.

Eoyang, G. H., & Dooley, K. J. (1996). Boardrooms of the future: The fractal nature of organizations. In C. Pickover (Ed.), *Fractal horizons: The future use of fractals* (pp. 195–203). New York: St. Martin's Press.

Evans, C. R., & Dion, K. L. (1991). Group cohesion and performance: A meta-analysis. *Small Group Research, 22*, 175–186.

Farmer, J. D., Ott, E., & Yorke, J. A. (1983). The dimension of chaotic attractors. *Physica D, 7*, 153–180.

Feigenbaum, M. J. (1978). Quantitative universality in a class of nonlinear transformations. *Journal of Statistical Physics, 19*, 25–52.

Feldhusen, J. F. (1995). Creativity: A knowledge base, metacognitive skills, and personality factors. *Journal of Creative Behavior, 29*, 255–268.

Feldman, D. H., Csikszentmihalyi, M., & Gardner, H. (1994). *Changing the world: A framework for the study of creativity*. Westport, CT: Praeger.

Fiedler, F. E. (1964). A contingency model of leadership effectiveness. In L. Berkowitz, (Ed.), *Advances in experimental social psychology* (Vol. 1, pp. 149–190). New York: Academic Press.

Fiedler, F. E., & Chemers, M. M. (1984). *Improving leadership effectiveness: The leader match concept* (2nd ed.). New York: Wiley.

Filardo, A. J. (1995). Has the productivity trend steepened in the 1990s? *Economic Review, 80*, 41–59.

Finke, R. A., & Bettle, J. (1996). *Chaotic cognition: Principles and applications*. Mahwah, NJ: Lawrence Erlbaum Associates.

Fisher, B. A. (1986). Leadership: When does the difference make a difference? In R. Y. Hirokawa & M. S. Poole (Eds.), *Communication and group decision-making* (pp. 197–218). Beverly Hills, CA: Sage.

Flache, A., & Macy, M. W. (1997). The weakness of strong ties: Collective action failure in a highly cohesive group. In P. Doreian & F. B. Stokman (Eds.), *Evolution of social networks* (pp. 19–44). Amsterdam: Gordon & Breach.

Fleishman, E. A., & Harris, E. F. (1962). Patterns of leadership behavior related to employee grievance and turnover. *Personnel Psychology, 15*, 43–56.

Frank, K. A., & Fahrbach, K. (1999). Organization culture as a complex system: Balance and information in models of influence and selection. *Organization Science, 10*, 253–277.

Frederickson, P., Kaplan, J. L., Yorke, E. D., & Yorke, J. A. (1983). The Lyapunov dimension of strange attractors. *Journal of Differential Equations, 49*, 185–207.

Freedman, C., & Kriesler, P. (1994). *Has the long run Phillips curve turned horizontal*? (Tech. Rep. No. 94/27). School of Economics, University of New South Wales, Sydney, Australia.

Freeman, L. C. (1979). Centrality in social networks: Conceptual clarification. *Social Networks, 1*, 215–239.

Freeman, W. J. (2000). *Neurodynamics: An exploration of mesoscopic brain dynamics*. New York: Springer-Verlag.

French, J. R. Jr., & Raven, B. H. (1959). The bases of social power. In D. Cartwright (Ed.), *Studies in social power* (pp. 150–167). Ann Arbor: University of Michigan Press.

French, W. L., & Bell, C. H. Jr. (1999). *Organization development* (6th ed.). Upper Saddle River, NJ: Prentice-Hall.

Friedman, J. W. (Ed.). (1994). *Problems of coordination in economic activity.* Boston: Kluwer.

Friedman, J. W., & Samuelson, L. (1994). The "folk theorem" for repeated games and continuous decision rules. In J. W. Friedman (Ed.), *Problems of coordination in economic activity* (pp. 103–128). Boston: Kluwer.

Friedman, M. (1968). The role of monetary policy. *The American Economic Review, 58*, 1–17.
Fulk, J., & DeSanctis, G. (1995). Electronic communication and changing organizational forms. *Organization Science, 6*, 337–349.
Gabrieli, J. D. E., Desmond, J. E., Demb, J. B., Wagner, A. D., Stone, M. V., Vaidya, C. J., & Glover, G. H. (1996). Functional magnetic resonance imaging of semantic memory processes in the frontal lobes. *Psychological Science, 7*, 278–283.
Galam, S. (1996). When humans interact like atoms. In. E. Witte & J. H. Davis (Eds.), *Understanding group behavior* (Vol. 1, pp. 293–312). Mahwah, NJ: Erlbaum.
Galbraith, J. K. (1994). Self-fulfilling prophets: Inflated zeal at the Federal Reserve. *American Prospect, 18*, 31–39.
Ganster, D. C., & Dwyer, D. J. (1995). The effects of understaffing on individual and group performance in professional and trade organizations. *Journal of Management, 21*, 175–190.
Gardner, H. (1993). *Creating minds*. New York: Basic Books.
Gelernter, D. (1995). *1939: The lost world of the fair*. New York: Free Press.
Gersick, C. J. G. (1991). Revolutionary change theories: A multilevel exploration of the punctuated equilibrium paradigm. *Academic of Management Review, 16*, 10–36.
Gillan, P. G. (1979). Island Commission: Group problem solving. In J. Pfeiffer (Ed.), *Structural experiences in human relations* (Vol. 7, pp. 99–104). San Diego: J. Pfeiffer and Associates.
Gilmore, R. (1981). *Catastrophe theory for scientists and engineers*. New York: Wiley.
Girault, P. (1991). Attractors and dimensions. In G. Cherbit (Ed.), *Non-integral dimensions and applications* (pp. 60–82). West Sussex, UK: Wiley.
Glance, N. S., & Huberman, B. A. (1994). The dynamics of social dilemmas. *Scientific American, 270*(3), 76–81.
Goertzel, B. (1994). *Chaotic logic*. Langhorne, PA: Gordon and Breach.
Goertzel, B. (1997). *From complexity to creativity: Explorations in evolutionary, autopoetic, and cognitive dynamics*. New York: Plenum.
Goldstein, J. (1994). *The unshackled organization*. Portland, OR: Productivity Press.
Goldstein, J. (1995). The tower of Babel in nonlinear dynamics: Toward the clarification of terms. In R. Robertson & A. Combs (Eds.), *Chaos theory in psychology and life sciences* (pp. 39–47). Mahwah, NJ: Lawrence Erlbaum Associates.
Goodman, L. A., & Kruskal, W. H. (1963). Measures of association for cross classifications. III. Approximate sampling theory. *Journal of the American Statistical Association, 58*, 310–364.
Gould, S. J. (1983). *Hen's teeth and horses toes*. New York: Norton.
Grassberger, P., & Proccaccia, I. (1983). Characterization of strange attractors. *Physics Review Letters, 50*, 346–349.
Graen, G. B, & Uhl-Bein, M. (1995). Relationship-based approach to leadership: Development of leader-member exchange (LMX) theory of leadership over 25 years: Applying a multi-level multi-domain perspective. *Leadership Quarterly, 6*, 219–247.
Greeley, L. (1986). The bumper effect dynamic in the creative process: The philosophical, psychological, and neurophysiological link. *Journal of Creative Behavior, 20*, 261–275.
Gregson, R. A. M. (1992). *n-Dimensional nonlinear psychophysics*. Hillsdale NJ: Erlbaum.
Gregson, R. A. M. (1995). *Cascades and fields in nonlinear psychophysics*. Singapore: World Scientific.
Gregson, R. A. M. (1998). Effects of random noise and internal delay in nonlinear psychophysics. *Nonlinear Dynamics, Psychology, and Life Sciences, 2*, 73–94.
Gregson, R. A. M. (1999). Confidence judgments for discrimination in nonlinear psychophysics. *Nonlinear Dynamics, Psychology, and Life Sciences, 3*, 31–48.
Gresov, C., Haveman, H. A., & Oliva, T. A. (1993). Organizational design, inertia, and the dynamics of competitive response. *Organization Science, 4*, 181–208.
Grigsby, J., & Stevens, D. (2000). *Neurodynamics of personality*. New York: Guilford Press.
Guastello, S. J. (1981). Catastrophe modeling of equity in organizations. *Behavioral Science, 26*, 63–74.
Guastello, S. J. (1982a). Color matching and shift work: An industrial application of the cusp-difference equation. *Behavioral Science, 27*, 131–137.

Guastello, S. J. (1982b). Moderator regression and the cusp catastrophe: Application of two-stage personnel selection, training, therapy, and program evaluation. *Behavioral Science, 27*, 259–272.

Guastello, S. J. (1985). Euler buckling in a wheelbarrow obstacle course: A catastrophe with complex lag. *Behavioral Science, 30*, 201–212.

Guastello, S. J. (1987). A butterfly catastrophe model of motivations in organizations: Academic performance. *Journal of Applied Psychology, 72*, 165–182.

Guastello, S. J. (1988). Catastrophe modeling of the accident process: Organizational subunit size. *Psychological Bulletin, 103*, 246–255.

Guastello, S. J. (1991). *The Artistic and Scientific Activities Survey*. Milwaukee, WI: Marquette University, Department of Psychology.

Guastello, S. J. (1992a). Clash of the paradigms: A critique of an examination of the polynomial regression technique for evaluating catastrophe theory hypotheses. *Psychological Bulletin, 111*, 375–379.

Guastello, S. J. (1992b). Accidents and stress-related health disorders: Forecasting with catastrophe theory. In J. C. Quick, J. J. Hurrell, & L. M. Murphy (Eds.), *Work and well-being: Assessments and interventions for occupational mental health* (pp. 262–269). Washington, DC: American Psychological Association.

Guastello, S. J. (1994). Catastrophe and chaos theory for NYSE stock prices: The crash of 1987 and beyond. In M. Michaels (Ed.), *Proceedings of the Third Annual Conference of the Chaos Network* (pp. 37–47). Urbana, IL: People Technologies.

Guastello, S. J. (1995a). *Chaos, catastrophe, and human affairs: Applications of nonlinear dynamics to work, organizations, and social evolution*. Mahwah, NJ: Lawrence Erlbaum Associates.

Guastello, S. J. (1995b). Facilitative style, individual innovation, and emergent leadership in problem solving groups. *Journal of Creative Behavior, 29*, 225–239.

Guastello, S. J. (1995c). The search for a natural rate of price inflation: US 1948–1995. *Chaos Network, 7*(3), 16–23.

Guastello, S. J. (1997a). The decline in world-wide oceanic fishing harvests. Lotka-Volterra and related dynamics. *Society for Chaos Theory in Psychology & Life Sciences Newsletter, 4*(3), 10–13.

Guastello, S. J. (1997b). Teoria del caos e sviluppo organizzativo. [Chaos theory and organizational development]. In M. Pigazzini & P. Terni (Eds.), *Nuove froniere della scienza* (pp. 49–76). Lecco, Italy: Giornale di Lecco.

Guastello, S. J. (1998a). Creative problem solving groups at the edge of chaos. *Journal of Creative Behavior, 32*, 38–57.

Guastello, S. J. (1998b). Self-organization and leadership emergence. *Nonlinear Dynamics, Psychology, and Life Sciences, 2*, 303–316.

Guastello, S. J. (1999a). Hierarchical dynamics affecting work performance in organizations. In W. Tschacher & J. P. Dauwaulder (Eds.), *Dynamics, synergetics and autonomous agents* (pp. 277–302). Singapore: World Scientific.

Guastello, S. J. (1999b). Hysteresis, bifurcation, and the natural rate of unemployment. In E. Elliott & L. D. Kiel (Eds.), *Nonlinear dynamics, complexity and public policy* (pp. 31–46). Commack, NY: Nova Science.

Guastello, S. J. (2000a). Symbolic dynamic patterns of written exchange: Hierarchical structures in an electronic problem solving group. *Nonlinear Dynamics, Psychology, and Life Sciences, 4*, 169–188.

Guastello, S. J. (2000b). Attractor stability in unemployment and inflation rates. In Y. Aruka & A. Matsumoto (Eds.), *Proceedings of the Japan Association for Evolutionary Economics* (pp. 23–26). Tokyo: Chuo University.

Guastello, S. J. (in press). An attenuated relationship between mathematical creativity and cognitive creativity. *Journal of Applied System Science*.

Guastello, S. J., & Bock, B. R. (2001). Attractor reconstruction with principal components analysis: Application to work flows in hierarchical organizations. *Nonlinear Dynamics, Psychology, and Life Sciences, 5*, 175–192.

Guastello, S. J., Bock, B. R., & Caldwell, P. (1999). *Effects of verbalization and personnel replacement on group coordination.* Unpublished manuscript.

Guastello, S. J., Bzdawka, A., Guastello, D. D., & Rieke, M. L. (1992). Cognitive abilities and creative behaviors: CAB-5 and Consequences. *Journal of Creative Behavior, 26*, 260–267.

Guastello, S. J., Craven, J., Zygowicz, K. M., & Bock, B. R. (2001). *A rugged landscape model for self-organization and emergent leadership in creative problem solving groups.* Unpublished manuscript.

Guastello, S. J., Dooley, K. D., & Goldstein, J. (1995). Chaos, organizational theory, and organizational development. In F. D. Abraham & A. R. Gilgen (Eds.), *Chaos theory in psychology* (pp. 267–278). Westport, CT: Praeger.

Guastello, S. J., Gershon, R. M., & Murphy, L. R. (1999). Catastrophe model for the exposure to blood-borne pathogens and other accidents in health care settings. *Accident Analysis and Prevention, 31*, 739–750.

Guastello, S. J., & Guastello, D. D. (1998). Origins of coordination and team effectiveness: A perspective from game theory and nonlinear dynamics. *Journal of Applied Psychology, 83*, 423–437.

Guastello, S. J., Hyde, T., & Odak, M. (1998). Symbolic dynamic patterns of verbal exchange in a creative problem solving group. *Nonlinear Dynamics, Psychology, and Life Sciences, 2*, 35–58.

Guastello, S. J., & Johnson, E. A. (1999). The effect of downsizing on hierarchical work flow dynamics in organizations. *Nonlinear Dynamics, Psychology, and Life Sciences, 3*, 347–378.

Guastello, S. J., Johnson, E. A., & Rieke, M. L. (1999). Nonlinear dynamics of motivational flow. *Nonlinear Dynamics, Psychology, and Life Sciences, 3*, 259–273.

Guastello, S. J., & Philippe, P. (1997). Dynamics in the development of large information exchange groups and virtual communities. *Nonlinear Dynamics, Psychology, and Life Sciences, 1*, 123–149.

Guastello, S. J., & Rieke, M. L. (1993). *Selecting successful salespersons with the 16PF: Form A validity studies* (Tech. Rep. 1). Champaign, IL: Institute for Personality and Ability Testing.

Guastello, S. J., & Rieke, M. L. (1994). Computer-based test interpretations as expert systems: Validity and viewpoints from artificial intelligence theory. *Computers in Human Behavior, 10*, 435–455.

Guastello, S. J., Rieke, M. L., Guastello, D. D., & Billings, S. W. (1992). A study of cynicism, personality, and work values. *Journal of Psychology: Interdisciplinary and Applied, 126*, 37–48.

Guastello, S. J., & Shissler, J. (1994). A two-factor taxonomy of creative behavior. *Journal of Creative Behavior, 28*, 211–221.

Guastello, S. J., & Shissler, J., Driscoll, J., & Hyde, T. (1998). Are some cognitive styles more creatively productive than others? *Journal of Creative Behavior, 32*, 77–91.

Guilford, J. P. (1967). *The structure of intellect.* New York: McGraw-Hill.

Hackman, J. R. (1992, June). *Where the variance lives: Continuity and change in social behavior.* Paper presented to the American Psychological Society, San Diego, CA.

Hackman, J. R., & Oldham, G. R. (1976). Motivation through the design of work: Test of a theory. *Organizational Behavior and Human Performance, 15*, 250–279.

Haken, H. (1984). *The science of structure: Synergetics.* New York: Van Nostrand Reinhold.

Haken, H. (1988). *Information and self-organization: A macroscopic approach to complex systems.* New York: Springer-Verlag.

Haken, H. (1999). Synergetics and some applications to psychology. In W. Tschacher & J.-P. Dauwaulder (Eds.), *Dynamics, synergetics and autonomous agents* (pp. 3–12). Singapore: World Scientific.

Hakstian, A. R., & Cattell, R. B. (1978). High stratum ability structures on a basis of twenty primary abilities. *Journal of Educational Psychology, 70*, 657–669.

Hamblin, R. L. (1958). Leadership and crises. *Sociometry, 21*, 322–355.

Hammer, M., & Champy, J. (1993). *Reengineering the corporation.* New York: Harper-Collins.

Hammer, M., & Champy, J. (1996). Reengineering the corporation: The enabling role of information technology. In J. M. Shafritz & J. S. Ott (Eds.), *Classics of organizational theory* (pp. 561–577). Belmont, CA: Wadsworth.

Harary, F., Norman, R. Z., & Cartwright, D. (1965). *Structural models: An introduction to the theory of directed graphs*. New York: Wiley.

Hardy, C. (1998). *Networks of meaning: A bridge between mind and matter*. Westport, CT: Praeger.

Haslett, T., Moss, S., Osborne, C., & Ramm, P. (2000). Local rules and fitness landscapes: A catastrophe model. *Nonlinear Dynamics, Psychology, and Life Sciences, 4*, 67–86.

Hausdoff, F. (1919). Dimension und ausseres mass. *Mathematical Annalen, 79*, 157–179.

Haustein, D. H. (1981). Human resources, creativity, and innovation: The conflict between Homo Faber and Homo Ludens. *Behavioral Science, 26*, 243–255.

Heath, R. (2000a, July). *Can people predict chaotic sequences*? Paper presented to the Tenth Annual Conference of the Society for Chaos Theory in Psychology & Life Sciences, Philadelphia.

Heath, R. (2000b). *Nonlinear dynamics: Techniques and applications in psychology*. Mahwah, NJ: Lawrence Erlbaum Associates.

Herrmann, H. J. (1996). Fractures. In A. Bunde & S. Havlin (Eds.), *Fractals and disordered systems* (2nd ed., pp. 201–231). New York: Springer-Verlag.

Herzberg, F., Mausner, B., & Snyderman, D. (1959). *The motivation to work*. New York: Wiley.

Hinds, P., & Kiesler, S. (1995). Communication across boundaries: Work, structure, and use of communication technologies in a large organization. *Organization Science, 6*, 373–393.

Hirokawa, R. Y. (1983). Group communication and problem solving effectiveness: An investigation of group processes. *Human Communication Research, 9*, 291–305.

Hirschleifer, J., & Coll, J. C. M. (1988). What strategies can support the evolutionary emergence of cooperation? *Journal of Conflict Resolution, 32*, 367–398.

Hitt, M. A., Keats, B. W., Harback, H. F., & Nixon, R. D. (1994). Rightsizing: Building and maintaining strategic leadership and long-term competitiveness. *Organizational Dynamics, 23*, 18–32.

Hocevar, D. (1981). Measurement of creativity: Review and critique. *Journal of Personality Assessment, 45*, 450–464.

Hogan, J., & Hogan, R. T. (1993, April). *The ambiguity of conscientiousness*. In F. L. Schmidt (Chair), The construct of conscientiousness in personnel selection. Symposium conducted at the annual convention of the Society for Industrial and Organizational Psychology, San Francisco.

House, R. J., & Mitchell, T. R. (1975). Path-goal theory of leadership. In K. N. Wexley & G. A. Yukl (Eds.), *Organizational behavior and industrial psychology* (pp. 177–186). New York: Oxford University Press.

Hoylst, J. A., Tagel, T., Haag, G., & Weidlich, W. (1996). How to control a chaotic economy? *Evolutionary Economics, 6*, 31–42.

Huber, J. C. (1998). Invention and inventivity as a special kind of creativity, with implications for general creativity. *Journal of Creative Behavior, 32*, 58–72.

Hubler, A. (1992). Modeling and control of complex systems. In L. Lam & V. Naroditsky (Eds.), *Modeling complex phenomena* (pp. 5–65). New York: Springer-Verlag.

Huberman, B. A., & Glance, N. S. (1993). Diversity and collective action. In H. Haken & A. Mikhailov (Eds.), *Interdisciplinary approaches to nonlinear systems* (pp. 44–64). New York: Springer-Verlag.

Inayatullah, S. (1999). Leading scientists and philosophers meet to consider the year 3000. *Humanity 3000 News* [Foundation for the Future], *2*(1), 1–2.

Isen, A. M., Daubman, K. A., & Nowicki, G. P. (1987). Positive affect facilitates creative problem solving. *Journal of Personality and Social Psychology, 52*, 1122–1131.

Jackson, E. A. (1991a). On the control of complex dynamic systems. *Physica D, 50*, 341–366.

Jackson, E. A. (1991b). Control of dynamic flows and attractors. *Physical Review A, 44*, 4839–4853.

Jarrett, R. F. (1948). Percent increases in output of selected personnel as an index of test efficiency. *Journal of Applied Psychology, 32*, 135–145.

Jaynes, J. (1976). *Origins of consciousness in the breakdown of the bicameral mind*. Boston: Houghton Mifflin.

Johnson-Laird, P. N. (1993). *Human and machine learning*. Hillsdale, NJ: Lawrence Erlbaum Associates.

Kaas, L. (1998). Stabilizing chaos in a dynamic macroeconomic model. *Journal of Economic Behavior and Organization, 33*, 313–332.

Kahneman, D., & Tversky, A. (1979). Prospect theory: An analysis of decision under risk. *Econometrica, 47*, 253–291.

Kagano, T., Nonaka, I., Sakabara, K., & Okumura, A. (1985). *Strategic versus evolutionary management*. Amsterdam: North Holland.

Kampis, G. (1991). *Self-modifying systems in biology and cognitive science*. Oxford, UK: Pergamon.

Kanter, D. L., & Mirvis, P. H. (1989). *The cynical Americans: Living and working in an age of discontent and disillusionment.* San Francisco: Jossey-Bass.

Kantowitz, B. H., & Sorkin, D. (1983). *Human factors: Understanding people-system relationships.* New York: Wiley.

Kanz, H., & Schreiber, T. (1997). *Nonlinear time series analysis*. New York: Cambridge University Press.

Kaplan, D., & Glass, L. (1995). *Understanding nonlinear dynamics*. New York: Springer-Verlag.

Kaplan, S. R. (1978). *The encyclopedia of tarot*. New York: U.S. Games Systems.

Kauffman, L. H., & Sabelli, H. C. (1998). The process equation. *Cybernetics and Systems: An International Journal, 29*, 345–362.

Kauffman, S. A. (1993). *The origins of orders: Self-organization and selection in evolution.* New York: Oxford University Press.

Kauffman, S. A. (1995). *At home in the universe: The search for laws of self-organization and complexity*. New York: Oxford University Press.

Keen, S. (1997). From stochastics to complexity in models of economic instability. *Nonlinear Dynamics, Psychology, and Life Sciences, 1*, 151–172.

Kelly, K. (1994). *Out of control: The new biology of machines, social systems and the economic world.* Reading, MA: Addison-Wesley.

Kelso, J. A. S. (1995). *Dynamic patterns: Self-organization of brain and behavior*. Cambridge, MA: MIT Press.

Kegan, D. L., & Rubinstein, A. H. (1973). Trust, effectiveness, and organizational development. *Journal of Applied Behavioral Science, 9*, 498–513.

Kets de Vries, M. R., & Miller, D. (1986). Personality, culture, and organization. *Academy of Management Review, 11*, 266–279.

Keynes, J. M. (1965). *General theory of employment, interest, and money* (2nd ed.). New York: Harcourt Brace. Originally 1936.

Kiel, L. D. (1994). *Managing chaos and complexity in government*. San Francisco: Jossey-Bass.

Kiesler, S. (Ed.). (1997). *Culture of the Internet*. Mahwah, NJ: Lawrence Erlbaum Associates.

King, D. A. (1996). Seeking the cure for ailing corporations *Organization Development Journal, 14*, 5–22.

Kirkpatrick, M. (1993). The evolution of size and growth in harvested natural populations. In T. K. Stokes, J. M. McGlade, & R. Law (Eds.), *The exploitation of evolving resources* (pp. 145–154). Berlin: Springer-Verlag.

Kirton, M. J. (1976). Adaptors and innovators: A description and measure. *Journal of Applied Psychology, 61*, 622–629.

Kirton, M. J., & DeCiantis, S. M. (1986). Cognitive styles and personality: The Kirton Adaption-Innovation and Cattell's Sixteen Personality Factor inventories. *Personality and Individual Differences, 7*, 141–146.

Knyazeva, H., & Haken, H. (1999). Synergetics of human creativity. In W. Tschacher & J.-P. Dauwalder (Eds.), *Dynamics, synergetics, and autonomous agents* (pp. 64–79). Singapore: World Scientific.

Kocic, L. (2001). AIFS: A tool for biomorphic fractal modeling. *Nonlinear Dynamics, Psychology, and Life Sciences, 5*, 45–65.

Koehler, G. (1995). Fractals and path-dependent processes: A theoretical approach for characterizing emergency medical responses to major disasters. In R. Robertson & A. Combs (Eds.), *Chaos theory in psychology and life sciences* (pp. 199–218). Mahwah, NJ: Lawrence Erlbaum Associates.

Koehler, G. (Ed.). (1996a). *What disaster response management can learn from chaos theory,* Sacramento, CA: California Research Bureau, California State Library.

Koehler, G. (1996b). What disaster response management can learn from chaos theory. In G. Koehler (Ed.), *What disaster response management can learn from chaos theory* (pp. 2–41). Sacramento, CA: California Research Bureau, California State Library.

Koehler, G. (1999). The time compacted globe and the high-tech primitive at the millennium. In L. D. Kiel & E. Elliott (Eds.), *Nonlinear dynamics, complexity, and public policy* (pp. 153–174). Commack, NY: Nova Science.

Kohonen, T. (1989). *Self-organization and associative memory.* (3rd ed.). New York: Springer-Verlag.

Kopel, M. (1997). Improving the performance of an economic system: Controlling chaos. *Evolutionary Economics, 7,* 269–289.

Koyama, A., Yoneyama, K., Sawada, Y., & Ohtomo, N. (Eds.). (1994). *A recent advance in time series analysis by maximum entropy method: Applications to medical and biological sciences.* Hokkaido: Hokkaido University Press.

Krau, E. (1995). Disempowering and downsizing middle management? International *Journal of Sociology & Social Policy, 15,* 91–119.

Kugiumtzis, D., Lillekjendlie, B., & Christophersen, N. (1994). *Chaotic time series, part I: Estimation of invariant properties in state space* (Tech. Rep.) University of Oslo, Department of Informatics.

Kuhn, T. (1972). *The structure of scientific revolutions.* New York: Freeman.

Labib, N., & Appelbaum, S. H. (1993). Strategic downsizing: A human resources perspective. *Human Resource Planning, 16,* 69–93.

Lange, R., Oliva, T., & McDade, S. (2000). An algorithm for estimating multivariate catastrophe theory models: GEMCAT II. Studies in Nonlinear Dynamics and Econometrics, 4:3, Massachusetts Institute of Technology.

Laszlo, E. (Ed.). (1991). *The new evolutionary paradigm.* New York: Gordon & Breach.

Latané, B., Nowak, A., & Liu, J. H. (1994). Measuring emergent social phenomena: Dynamism, polarization, and clustering as order parameters of social systems. *Behavioral Science, 39,* 1–24.

Latané, B., Williams, K., & Harkins, S. (1979). Many hands make light the work: The causes and consequences of social loafing. *Journal of Personality and Social Psychology, 37,* 822–832.

Lathrop, D. P., & Kostelich, E. J. (1989). Characterization of an experimental strange attractor by periodic orbits. *Physics Review A, 40,* 4028–4031.

Laughlin, P. R. (1988). Collective induction: Group performance, social combination processes, and mutual majority and minority influence. *Journal of Personality and Social Psychology, 54,* 254–267.

Laughlin, P. R. (1996). Group decision making and collective induction. In E. Witte & J. H. Davis (Eds.), *Understanding group behavior: Consensual action by small groups,* Vol. 1., pp. 61–80). Mahwah, NJ: Lawrence Erlbaum Associates.

Laughlin, P. R., Chandler, J. S., Shupe, E. I., Magley, V. J., & Hulbert, L. G. (1995). Generality of a theory of collective induction: Face-to-face and computer-mediated interaction, amount of potential information, and group versus member choice of evidence. *Organizational Behavior and Human Decision Processes, 63,* 98–111.

Laughlin, P. R., & Futoran, G. C. (1985). Collective induction: Social combination and sequential transition. *Journal of Personality and Social Psychology, 48,* 608–613.

Laughlin, P. R., & McGlynn, R. P. (1986). Collective induction: Mutual group and individual influence by exchange of hypotheses and evidence. *Journal of Experimental Social Psychology, 22,* 567–589.

Laughlin, P. R., & Shippy, T. A. (1983). Collective induction. *Journal of Personality and Social Psychology, 45,* 94–100.

Laughlin, P. R., VanderStoep, S. W., & Hollingshead, A. B. (1991). Collective versus individual induction: Recognition of truth, rejection of error, and collective information processing. *Journal of Personality and Social Psychology, 61,* 50–67.

Lea, M., O'Shea, T., & Fung, P. (1995). Constructing the networked organization: Content and context in the development of electronic communications. *Organization Science, 6,* 462–278.

Leedom, D. K., & Simon, R. (1995). Improving team coordination: A case for behavior-based training. *Military Psychology, 7*, 102–122.

Leon, F. R. (1981). The role of positive and negative outcomes in the causation of motivational forces. *Journal of Applied Psychology, 66*, 45–53.

Lerner, A. (1951). *Economics of employment*. New York: McGraw-Hill.

Levine, J. H., & Spedaro, J. (1988). Occupational mobility: A structural model. In B. Wellman & S. D. Berkowitz (Eds.), *Social structures: A network approach* (pp. 452–475). New York: Cambridge University Press.

Levinger, G. (1980). Toward the analysis of close relationships. *Journal of Experimental Social Psychology, 16*, 510–544.

Levinthal, D. A., & Warglien, M. (1999). Landscape design: Designing for local action in complex worlds. *Organization Science, 10*, 342–358.

Levy, S. (1992). *Artificial life: A report from the frontier where computers meet biology*. New York: Random House.

Lewin, K. (1947). Frontiers in group dynamics. *Human Relations, 1*, 5–41.

Lewin, K. (1951). *Field theory in social science*. New York: Harper & Row.

Lewin, K., Lippitt, R., & White, R. (1939). Patterns of aggressive behavior in experimentally created "social climates" *Journal of Social Psychology, 10*, 271–299.

Leydesdorff, L., & van den Besselaar, P. (Eds.). (1994). *Evolutionary economics and chaos theory*. New York: St. Martin's Press.

Li, T.-Y., & Yorke, J. A. (1975). Period three implies chaos. *American Mathematical Monthly, 85*, 985–992.

Likert, R. (1961). *New patterns of management*. New York: McGraw-Hill.

Lind, M. R., & Sulek, J. M. (1994). A Newtonian metaphor for organizational change. *IEEE Transactions on Engineering Management, 41*, 375–383.

Lindell, M., & Rosenqvist, G. (1992). Management behavior dimensions and development orientation. *Leadership Quarterly, 3*, 355–377.

Linz, S. J., & Sprott, J. C. (1999). Elementary chaotic flow. *Physics Letters A, 259*, 240–245.

Liu, X., Dooley, K. J., & Anderson, J. C. (1995). Combining process knowledge for continuous quality improvement. *IIE Transactions, 27*, 811–819.

Locke, E. A., & Latham, G. P. (1990). Work motivation and satisfaction: Light at the end of the tunnel. *Psychological Science, 1*, 240–246.

Lord, F. M., & Novick, M. R. (1968). *Statistical theories of mental test scores*. Reading MA: Addison-Wesley.

Lorenz, E. N. (1963). Deterministic nonperiodic flow. *Journal of Atmospheric Sciences, 20*, 130–141.

Lotka, A. J. (1926). The frequency distribution of scientific productivity. *Journal of the Washington Academy of Sciences, 16*, 317–323.

Loye, D. (1978). *The knowable future: A psychology of forecasting and prophesy*. New York: Wiley Interscience.

Loye, D. (1995). How predictable is the future: The conflict between traditional chaos theory and the psychology of prediction, and the challenge for chaos psychology. In R. Robertson & A. Combs (Eds.), *Chaos theory in psychology and life sciences* (pp. 345–358). Mahwah, NJ: Lawrence Erlbaum Associates.

Loye, D. (2000). *An arrow through chaos: How we see into the future*. Rochester, VT: Park Street Press.

Luhmann, N. (1986). The autopoiesis of social systems. In F. Geyer & J. van der Zouwen (Eds.), *Sociocybernetic paradoxes: Observation, control and evolution of self-steering systems* (pp. 172–192). London: Sage.

Lund, R. A. (1995). [Remark on boundaries in the creative process]. Posting to the LISTSERV discussion group, CREA-CPS@HEARN.NIC.SURFNET.NL, March 8.

Lundberg, C. C. (1985). On the feasibility of cultural interventions in organizations. In P. J. Frost, L. F. Moore, M. R. Louis, C. C. Lundberg, & J. Martin (Eds.), *Organizational culture* (pp. 169–186). Newberry Park, CA: Sage.

MacCormac, E., & Stamenov, M. I. (1996). *Fractals of brain, fractals of mind: In search of a symmetry bond.* Philadelphia: Benjamins.

Maehr, M. L., & Braskamp, L. A. (1986). *The motivation factor: A theory of personnel management.* Lexington, MA: Lexington.

Mandelbrot, B. B. (1966). Forecasts of future prices, unbiased markets, and 'Martingale' models. *Journal of Business, 39*, 242–255.

Mandelbrot, B. B. (1977). Fractals and turbulence: Attractors and dispersion. In P. Bernard & T. Raiu (Eds.), *Turbulence seminar Berkeley 1976/1977* (pp. 83–93). New York: Springer-Verlag.

Mandelbrot, B. B. (1983). *The fractal geometry of nature.* New York: Freeman.

Mannell, R. C., Zuzanek, J., & Larson, R. (1988). Leisure states and "flow" experiences: Testing perceived freedom and intrinsic motivation hypotheses. *Journal of Leisure Research, 20*, 289–304.

Marks-Tarlow, T. (1999). The self as a dynamical system. *Nonlinear Dynamics, Psychology, and Life Sciences, 3*, 311–346.

Maturana, H., & Varela, F. G. (1980). *Autopoiesis and cognition: The realization of the living.* Dordrecht: Reidel.

Mawhinney, T. C. (1979). Intrinsic X extrinsic work motivation: Perspectives from behaviorism. *Organizational Behavior and Human Performance, 24*, 411–440.

May, R. M. (1976). Simple mathematical models with very complicated dynamics. *Nature, 261*, 459–467.

May, R. M., & Oster, G. F. (1976). Bifurcations and dynamic complexity in simple ecological models. *American Naturalist, 110*, 573–599.

Mayer-Kress, G. (1994, November). *Global brains as paradigm for a complex adaptive world.* Paper presented to the conference Evolving Complexity. Challenges to Society, Economy and the Individual, University of Texas at Dallas, Richardson, TX.

Maynard Smith, J. (1982). *Evolution and the theory of games.* Cambridge, UK: Cambridge University Press.

McCain, R. A. (1992). Heuristic coordination games: Rational action equilibrium and objective social constraints in a linguistic conception of rationality. *Social Science Information, 31*, 711–734.

McClelland, D. C. (1961). *The achieving society.* Princeton NJ: Van Nostrand.

McClelland, D. C. (1975). *Power: The inner experience.* New York: Irvington.

McClelland, D. C., Atkinson, J. W., Clark, R. A., & Lowell, E. L. (1953). *The achievement motive.* New York: Appleton-Century-Croft.

McClelland, D. C., & Boyatsis, R. E. (1982). Leadership motive pattern and long-term success in management. *Journal of Applied Psychology, 67*, 737–743.

McClure, B. A. (1998). *Putting a new spin on groups: The science of chaos.* Mahwah, NJ: Lawrence Erlbaum Associates.

McCullers, J. C., Fabes, R. A., & Moran, J. D. III (1987). Does intrinsic motivation theory explain adverse effects of rewards on immediate task performance. *Journal of Personality and Social Psychology, 52*, 1027–1033.

McGregor, D. M. (1960). *The human side of enterprise.* New York: McGraw-Hill.

McKelvey, B. (1999). Avoiding complexity catastrophe in coevolutionary pockets: Strategies for rugged landscapes. *Organization Science, 10*, 294–322.

Mead, G. H. (1934). *Mind, self, and society.* Chicago: University of Chicago Press.

Meadows, D. H., Meadows, D. L., Randers, J., & Behrens, W. W. III (1972). *The limits to growth.* New York: Universe.

Medvinsky, A. B., Tikhov, D. A., Enderlein, J., & Malchow, H. (2000). Fish and plankton interplay determines both plankton spatio-temporal pattern formation and fish school walks. *Nonlinear Dynamics, Psychology & Life Sciences, 4*, 135–152.

Mentzer, M. S. (1996). Corporate downsizing and profitability in Canada. Canadian *Journal of Administrative Sciences, 13*, 237–250.

Meltzer, H. (1942). Explorations in humanizing relations of key people in industry. *American Journal of Orthopsychiatry, 12*, 517–528.

Metzger, M. A. (1994). Have subjects been shown to generate chaotic numbers? Commentary on Neuringer and Voss. *Psychological Science, 5*, 111–114.

Metzger, M. A. (1997). Applications of nonlinear dynamical systems theory in developmental psychology: Motor and cognitive development. *Nonlinear Dynamics, Psychology, & Life Sciences, 1*, 55–68.

Michaels, M. D. (1989). The chaos paradigm. *Organizational Development Journal, 7(2)*, 31–35.

Michaels, M. D. (1991). Chaos constructions: A neural net model of organization. In M. D. Michaels (Ed.), *Proceedings of the first annual Chaos Network conference* (pp. 79–83). Urbana, IL: People Technologies.

Michaels, M. D. (1992). *The Chaos Exercise*^{Tm}. Savoy, IL: People Technologies.

Mick, S. S., & Wise, C. G. (1996). Downsizing and financial performance in rural hospitals. *Health Care Management Review, 21*, 16–25.

Miller, J. G. (1978). *Living systems*. New York: McGraw-Hill.

Mitroff, I. (1993, April). *Radical surgery: Why organizations of tomorrow wo't look anything like those of today.* Paper presented to the Society for Industrial and Organizational Psychology, San Francisco.

Morel, B., & Ramanujam, R. (1999). Through the looking glass of complexity: The dynamics of organizations as adaptive and evolving systems. *Organization Science, 10*, 237–253.

Morris, C. (1906). *The San Francisco calamity, earthquake, and fire*. City Unknown: W. E. Scull.

Mosekilde, E., Larssen, E., & Sterman, J. (1991). Coping with complexity: Chaos in human decision making behavior. In J. Casti & A. Karlqvist (Eds.), *Beyond belief: Randomness, prediction, and explanation in science* (pp. 199–299). Boca Raton, FL: CRC Press.

Mudd, S. (1995). Suggestive parallels between Kirton's A-I theory of creative style and Koestler's bisociative theory of the creative act. *Journal of Creative Behavior, 29*, 240–254.

Mullen, B., & Copper, C. (1994). The relation between group cohesiveness and performance: An integration. *Psychological Bulletin, 115*, 210–217.

Nash, J. (1951). Non-cooperative games. *Annals of Mathematics, 54*, 286–295.

Neuman, G. A., & Wright, J. (1999). Team effectiveness: Beyond skills and cognitive ability. *Journal of Applied Psychology, 84*, 376–389.

Neuringer, A., & Voss, C. (1993). Approximating chaotic behavior. *Psychological Science, 4*, 113–119.

Newhouse, R., Ruelle, D., & Takens, F. (1978). Occurence of strange attractors: An axiom near quasi-periodic flows on T^m, $m \geq 3$. *Communications in Mathematical Physics, 64*, 35–41.

Nicolis, G., & Prigogine, I. (1989). *Exploring complexity*. New York: Freeman.

Oliva, T. A., Desarbo, W. S., Day, D. L., & Jedidi, K. (1987). GEMCAT: A general multivariate methodology for estimating catastrophe models. *Behavioral Science, 26*, 153–162.

Oliva, T. A., Peters, M. H., & Murthy, H. S. K. (1981). A preliminary empirical test of a cusp catastrophe model in the social sciences. *Behavioral Science, 26*, 153–162.

O'Neill, B. (1984). Structures for nonhierarchical organizations. *Behavioral Science, 29*, 61–77.

Ott, E., Grebogi, C., & Yorke, J. A. (1990). Controlling chaos. *Physical Review Letters, 64*, 1196–1199.

Ott, E., Sauer, T., & Yorke, J. A. (Eds.). (1994). *Coping with chaos*. New York: Wiley.

Orlikowsky, W. Y., Yates, J., Okamura, K., Fujimoto, M. (1995). Shaping electronic communication: The metastructuring of technology in the context of use. *Organization Science, 6*, 423–444.

Orsucci, F. (1998). *Complex matters of the mind.* Singapore: World Scientific.

Ouchi, W. G. (1980). *Theory Z: How American management can meet the Japanese challenge*. Reading, MA: Addison-Wesley.

Packard, N. H., Crutchfield, J. P., Farmer, J. D., & Shaw, R. S. (1980). Geometry from a time series. *Physics Review Letters, 45*, 712–716.

Papadimitriou, D. B., & Wray, L. R. (1994). *Flying blind: The Federal Reserve's experiment with unobservables.* (Tech. Rep.) Public Policy Brief, The Jerome Levy Economic Institute, Bard College.

Parkhurst, H. B. (1999). Confusion, lack of consensus, and the definition of creativity as a construct. *Journal of Creative Behavior, 33*, 1–21.

Pearlman, K. (Chair). (1995, May). *Is the "job" dead: Implications for changing concepts of work for I/O science and practice.* Symposium presented to the Society for Industrial and Organizational Psychology, Orlando.

Pearson, C. A. L. (1992). Autonomous work groups: An evaluation at an industrial site. *Human Relations, 45*, 905–936.

Peters, E. E. (1991). *Chaos and order in capital markets*. New York: Wiley.

Peters, E. E. (1994). *Fractal market analysis: Applying chaos theory to investment and economics.* New York: Wiley.

Phelps, E. S. (1967). Phillips curves, expectations of inflation and optimal unemployment. *Economica, 34.*

Pherigo, R., Lee, M. L., Nehman, G., & Eve, R. A. (1999). Self-regulation: Implications of complex adaptive systems theory to regulatory policy. In L. D. Kiel & E. Elliott (Eds.), *Nonlinear dynamics, complexity, and public policy* (pp. 139–152). Commack, NY: Nova Science.

Philippe, P. (2000). Epidemiology and self-organized critical systems: An analysis in waiting times and disease heterogeneity. *Nonlinear Dynamics, Psychology, and Life Sciences, 4*, 275–295.

Phillips, A. W. (1954). *Stabilisation policy in a closed economy*. London: Norton.

Piaget, J. (1952). *The origins of intelligence in children*. New York: W. W. Norton.

Pickering, J. M., & King, J. L. (1995). Hardwiring weak ties: Interorganizational computer-mediated communication, occupational communities, and organizational change. *Organization Science, 6*, 479–486.

Pincus, D. (2001). A framework and methodology for the study of nonlinear self-organizing family dynamics. *Nonlinear Dynamics, Psychology, and Life Sciences, 5*, 139–174.

Policansky, D. (1993). Fishing as a cause of evolution in fishes. In T. K. Stokes, J. M. McGlade, & R. Law (Eds.), *The exploitation of evolving resources* (pp. 1–18). Berlin: Springer-Verlag.

Poole, M. S., Van de Ven, A. H., Dooley, K., Holmes, M. E. (2001). *Organizational change and innovation processes*. New York: Oxford University Press.

Porter, L. W., & Lawler, E. E. III. (1965) Properties of organizational structure related to job attitudes and behavior. *Psychological Bulletin, 64*, 23–51.

Poston, T., & Stewart, I. (1978). *Catastrophe theory and its applications*. London: Pitman.

Premack, D. (1971). Catching up with common sense or two sides of a generalization: Reinforcement and punishment. In R. Glaser (Ed.), *The nature of reinforcement* (pp. 121–150). New York: Academic Press.

Pressing, J. (1999). Referential dynamics of cognition and action. *Psychological Review, 106*, 714–747.

Prichard, R. D., Campbell, K. M., & Campbell, D. J. (1977). Effects of extrinsic financial rewards on intrinsic motivation. *Journal of Applied Psychology, 62*, 9–15.

Priesmeyer, H. R., & Cole, E. G. (1996). Nonlinear analysis of disaster response data. In G. Koehler (Ed.), *What disaster response management can learn from chaos theory* (pp. 60–79). Sacramento, CA: California Research Bureau, California State Library.

Prigogine, I., & Stengers, I. (1984). *Order out of chaos: Man's new dialog with nature*. New York: Bantam.

Puu, T. (1993). *Nonlinear economic dynamics* (3rd ed.). New York: Springer-Verlag.

Puu, T. (2000a). *Attractors, bifurcations, and chaos: Nonlinear phenomena in economics*. New York: Springer-Verlag.

Puu, T. (2000b). Economic development, Darwin, and catastrophe theory. In Y. Aruka & A. Matsumoto (Eds.), *Evolutionary economics in Tokyo: Papers of the fourth annual conference of the Japan Association for Evolutionary Economics* (pp. 7–10). Tokyo: Chuo University.

Ramaprasad, A. (1982). Revolutionary change and strategic management. *Behavioral Science, 27*, 387–392.

Rankin, F. W., Van Huyck, J. B., & Battalio, R. C. (2000). Strategic similarity and emergent conventions: Evidence from similar Stag Hunt games. *Games and Economic Behavior*, *32*, 315–337.

Reber, A. S., Kassin, S. M., Lewis, S., & Cantor, G. (1980). On the relationship between implicit and explicit modes of learning a complex rule structure. *Journal of Experimental Psychology: Human Learning and Memory*, *6*, 492–502.

Redmond, M. R., Mumford, M. D., & Teach, R. (1993). Putting creativity to work: Effects of leader behavior on subordinate creativity: *Organizational Behavior and Human Decision Processes*, *55*, 120–151.

Reynolds, C. W. (1987). Flocks, herds, and schools: A distributed behavioral model. *Computer Graphics*, *21*, 25–34.

Richey, M. W. (1992). The impact of corporate downsizing on employees. *Business Forum*, *17*(3), 9–13.

Rieke, M. L., Guastello, S. J., & Conn, S. R. (1994). Leadership and creativity. In S. R. Conn & M. L. Rieke (Eds.), The *Sixteen Personality Factor Questionnaire*: *Fifth edition technical manual* (pp. 183–212). Champaign, IL: Institute for Personality and Ability Testing.

Rinaldi, S., Cordone, R., & Casagrandi, R. (2000). Instabilities in creative professions: A minimal model. *Nonlinear Dynamics, Psychology, and Life Sciences*, *4*, 255–273.

Rinaldi, S., & Gragnani, A. (1998). Love dynamics between secure individuals: A modeling approach. *Nonlinear Dynamics, Psychology, and Life Sciences*, *2*, 283–302.

Robinson, J. (1933). *Economics of imperfect competition*. Cambridge, UK: Cambridge University Press.

Rosser, J. B. Jr. (1991). *From catastrophe to chaos: A general theory of economic discontinuities*. Boston: Kluwer.

Rosser, J. B. Jr. (1997). Speculations on nonlinear speculative bubbles. *Nonlinear Dynamics, Psychology, and Life Sciences*, *1*, 275–300.

Rosser, J. B. Jr. (1999). On the complexities of complex economic dynamics. *Journal of Economic Perspectives*, *13*, 169–192.

Rosser, J. B. Jr. (2000a). *From catastrophe to chaos: General theory of economic disequilibrium, I: Mathematics, microeconomics, macroeconomics, finance* (2nd ed.). Boston: Kluwer.

Rosser, J. B. Jr. (2000b). Self-fulfilling chaotic mistakes: Some examples and implications. *Discrete Dynamics in Nature and Society*, *4*, 29–37.

Rosser, J. B. Jr., Folke, C., Gunther, F., Isomaki, H., Perrings, C., & Puu, T. (1994). Discontinuous change in multilevel hierarchical systems. *Systems Research*, *11*, 77–94.

Rosser, J. B. Jr., Rosser, M. V., Guastello, S. J., & Bond, R. W. Jr. (2001). Chaotic hysteresis and systemic economic transformation: Soviet investment patterns. *Nonlinear Dynamics, Psychology, and Life Sciences*, *5*, 345–368.

Ruelle, D. (1991). *Chance and chaos*. Princeton, NJ: Princeton University Press.

Rushkin, H. J., & Feng, Y. (1997). Self-organized criticality in some dissipative sandpile models. *Physica A*, *245*, 453–460.

Rummel, R. J. (1970). *Applied factor analysis*. Evanston, IL: Northwestern University Press.

Saal, F. E., & Knight, P. A. (1988). *Industrial/organizational psychology: Science and practice*. Belmont, CA: Wadsworth.

Sabelli, H. C. (2001). Novelty, a measure of creative organization in natural and mathematical time series. *Nonlinear Dynamics, Psychology, and Life Sciences*, *5*, 89–114.

Sabelli, H. C., & Kauffman, L. H. (1999). The process equation: Formulating and testing the process theory of systems. *Cybernetics and Systems: An International Journal*, *30*, 261–274.

Sadtchenko, K. (2000). Universal laws in application to evolutionary economics. In Y. Aruka & A. Matsumoto (Eds.), *Evolutionary economics in Tokyo: Papers of the fourth annual conference of the Japan Association for Evolutionary Economics* (pp. 49–53). Tokyo: Chuo University.

Saltzman, E. L. (1995). Dynamics and coordinate systems in skilled sensorimotor activity. In R. F. Port & T. van Gelder (Eds.), *Mind as motion* (pp. 149–173). Cambridge, MA: MIT Press.

Samurcay, R., & Rogalski, J. (1993). Cooperative work and decision making in emergency management. *Le Travail Humain*, *56*, 53–77.

Sashkin, M. (1984). *The leader behavior questionnaire*. King of Prussia, PA: Organization Design and Development.
Sashkin, M., & Burke, W. W. (1990). Understanding and assessing organizational leadership. In K. E. Clark & M. B. Clark (Eds.), *The measurement of leadership* (pp. 297–325). West Orange, NJ: Leadership Library of America.
Schacter, S. (1959). *The psychology of affiliation*. Stanford, CA: Stanford University Press.
Schein, E. (1988). *Process consultation: Its role in organizational development*. Reading, MA: Addison-Wesley.
Schein, E. (1990). Organizational culture. *American Psychologist, 45*, 109–119.
Scheper, W. J., & Scheper, G. C. (1996). Autopsies on autopoiesis. *Behavioral Science, 41*, 3–12.
Schlesinger, A. (1988). On leadership. In L. R. Hartenian, Benito Mussolini (pp. 7–11). New York: Chelsea House.
Schultze, C. L. (1959). *Prices, costs, and output for the postwar decade: 1947–1957*. New York: Center for Economic Development.
Seccareccia, M. (1991). An alternative to labour-market orthodoxy: The post-Keynesian institutionalist policy view. *Review of Political Economy, 3*, 43–61.
Seger, C. A. (1994). Implicit learning. *Psychological Bulletin, 115*, 163–196.
Senge, P. M. (1980). *The fifth discipline*. New York: Doubleday.
Sexton, P. C. (1991). *The war on labor and the left*. Boulder, CO: Westview.
Shannon, C. E. (1948). A mathematical theory of communication. *Bell System Technical Journal, 27*, 379–423.
Shaw, J. B., & Barrett-Power, E. (1997). A conceptual framework for assessing organization, work group, and individual effectiveness during and after downsizing. *Human Relations, 50*, 109–127.
Sheridan, J. E., & Abelson, M. A. (1983). Cusp catastrophe model of employee turnover. *Academy of Management Journal, 26*, 418–436.
Shepperd, J. A. (1993). Productivity loss in performance groups: A motivation study. *Psychological Bulletin, 113*, 67–81.
Siegel, S. M., & Kaemmerer, W. G. (1978). Measuring the perceived support for innovation in organizations. *Journal of Applied Psychology, 63*, 43–48.
Simonton, D. K. (1988). Creativity, leadership, and change. In R. J. Sternberg (Ed.), *The nature of creativity: Contemporary psychological perspectives* (pp. 386–426). Cambridge, MA: MIT Press.
Simonton, D. K. (1989). Age and creative productivity: Nonlinear estimation of an information processing model. *International Journal of Aging and Human Development, 29*, 23–37.
Smale, S. (1964). Diffeomorphisms with many periodic points. In S. S. Cairns (Ed.), *Differential and combination topology in honor of Marsten Morse* (pp. 63–80). Princeton, NJ: Princeton University Press.
Smith, C., & Comer, D. (1994). Self-organization in small groups: A study of group effectiveness within non-equilibrium conditions. *Human Relations, 47*, 553–581.
Smith, G. F. (1998). Idea-generation techniques: A formulary of active ingredients. *Journal of Creative Behavior, 32*, 107–133.
Smith, J. B. (1994). *Collective intelligence in computer-based collaboration*. Hillsdale, NJ: Lawrence Erlbaum Associates.
Smith, T. S., & Stevens, G. T. (1997). Biological foundations of social interaction: Computational explorations of nonlinear dynamics. In R. A. Eve, S. Horsfall, & M. E. Lee (Eds.), *Chaos, complexity, and sociology: Myths, models, and theories* (pp. 197–214). Thousand Oaks, CA: Sage.
Smithson, M. (1997). Judgment under chaos. *Organizational Behavior and Human Decision Processes, 69*, 59–66.
Sprott, J. C. (1997). Simplest dissipative chaotic flow. *Physics Letters A, 228*, 271–274.
Sprott, J. C. (2001, August). *Can a monkey with a computer create art?* Paper presented to the 11th Annual conference of the Society for Chaos Theory in Psychology & Life Sciences, Madison, WI. http://sprott.physics.wisc.edu

Sraffa, P. (1960). *Production of commodities by means of commodities: Prelude to a critique of economic theory.* London: Cambridge University Press.
Stacey, R. D. (1992). *Managing the unknowable: Strategic boundaries between order and chaos in organizations*. San Francisco: Jossey-Bass.
Stacey, R. D. (1993). Strategy as order emerging from chaos. *Long Range Planning, 26*, 10–17.
Stacey, R. D. (1996). *Complexity and creativity in organizations*. San Francisco: Berrett- Kohler.
Staudenmeyer, N., & Lawless, M. W. (1999, November). *Organizational decay: How innovation stresses organizations*. Paper presented to INFORMS' 99, Philadelphia.
Steers, R. M., & Rhodes, S. R. (1978). Major influences on employee attendance: A process model. *Journal of Applied Psychology, 63*, 391–407.
Steiner, I. D. (1972). *Group process and productivity*. New York: Academic Press.
Sterman, J. (1988). Deterministic models of chaos in human behavior: Methodological issues and experimental results. *System Dynamics Review, 4*, 148–178.
Sternberg, R. J., & Lubart, T. I. (1991). An investment theory of creativity and its development. *Human Development, 34*, 1–31.
Sternberg, R. J., & Lubart, T. I. (1995). *Defying the crowd: Cultivating creativity in a culture of conformity*. New York: Free Press.
Stewart, I. (1989). *Does God play dice? The mathematics of chaos*. Cambridge, MA: Blackwell.
Storfer, M. D. (1990). *Intelligence and giftedness: The contributions of heredity and early environment*. San Francisco: Jossey Bass.
Stout, R. J., Salas, E., & Carson, R. (1994). Individual task proficiency and team process behavior: What's important for team functioning? *Military Psychology, 6*, 177–192.
Sugihara, G., Garcia, S., Gulland, J. A., Lawton, J. H., Maske, H., Paine, R. T., Platt, T., Rachor, E., Rothschild, B. J., Ursin, E. A., & Zeitzschel, B. F. K. (1994). Ecosystem dynamics. In R. M. May (Ed.), *Exploitation of marine communities* (pp. 131–153). Berlin: Springer-Verlag.
Sulis, W. (1997). Fundamental concepts of collective intelligence. *Nonlinear Dynamics, Psychology, and Life Sciences, 1*, 35–54.
Sweney, A. B. (1970). Organizational power roles. *Professional Management Bulletin, 10*, 5–13.
Tabachnick, B. G., & Fidell, L. S. (1989). *Using multivariate statistics* (2nd ed.). New York: Harper & Row.
Taylor, H. C., & Russell, J. T. (1939). The relationship of validity coefficients to the practical effectiveness of tests in selection: Discussion and tables. *Journal of Applied Psychology, 23*, 565–578.
Tenner, E. (1996). *Why things bite back.* New York: Knopf.
Terkle, S. (1984). *The second self: Computers and the human spirit.* New York: Knopf.
Terpstra, D. E. (1981). Relationship between methodological rigor and reported outcomes in organizational development evaluation research. *Journal of Applied Psychology, 66*, 541–543.
Thelen, E. (1992). Development and a dynamic system. *Current Directions in Psychological Science, 1*, 189–192.
Thieler, J., & Eubank, S. (1993). Don't bleach chaotic data. *Chaos, 3*, 771–782.
Thom, R. (1975). *Structural stability and morphegenesis*. New York: Benjamin-Addison- Wesley.
Thom, R. (1983). *Mathematical models of morphegenesis*. New York: Halsted.
Thompson, J. M. T. (1982). *Instabilities and catastrophes in science and engineering*. New York: Wiley.
Thompson, J. M. T., & Stewart, H. B. (1986). *Nonlinear dynamics and chaos*. New York: Wiley.
Thompson, R. G. (1993). Study notes separability of oil company profitability, efficiency. *Oil & Gas Journal, 91*(45), 62–70.
Tilman, D. (1994). Competition and biodiversity in spatially structured habitats. *Ecology, 75*, 2–16.
Tilman, D., May, R. M., Lehman, C. L., & Nowak, M. A. (1994). Habitat destruction and the extinction debt. *Nature, 371*, 65–66.
Tolman, E. C. (1932). *Purposive behavior in animals and man*. New York: Century.
Tong, H. (1990). *Non-linear time series: A dynamical system approach.* Oxford, UK: Oxford University Press.

Torre, C. A. (1995a). Chaos in the triadic theory of psychological competence in the academic setting. In. F. Abraham & A. Gilgen (Eds.), *Chaos theory in psychology* (pp. 279–294). Westport, CT: Praeger/Greenwood.

Torre, C. A. (1995b). Chaos, creativity, and innovation: Toward a dynamical model of problem solving. In R. Robertson & A. Combs (Eds.), *Chaos theory in psychology and life sciences* (pp. 179–198). Mahwah, NJ: Lawrence Erlbaum Associates.

Tracy, L. (1996). Genes, memes, templates, and replicators. *Behavioral Science, 41*, 205–214.

Trist, E., & Bamforth, K. (1951). Some social and psychological consequences of the longwall method of coal getting. *Human Relations, 4*, 3–38.

Trofimova, I. (1996, June). *Fractal functionality in differential psychology*. Paper presented to the sixth annual international conference of the Society for Chaos Theory in Psychology & Life Sciences, Berkeley, CA.

Tschacher, W., & Dauwalder, J.-P. (1999). (Eds.), *Dynamics, synergetics, and autonomous agents* (pp. 277–302). Singapore: World Scientific.

Tucci, J. E., & Sweo, R. (1996). Strategic groups: Firm structure, industry diversification, and performance determinants. *American Business Review, 14*, 73–79.

Turvey, M. T. (1990). Coordination. *American Psychologist, 45*, 938–953.

Ueda, Y. (1983). *The road to chaos*. Santa Cruz: Aeriel Press.

Vaill, P. (1989). *Managing as a performing art*. San Francisco: Jossey-Bass.

Vandaveer, V. V. (Chair). (1995, May). *Giving back to the field: Prestigious practitioners return*. Panel discussion presented to the Society for Industrial and Organizational Psychology, Orlando.

van der Maas, H., & Molenaar, P. (1992). A catastrophe-theoretical approach to cognitive development. *Psychological Review, 99*, 395–417.

van Geert, P. (2000). The dynamics of general developmental mechanisms: From Piaget and Vygotsky to dynamic systems models. *Current Directions in Psychological Science, 9*, 64–68.

Van Maanen, J., & Barley, S. R. (1985). Cultural organization: Fragments of a theory. In P. J. Frost, L. F. Moore, M. R. Louis, C. C. Lundberg, & J. Martin (Eds.), *Organizational culture* (pp. 31–54). Newberry Park, CA: Sage.

Vespignani, A., & Zapperi, S. (1997). Order parameter and scaling fields in self-organized criticality. *Physical Review Letters, 78*, 4793–4796.

Vetter, G., Stadler, M., & Haynes, J. D. (1997). Phase transitions in learning. *Journal of Mind and Behavior, 18*, 335–350.

von Bertalanffy, L. (1968). *General systems theory*. New York: Braziller.

von Neumann, J., & Morgenstern, O. (1953). *Theory of games and economic behavior*. Princeton, NJ: Princeton University Press.

von Oech, R. (1992a). *Creative Whack Pack*. Stamford, CT: U.S. Games Systems.

von Oech, R. (1992b). *A whack on the side of the head*. Menlo, CA: Creative Think.

Vroom, V. H. (1964). *The motivation to work*. New York: Wiley.

Wahba, M. A., & House, R. J. (1974). Expectancy theory in work and motivation: Some logical and methodological issues. *Human Relations, 27*, 121–147.

Waldrop, M. M. (1992). *Complexity: The emerging science at the edge of chaos*. New York: Simon and Schuster.

Walker, C. C., & Dooley, K. J. (1999). The stability of self-organized rule-following work teams. *Computational and Mathematical Organization Theory, 5*, 5–30.

Wall, T. D., Kemp, N. J., Jackson, P. R., & Clegg, C. W. (1986). Outcomes of autonomous work groups: A long-term field experiment. *Academy of Management Journal, 29*, 280–304.

Walther, J. B. (1996). Computer-mediated communication. Impersonal, interpersonal, and hyperpersonal interaction. *Communication Research, 23*, 3–45.

Walther, J. B., Anderson, J. F., & Park, D. W. (1994). Interpersonal effects in computer-mediated interactions: A meta-analysis of social and antisocial communication. *Communication Research, 21*, 460–487.

Ward, E. A. (1997). Autonomous work groups: A field study of correlates of satisfaction. *Psychological Reports, 80*, 60–62.

Ward, L. M., & West, R. L. (1994). On chaotic behavior. *Psychological Science,* 5, 232–236.

Ward, L. M., & West, R. L. (1998). Modeling human chaotic behavior: Nonlinear forecasting analysis of logistic iteration. *Nonlinear Dynamics, Psychology, and Life Sciences, 2*, 261–282.

Watson, T. W., Alley, W. E., & Southern, M. E. (1979, October). *Initial development of the operational composites for the Vocational Interest-Career Examination.* Paper presented at the 21st annual conference of the Military Testing Association, San Diego.

Weber, M. (1946). *Theory of economic and social organization.* New York: Oxford University Press.

Weber, P. (1994). *Net loss: Fish, jobs, and the marine environment* (Tech. Rep. No. 120). Washington, DC: Worldwatch Institute.

Weick, K. E. (1996). Technology as equivoque: Sensemaking in new technologies. In J. M. Shafritz & J. S. Ott (Eds.), *Classics of organizational theory* (pp. 561–577). Belmont, CA: Wadsworth.

Weintraub, E. R. (1983). Zeeman's unstable stock exchange. *Behavioral Science, 28*, 79–83.

Weiss, P. (1999). Sandpile style: Poured or rained. *Science News, 156*, 367.

Weller, L. D. (1995). School restructuring and downsizing: Using TQM to promote cost effectiveness. *TQM Magazine, 7* (6) 11–16.

Wellman, B. (1977). An electronic group is virtually a social network. In S. Keisler (Ed.), *Culture of the Internet* (pp. 179–205). Mahwah, NJ: Erlbaum

Wellman, B., & Berkowitz, S. D. (Eds.). (1988). *Social structures: A network approach.* New York: Cambridge University Press.

West, B. J., & Deering, B. (1995). *The lure of modern science: Fractal thinking*. Singapore: World Scientific.

Wheatley, M. (1992). *Leadership and the new science*. San Francisco: Berrett-Kohler.

White, R., & Englen, G. (1997). Cellular automata as the basis of integrated dynamic regional modeling, *Environment and Planning B, 24*, 235–246.

White, R., Englen, G., & Uljee, I. (1997). The use of constrained cellular automata for high-resolution modeling of urban land use dynamics. *Environment and Planning, B, 24*, 323–343.

Wiersema, M. F., & Liebeskind, J. P. (1995). The effects of leveraged buyouts on corporate growth and diversification in large firms. *Strategic Management Journal, 16*, 447–460.

Wiggins, S. (1988). *Global bifurcations and chaos.* New York: Springer-Verlag.

Willingham, D. B., & Goedert-Eschmann, K. (1999). The relation between implicit and explicit learning: Evidence for parallel development. *Psychological Science, 10*, 531–534.

Woodcock, A. E. R., & Davis, M. (1978). *Catastrophe theory*. New York: Avon.

Woodman, R. W., & Sherman, J. J. (1980). The role of team development in organizational effectiveness: A critical review. *Psychological Bulletin, 88*, 166–186.

Xiao, Y., Patey, R., & Mackenzie, C. F. (1995). *A study of team coordination and its breakdowns in a real-lift stressful environment examined through video analysis*. (Tech. Rep). University of Maryland, School of Medicine, Department of Anesthesiology.

Yee, H. C., Sweby, P. K., & Griffiths, D. F. (1991). Dynamical approach study of spurious steady-state numerical solutions on nonlinear differential equations I: The dynamics of time discretization and its implications for algorithm development in computational fluid dynamics. *Journal of Computational Physics, 97*, 249–310.

Zack, M. H., & McKenney, J. L. (1995). Social context and interaction in ongoing computer-supported management groups. *Organization Science, 6*, 394–422.

Zagare, F. C. (1984). *Game theory: Concepts and applications.* Quantitative Applications in the Social Sciences Paper Series, No. 41. Newbury Park, CA: Sage.

Zander, A. (1994). *Making groups effective* (2nd ed.). San Francisco: Jossey-Bass.

Zaror, G., & Guastello, S. J. (2000). Self-organization and leadership emergence: A cross-cultural replication. *Nonlinear Dynamics, Psychology, and Life Sciences, 4*, 113–119.

Zaslavsky, G. M. (1999). Chaotic dynamics and the origin of statistical laws. *Physics Today, v*, 39–45.

Zausner, T. (1996). The creative chaos: Speculations on the connection between non-linear dynamics and the creative process. In W. Sulis & A. Combs (Eds.), *Nonlinear dynamics and human behavior* (pp. 343–349). Singapore: World Scientific.

Zeeman, E. C. (1974). On the unstable behavior of stock exchanges. *Journal of Mathematical Economics, 1*, 39–49.

Zeeman, E. C. (1977). *Catastrophe theory: Selected papers (1972–1977)*. Reading, MA: Addison-Wesley.

Zeggelink, E. P. H., Stokman, F. N., & van de Bunt, G. G. (1997). The emergence of groups in the evolution of friendship networks. In P. Doreian & F. B. Stokman (Eds.), *Evolution of social networks* (pp. 45–71). Amsterdam: Gordon & Breach.

Zhang, W.-B. (1996). *Knowledge and value: Economic structures with time and space*. Umea, Sweden: Umea University Press.

Zimmerman, B., Lindberg, C., & Plsek, P. (1998). *Edgeware: Insights from complexity science for health care leaders*. Irving, TX: VHA Inc.

Zornoza, A., Prieto, F., Marti, C., & Peiro, J. M. (1993). Group productivity and telematic communication. *European Work and Organizational Psychologist, 3*, 117–127.

Author Index

A

B

D

E

F

G

T

U

V

W

X

Y

Z

Subject Index

A

B

C

D

E